Praise for *Racism and the Making of Gay Rights*

"This beautifully crafted narrative weaves toge
tionship of Magnus Hirschfeld and Li Shiu Ton
Hirschfeld's complex but ultimately racist thinking about homosexuality, race, and empire. It's hard to do justice to the power of this book. Let me just say that once you open it, you'll have trouble tearing yourself away, and not only because you'll want to know what happened to Li's manuscript."

Leila J. Rupp, Professor of Feminist Studies,
University of California Santa Barbara

"Fascinating, important, pioneering! Homophobia and queer liberation, racism and anti-racism, sexism and anti-sexism, colonialism and anti-colonialism – they're all profoundly entangled in Marhoefer's lively, original study of Magnus Hirschfeld's life and times."

Jonathan Ned Katz, author of
The Daring Life and Dangerous Times of Eve Adams

"*Racism and the Making of Gay Rights* decentres Magnus Hirschfeld, long revered as a 'founding father' of gay liberation, by revealing the racist and imperialist investments behind his overfocus on white, cisgendered men, a still-too-common feature of queer representation. Crucially, Laurie Marhoefer introduces the possibility of a better, queerer liberation in the thought of Hirschfeld's Chinese research assistant and perhaps lover, Li Shiu Tong. This is queer history for a better future."

Angela Zimmerman, Professor of History, George Washington
University and author of *Alabama in Africa: Booker T. Washington,
the German Empire, and the Globalization of the New South*

"In this stunning new analysis of Magnus Hirschfeld's writing and legacy, Laurie Marhoefer asks what might have been had the sexological giant opened himself up to the anti-racist arguments in his midst. We will be sorting these questions for years to come. A trenchant critique of the myths surrounding Magnus Hirschfeld, asking us to wrestle with the implications of a queer life built on anti-black racism and empire. "

Jennifer Evans, Professor of History, Carleton University

"This is the book that German history and queer history need right now. *Racism and the Making of Gay Rights* will be a hugely important intervention."

Katie Sutton, Associate Professor of German and Gender
Studies, Australian National University

Racism and the Making of Gay Rights

A Sexologist, His Student, and the Empire of Queer Love

LAURIE MARHOEFER

UNIVERSITY OF TORONTO PRESS
Toronto Buffalo London

ISBN 978-1-4875-0581-3 (cloth)   ISBN 978-1-4875-3275-8 (EPUB)
ISBN 978-1-4875-2397-8 (paper)   ISBN 978-1-4875-3274-1 (PDF)

Library and Archives Canada Cataloguing in Publication

Title: Racism and the making of gay rights : a sexologist, his student, and the
    empire of queer love / Laurie Marhoefer.
Names: Marhoefer, Laurie, author.
Description: Includes bibliographical references and index.
Identifiers: Canadiana (print) 20220130795 | Canadiana (ebook) 20220134073 |
    ISBN 9781487505813 (hardcover) | ISBN 9781487523978 (softcover) |
    ISBN 9781487532758 (EPUB) | ISBN 9781487532741 (PDF)
Subjects: LCSH: Hirschfeld, Magnus, 1868–1935. | LCSH: Li, Shiu Tong. |
    LCSH: Gay rights – History – 20th century. | LCSH: Racism – History –
    20th century. | LCSH: Sexual minorities – Social conditions – 20th century. |
    LCSH: Minorities – Social conditions – 20th century. | LCSH: Sexual minorities –
    Identity. | LCSH: Gay men – Biography.
Classification: LCC HQ76.5 .M37 2022 | DDC 306.76/6–dc23

We wish to acknowledge the land on which the University of Toronto Press
operates. This land is the traditional territory of the Wendat, the Anishnaabeg,
the Haudenosaunee, the Métis, and the Mississaugas of the Credit First Nation.

University of Toronto Press acknowledges the financial support of the
Government of Canada, the Canada Council for the Arts, and the Ontario Arts
Council, an agency of the Government of Ontario, for its publishing activities.

Canada Council   Conseil des Arts
for the Arts   du Canada

ONTARIO ARTS COUNCIL
CONSEIL DES ARTS DE L'ONTARIO
an Ontario government agency
un organisme du gouvernement de l'Ontario

Funded by the   Financé par le
Government   gouvernement
of Canada   du Canada

To Hattie. Now we can say mosquito pants.

Contents

Illustrations

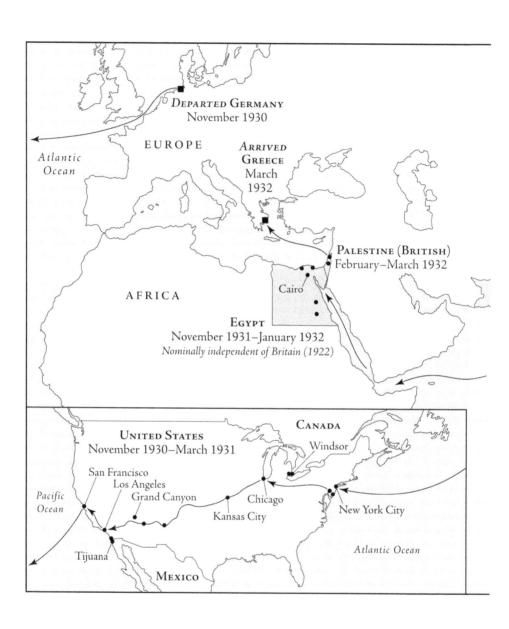

DEPARTED GERMANY
November 1930

EUROPE

ARRIVED
GREECE
March
1932

Atlantic
Ocean

PALESTINE (BRITISH)
February–March 1932

AFRICA

Cairo

EGYPT
November 1931–January 1932
Nominally independent of Britain (1922)

CANADA

UNITED STATES
November 1930–March 1931

Windsor

San Francisco
Los Angeles
Grand Canyon

Chicago

Pacific
Ocean

Kansas City

New York City

Tijuana

Atlantic Ocean

MEXICO

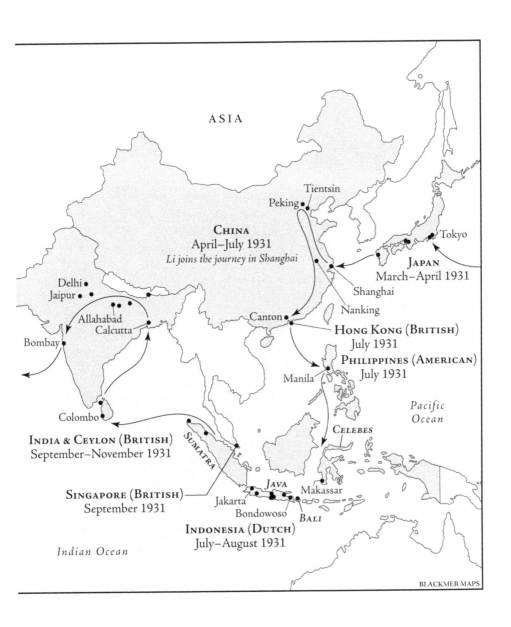

ASIA

Tientsin

Peking

CHINA
April–July 1931
Li joins the journey in Shanghai

Tokyo

JAPAN
March–April 1931

Shanghai

Nanking

Delhi
Jaipur

Allahabad
Calcutta

Bombay

Canton

HONG KONG (BRITISH)
July 1931

PHILIPPINES (AMERICAN)
July 1931

Manila

*Pacific
Ocean*

Colombo

CELEBES

INDIA & CEYLON (BRITISH)
September–November 1931

SUMATRA

SINGAPORE (BRITISH)
September 1931

Jakarta

JAVA

Makassar

Bondowoso

BALI

INDONESIA (DUTCH)
July–August 1931

Indian Ocean

BLACKMER MAPS

Map 1. Hirschfeld and Li's World Journey (abbreviated), 1930–2.
(© Kate Blackmer)

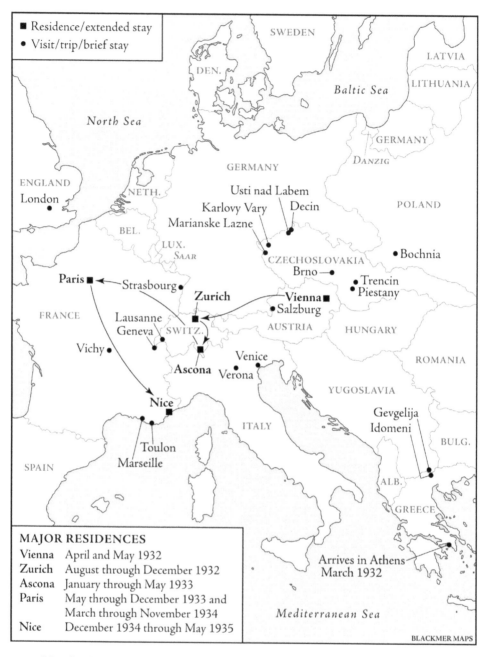

Map 2. The Exile: Hirschfeld's Itinerant Life in Europe (abbreviated), 1932–5.
(© Kate Blackmer)

Figure 1. Li and Hirschfeld at the 1932 meeting of the World League for Sex Reform in Brno, Czechoslovakia. (Photo by E. Elkan. Wellcome Library. CC-BY 4.0 License)

李
兆
堂

Figure 2. Drawing of Li that was found in his papers with his name written at upper right; artist's signature and date at lower right are difficult to make out but the year appears to be 1932. (MHG)

Figure 3. Hirschfeld lecturing in 1931 at the University of Tokyo. This photo ran in his book *World Journey*. In the course of his world tour he gave 178 lectures, he later told *Voilà* magazine.

Figure 4. Members of the Chinese Women's Club and other audience members for Hirschfeld's lecture, on the day that Hirschfeld met Li. Though Li was present, he is not in the photo; the club's president, Mrs. Ma, assumedly is. The original caption does not identify the people in the picture. (From *World Journey*)

Figure 5. Li, Hirschfeld, and sailors, Peking, 1931. The photograph is in the papers of Max Reiss, a friend of Hirschfeld and Li's from the exile. The original caption, which appears to have been written by Li, is "Forbidden City Peking/Probably middle bridge across the Golden River towards the Gate of Great Harmony." (MHG)

Figure 6. Chinese students with Hirschfeld after one of his lectures, 1931. Li is on the right in the dark suit. (From *World Journey*)

Figure 7. Hirschfeld as the sexologist doing research, on Java, 1932; probably taken by Li. The original caption is "Phallic stones near Borobudur." (From *World Journey*)

RACISM AND THE MAKING OF GAY RIGHTS

The problem of the Twentieth Century is the problem of the color line.
                                    – W.E.B. Du Bois, *The Souls of Black Folk*, 1903

But when were the Jews in Germany ever as persecuted as the homoerotics? Does the penal code contain an exceptional law against the *racial* minority like the infamous exceptional law against the *sexual* minority? The shame of the century is homophobia; the shame of the century is Paragraph 175 [Germany's law against sodomy].
                                    – Kurt Hiller, *§175: Die Schmach des Jahrhunderts!*
                                    [Paragraph 175: Shame of the Century!], 1922

Introduction

Manila, Philippines, July 1931

On July 6, 1931, the American steamship *President Cleveland* sailed into the mouth of Manila Bay at the end of an uneventful two-day journey from Hong Kong across the South China Sea. One passenger was already such a sensation in Manila that the reporters and photographers from the newspapers did not wait until the *President Cleveland* had docked and instead rode along on the harbor pilot's boat to meet the ship. The man they were rushing to interview was a rumpled, diabetic, white-and-gray-haired German doctor. They found him on board, most likely in the company of his sole traveling companion, a dapper and much younger man, a Chinese medical student who only days before had quit school and bade farewell to his family and his homeland in order to follow the doctor around the world. The student's name was Li Shiu Tong (李兆堂). The doctor, Magnus Hirschfeld, was a sexologist, a scientist of human sexuality. He was also the world's best-known, most committed defender of homosexuals. With Li at his side, he was on a peripatetic global lecture tour.[1]

Magnus Hirschfeld made the modern homosexual. Although no one that day in Manila Harbor probably thought so, looking back from almost one hundred years later, it is clear. He cofounded the world's first gay rights group, the Scientific Humanitarian Committee (Wissenschaftlich-Humanitäres Komitee, or WhK), in Berlin in 1897. But what is far more important is that he and his colleagues came up with an enormously influential concept of what same-sex desire *was*, what it meant and how it fit into the wider world. If you think homosexuality is an inborn quality that cannot be changed and has a biological root but is not an illness, and if you think gay people are a "sexual minority" who are born that way and who deserve legal protections just as racial minorities do, you owe those ideas to Hirschfeld and a handful of others. Hirschfeld was among the first to articulate that conceptual model of what it means to be gay in print in 1896. Between that year and 1935, the year he died, he did more than anyone else to spread an idea that is now widely accepted but at the time was a radical heterodoxy – the idea that same-sex-desiring people were not sick or criminal but rather were blameless and respectable members of a sexual minority, a sliver of the otherwise mostly heterosexual population, and that homosexuality was a natural, inborn variation, not a disease or diabolical impulse and not something that one ought to try to change or that one could change if one wished to do so.

This history is largely lost today, but in 1931, Hirschfeld was an internationally famous sex expert, a celebrity scientist renowned not just for his insights about same-sex desire but for his encyclopedic knowledge of sex in all of its varieties.[2] When the reporters found him on the *President Cleveland*, they pulled out their pens and peppered him with question after question: What did he think about the new idea of "companionate marriage" – that marriage ought to mean a fulfilling sex life and romantic bond? What did he think about the celibacy of Catholic priests? "And what about women?" they wanted to know. Hirschfeld was not a man for pithy explanations. He had recently published a 3,000-page, multivolume tome on these topics. He was used to the press by now and found the reporters bemusing and silly, though he loved the attention, too. One can easily imagine him turning to Li as their ship sailed through the port and making a wry remark about how, as he put it when he wrote about the scene years later in his travel memoir, "obviously," the journalists "had no clue as to just how complex" the matters they were asking about really were.[3]

Though the two men were inseparable, Li and Hirschfeld had been strangers only a few months before. Li had introduced himself to Hirschfeld after the older man gave a public lecture to a Chinese feminist club in Shanghai. Soon after, the twenty-four-year-old Li quit medical school to act as an assistant to the sixty-three-year-old Hirschfeld, who had been traveling alone and was not always in good health. Together, the two men journeyed through a world scarred by colonialism, across the American, British, and Dutch empires (see map 1). Li planned to arrive, finally, in Berlin, to study with the great man at his celebrated Institute for Sexual Science. Li wanted to become an important sexologist himself. For his part, Hirschfeld believed that, in Li, he had discovered the long-sought-after disciple who would continue his life's work after his death, his life's work being the ambitious goal of liberating all of humanity from oppressive, unscientific beliefs about sex and love. By the time they reached Manila Bay he was also, one suspects, in love with the younger man. Certainly, sometime during their world journey, he fell in love.

Yet as Hirschfeld and Li made ready to leave the *President Cleveland*, their hopes for the future were thrown into doubt. The Americans refused to let Li off the ship. The Philippines had been an American colony since 1898. The United States conquered the archipelago in a bloody war that killed more than a quarter of a million people, most of them Filipinos, many of them civilians. White Americans in Manila in 1931 had strict, racist views of white superiority like those that prevailed at the time in the United States. The US had extended the Chinese Exclusion Act to the Philippines. It barred immigrants from China despite the fact that tens of thousands of people had migrated to the Philippines in the nineteenth century from China, especially from Fujian, and that Chinese communities had existed in some cities for hundreds of years before that. "American territory is closed to the yellow race," the immigration officer told Hirschfeld and Li when they tried to disembark.[4]

Hirschfeld and Li's story opens up a window onto how racism – as well as antiracism – and colonialism – together with anticolonialism – were all present at the very beginning of gay politics. Indeed, the ties between racialization and gay politics go even deeper: ideas about "the races" shaped homosexuality as we know it. European and American empires were central sites of queer (and trans) self-fashioning and self-imagining. Anticolonial rhetoric also inspired some queer liberationist rhetoric, and it did so from the get-go, well before the 1970s. Histories of gay rights often begin in the United States, with the Stonewall riots of 1969. The real first chapter of gay rights is a century-long chapter that took place in Europe and its colonies between roughly 1830 and 1933. The most important person in that chapter was Hirschfeld. His story is, quite centrally, about the interwovenness of race and empire and sexuality and gender. This is clear when the story begins in Manila in 1931.

Magnus Hirschfeld fashioned the "homosexual" out of existing ideas about "the races," about empire, and moreover about Jews and about disability. He borrowed promiscuously as he built his model. Aspects of the new theory of homosexuality came from scientific racism. Other aspects came from antiracist thought. Hirschfeld tied his model to claims about the whiteness of Jews, a challenge to rising antisemitism around the globe. The model also owes substantial debts to the intellectual apparatus of empire – one of Hirschfeld's major arguments in favor of his model depended on imperial notions of "race" and "civilization." Yet at times, Hirschfeld marshaled anticolonialism, claiming that the fight against empire and the fight against the oppression of homosexuals were the same fight. "The homosexual" owed its design to eugenics as well, in profound ways. It was, moreover, implicitly male, marked by the gender politics of its day. Roderick Ferguson, writing about the era of Stonewall, argues that the story of gay rights has been told as if gay activists only came to questions about racism and colonialism (Ferguson includes incarceration and capitalism here) "later," after the initial development of gay rights around separate questions of sexual freedom, but in fact, "a multidimensional host of concerns were there from the very beginning only to be excised later on."[5] This book shows a similar dynamic at the very outset of gay rights, decades before Stonewall. The title, *Racism and the Making of Gay Rights*, is meant to reflect this, though only partially. The title would have grown too long if it included all the other ideologies at play here, but they are important too: imperialism, antiracism, the fight against antisemitism, anticolonialism, eugenics, and gender ideologies were all indispensable in the making of gay rights at its very beginnings.

In part, there is hope in this story for an expansive gay politics, one that fights racism and imperialism. Hirschfeld and Li's story shows that gay politics did not have to be implicitly white or consistently bad at antiracism. Hirschfeld loved Li, saw the evils of empire and racism as he traveled at Li's side, and chose Li to carry on the work of gay rights as his heir. After Hirschfeld died, Li did carry on with Hirschfeld's research. Nevertheless, what endured of Hirschfeld's work was a political movement that assumed that empire and racism were issues separate from queer liberation. This left out a lot of queers, indeed the majority, and it left out Li.

The scene as Hirschfeld and his protégé tried to disembark in Manila probably did not shock Li. Being on the wrong side of the "color line" was not new to him. Shanghai, where he had been at university, was a racially and nationally stratified, and partially colonized, city, and Hong Kong, where he had grown up, was a British colony. Hirschfeld, however, living for most of his life as a Jew in Europe, had not had many such experiences of quotidian apartheid. He had experienced murderous racism when he had been physically attacked by antisemites in Munich about a decade before. That violence was exceptional though. He grew up Jewish in Germany following the abolition of formal legal restrictions on Jews. Antisemitic attitudes still prevailed in conservative circles, but overt legal restrictions on one's movement in space were things of the past. Yet Hirschfeld was learning all about this sort of racism lately thanks to his relationship with Li. In China, Hirschfeld and Li had entered more than one white European space together only to be thrown out. The manager of a European club in Shanghai where Hirschfeld and (most likely) Li had gone to meet a colleague of Hirschfeld's barred Li at the door. Hirschfeld turned around and left, telling the manager on his way out, "You seem to forget that you are a guest in China." The manager snapped back, "We are not afraid of the Yellow Peril."[6]

Hirschfeld had lecture engagements to keep in Manila, but he had no intention of abandoning his protégé. Did the immigration officer know that Li had a transit visa made out by the American vice-consul in Hong Kong? Did he realize that Li, born in Hong Kong, was a British colonial subject? None of this changed the officer's mind. Neither did Hirschfeld's paternalistic assurance that he would supervise the younger man, keeping him "in my company." It was to no avail. "We could not deny that Li was Chinese, and that was enough."[7]

Racism had disrupted Hirschfeld and Li's mutual pledge to travel the world together as teacher and pupil, spreading news of the non-pathological, innate nature of homosexuality.

Over the past thirty years, one of the biggest questions in queer politics has been what, if anything, gay rights has to do with a broader left-of-center agenda, especially the struggles against racism and imperialism. This puzzle often gets posed something like this: Is equality for gay people intimately connected to other political goals, or is it a stand-alone issue?[8] At the heart of the conundrum has been the relationship between gay rights and antiracism. Activist movements in Germany, the United States, Canada, and elsewhere have split apart over this. Some activists argue that any movement for gay rights is fundamentally a movement against racism and a struggle for a broader vision of social justice. After all, most people who feel same-sex desires are not "white."[9] A political movement on behalf of queer people thus has to fight racism, and queer-of-color activism has a long and rich history. We increasingly remember Stonewall, often claimed as the original moment of gay politics, as a radical uprising led by trans women of color whose agenda included prison abolition, an end to police violence, and wealth redistribution.[10] Black Lives Matter, with its explicitly pro-queer and pro-trans chapters, is a recent example of powerful Black antiracist queer and trans organizing.[11] Yet over the decades, many white activists have not believed that to fight for gay rights necessarily means to fight racism. There has been a fork in the road, and a lot of the movement – in particular, white people who *could* ignore racism – has gone the route of assuming that antiracism and gay rights are not intrinsically connected.

Surprisingly, this fork in the road is not a creation of the 1990s. In fact, it is as old as gay rights itself. The choice between a broader, antiracist movement and a narrower one that (at best) ignores racism is "baked in" to gay politics. It was staring Hirschfeld and Li in the face in Manila in 1931.

In the end, they found a way around the immediate problem. Hirschfeld appealed to the Chinese consul in Manila. After they underwent "many cumbersome formalities" and agreed to leave their passports, Li was allowed "to set foot on the Philippines under American colonial control" until the next ship sailed.[12] The American Chinese Exclusion Act barred coolies, contract laborers specifically, from the colony. A number of other occupations were exempted, including students and travelers, who could enter if they applied for a certificate; likely this is what the Chinese consul helped Li to do.[13] As a wealthy man, Li was entitled to cross this color line. Hirschfeld, however, reports that the Americans granted Li only four days in their colony; luckily, Hirschfeld does not seem to have planned to stay any longer than that. Had it been known that either of the two men was queer, they might have had other troubles. American immigration officials at times stopped homosexuals at the border. Hirschfeld was aware of this. As he put it, "homosexual men and women are barred from the land of Walt Whitman," though in reality it was most often poor people who ran into this problem, not wealthy men like Hirschfeld and Li.[14] As they argued with the American officials in Manila, no one but the two men themselves knew that homosexuality had anything to do with the matter. The problem of racism, of course, remained unresolved, and would haunt the remainder of both of their lives.

A few years later, Hirschfeld and Li sat together in the library of the University of Zurich, working on a book about their trip around the world, a trip that had taken them through the Dutch, American, and British empires.[15] The book was *World Journey of a Sexologist.* Though Li is not credited as an author of *World Journey,* he acted as Hirschfeld's secretary as the older man wrote it. The book is suffused with stories of their time together, even as Li appears infrequently – *World Journey* maintains the fiction that they had merely a conventional teacher-student relationship. Neither man could afford to make his queerness public. The book is also shot through with anti-imperialist sentiment and with a queer critique of racism. In the chapters on their time in Manila, Hirschfeld portrays himself as passionately inspired to go left at the fork, that is, to think about what he called "homosexual emancipation" as part of a larger, greater global struggle for justice. He calls himself "someone who was fundamentally on the side of the unjustly oppressed, whether that oppression was against their nationality, race, religion, social status, or sexuality."[16]

The largest of Hirschfeld's three lectures in Manila was at the university, where he spoke outside on a lawn to several thousand Filipino students, including some female students. The president of the university presided over the late-afternoon event. Hirschfeld stood on a stage to deliver his lecture on sexology. Often when Hirschfeld lectured, Li was amid the listeners in the audience, operating a slide projector for the accompanying images, but at this event that must not have been the case, as the lecture happened during the day and projecting slides would not have worked. Perhaps Li watched from the audience. Behind Hirschfeld sat most of the university faculty as well as important Manila personalities, both American and Filipino. Toward the end of his lecture a thundershower began, but it lasted only ten minutes and did not disrupt things too badly.[17]

Afterward, a student came up and asked Hirschfeld if he could come to see him the following day to show him around the city. The student was a member of the "Philippine independence movement," Hirschfeld reported. He was pleased by the invitation – he was always eager to meet with "as many natives [*Inländern*] as possible" as he put it. He had noticed that most Europeans in Asia did their socializing with other Europeans, almost exclusively. They learned nothing about the "ways of the natives [*Eingeborenen*]." Not so Hirschfeld. He took pride that he got beyond white European circles. He did not only lecture to white European audiences – for instance, later, on Java, he spoke to a mostly Javanese audience of men and women at a private house in Samarang, which antagonized the Dutch colonists who found out about it. Yet the sexologist never entirely dispensed with his paternalizing, Eurocentric worldview when it came to "natives."[18]

The next morning, the "young Filipino" (Hirschfeld does not give his name, probably to protect him from the Americans) led him on a walk through the Intramuros, the old Spanish walled city. The student quickly turned the talk to Filipino independence. Hirschfeld listened sympathetically. One assumes that Li was listening, too – he was a student who had grown up in a British colony, had gone to school in a multinational colonial city, and was, I suspect, interested in anticolonialism, and he probably had lots to say to the Filipino student – but Hirschfeld's account does not mention Li.[19] The Filipino student believed Hirschfeld was an obvious ally. "You are an advocate for the idea that the natural rights of individuals and of peoples should not be violated, so perhaps you can raise your voice for us Filipinos too," Hirschfeld reports that he said.[20] This pleased Hirschfeld. As he traveled the world with Li at his side, Hirschfeld passionately believed that the injustices he had spent his adult life fighting – the unjust oppression of people by backward ideas about sex and gender – were part of a larger unjust oppression of people around the world: imperialism. Hirschfeld weaves this theme through his account of his morning walk with the Filipino student. Because Hirschfeld is an advocate for homosexuals, the student thinks, he will also be an advocate for Filipino independence.

They walked through Manila to the place where the Filipino national hero José Rizal had been shot by the Spanish in 1896. Standing by the memorial to Rizal, the student made a speech. He likened Rizal to the American president Abraham Lincoln, who had said that no people was exalted enough to rule over another, and he invoked another American president, Woodrow Wilson, who had called for the self-determination of nations.[21] This resonated powerfully with the rhetoric of the homosexual emancipation movement that Hirschfeld led. Many activists in that movement thought of homosexuals as analogous to a colonized people. Homosexuals, in this view, were like the enslaved Black Americans whose emancipation Abraham Lincoln proclaimed. They were like the racial, ethnic, and national minorities whose right to self-determination Wilson had defended. Wilson was especially significant for Hirschfeld – his rhetoric an important model for the interwar gay rights movement, which styled itself as representing a "sexual minority" analogous to ethnic and national minorities.

Yet the tradition of gay rights activism that Hirschfeld helped create ultimately rejected the idea that anti-imperialism and homosexual emancipation were the same struggle. It went right at the fork. Hirschfeld helped build a gay rights movement where sex had conquered race, so to speak – that is, where it was easy to assume a white subject and ignored racism, at least so long as one was white oneself. Hirschfeld met some prominent African American foes of racism: Langston Hughes, James Weldon Johnson, and William Pickens. Hirschfeld and Li stayed at Jawaharlal Nehru's house and met the teenaged Indira Gandhi. But Hirschfeld did not read Hughes, Johnson, Pickens, or Nehru. He did not cite them. He ignored and dismissed them – in the case of the three Black Americans, in racist language. He stuck to his own watered-down and problematic antiracism. To Hirschfeld, "racism" meant, narrowly, scientific racism; in the 1930s and today, however, many people have a broader concept of "racism" as the denigration of a group defined as a "race," regardless of whether that denigration adheres to the terms of scientific racism. The concept that Hirschfeld popularized around the world, "homosexuality," is haunted by flawed antiracism, and Hirschfeld's many publications are haunted by a visceral anti-Blackness that contradicts his claim to oppose racism. One sees this in the story of his world journey, too. Hirschfeld's racialized erotic vision of Li was in part what drew him to the younger man.

A few hours after the stirring speech at the site of Rizal's execution, Hirschfeld and Li sailed from Manila on the Dutch ship *Tjinegara*, then in its first year of service. Hirschfeld found the ship very modern and elegant. It had saloons of ebony and marble. Its wireless technology kept them abreast of the events of the world even as they glided through still waters among islands that Hirschfeld had been taught as a boy at school were the homes of cannibals. That first night on board he and Li sat together in the ship's dining room, which was on an upper deck, its windows opening on expansive views of the sea. Hirschfeld was charmed. He loved the sea. To dine, he and Li were in the requisite attire – in summer, a short white "tropical dinner jacket [*Tropensmoking*]" and black trousers. Hirschfeld appreciated his dinner companion, Li, who was good-looking and was, as Hirschfeld later wrote, "highly cultured," a young man from one of China's most "distinguished" families. They almost certainly dined at a table with others. Li could be a very amusing dinner companion – he was vivacious, a teller of funny stories, though perhaps that night he was not at his ease, having only newly become the young assistant of a famous man; perhaps he left the conversation mostly to Hirschfeld. The sexologist was a celebrity on board. Later, the ship's captain asked Hirschfeld to give a lecture to the first-class passengers and ship's officers, and he happily did so, speaking on sexual ethnology.[22]

Whether any of their other companions that night sensed the older man's desire for the younger man, I cannot say for certain. Probably not. Among strangers, they presented themselves as teacher and student, much as they appear in a group photograph taken earlier that year, in China after one of Hirschfeld's lectures, though in that photograph Li is among a group of students, while in reality he was Hirschfeld's only student (figure 6). Hirschfeld called their bond "the ideal teacher-student relationship," and his contemporaries often referred to Li as Hirschfeld's "Chinese pupil."[23] Queer male-male affections often went thus unspoken and unnoticed in the first-class cabin in this time and place.[24] The wealthy white passengers and white European crew did pay intense attention to racialized norms of gender and sexuality, but it was almost always heterosexual behavior that broke these norms – white women wearing shorts in the dining room, or white men drunkenly harassing or assaulting white, Chinese, and Indonesian women.[25] All the better for Hirschfeld and Li. Had their relationship been public, it would have ruined Hirschfeld's career and threatened Li's. In the 1930s, almost no one was "out," as we would say.

Yet the other first-class diners that night may have sensed something queer about Hirschfeld and Li. More so because Li was so much younger and Chinese. For many decades, white Europeans and Americans had told themselves that Chinese men, and indeed all East and South Asian men, were feminine.[26] Europeans also wrote about how Chinese men were prone to same-sex desires.[27] Hirschfeld, quite pointedly, did not endorse either idea.[28] Yet at the time, many white Europeans went after younger Asian men, or boys, in the colonies, giving rise to a trope that persisted into the 1990s if not beyond.[29] Moreover, elite white Europeans and Americans often – perhaps always – noted Hirschfeld's Jewishness, despite Hirschfeld himself not having much in the way of Jewish identity. He did not practice or, for most of his life, really consider his Jewish upbringing as a major part of who he was, and though he did think he was a Jew by race, this meant very little to him until his years of exile, as I will explain later. Nevertheless, there was in the 1930s an association between Jews and "sexual disorder," particularly for people of a conservative mindset from German-speaking Europe, so it may be that Hirschfeld's Jewishness made some people wonder what the younger man meant to the older one.

Thus racism was subtly a part of perceptions of queer love. The perceived races of our two protagonists made them more perceptible as lovers, I would guess.

Or perhaps there was another white man who felt queer desires in the first-class cabin. He might have thought that he understood right away. Some rich white queer European men saw China as more tolerant of homosexuality than Europe was (a view Hirschfeld shared) and moreover believed it to be home to beautiful, subservient men who, thanks to their feminine natures, were more open to same-sex affairs than were Europeans back home.[30]

Indeed, the colonies were understood by men with queer desires to be especially queer places. Colonial officialdom was not without its share of men who had fled Europe for sexual freedom in the empire. Far from critiquing the imperialist underpinnings of such queer longings, much of Hirschfeld's work prior to the book he wrote with Li by his side played into those longings. One of his books was so detailed on sex with colonized people in the empires that people could easily use it as a guide for queer imperial sex tourism. He moreover mined the stories of queer colonial officials for evidence to support his theories. This vision of an empire of queer love may have been part of what brought Hirschfeld on the world tour in the first place.[31] Perhaps on his journey, he had hoped to find someone like Li. This empire of queer love existed thanks to empire writ large: it was colonial power and violence, not the primitive toleration of "natives" for homoeroticism, which made the colonies spaces of relative queer sexual freedom for white European men. Empire created gay liberation, of a sort, and Hirschfeld enjoyed it.

The *Tjinegara* was heavily encoded by intersecting, often unspoken, but nonetheless intense rules about race, class, and gender. Dutch shipping companies went to great lengths to make shipboard spaces into a microcosm of the proper colonial order, for example by ensuring that white Europeans held the top crew spots, overseeing a workforce of colonized people. At the same time, the liminal space of the ship, with strangers thrown together at close quarters, tempted white wealthy Europeans to transgress some of those rules.[32] Hirschfeld and Li were among about twenty people traveling in first class, most of them Dutch and German. Dutch ship lines often tried to keep first class all white, on one occasion denying passage to a prominent Black American family.[33] The lines from Hong Kong to Indonesia welcomed wealthy Chinese passengers, initially into first class, but as time went on, the company that owned the *Tjinegara* decided to designate first class for white Westerners and second class for wealthy Asians.[34] They made exceptions, however, for just the sort of Chinese man Li was – wealthy, Westernized, and "civilized," in the view of ticket agents. All the more so if Hirschfeld had gone to the ticket office in Hong Kong and bought their passages together. Traveling with a white European luminary would be seen as a guarantee of Li's suitability for first class. His presence probably did not raise the racial hackles of white fellow passengers. White racial aggression on these ships was more often aimed at working-class Chinese and Indonesian people. In Li, white first-class travelers may have even seen evidence of the justice of empire: here was a "civilized" Chinese man. He proved that the civilizing mission could work; most colonized people were not yet civilized like he was, thus empire had to persist.[35] At dinner, he and Hirschfeld were attended by an all-Indonesian waitstaff; the company had previously employed Chinese waiters on some ships but a few years before had stopped doing that because Dutch officials believed Indonesians to be more pliant and docile.[36] The sacking of Chinese waitstaff had been fueled by Dutch paranoia about Chinese political radicalism spreading to their Indonesian colony.[37] The ship had hundreds of Chinese passengers in second and third class. Most, Hirschfeld thought, were returning to Java from a visit to Canton.[38] Many were doubtless among the approximately half a million coolies (contract laborers) working in colonial Indonesia at the time.[39]

The shipping companies sometimes invited passengers in first class to step into third- and fourth-class spaces in order to observe the lower-class passengers, a sort of anthropological tour, an exercise in colonial "slumming."[40] Hirschfeld gladly went to see the Chinese passengers. Perhaps Li went too; perhaps he did not, given the odd racial situation it would have put him in. Hirschfeld enjoyed it and remembered the "sparkling dark eyes" of Chinese people traveling in third and fourth class, eyes that he thought held bitterness at the suffering of their nation under foreign domination. Writing about the scene years later, Hirschfeld waxed poetic about those eyes and about the Chinese character, as he put it. In comparison to Europeans, the Chinese were "more even-tempered, softer, more sweet-tempered [*gutmütiger*], more devoted."[41] Devotion was something that meant a tremendous amount to Hirschfeld. It was what he had always wanted in a pupil and intellectual heir. Generalizing about "the Chinese" as a homogenous group of people, and based on a short stay in China – during which he fancied he had gotten to know the soul of the nation better than most European visitors did because he had been with Li – Hirschfeld displayed some of his Eurocentric myopia.[42] This sort of imagination of intimacy with Chinese people was not an uncommon fantasy for white first-class passengers when they slummed in third and fourth class.[43] He was also, I suspect, writing a tacit, racialized tribute to Li. A few months before, he had explained in a newspaper interview that when whites like himself fell in love with people of other races, they almost always fetishized some physical "racial characteristic" about the beloved.[44] Li's were the Chinese eyes that Hirschfeld knew best, and Li's unwavering devotion was his great solace. Hirschfeld's desire for his student was in part about race.

Though Hirschfeld hated "racism" as he defined it, as you can see, he never entirely got away from it. He believed in "races," and more than that – he had a theory of "the races." It was closely related to his theory of homosexuality and indeed supported it. There is a large scholarship on Hirschfeld, but very little of it considers his position on "the races," and none of it treats his ideas as a coherent theory intersecting his theory of homosexuality.

How Li, for his part, felt about the sexagenarian sexologist is something of a mystery. He wanted to go to Berlin to study at the Institute for Sexual Science. Hirschfeld had offered him a stipend and a position there. Hirschfeld had even promised to groom Li to be his successor.[45] But did Li love his mentor? Did he agree with his theories? What did Li make of his mentor's racialized desire for him? Only a scant record of Li's views on all of this survived after his death, and many of those papers were tossed into the garbage in Vancouver, British Columbia, in 1993. Yet Li's voice rings out from the archive. He was a central player in the canonical history of gay rights, though that history in the 1920s and 1930s has almost always been told as a story of white Europeans. Right at the center of gay politics, on the contrary, was a Chinese European Canadian man, a man who was discreetly but very artfully queer and who negotiated the racism all around him in order to become a sexologist himself. Li in fact came to reject Hirschfeld's theories. In a manuscript he wrote in Vancouver late in his life, he described how his own decades of research after Hirschfeld's death had shown him a very different model of queerness: one that had same-sex desire as a nearly universal human experience, not the sole possession of a lonely minority. In his model, people were not born gay. Li became a dissident sexologist, but he never published. This book tells his story as well.

I wrote this book for four reasons. The first, and probably the foremost, is that I wanted to examine how and why gay politics can be so white, how and why white activists can continue, despite decades of critiques and despite the bald and brutal reality of racism, to do gay politics in a way that assumes that the subject of gay politics is a person who is not plagued by racism but rather benefits from it. In 2010, in the course of a debate about racism in white-led Berlin gay rights groups, Tülin Duman of Gays and Lesbians from Turkey identified the problem as stemming from the assumed model of homosexuality: "While the gay and lesbian civil rights movement has a one-dimensional model of identity, there are more and more people [coming out] who are not *only* homosexual. Skin color, ancestry, sex, religion, age, disability and many other markers form our identities too."[46] For many decades, people have made a related point: there is no generic homosexual, no one is *only* homosexual, and everyone has other relevant things about them, such as racialization. Why are the assumptions that to be gay is to be white and that racism (not to mention sexism and anti-disability politics) is a side issue nevertheless so persistent, surviving without question in some white circles into the twenty-first century?[47]

These questions draw my attention because I am a student of the many scholars who have argued that sexuality and racism are inseparable.[48] As David Eng puts it, "sexual and racial difference cannot be understood in isolation … as separate discourses or distinct spheres of analysis," but rather "they must be understood as mutually constitutive, as drawing their discursive legibility and social power in relation to one another."[49] To writers and readers in the broad interdisciplinary field of queer theory and queer-of-color critique, the point that we miss something when we analyze queer sexuality without analyzing race, when we are looking at times and places where racism exists, was made forcefully in the 1990s and 2000s and is now so well established as to be self-evident.[50] Some scholars have analyzed the co-constitution of queerness and racism in Germany; I am indebted to their insights.[51] Yet a lot of the scholarship on queer sexuality in metropolitan Europe has not. Oddly so. The history of imperialism and racism is a story about Europe, too.[52]

A related point: it may be that same-sex desire is something that everybody feels at one time or another – with the caveat that what people understand by "same sex" varies wildly,[53] and the additional caveat that feeling same-sex desire is not the same for everyone.[54] But the experience of being the target of homophobia is not universal. In times and places where racism exists, animosity against queerness is inflected by racism. People who are upset about same-sex desire, moved to disgust or to violence, perceive same-sex sexuality as a racialized thing. On the other side of this bad dynamic, the people who are the targets of homophobia are always already faced with interrelated anxieties about race (or the lack thereof, if whiteness protects them). "Black lesbians do not experience homophobia in the same way as white lesbians do," writes

Evelynn Hammonds. "Here, as with other oppressions, the homophobia experienced by black women is always shaped by racism."[55] On the world journey, Hirschfeld qualified as white and thus dodged racism almost entirely. It dogged Li's footsteps across three empires. Later, because Hirschfeld was a Jew in Europe in the era of fascism, his life was upended by racism, and moreover by racist homophobia. Li, in contrast, could still live in German-speaking Europe after 1933, when Hirschfeld feared for his life there. But before his exile, Hirschfeld thought whiteness protected him from racism, and he was mostly right.

The relationship between racism and homosexuality in nineteenth- and early twentieth-century science is a hot topic. An influential body of scholarship has tended to imply that the biologicalization of identity in the nineteenth century – in scientific racism as well as in scientific accounts of sex – placed people racialized as non-white (be they queer or not) and white sexual deviants in similarly pathologized positions; in the past, this finding suggests, white queers and non-white citizens or colonial subjects were the targets of meaningfully similar ideological violence.[56] In fact, though occasionally the two groups were pathologized in similar terms, most often they were not; moreover, when things were similar, the power of whiteness was rarely, if ever, truly stripped from white queers.[57] That was on purpose. White queers fought to put themselves in such a position, even as they used the existence of non-white queers as evidence for their campaign. Nor would the white heterosexuals who wrote about homosexuality find any joy in undermining the power of whiteness, upon which the colonial order relied, by implying that it was so fragile that queerness could erode it. For most authors who wrote against homosexual liberation, "the homosexual" was implicitly white and white people were always profoundly distinct from non-white people, whether they indulged their queer desires or not.[58]

This book sets out to investigate how and why homosexuals who considered themselves "white" proceeded to act as if sexuality and racism were in fact not related at all. Hirschfeld is my example of such a homosexual, and he was an important architect of this conceptual move, but he certainly is not unique. Part of the answer is that some gay activists were white supremacists. There is, in fact, a tradition of fascist queer activism with roots in the nineteenth century.[59] Some white gay activists who are not on the extreme right are racist, too. Gay rights movements have diverse political ideologies, but they often tend to be liberal and moderate.[60] Classical liberalism, the ideology of the transatlantic slave trade and of settler colonialism, is not antiracist. Yet there are also white queers who, like Hirschfeld, self-identify as antiracist and who are blithely, blatantly terrible at fighting racism. It is the inability, or refusal, of seemingly well-meaning white queers to think of queer politics and antiracism together that most interests me here. Without covering over the history of gay white racism, it seems crucial to point out that some of the failings of white gay activists stem in part from the modern notion of homosexuality, a concept that did not appear explicitly racist, that indeed was popularized by the avowedly antiracist Hirschfeld, but that, when one teases out its threads, tends to make the homosexual white and to make racism a side issue, at best, rather than an intrinsic problem for gay people. I hope showing this will help explain why Hirschfeld's biological model can still be so problematic and exclusionary – it was built to serve implicitly white, male, and able-bodied subjects.

The second reason I wrote this book was to show that it did not need to be so. Hirschfeld had moments in which he saw clearly the interrelatedness of antiracism and sexual liberation. He often cast those moments in biological terms, which makes me uneasy, given his trouble divorcing himself from a biologically grounded racism and, moreover, his infatuation with eugenics. Yet even he saw how antiracism is intrinsic to gay rights. I have much less information on what Li thought. Yet he had his own ideas about what same-sex desire was, and in his admittedly fragmentary work, racialization has a different emphasis.

The third reason I wrote this book was to reassess Hirschfeld and to give Li his due. The older man has several biographers, but almost no one has written about the younger man.[61] Yet their years together are an important moment in the history of sexuality. That moment shows the tension between antiracism and racism in the biological model of homosexuality, and it shows paths not taken. Li is also a fascinating person in his own right. He deserves to be more than an afterthought. His story complicates the history of the first century of gay rights, showing how central racism was to gay politics in the life of a young Chinese man traversing three empires, then making his home in Europe, Hong Kong, the United States, and Canada. It shows how central that young man was to German homosexual emancipation, a movement that scholars often assume was white. Moreover, though most people in the English-speaking world have not heard of Hirschfeld, he had a big impact on the gay politics that came after him – a bigger impact, I argue here, than most people have acknowledged. More and more, Hirschfeld is famous again. He is, to quote Jennifer Evans, "lionized" in Germany, where most queer people know his name and recently lots of things have been named for him.[62] Increasingly, people who study gay and trans politics outside of Germany are adding him into their narratives.[63] He, however, had a troubling theory of "the races," a large debt to eugenics, a persistent anti-Black racism pervading his thought, and an inability to really consider the plight of people with queer desires who were not male. We ought to take all that into account, not only in order to acknowledge that he was a problematic gay hero, but also in order to check how these troubles might still be shaping gay politics, which he did so much to set on its present course.[64] Gay history is not usually told as a transnational story that begins in the nineteenth century. Most historians have written about the United States and have begun their books in the twentieth century.[65] Most of gay history has overlooked the German-speaking first chapter entirely and therefore has not noted the deep connections between modern homosexuality and the politics of race, empire, gender, eugenics, and antisemitism.

My final reason for writing this book was to show what Hirschfeld and Li's relationship was like, as a way to see the history of queerness, racialization, and empire up close, to better comprehend it. Perhaps history's swirling complexities are best transmitted to the reader by telling a story. Perhaps there is radical theoretical potential there, in telling in lavish detail of very complex lives lived across sprawling decades, lives that do not reduce into easy maxims.[66] This accounts for the book's odd structure. It is half narrative co-biography and half intellectual history. The chapters often take a moment in the world journey as a starting place. Some chapters mostly tell about the two men; other chapters mostly analyze Hirschfeld's or Li's thought. Beyond my theoretical concerns, I did this out of consideration for the reader. The intellectual history seems necessary to conclusively demonstrate what I am saying about Hirschfeld's ideas, to convince the small world of Magnus Hirschfeld studies that we can no longer look away from his less-than-heroic moments, and to show what kind of an alternative sexology Li put forward. As a reader, however, I find intellectual history dry, and I love narrative. I have, moreover, a historical reason for the biography: early gay history sought to push back against homophobia and thus understandably celebrated agency and world-making and often brushed aside the things that made queer life so hard.[67] Now most of the people who were adults in the 1930s are gone. We forget, I think, just what it was like to be a celebrity sexologist traveling the world in the 1930s while secretly in love with one's male student and companion, and just what it was like to be a very wealthy young Chinese medical student working as the assistant on a one-man lecture tour around the globe, a somewhat scandalous lecture tour promoting the idea of biological homosexuality. We cannot readily call to mind what it meant for a twenty-four-year-old queer man from Hong Kong to leave China to study in Europe at the side of a much older, famous man in failing health who desired him desperately. Li's and Hirschfeld's lives informed their thinking on sex and politics, and we ought to see how that worked, in part to comprehend just how much things changed for the better later in the twentieth century and to remember what the 1930s were like. Hirschfeld was not out, not openly gay, for example, though more and more people assert that he was.[68] Far from it, in fact. Yet, in his left-leaning social and professional world, it was quite possible to be – very discreetly – queer. There was nevertheless a price to be paid.

Moreover, biography is a good way to show the complex, interwoven, and sometimes contradictory ways in which queerness and racism co-existed and were co-constituted. It can be complicated. Antiracism and anti-imperialism were not the same thing. Hirschfeld both loved Li and racialized him. He both decried empire and retained Eurocentric and racist views, as one can see in the story about Manila. He was a foe of empire, but not a consistent one. He was uncritical of settler colonialism in the US, though he apparently visited at least one Native nation. He thought non-white races ought to rule themselves in India and Egypt, even as he thought some "primitive" non-white races were fated to ex-tinction. He harbored a persistent anti-Black racism even as he wrote of himself as an antiracist. He was also Jewish, though as he toured the segregated United States and hobnobbed with arch white supremacists, it seemed that he had successfully claimed whiteness. Later, in 1933, his own beloved Germany began to strip that whiteness away. Yet it was not exactly his "race" that determined that he could never go home to Ber-lin, even in 1932, when Hitler was not yet in power and very few German Jews had fled the country. Berlin was too dangerous even in 1932 for Hirschfeld because of the interrelated dynamics of sexuality, gender, and racism: to the fascists, he was a Jewish champion of homosexuality, a liv-ing symbol of the Jewish conspiracy to undermine "Aryan" masculinity. That made him a particular target. He had trouble living in exile in Paris because he was queer – his other boyfriend, Karl Giese, a white non-Jew, was arrested for queer acts by the Paris police and expelled from the country, forcing Hirschfeld to abandon his plans to restart his own ca-reer in exile. To my eye, the best way to lay all this out in its complexity is to tell the story in all of its lovely, contradictory, and maddening detail, so that readers can think through it for themselves.

The first chapter introduces Hirschfeld while he was crossing the North Atlantic at the outset of his impromptu world tour and tells the story of his career to that point, explaining why he was so important. In the second chapter, we see Hirschfeld's debt to empire: he and others built the model of "homosexuality" on an imperial foundation, feeding on imaginings of an empire of queer love. We meet Li in chapter 3 in Shanghai in 1931 and examine his relationship with Hirschfeld. The fourth chapter, set in Jawaharlal Nehru's house in Allahabad, India, shows how Hirschfeld's views of empire changed, in part I suspect thanks to Li. The older man had been blithely unconcerned about imperialism, but he became its die-hard foe. Chapter 5 is an intellectual history of the concept of a "sexual minority" and the gay analogy to race; it recounts the enormous debts early gay politics owed to ideas about Jews, about race, and about ethnicity. It shows how early gay rights constructed an implicitly white homosexual. The next three chapters (6, 7, and 8), take readers to New York City in the winter of 1930/1 and to Tel Aviv, Palestine, in the winter of 1932 to examine Hirschfeld's theory of "the races," his racist asides about Black people, including those he met (such as Langston Hughes) who were active in Black queer politics, and his insistence that Ashkenazi Jews such as himself were white. Hirschfeld's ideas about "the races," about empire, and about "civilization" made his model of the homosexual. However, he also believed in biological inequality quite apart from racialization. Chapter 9 examines his eugenics. It is, at least to me, a long-overdue exhaustive account of what he thought about eugenics, what he did about it, and what that means for gay history. And it did mean something for gay history: Hirschfeld formulated a queer eugenics. He used eugenics to violently control some queers while at the same time also using eugenics to justify the existence of other queers. Chapter 10 asks where women fit in to Hirschfeld's work and finds his feminism lacking. Chapter 11 is a more biographical interlude that examines the exile years from Li's perspective, showing how Hirschfeld's tribulations put Li in a difficult bind. The last two chapters, 12 and 13, are Li's. They show how after Hirschfeld's death he became a sexologist in his own right and defied his teacher. They show how he navigated the racialized sexual politics of his day by performing queer masculinities and writing fiction. Li's own theory of sexuality, which he began to elaborate in an unpublished, unfinished manuscript late in his life, is a rejection of Hirschfeld – he found nearly universal queerness, with bisexuality being a near-majority sexuality. He also found that sexual fluidity was a defining part of human life, and he noted widespread transness. Li, however, never published. He may have been hampered in his work by the legacy of his mentor's implicitly white homosexual subject. Li's theory was nearly lost when his manuscript was thrown into the garbage after he died in Vancouver in 1993. It has not been examined as a theory of sexuality until now.[69]

A final note on this book's limits: it almost entirely ignores women, as Hirschfeld did when it came to queer women and as the field of gay history too often has done.[70] More on this in chapter 10. This book is also weak on trans history.[71] Hirschfeld was a pivotal figure in early trans politics, as was Harry Benjamin, who appears throughout this book. Well before the 1930s, Hirschfeld helped people who sought to live as their true sex, not their birth-assigned sex, to legally change their names and to get police permits to dress in clothing that fit their sex. His 1910 book on "transvestitism" presented a transgender identity category; it is among the first works to do so.[72] Today "transvestite" is a term of abuse in the eyes of many trans people, but in Hirschfeld's day it was an umbrella term that included people who considered themselves to be cross-dressing for fun as well as people who explained that their birth-assigned sex was not their actual sex and sought to live as their actual sex, at times enlisting Hirschfeld to help them do that. Such people, who fit our contemporary notions of "trans" and "transgender," used "transvestite" as a term of positive self-identification, hence I also use it at times in its historical sense.[73] Queer and trans politics overlapped, fellow-traveled, were at times one and the same, and also conflicted and diverged. Trans history does fit within the parameters of queer history; trans history does not reduce (as if we were talking about math equations) to queer history and ought not to be so reduced.[74] Yet a fuller account of queer history would incorporate more trans history. At times – particularly in chapter 2 – I have evidence about trans politics, and I have included it, but as a possible help to other researchers, not as a definitive statement. All this having been said, there are some conclusions here that do apply to trans history.

What is new in this book is this: from the very beginning of gay politics – that is, from the "invention" of homosexuality as such – ideas about race and empire, about disability, about Jewish identity and the struggle against antisemitism, and about sex and gender were front and center, used to fashion the modern homosexual.[75] With respect to racism, this could have made gay rights fundamentally antiracist, but somewhat ironically, it could also do the opposite.

1 "Einstein of Sex": Magnus Hirschfeld at the End of the First Century of Gay Rights

North Atlantic Ocean, November 1930

Magnus Hirschfeld loved being aboard a ship. A ship was a floating laboratory for a sexologist. It was November 19, 1930, and the German steamer *Columbus* was five days out from Bremerhaven, sailing for New York Harbor. That morning, an icy wind had gotten up, the tail end of storms in Greenland and Newfoundland, and it blew through the day. Then, toward evening, people aboard the ship sighted the first seagulls. Still hundreds of miles out in the Atlantic, they were approaching land again. As Hirschfeld gazed out at the North Atlantic, he perhaps felt other things beneath the anticipation of reaching New York – grief at the faithlessness of younger men, men he had loved, and the agonizing stirrings of despair about the future of his life's work.[1]

The trip to New York was an escape from troubles in Berlin. The lecture tour of the world was not planned far in advance. Later, in his book, he made it seem as if it began almost by chance. He suddenly got a telegraph inviting him to lecture to a German American medical society in New York.[2] What really happened is that Hirschfeld wrote Harry Benjamin, a German American doctor who practiced in New York, whom he knew through the leftist World League for Sexual Reform. He asked Benjamin to get a medical society to invite him to lecture, which Benjamin did.[3] When the invitation came, Hirschfeld only had a few days to think it over before sailing on the *Columbus*.[4] He had happier motives for going. Hirschfeld liked the United States and wanted to see it again. He had toured it as a young man thirty-seven years before. He had earned a break, too. He had just finished what he considered "my greatest life's work," the multivolume *Sexology*, which he intended to be the foundational text for the new science he was helping to build.[5] Yet something deeper made him seek diversion – the pain of betrayal.

Hirschfeld had been kicked out of the leadership of the world's first homosexual emancipation group, the Scientific Humanitarian

Committee (WhK), a group he had cofounded decades before and had led for most of his adult life. Other men on the WhK's executive committee had forced his resignation because they wanted to go in a new, more left-of-center direction and because they found Hirschfeld's leadership domineering.[6] The men who forced him to resign had been his friends and protégés. He had not seen it coming. In the autumn of the previous year, a young man who had for years worked for Hirschfeld at his Institute for Sexual Science had conspired with other old allies and friends to force him out. Then, that same man orchestrated what Hirschfeld thought of as a "smear campaign" as he tried to get Hirschfeld booted from the other major organization that he controlled, the World League for Sexual Reform (WLSR).[7] The WLSR was an international network of left-of-center men and women, many of them doctors and some of them feminists, who wanted to change unscientific attitudes and laws about sexuality and gender.[8] Hirschfeld kept control of the WLSR. But the struggle had gone on all year, from the fall of 1929 through the summer of 1930.[9]

His health had been bad that year, too. He feared his own death. He did not know whom to trust. His colleagues had turned on him. He raged in his journal. He worried about money as well. The worst of it was that he still had no successor, no one to continue his work after he died or to safeguard his legacy. These colleagues who were turning on him, they were turning away from his ideas, too, and from his theory of homosexuality. "I could really despair for my life's work," he wrote in his journal, then consoled himself that his lover, Karl Giese, would carry on his work after his death.[10]

Yet he knew that was impossible. Hirschfeld of course trusted Giese, the Institute for Sexual Science's archivist and his assistant. Giese was a much younger man whom Hirschfeld had met at least a decade before. In Berlin, Giese looked after Hirschfeld.[11] To the public, and even to close allies in the sex reform movement, their relationship was a professional one, but intimates knew they were partners who lived together in a private apartment at the Institute.[12] When he died, Hirschfeld wanted Giese to act as administrative head of the Institute, together with a second confidant who would look after the business side.[13] But Giese could not be the public face of sexology. He did not have a medical degree.

Happily, despite his worries, there was much on the ship to distract Hirschfeld. He turned his sexologist's eye on the first-class passengers. An older, distinguished man was traveling with a much younger woman. She looked to Hirschfeld to be from a working-class part of East Berlin – a prostitute, he guessed. An older woman in elaborate makeup that made her look like "a mummy" from a crypt, he wrote, traveled with a little Japanese dog and a young French "gigolo," an elegant fellow with a stylish moustache. For the evening dancing following the afternoon movie, the older woman and the "little Berlin tart [*Nutte*]" donned expensive ball gowns and diamonds and pearls. Hirschfeld watched them, perhaps from a chair set to the side of the dance floor, probably wearing a rumpled dark suit. He silently memorized details to color the snarky letters he would write to his friends back in Berlin. He found his rich shipmates ostentatious, "the ladies in their newest Paris and Berlin costumes – a true orgy of narcissism, exhibitionism and fetishism – the men, nine-tenths of them in tuxedos with white vests and starched shirts."[14] He saved his sharpest words for the women. Hirschfeld did not have a lot of genuine empathy for women, despite his official feminism.[15] Amid the glamour, he himself refused to put on a tux, though he could not escape "a certain sense of sartorial inferiority [*Kleidungsminderwertigkeitsgefühl*]" and a begrudging admiration for those who did dress up – with the rocking of the ship, he had trouble getting his foot into the correct trouser leg.[16]

Some wealthy fellow passengers in first class probably had snarky things to say about the sexologist. They probably saw Hirschfeld as the wealthy British writer Christopher Isherwood had seen him when they met in Berlin a few years before. Isherwood's description, laced with antisemitism and disdain, was of "the silly solemn old professor with his doggy mustache, thick peering spectacles, and clumsy German-Jewish boots," though Isherwood later came to appreciate Hirschfeld.[17] In a much friendlier description by another writer, from a 1933 interview, Hirschfeld was "stocky and vigorous, alert and energetic, his lips under the thick mustache light[ing] up with a smile … The clear eyes, extraordinarily attentive behind the golden glasses, have an expression both gentle and full of authority."[18]

Hirschfeld was much happier studying the homosexuality of the sailors than watching the fancy ladies of first class. He roamed the ship and met an older steward who, to Hirschfeld's surprise, told him "totally unselfconsciously" that he, the steward, was a homosexual.[19] In those days, one did not often admit that to a stranger.

Hirschfeld had bought a first-class ticket hoping to make the American press take note of him when he disembarked. Maybe he could drum up some interest, give more public lectures, and stay abroad longer, bankrolling the trip with the honorariums. He thought, too, that as he was representing sexology, he ought to represent it well, in first class.[20]

Sexology, a scientific and medical subfield, came together especially in the German-speaking world in the first decade of the twentieth century.[21] The word "sexology" did not at the time mean everything that was published about sex from the perspective of science and medicine; it rather meant a small, new, struggling subfield.[22] Hirschfeld was among its founders and great men. The idea was to have a broad science of sexuality, encompassing not just "the perversions" that had fascinated an earlier generation but also "normal" sexuality, everything from hormones to sexually transmitted infections to reproduction. In Hirschfeld's mind, sexology was foundationally a European project – though this was not in fact the case, as it flourished around the world.[23] Sexology was supposed to become its own discipline, like psychiatry, with academic departments in medical schools, or so Hirschfeld and others hoped. It never did.[24]

As far as first class went, he did not regret the lavish food either.[25] Hirschfeld had a sweet tooth that he was ever at odds with after he developed diabetes as an adult.[26] But the main justification for traveling in high style was to seduce the press. Hirschfeld wondered in one letter if Benjamin ought to arrange a press conference for his arrival.[27] He wrote as well to the celebrated German American writer George Sylvester Viereck, the son of a friend.[28] Viereck was queer and took an interest in Hirschfeld's work.[29] That was a fortuitous connection – Viereck knew how to work the American press.[30]

Yet if the American press did take notice, what would the reporters make of him? In Europe, where he was better known, Hirschfeld had a mixed reputation, though unfairly so, he thought. In a world where any public discussion of sex was breaking a taboo, a strong whiff of scandal clung to sexology.

He had antisemitism to contend with as well. Hirschfeld was a secular person for whom the Judaism of childhood meant little now. Yet whenever he raised his voice in public, antisemitism kept many people from taking him entirely seriously. This was true of some relatively left-of-center people too. "I have even heard in serious circles that mostly Jews are concerned with Sexual [*sic*] reform because they have not so strong principles in morals," a Czech birth control advocate wrote to Margaret Sanger, the famous American leader of birth control activism. This letter was written a few days before Hirschfeld's World League for Sexual Reform held its fifth international congress in Brno, then in Czechoslovakia. There were several Jews in the WLSR leadership in addition to Hirschfeld. The letter's author had taken note of reactions to this in the run-up to the congress: "I see now with the congress for sexual reform that most people object to the participation of so many Jews." He told Sanger he wanted to keep Jews out of his work for birth control in Czechoslovakia, and apparently he thought she agreed.[31] Indeed, both sexology and psychoanalysis were nascent fields that had to contend with antisemitism. It drove Jewish practitioners into less-prestigious specialties and inspired them to found new fields such as sexology, yet it dogged them when they did so.[32]

Hirschfeld maintained a heterosexual façade, but rumors of his covert homosexuality had proved to be an enduring drag on his reputation as well, no matter how discreet he was about his affairs – and as readers will note as this book progresses, he was ultra-discreet, even in his private papers. "Now as to Hirschfeld, I like him all right and believe that he can do a certain amount of good, but I am absolutely with you as to connecting his name with Birth Control," Margaret Sanger wrote in 1928 to a colleague who ran a birth control clinic in Berlin. Sanger was referring to Hirschfeld's homosexuality. The colleague had told Sanger that "he is so widely known as a homosexual and as a student of homosexuality" that it would be a mistake to associate with him.[33] Freud, who had lots of professional contact with Hirschfeld, wrote of his "well-sublimated homosexuality."[34] When Hirschfeld opened the Institute for Sexual Science in 1919, a right-extremist newspaper went on the attack, claiming the Institute was nothing but a homosexual bordello. The Institute had no university affiliation, they pointed out. It was nothing but "homosexuals" carrying out their "shameless" activities "under the cover of science."[35] The Berlin police looked into the accusation and pronounced it silly. However, in the course of their investigation, both the police and two doctors who knew Hirschfeld through professional channels stated in memos that they believed he was a homosexual.[36] One of the doctors even echoed the fantastic allegation that Hirschfeld had made the Institute into a sex club.[37] Hirschfeld's enemies used his homosexuality to get at him. Ahead of the 1929 London congress of the WLSR, a rival sexologist wrote to people alleging that Hirschfeld was homosexual and advising them not to attend the meeting.[38]

What would the Americans, notorious prudes, make of him?

The *Columbus* reached New York Harbor late in the day. Hirschfeld and the other passengers went through passport control and medical screening. As soon as they were done, a scrum of reporters came on board. They "turned their cameras and fountain pens" on Hirschfeld, as he wrote later, and branded him with the headline "Einstein of Sex."[39] The clever moniker was in fact the work of Viereck.[40] It was a calculated effort to stir up the kind of celebrity enjoyed by Albert Einstein, then living in California. The name alone did not make Hirschfeld a celebrity, but a celebrity he was – a celebrity sex expert.[41] The first headlines were a taste of what was to come. Invitations to lecture poured in.

Even before his world tour, Hirschfeld was much better known in the United States than he is today. In 1920, he was already "the well-known expert on sexual science" in the American press.[42] The US's anarchist sex radicals loved him; later, while he was in exile in Paris, one of them, Emma Goldman, came to visit him.[43] But the wider public knew him as well. In 1924, he came up in the press during the murder trial of Nathan Leopold and Richard Loeb, rich Chicagoans rumored to be homosexual. A story erroneously claimed that Hirschfeld, as well as Sigmund Freud, would be witnesses for the defense.[44] The reporter credited Hirschfeld with the discovery of the "third sex," that is, homosexuals.[45] Americans also recognized Hirschfeld from advertisements for Titus Pearls, the rejuvenation pills he fronted. Those ads called him "the world-known authority on Sexology and Director of the Institute for Sexual Science of Berlin, Germany."[46] The *New England Journal of Medicine* implied he was a quack because of Titus Pearls.[47] The advertising he did for Titus Pearls did not help his credibility with other doctors.[48] It did, however, spread his fame.

In 1930, at the outset of his world tour, Hirschfeld reached a new height of celebrity, his reputation seemingly unsullied. In the American press, and then afterward in the press of other countries, he was what he had always thought himself to be – a world-renowned expert on human sexuality. He was a smash hit, though not everyone was enthused. "Wild Sex Talk Has Not Been Helpful," editorialized the *Modesto News-Herald*.[49] The American press photographed him over one hundred times.[50] He would be the "Einstein of Sex" at the end of his circumnavigation of the world, in Greece, too.[51]

He felt "astonishment." He had not known "how far beyond the borders of Germany and Europe the gospel of research on human sexual life and love life that I represented had already spread." He realized he could travel the world advancing his life's work – spreading scientific information about sexuality. He lectured across the United States. He was briefly in Mexico at one point, in Canada at another, and he sailed from San Francisco on March 5, 1931, on the Japanese steamer *Asamu Maru*. After seven weeks, most of them spent in Tokyo, and many public lectures, he sailed for China, where he would meet Li.[52]

Hirschfeld's lecture tour of the world was the first time that anyone had told so many people in so many different places that same-sex desire indicated a state of being called "homosexuality," which was a natural, non-pathological condition. The lecture tour was the high point of the first century of gay rights. Beginning in the 1830s, that century had been marked by the unsuccessful fight against sodomy laws.

Magnus Hirschfeld was born in 1868, about thirty years after an obscure Swiss hatmaker published the first book defending male-male love. Hirschfeld was born into a world in which being accused of sodomy, as male-male sex was often called, was such a grave blow that men took their own lives rather than face a public trial. After he grew up and became a doctor, Hirschfeld was once called in to consult with a man who had been arrested for sodomy. He and the jailer arrived at the accused man's cell to find that he had just hung himself. The body was still warm.[53]

Sodomy, the crime that Hirschfeld would spend his life arguing was in fact no crime at all, had very long roots in European history. To the medieval Catholic Church, "sodomy" was a collection of supposedly grievously sinful sex acts including penetrative anal sex, sexual contact between a human and an animal, and other sex acts that were thought to have no chance of leading to conception, such as what we would call oral sex.[54] In the Middle Ages, "sodomy" was not "homosexuality." Though when they spoke of "the sodomitic sin" early medieval monastics probably often had male-male anal intercourse in mind, they were worried about an act, not a special type of person; moreover, sodomy laws applied to male-female couples as well and also (more rarely) to female-female couples – they, too, were thought by many authorities to be capable of "sins against nature."[55] People were not often convicted of sodomy, but the penalty was burning alive.[56] Though the Protestant Reformation did little to alter the prosecution of sodomy across Europe, the Enlightenment did.[57] Secularism and a new zeal for the evidence-based study of the natural world changed how people thought about medicine, the body, and politics. To Enlightenment writers, male-male sex was a crime against nature.[58] But they thought religion should not make law. They thought it grotesque to burn people at the stake for an act that was disgusting but not dangerous.[59]

The French Revolution made men citizens with natural rights that even the king could not violate and emphatically made one's religion a part of one's private, not public, self. So, on the one hand, French revolutionaries penned pornographic screeds about Marie Antoinette's alleged "tribadism" (sex with women) and her other supposed debaucheries, like participation in orgies and masturbation, because all of that bad sex demonstrated the corruption of the monarchy.[60] Then they decapitated her. On the other hand, those same revolutionaries rewrote the French law code and simply left out a host of crimes they considered religious superstitions that had no business in a secular penal code – blasphemy, heresy, witchcraft, bestiality, and sodomy, to name a few.[61] Sodomy was not a crime in Napoleon's empire, and as Napoleon added large swaths of central Europe to that empire, sodomy laws fell. (The Napoleonic Code did have laws against public indecency, corrupting the young, and similar vague offenses that were used against adult men who had same-sex sex in public; such laws would later bring down Karl Giese.)[62] Sodomy laws stayed on the books elsewhere, however, such as in German-speaking Prussia. As time went on and penal law changed, however, no one burned anyone at the stake anymore – the last execution for female-female sex was in 1721.[63] Rather, the punishment was prison, and life-destroying public shame.

The French Revolution also removed medieval legal restrictions on French Ashkenazi Jews, which is important because shortly after this, same-sex-desiring people took the struggle of Jews for civil rights as a model for themselves.[64] France became the first European nation to grant full civic equality to Jewish men. Religious views were a matter of individual conscience.[65]

When Hirschfeld was a child, the monarch of Prussia went to war to establish a nation-state called "Germany" for the first time, uniting many of Europe's smaller German-speaking kingdoms. Hirschfeld's earliest memories were of riding in a wagon with his father, who was a doctor, to visit a military hospital during one of those wars.[66] Like many Jewish German families, Hirschfeld's celebrated the new German empire – its law code struck away the remaining legal discriminations against Jews.[67] Prussia still had a sodomy law, however, and that law became the law of the new German empire.

Yet by the 1860s many progressive, secularly minded people saw another good reason to dispense with laws against sodomy altogether: medicine.[68] By the 1850s, a new subspecialty, psychiatry, was claiming that people who enjoyed same-sex sex did so because they suffered from a mental illness and that they ought to be viewed not as sinners or criminals but as patients in need of care.[69] Psychiatry would define homosexuality as a mental illness well into the second half of the twentieth century.

In 1869, the year after Hirschfeld was born, a blue-ribbon commission of medical experts told the government to strike down the criminalization of sodomy and bestiality. The commission was led by the Berlin anthropologist, doctor, and politician Rudolf Virchow, a liberal foe of antisemitism who was later one of Hirschfeld's professors in medical school and who influenced him a good deal in his thinking on "the races." Virchow's commission did not make any reference to an idea that would become important later, in part thanks to Hirschfeld – that is, the idea that men who had same-sex sex were a special type of person with an innate predisposition. The commission did not need to. In 1869, there were better-established, far more respectable arguments against sodomy laws. Virchow's commission made what now seems a rather mild, somewhat agnostic, and narrowly medical argument against the criminalization of male-male "sodomy" (*Unzucht*) and bestiality: though neither were lovely, from a medical perspective neither were any worse than other unsavory sex acts that were not criminal, such as "sodomy" done by female-male couples, or indeed by female-female couples.[70] (Prussia had by then revised its sodomy law so that lesbian sex was not covered; this seems to have been an oversight rather than a purposeful move to decriminalize female-female sex.)[71] The commissioners protested that they were not qualified to weigh in on whether male-male sodomy "is a particularly pronounced denigration [*Herabwürdigung*] of human beings, a particularly dire instance of immorality, as opposed to other types of sodomy."[72] They were merely pointing out that from a public health perspective, the law made no sense. Anticipating an idea that came to fruition almost sixty years later in Germany, the commission ended its short report by suggesting that perhaps the law against male-male sex could be replaced with a law against male prostitution.[73] A similar commission in Austria-Hungary made the point that most people who had same-sex sex were either in circumstances of extreme sexual depravation or mentally ill.[74]

Neither commission succeeded. Austria and Germany both kept their sodomy laws well into the twentieth century. Yet the fact that, on its own, medicine was gradually turning against sodomy laws helps explain why Hirschfeld, whose decision to study medicine was probably not unrelated, was so successful so quickly.

In 1868, Germany also had what we might call a very small, marginalized gay or trans rights movement, though it did not use those terms.[75] When Hirschfeld was a child, scattered rogue voices among the German-speaking bourgeoisie already called out in print for the liberation of men who desired other men, and on terms quite different from what the doctors envisioned. In a moment when literacy was rising and print technology was getting cheaper, people who thought same-sex desire perfectly natural began to publish their thoughts. These were not the first people to have assumed that their same-sex desires or gender nonconformity characterized them as individuals, nor were they the first to decide that such things ought not to be the basis of their oppression. What was new were the public politics of this, the calls in print for an end to oppression and the comparisons to the unjust oppression of other groups in post-Enlightenment society. Privately, in 1823, a rich, masculine Englishwoman who loved other women riffed on Rousseau in order to explain her nature, but she was not writing for publication.[76] That appears to have first been done by a wealthy hatmaker named Heinrich Hössli in a Swiss alpine village. He wrote two volumes on male-male love, in 1836 and 1838.[77] Then, in the 1860s and 1870s, a firebrand lawyer named Karl Heinrich Ulrichs did a series of pamphlets defending female souls in male bodies (and vice versa): "Urnings," he called them. Both authors sounded nothing like Virchow and the other doctors. Hössli pointed to the ancient world, to biology, and to post-Enlightenment politics: Jews and witches had been unfairly persecuted, and now in more rational times, they were not. (This was more true of witches than of Jews at the time, though the Enlightenment had improved things for Jews west of the Russian Empire.) Same-sex-loving men were still suffering irrational persecution. This ought to cease. No one burned witches anymore. He also pointed to another disenfranchised class of persons as an example: women.[78] But Hössli did not find much of an audience. Ulrichs did not know of Hössli's work until after he had begun his own.[79]

Ulrichs, a lawyer, civil servant, and journalist with a passion for classicism, was a more important figure than Hössli because more people read him.[80] He had his own theories, but he drew on the same mix of precedents one finds in Hössli – ancient Greece, biology, and the idea of same-sex-desiring people as an unfairly persecuted class. In Ulrichs's theory, same-sex desire comes from gender inversion. Urnings who loved men were not actually loving the same sex, because Urnings were a third sex. Rereading him today, it is not clear whether he belongs more to trans history or to gay history.

Ulrichs was courageous. He self-identified in public as an "Urning" – Hössli had not (he was married).[81] Hirschfeld never did either, though a few of his contemporaries did.[82] Ulrichs went to a legal convention in Munich in 1867 and attempted to make a public speech against sodomy laws. The other lawyers found what he was saying so objectionable that they shouted him down. And though not many people read Ulrichs, he found a larger audience than Hössli had. Karl Marx and Friedrich Engels read him, though he did not change their minds.[83] "The paederasts are beginning to count themselves, and discover that they are a power in the state," a dismissive Engels wrote to Marx in 1869, echoing Ulrichs's claim that Urnings were a class. Though Engels deemed the notion "smut," he apprehended what was happening – queer men were organizing on the new political model, as a group with democratic political power.[84] Around the same time, a few other authors wrote against the sodomy law too.[85] One, a Hungarian then living in Berlin named Karl Maria Kertbeny, coined the term "homosexuality [*Homosexualität*]" in 1869.[86] This was all possible only in German-speaking Europe, with its relaxed censorship. Other countries did not allow the topic to be discussed in print.[87] By the 1880s, British authors were quietly making pro-homosexuality arguments similar to those of Hössli and Ulrichs, but they could only publish them privately and in small editions.[88]

These sex and gender radicals lurking within the bourgeoisie were not geniuses who suddenly hit upon an entirely novel idea. Their arguments were built from the commonplaces of a European bourgeoisie education – the principles of the Enlightenment and liberal nineteenth-century politics, the example of classical Greece – as well as from very general notions of biology.[89] Probably many people came up with similar ideas. Maybe some published them in now-forgotten, poorly circulated texts. At the same time, their ideas varied quite a lot and in some ways were radically alien from what gay rights would become later. Hössli did not write about women at all; it is not clear that his model applies to them.[90] Ulrichs's Urnings, female souls in male bodies and vice versa, seem to be proto-trans people even more than they seem like early examples of gay identity.

Most important: they were not very successful. Ulrichs did not change many minds.[91] He never founded an organization, though he thought about doing so.[92] His fight to strike down the sodomy law failed. He helped swayed Richard von Krafft-Ebing, one of the day's leading psychiatrists, who came around at the end of his life and wrote that in some people, same-sex desire was no mental illness but was an inborn predisposition.[93] It was not, however, until after Ulrichs's death that Krafft-Ebing changed his position, and he did so in an article published in Hirschfeld's journal, after having agreed to add his name to a petition drawn up by Hirschfeld's Scientific Humanitarian Committee.[94] Ulrichs eventually gave up, moved to a town on the Italian peninsula (where sodomy was not a crime), and threw himself into his other passion, classicism, editing a tiny journal. Ulrichs's importance has been overemphasized in my view. Hirschfeld was the real game-changer.[95] When Hirschfeld was first publishing on homosexuality in the 1890s, Ulrichs was forgotten. Hirschfeld could barely find Ulrichs's pamphlets – the few people who had read them decades before had burned them for fear of incriminating themselves, Hirschfeld thought.[96]

Hirschfeld grew up in a large family in a seaside Baltic spa town. Today it is the Polish city Kołobrzeg; at the time it was the German city Kolberg. His was an observant, liberal, assimilated Jewish family. His father was a prominent doctor. Hirschfeld seems to have had a happy childhood and to have enjoyed loving relationships with his parents and siblings. His father made a large impression, and the desire to help others was strong in the younger Hirschfeld. This is probably why in his youth he was drawn to social democracy. He followed his two older brothers to medical school. The profession of a doctor was one of the few prestigious positions open to a middle-class German Jew; lingering antisemitism kept Jews out of the civil service and other posts. None of his four sisters had opportunities for higher education. In Kolberg, girls from wealthy families might study at the equivalent of the high school level, but not at the prestigious *Gymnasium* that prepared Hirschfeld and his brothers for university and the professions. Hirschfeld finished his medical studies at Berlin University (now Humboldt) in 1892. His doctoral thesis was on influenza. He traveled after graduation – Morocco, Algeria, Italy, and America. Then, in 1894, he opened a private practice as a doctor specializing in experimental natural methods.[97]

In his years in medical school, from 1887 to 1893, Hirschfeld learned almost nothing about sexuality. "I barely ever heard a professorial mouth utter the word 'sexuality,'" he wrote. Yes, the medical students at Berlin University learned about syphilis and gonorrhea, about birth, and about the anatomy of the sex organs. At the end of classes on the sex organs any drawings of anatomy would be erased from the chalkboard, so that no unauthorized eyes would glimpse scandalous images. But save for a brave junior lecturer in zoology, no one said anything about sexual sensation or need. No one spoke of the normal sex drive, let alone the abnormal sex drive. "I remember only a single exception to this," Hirschfeld wrote.

> In a large, over-filled lecture hall ... the most popular psychiatrist in Berlin, Professor Emanuel Mendel, gave a weekday evening lecture for doctors and lawyers on legal incapacity due to insanity, with demonstrations. The young academics met the moral criminals and the pederasts. It began with the explanation of the physical signs of an "active" or "passive" pederast: an anus with a funnel shape and a correspondingly tapered penis ... Not infrequently, the professor went on, pederasts assaulted children too, as the next case, a child molester, showed ... The medical exam for the court had found in this case that the accused had feeblemindedness and moral insanity. The lecture's final case was an old man who had exposed his sex organs to a grieving widow at a suburban cemetery ... the professor explained that he was epileptic.[98]

More than twenty years later, as Hirschfeld sat writing these recollections, probably in his study at the Institute for Sexual Science, the scene was still clear in his mind. There stood the three "cases" at the front of the packed auditorium: the pederast, the child molester, and the exhibitionist. The three men listened with rapt attention as the professor explained their failings, just as captivated by the lecture as were the students.[99]

How painful was it for a medical student who desired other men to sit out in that audience, as a renowned authority equated the desire of an adult man for another adult man with child molestation and exposing oneself to a grieving widow in a cemetery? The professor blamed all of it on feeblemindedness, moral insanity, and epilepsy, which at the time were themselves considered shameful conditions, the results of heredi-tary degeneration.[100] The moment seared Hirschfeld's consciousness, it seems – hence the clear memory. So much was at stake. He thought that medical opinion on homosexuality was the single most important thing standing between homosexuals and freedom.[101] And medical opinion was not exactly friendly: in the late nineteenth century, the leading ex-perts on homosexuality were recommending hypnosis as a cure, or even lobotomy.[102]

Hirschfeld fought back. A transparent, frank, scientific, public ap-proach to sex could cure many of society's ills, he thought. That idea was not an uncommon one in the left-of-center circles in which he traveled as a young man. Late nineteenth-century Germany was a place where lots of people wanted to harness science to change lives. Reform groups sprang up. They wanted to use science to build better public health systems or to argue for equality for women. There were nudist societies that promoted natural, non-erotic nakedness for health and well-being. People were experimenting with modern dance and call-ing for vegetarianism, more sensible clothing for women, and physical fitness. Left-wing teachers wanted honest sex education for young peo-ple. "Neo-Malthusians" wanted birth control. Conservative Christians were horrified by the whole lot of reformers. Hirschfeld's initial efforts were not about homosexuality, however. He made a few forays at public education on other topics – articles on medicine and public health in magazines, warning of the dangers of alcoholism and opining on other matters.[103]

Then, something galvanized the young doctor's will. Something drove him to take a remarkable step, one that arguably changed the world, and for sure changed German sex politics for the next three dec-ades. In 1896, Hirschfeld published a thirty-five-page pamphlet called *Sappho and Socrates, or, How Can We Explain the Love of Men or Women for Persons of the Same Sex?*[104] What inspired him? He said himself that it was the suicide of a lieutenant whom he had treated for depression. The young man took his own life shortly after his wedding. He wrote in a farewell letter to Hirschfeld that he did not have the strength to tell the truth about himself to his parents, who had so wished for him to marry, and that therefore he had decided to end it all.[105] "How many similar 'farewell letters' I have received since!"[106] Hirschfeld wrote dec-ades later. Suicide was a common response to one's own homosexuality. Among the many men who died that way was Eduard Oberg, who along with Hirschfeld was one of the founders of the world's first gay rights group.[107] Oscar Wilde's 1895 trial drove Hirschfeld to act, too. He and other queer men across Europe were profoundly shaken by Wilde's martyrdom.[108] However, *Sappho and Socrates* had a longer history. It was very like the work of an up-and-coming English sexologist, Havelock Ellis, and a queer English poet and cultural historian, John Addington Symonds; they and Hirschfeld were reading some of the same things, and that same year, 1896, Ellis and Symonds published the first German edition of their book *Sexual Inversion*, which was very like Hirschfeld's pamphlet.[109] Hirschfeld must have been working out his ideas for some time, perhaps since that day in the lecture hall in medical school – his theory was detailed and comprehensive.[110] Surely he had been talking to people about it. The work of the two Brits demonstrates that many people were thinking along these lines at the time. Yet Hirschfeld's pamphlet was also an answer to the image of the homosexual that had haunted him since medical school, if not before. It was the picture of the homosexual as pathological, deranged, and physically marked in a humiliating way.

In *Sappho and Socrates*, the ambitious young doctor put forward a scientific theory of same-sex desire's innate, biological nature, in both men and women. Same-sex desire was not a mental illness. It was caused by an inborn biological condition. That condition was not a disease. Indeed, it fit beautifully within the broader system of human sexuality. Same-sex-loving people were therefore an unjustly oppressed group. Europeans used to burn witches and heretics. That had been a cruel violation of scientific rationality and the rights of people. So, in the same way, were convictions for sodomy.[111] This was remarkably close to what Hirschfeld would argue for the rest of his life. In the pamphlet, as in all of his public advocacy, Hirschfeld claimed to be a neutral scientist who was merely conveying the facts. This strategy won him more public influence than anyone before him had wielded.

Sappho and Socrates was groundbreaking because it reconciled earlier claims of homosexuals as a class of people with a rigorous medical/biological approach, which the earlier authors had not had. In Hirschfeld's model, homosexuals were a class defined by an unusual, but not pathological, biological trait. The pamphlet was marked throughout by the trappings of serious science. It had charts and graphs. It had erudite discussions of embryology and endocrinology and evolution. It broke with the leading medical authorities on homosexuality, who all thought it was pathological.[112]

Sappho and Socrates was, to borrow a term from the Hirschfeld biographer and German English lesbian sexologist Charlotte Wolff, "a landmark." Wolff has it as a landmark in "sexological history" but I would go further: it was a landmark in the history of sexuality and in what would later be called gay politics.[113] Two things make the pamphlet an important point of historical rupture, that is, a point where the incredibly complex system of human interactions suddenly lurched in a new, though not unprecedented, direction. The first was that it launched Hirschfeld's career. No one had ever had a career like it. It was not foreordained that anyone would. That someone would come along at the end of the nineteenth century and publish an argument that was not unlike those of Ulrichs and Hössli was, I would submit, well within the realm of possibility given what was going on in the 1890s. That someone would do that and single-handedly, without much support from the scientific establishment, forge themselves into a semi-credible scientific expert with an international public profile and their own research institute was less likely. Yet that is what Hirschfeld eventually did. The second way in which this was a lurch in a new direction was the content of the pamphlet, which married gay politics to science, in particular to biology as opposed to psychiatry.[114] Hirschfeld's model was not entirely new, yet the spin he put on ideas that had popped up in the work of others was a very lasting one. Here, for the first time, was biological, non-pathological homosexuality, a condition that a small minority of the population was born with, and science proved this, he asserted. Among other things, as Leila Rupp notes, the model contained an important change in gender. Female and male queerness had often in the past been seen as quite distinct, but now both arose, supposedly, from a single condition that "defined certain individuals" in a way it had previously not been thought to do.[115] That Hirschfeld was working in Germany augmented the global impact of what he did. At the time, the natural sciences in the German-speaking world were cutting edge.[116]

What nature had done, Hirschfeld wrote in the 1902 reprint of *Sappho and Socrates*, was "created a class of people [*Menschenklasse*] that she did not intend for physical reproduction," and by 1902 he thought that idea "has spread very far."[117] It was a powerful idea, combining as it did the claim that homosexuals were a class of people with biology. Yet it remained a fringe idea throughout Hirschfeld's life. Thanks to decades of labor by him and others, however, the model was widely cited and discussed by the mainstream. For example, when a committee of the German Parliament voted to decriminalize sodomy in 1929, many politicians took the time to remark on how they thought Hirschfeld's theory was wrong and that, in fact, homosexuality was contagious or a mental illness. That effort to repeal the sodomy law stalled, though the vote went Hirschfeld's way.[118]

Hirschfeld's work was paralleled to a certain extent by the work of Havelock Ellis in the English-speaking world, though Ellis was never the political advocate that Hirschfeld would become.[119] Hirschfeld got much more political and, arguably, more publicly associated with the homosexual cause then Ellis did. A leading British medical journal dismissed Ellis and Symonds's claim that homosexuality was a natural anomaly, asserting that it was a depravation that one acquired, and the book was later banned in the United Kingdom.[120] German-speaking Europe was far friendlier to this nascent gay rights advocacy, and Hirschfeld envisioned a different sort of career, that of a public advocate.

Medical expertise formed the core of the strategy. He would use research to convince the public and the government that homosexuals were a naturally occurring minority. It was going to take money, "copious funding [*Mittel in Menge*]," he wrote in 1902.[121] But the mainstream scientific community was not going to make a place for him. He would never hold a university post, because of antisemitism, because of the radical nature of his theory, and because of the rumors about his own homosexuality. He had to raise the money to found his own research institute, which he did. In 1919 he opened the Institute for Sexual Science in Berlin. "Urnings" had to help themselves. The heterosexual majority cursed them not out of ill will "but out of ignorance – they do not understand that they are a minority [*Minderheit*]," naturally predisposed to same-sex desire.[122]

It is not just the novelty of his theory that makes the arrival of Hirschfeld on the stage of gay politics a momentous moment.[123] Hirschfeld was more than a theorist. Indeed, his theories have not held up all that well. *Sappho and Socrates* is full of theoretical holes, and no one has proven that homosexuality is inborn, despite lots of attempts to do so.[124] But his practical qualities were as significant as his ideas. He had organizational talents and the sagacity to judge his moment. He was also at the right place at the right time. Momentum for his cause was building independent of himself. The Wilde trial spurred public discussion. Between 1898 and 1908, Hirschfeld would later reckon, there were 10,000 German-language publications on homosexuality.[125] Other authors began to defend male-male love. Globally, scientific approaches to sexuality were gaining traction, not only in Europe but in India, China, and elsewhere – at the end of his career, the growth of this transnational field of sexual science paved the way for Hirschfeld's lecture tour, though he was terrible at recognizing the contributions of non-Europeans to sexual science.[126]

In 1897, Hirschfeld gathered three other men in his apartment in Charlottenburg, then a suburb of Berlin, to found the Scientific Humanitarian Committee, with its goal the humane and scientific reform of sodomy laws. They were a group of buttoned-down, respectable, middle-class and aristocratic men, and they advocated democratic reform, not revolution, but their ideas were shockingly radical for their day. Nevertheless, the Scientific Humanitarian Committee's clout was visible right away. Two of the four men had formidable connections. Max Spohr ran a publishing house and already specialized in pro-homosexual literature. He had published *Sappho and Socrates*. He would go on to help Hirschfeld publish a journal and to reprint Ulrichs's pamphlets.[127] Franz Josef von Bülow was a wealthy former colonial official from an important political family.[128] Von Bülow is an interesting fellow for another reason. Shortly before the Committee's first meeting, he had been shot in the head fighting the Herero people in Germany's colony in southwestern Africa.[129] Some years later, the German military responded to an uprising by the Herero with a campaign of genocide against them and the Nama people, a mass murder that nearly wiped out the Herero and Nama.[130] Hirschfeld apparently lost no sleep over von Bülow's bloody time in the colony.[131] The least-illustrious of the four founders was Eduard Oberg, a lawyer and civil servant who worked tirelessly for the Committee for decades until, in the dark Berlin winter of 1917, he died by suicide.[132] Spohr was married and, according to Hirschfeld, not homosexual.[133] The other three quietly were.[134] This was a mobilization of wealthy, well-connected men prepared to fight for their lives.

They got results. They were rapidly joined by other men, including a high-ranking official in the Berlin police department.[135] The group wrote a petition to the Reichstag calling for the sodomy law's abolition. It was signed by famous men, including Krafft-Ebing, the Austrian psychiatrist, and one of Germany's top politicians, the leader of the Social Democratic Party August Bebel.[136] Hirschfeld knew Bebel from his student days. Bebel even made a speech in favor of the petition in the Reichstag in 1898.[137] The parliament did not strike the law, but this was remarkable progress for the cause. The WhK did a second petition, signed by 2,000 important people, among them Rainer Maria Rilke, Heinrich and Thomas Mann, and Frank Wedekind (author of the play *Spring Awakening*, which in the 2000s found improbable new life as a Broadway musical).[138]

This advocacy for homosexuals was unprecedented and unparalleled. In Great Britain at the time, a few authors defended same-sex desire and Havelock Ellis built a towering reputation as a sexologist who supported the decriminalization of sodomy. None of that went nearly as far as the Germans. Nowhere else was there a dedicated reform group petitioning the parliament. Nowhere else did a leading political figure of Bebel's stature speak out on behalf of that group, even if his speech spun his defense of homosexuals into a veiled attack on his enemies.

It was not, however, what gay rights would become. The dramatic success at the start of Hirschfeld's career – he turned twenty-nine the day before he cofounded the Scientific Humanitarian Committee – cemented his opinion about the best way to fight for homosexual emancipation.[139] He stuck to the path stubbornly for the rest of his life. A scientist, a public intellectual, ought to lead efforts to educate the masses and lobby the government. He and his allies ought to use their connections to influence important people. Above all, they ought to maintain their respectability, because their power came from their status. Open homosexuality would destroy that status. In the first half of the twentieth century, indeed, to publicly argue for homosexual liberation *as a self-identified homosexual* was to mark oneself as a marginal and inconsequential figure of fun, an alarming clown.[140]

Gay rights became a mass movement in the twentieth century. Scientists did not lead it. It drew its legitimacy from the sheer numbers of people it marshaled to its cause, though also sometimes from science and often from quiet, wealthy donors. Increasingly, people declared their homosexuality in public as a way to fight stigma. By the end of Hirschfeld's life, those developments were under way, and he resisted them.[141]

Hirschfeld's career from the 1890s to the day he met Li Shiu Tong in 1931 was an eventful one. He had a preternatural ability to build institutions like journals and scientific societies. He ran a privately funded research institute. He published a very long list of books and articles. He helped make a feature film about the injustice of the sodomy law, in which he played himself. He kept up a private practice too, seeing patients, including many unhappy homosexuals and trans people (who at the time called themselves "transvestites"). He helped trans men and women get police permission to live as their self-confirmed sex. He testified on behalf of men accused of sodomy. He saved many from the ruin that overcame the man who took his own life on the day the young Hirschfeld went to meet him in his jail cell. Hirschfeld's was a career with lows and highs. His reputation suffered after he meddled in a scandal about alleged homosexuality in the kaiser's inner circle in the early twentieth century. It rebounded internationally as the World League for Sexual Reform flourished after the First World War.[142]

By 1931, Hirschfeld was also one of the world's leading sexologists. He helped found the discipline of sexology. Though this would not become clear until after his death, sexology flopped. It never gained the trappings of a discipline, like dedicated university departments and PhD programs. It remained outside the scientific establishment. Yet in the 1930s sexology looked like it might make it as a new branch of science, with its own journals and conferences. That lent lots of power to Hirschfeld's advocacy.

The Magnus Hirschfeld who arrived in New York was standing at the apex of a small social movement for homosexual rights. He was a major expert on homosexuality and "transvestitism," as well as the single most important advocate of the rights of homosexuals in the world in the first half of the twentieth century. An American author wrote in 1922 that Hirschfeld's theory of homosexuality "has had more influence on modern thought than any other theory of homosexualism" and had "unfortunately … been accepted as gospel truth by many homosexuals."[143] It was this celebrity sex radical to whom a young Li Shiu Tong introduced himself in Shanghai in 1931. Yet well before he met Li in Shanghai's International District, a foreign-controlled enclave within the city, Hirschfeld's theory was steeped in the politics of empire.

2 The Empire of Queer Love

As he traveled the world on his lecture tour, often in Li's company, Hirschfeld saw the violence and injustice of imperialism. Yet he already knew plenty about empire. He had used it to create his model of homosexuality. Empire was a source of data, data that came directly out of the mouths of Europeans who were cheerfully employed by the imperial project. Empire offered a conceptual element, too – the idea of "civilization" – with which Hirschfeld built his model.[1] He was not alone in this.[2] Homosexual emancipation was usually tacitly or even explicitly in favor of empire. Recall that a founder of the Scientific Humanitarian Committee fought Germany's rebellious colonial subjects with his own hands.

Many years before he met Li, sometime between 1910 and 1914, Hirschfeld was living in Berlin and working on his mammoth book *The Homosexuality of Men and Women*, an exhaustive sexological study of homosexuality. Once finished it tipped the scales at over 1,000 pages and became a "Bible" for homosexuals.[3] The point of the book was twofold: First, to show "heterosexuals" that prejudice against homosexuals was "an injustice." Second, to lift homosexual men and women out of their feelings of shame and guilt, to valorize their same-sex love, and to rescue them from isolation by showing them how many people in human history and at present in all parts of the globe were also homosexual.[4] To this end, Hirschfeld spent over one hundred pages reporting instances of homosexuality around the world. He often relied on reports from men he knew through homosexual political circles and who were working abroad. Many of these men were working in the European colonial empires, including Germany's empire, which still existed when the book was published in 1914. (Germany lost its colonies in the First World War.)

When he came to the section on China, Hirschfeld relied on a letter he had received from a man who lived and worked in Peking (Beijing). At the time, Germany had a substantial colonial footprint in China. It held a city-state colony, Kiaochow (around Jiaozhou Bay on the coast, with its center at Tsingtau).[5] Hirschfeld's informant, who is not named, does not seem to have been a colonial civil servant; his profession goes unnoted in his letter. He may have worked in private industry. Nevertheless, he was a "foreigner" in China, working under the auspices of what many Chinese perceived as a hostile imperialist state and enjoying the privileges of "foreigners" in the treaty ports. In particular he mentions time spent in Tianjin (Tientsin), a city that Hirschfeld and Li visited together years later.

This German in China wrote a long, vivid description of homosexual subcultures in Peking and Tianjin. Almost all of what he wrote was about Chinese men who sold sex to other Chinese men and to foreign men. It was detailed enough, giving locations and prices charged, that one could use it as a sort of travel guide, which I suspect some people did. He told of his visit to a "boy bordello [*Knabenbordell*]" in Tianjin, where he met three handsome youths. The youngest was twelve, he thought, and the oldest between sixteen and seventeen. Hirschfeld published a long passage of his letter without comment.[6]

An aside about pedophilia: in historical discussions of "homosexuality," not only by homosexual emancipation's enemies but also by homosexuals themselves, there often was a lack of distinction between what we would consider the sexual abuse of children and what we would consider "homosexuality" – that is, consensual adult sex.[7] In Hirschfeld's work one sees references to sex between adult men and girls as well as boys. Hirschfeld does not comment on what might trouble us about the boy bordello in Tianjin, except, later, to offer a mild condemnation not of Europeans but of Chinese parents. He argues that the lack of prejudice in China against homosexuality is demonstrated by the fact that poor parents offer their daughters and sons to brothels and that this practice may seem "ignominious" to Hirschfeld's readers but does not seem so to the Chinese.[8] The conflation of a twelve-year-old working in a bordello, in this case, and "homosexuality" is an under-studied part of homosexual emancipation – willfully so, scholars generally do not want to see this – and of twentieth-century gay (mostly male) politics, one that deserves more examination. It comes up less in Hirschfeld's work than in other German homoerotic thought in this period, but one finds it in Hirschfeld as well, at times, such as in this example.[9] One of the central charges against homosexual emancipation was that all homosexuals were really pedophiles, bent on seducing children.[10] Yet the homosexual emancipation movement at times included men who eroticized boys. This was a problem not just for German homosexual emancipation in Hirschfeld's day but for other twentieth-century gay rights movements as well.[11]

Yet I want to draw the reader's attention to something else in this letter: the effortless way in which Hirschfeld sidestepped the question of whether empire was right or wrong. Another vivid example that Heike Bauer gives is a moment when Hirschfeld wrote about the possible homosexuality of a soldier who had taken part in the genocide of the Herero and Nama peoples in German South West Africa (Namibia today) in 1904–8. He wrote about the person's sexuality without commenting on the genocide. Bauer notes that, moreover, a major event in homosexual emancipation – the accusations by journalist Maximilian Harden of male homosexuality in Kaiser Wilhelm II's inner circle and the ensuing public trials – was in fact all about the colonial project. Harden became vexed about (alleged) male homosexuality around the kaiser after the kaiser displayed what Harden took to be imperial weakness: the kaiser decided not to fight the French over Morocco in 1905.[12] All in all, in Bauer's account Hirschfeld isn't much of a decolonialist at all. In his early and middle career, he wrote almost nothing that was critical of empire, though empire was right before his face.

In his early and middle career, Hirschfeld, moreover, *needed* the empire. He used the stories this European exponent of empire told him to make what was to him a crucial point. The point was that homosexuality existed around the globe and therefore must be a natural, innate, biological phenomenon. He had other informants in the colonies, too, such as a forestry official who worked in the Dutch colonial administration in Indonesia, who came to Berlin and told Hirschfeld about his eventful sex life with "the natives."[13] The Dutch civil servant told of more than fifteen years in the empire, during which he had had over one hundred sexual encounters with men from Java. He often paid them. Cab drivers, for instance, were "almost all willing to have sex for money," Hirschfeld wrote that the civil servant told him. I assume these were animal carts, not automobiles. The Dutch man apparently said that "one sits side-by-side or back-to-back with the driver, in close contact, and the bodily contact gradually develops into intimate acts."[14]

The fact that homosexuality existed not only in Berlin but also in Peking and even on Java, among men supposedly less civilized than Europeans, was proof of Hirschfeld's model of the modern homosexual. He wrote, "The uniform face that homosexuality wears far and wide, that appears in each place so fully independent of other places, has for me always been one of the most resounding proofs of its purely biological causation."[15] When it came to homosexuality, it was sexual orientation, not race, that had overriding importance: "Beyond question, the sexual type conquers the racial type."[16]

Homosexuality existed independent of environment, and in an identical form, even across radical differences. This was a compelling argument for Hirschfeld's model. What made it so compelling were the imagined vast differences between the peoples of the world and among the "races." It wouldn't be worth mentioning that homosexuality existed in the colonies as well as among all the "races" if it were not somewhat counterintuitive that it did. Underlying the "resounding" nature of this proof, for Hirschfeld, was the assumption that Chinese men and white European men, for example, were quite different in other respects.

One big difference was "civilization." The imperial project relied on the contention that Europeans had achieved a higher level of civilization and that they had an obligation, or a right, to help less-developed peoples or to rule over them, or both. Europeans were civilized. Other people were savage or primitive. Still others, such as the Chinese, were somewhat civilized but still lagged behind Europe. Hirschfeld and other homosexual emancipationist authors used this intellectual framework to bolster their model of homosexuality. At the same time, many white European queers imagined the colonies as spaces of relative sexual freedom, an empire of queer love, and that, too, depended on the violent power politics of empire. Imperialism was profoundly bound up with queer liberation in this early moment.

Like many people in his day, Hirschfeld thought of progress as a pre-ordained path along which different groups of humans advanced at different paces, arriving at different "level[s] of civilization," as he put it.[17] Some "peoples and races ... appear childlike when contrasted with their more advanced, more adult brethren."[18] Groups did not lag behind because they were biologically inferior; rather, circumstance accounted for most of the difference.[19] Liberal anthropology, a major influence on Hirschfeld's thought (see chapter 6), also had a concept of a trajectory along which groups of people (they might very well be racially heterogeneous groups) went forward at uneven rates. Liberal anthropologists attributed the "speeds" with which groups "advanced" to beneficial circumstances in the local environment and in a group's position in trade networks – that is, to geography, economics, and history.[20] While acknowledging the existence of more or less "civilized" peoples, Hirschfeld carefully detached homosexuality from culture: "Though societies respond differently to homosexuality, the sameness of the form in which homosexuality manifests itself and the sameness of homosexual life from the most primitive to the most cultured peoples and among all races and classes is so extraordinarily pronounced that it is completely impossible that homosexuality is caused by anything but a natural law that is deeply rooted in humanity."[21]

By claiming that homosexuality had a uniform face across divisions of civilization, Hirschfeld and others in his circle were striking back at a powerful argument against homosexual emancipation: the claim that "decadence" and overcivilization caused homosexuality. Eighteenth- and nineteenth-century European authors had assumed that savage peoples were in fact prone to same-sex sex acts and indeed to all sorts of sexual and gender disorder because they lacked civilization and Christianity.[22] But around the turn of the twentieth century, critics of homosexuality began to attribute same-sex sexuality and gender-crossing to overcivilization.

This thinking drew on the anthropology of its day. From the nineteenth century into the twentieth, anthropologists generally observed a distinction between civilized and uncivilized people. In the German-speaking world, anthropologists divided humanity into "cultural peoples" (*Kulturvölker*) and "natural peoples" (*Naturvölker*). The former were supposedly highly civilized while the latter lived in a primitive state of nature. Conveniently overlooking all the stories of the sexual "immorality" of the "uncivilized" brought back by eighteenth-century missionaries, anthropologists claimed that homosexuality did not exist in people who lived in a state of nature. It thus had to be a product of too much culture, of European cultural decline and degeneration.[23]

But this was not true. "Just as the love between men and women has nothing to do with geographic borders or racial differences, homosexuality, this biological phenomenon, has nothing to do with geographic borders or racial differences," wrote Hirschfeld.[24] "The opinion, which one encounters not infrequently in literature claiming to be scientific, that homosexuality is a product of overcivilization and a stigma of racial [*völkischer*] decadence, is contradicted by reliable observations of peoples [*Völkern*] for whom we can rule out the possibility that the refinement of morals or overcivilization ... has been any influence on them at all ... Already in 1875 Friedrich von Hellwald wrote that homosexuality was nowhere more common than among the wild tribes [*Stämmen*]."[25] Hirschfeld was far from alone in this view. Beginning with Ulrichs if not before, the men of moderate-centrist homosexual emancipation worked hard to amass a trove of evidence that purported to show that homosexuality was evenly distributed around the globe.[26] This was no small part of the homosexual emancipationist argument. They repeated it often. It showed they were not "degenerate" or "decadent."

For example, the homosexual emancipationist magazine *Friendship* (*Freundschaft*) published a series of articles on the topic in 1920 by an author identified as Richard B.C. Vogel (*Friendship* authors often used pseudonyms). Vogel began one of these essays, headlined "Homosexual Negro Tribes [Homosexuelle Neger-Stämme]," by noting that "among heterosexuals it is often claimed that homosexuality is related to degeneration, a result of decadence and of the corruption of morality by over-civilization [*Überkultur*]. The strongest argument made for this is the lack of homosexuality among the natural peoples [*Naturvölkern*]." But this was unsubstantiated. "Same-sex orientation [*Gleichgeschlechtlichkeit*] exists in all times" as well as "among all peoples, without exception – Australian aborigines, Indian tribes, African and American Negros, Mongolians and Malaysians, Turks and Eskimos."[27] He offered example after example of especially male homosexuality in Africa and then concluded that such proof "disputes the idea that homosexuality results from 'over-civilization.'"

This argument could only take place in the way that it did because both sides agreed that some people were "civilized" and others were not. All agreed, likewise, that the "negros" of Africa were uncivilized.

Hirschfeld's Scientific Humanitarian Committee published some of the output of this multi-researcher scholarly project, the project that sought to prove that homosexuality existed in all races and among "primitive" peoples around the globe.[28] The Scientific Humanitarian Committee member Ferdinand Karsch-Haack wrote a nearly 700-page book making this point.[29] He ends it by declaring that same-sex sexuality is "fundamentally natural" and that "incontrovertible facts" demonstrated the preposterousness of the notion that "pederasty and tribadism are vices that only develop among depraved [*verderbten*] cultural peoples."[30] Hirschfeld's *Homosexuality of Men and Women* contained a mountain of evidence of homosexuality and gender-crossing across the entire globe, some of it, ironically, coming from the earlier missionary reports of the shocking practices prevailing among the pagans, as when Hirschfeld repeated a seventeenth-century report by Louis Hennepin, explorer and missionary from France and Belgium in North American, about "the Illinois," their "'shameless'" indulgence in sodomy and their practice of dressing boys in women's clothing.[31]

Yet these stories of sex among primitive peoples could suggest something else, something dangerous: that homosexuality, as well as transness, were in fact *more* common in the less-civilized world. This idea was dangerous because it undermined the claim that homosexuality was uniform around the globe and that therefore there was nothing intrinsically wrong with white European homosexuals.

It was a sexy idea though. Everyone involved in homosexual emancipation seems to have agreed that non-Europeans were often more open to same-sex sex than were many uptight (white) Europeans. Even Hirschfeld thought so. Lots was written on how relatively accepting less-civilized people were of same-sex affairs and of gender transition, too. A collectively imagined queer empire, a place of erotic and transgender possibilities far beyond what Europe would allow, took shape in the pages of books and magazines.

"In Sudan," for example, "as unbelievable as it may sound, homosexuality is a national custom [*Volkssitte*]."[32] A "negro" king in the Sudan had "an official male harem." Other examples abound. "In Zanzibar there is a regular practice of male prostitution by freed Arabic slaves and by other negros," wrote Vogel. "These male prostitutes ply their trade totally openly and are quite beloved and sought-after by the Zanzibar negros. The law is very accommodating and tolerant of these relationships, and more reasonable than the laws of some of the so-called 'civilized' countries like Germany, where the infamous blackmail law §175 [the sodomy law] is still claiming countless victims."[33]

What we might call transness – gender-bending, gender nonconformity, and the crossing from one gender to the other – flourished among the uncivilized as well in the queer white European imagination.[34] Take, for example, Vogel's reports about "the tribes of Madagascar." He considered men in women's clothing there an expression of "the desire for the same sex" rather than a separate condition, "transvestitism," as people termed transness at the time. But he was writing in 1920, a decade after Hirschfeld's theory of transvestitism, and many of his readers probably recognized the people he described as transvestites. He wrote that in Madagascar there were "feminine, delicate, slight [*schwächliche*] men, who declare that they can only consort with their own sex; they are viewed and treated fully as women and, as women, they are allowed to wear women's clothing, which most of them happily do."[35]

Hirschfeld reported many cases of gender-crossing among primitive peoples. For example, a Siberian people living on the border of the Arctic Circle whom he terms "the Hyperboreans [*Hyperboräer*], whose racial composition has not yet been unraveled," had male shamans who sometimes changed their sex, becoming women, and then married men; occasionally women among them became men.[36] A Dutch ethnologist told him that he had repeatedly met tribes where a number of men dressed in women's clothing and some women dressed as men. "The whole village knows and respects these two-sexed individuals [*Zweigeschlechtlichen*]," Hirschfeld reported.[37] In *World Journey*, he included a photograph, possibly taken by Li, of "Javanese transvestites (men in women's clothing)."[38]

Yet how could homosexuality and transvestitism have uniform faces and at the same time be rampant in certain less-civilized corners of the globe? Hirschfeld squared the circle in this way: Neither homosexuality nor transvestitism were more common in the world beyond Europe's borders. What differed was the way in which the local population reacted to them. There were "three phases," three distinct modes of response to homosexuality, which societies adopted in chronological succession as they developed.[39] That is, groups of humans proceeded from phase to phase as they rose from a primitive state to a civilized one. In the first phase, the most primitive, people "naïve[ly]" tolerated homosexuality and even made use of it.[40] Homosexuality might have a religious function for priests or magicians, or a pedagogic function, as in ancient Greece.[41]

In the second phase, "the majority's instinctive opposition [*Kontrainstinkte*] gets the upper hand."[42] Anxious heterosexuals criminalized same-sex sex. The police, however, couldn't arrest every homosexual; in practice, it was only in "exceptional cases" that people were called to answer before the law.[43] (Indeed, this was basically true of every regime under which homosexual sex had ever been a crime – most people who had same-sex sex were not caught.) Hirschfeld argued that the worst thing about criminalization was that it made it difficult for homosexuals to have "monogamous" relationships and drove them, rather, to pay for sex, increasing the amount of same-sex sex while diminishing its "quality."[44] What changed this dismal state of affairs, according to Hirschfeld, was the rise of science, with scientific research on homosexuality marking the third phase.[45] Though he oddly neglects to really describe phase three in the passage in *The Homosexuality of Men and Women* where he explains all this, one assumes that this stage brings toleration, as well as monogamy.

Therefore, any group of people who were "primitive" in the 1920s would be more accepting of homosexuality than were civilized peoples such as white Europeans. This was probably what Vogel meant when he noted that Zanzibar was more open to homosexuality than was Germany, with its notorious sodomy law.

China had no law against homosexuality.[46] It was the foreign powers who made it illegal in their zones. The British were severe about sex in all of their colonial possessions, Hirschfeld saw again and again as he traveled, exporting their laws against same-sex sex to places that had not previously had such laws.[47] But China was also more tolerant because it had always been so – having not yet reached the level of civilization that Europe had (despite pockets of technological advance such as at universities and Westernized elites like Li).[48] Hirschfeld wrote about women in Canton Province who avoided marriage and lived together, supporting themselves by harvesting silkworm thread. Some built houses and lived with female partners. Local authorities did not like this and had tried to stop it, he wrote, but with no success. These lesbian households, this "custom of marital comradeship between women," was not some new way of life but rather was an "ancient" custom.[49] Lesbianism was ancient. It was the repression of lesbianism that was modern.

This logic also applied to transvestites. Hirschfeld argued that transvestitism existed "among the oldest and more recently civilized peoples, the Asiatic as well as the European," and was "not limited by place, time, race, origin, or religion."[50] Like homosexuality, it too must therefore be an innate, non-pathological, biological condition.

Other queer white European authors in Hirschfeld's day were murky on what exactly made less-civilized people more sexually fluid – was it stages of civilization, racial difference, or something else? They were, however, very clear that this was the case. The idea fascinated them. It made for captivating fiction and real-life erotic adventure.

The idea that colonized people were more open to same-sex affairs fired homoerotic fantasies of empire, and those fantasies inspired sojourns in the actual empire, be they pleasure trips or careers of many years. Numerous Dutch gay men told Hirschfeld they sought out jobs in the colonies, preferably as civil servants but also as salesmen and doctors, in order to have sexual adventures with colonized men.[51] Hirschfeld's work on global homosexuality was an unintended queer travel guide. The informant in China explained where in Peking one ought to go to pay men for sex – a specific stretch of the city wall – but noted that there were better sex workers in the embassy quarter. One could recognize them by their black robes. He also recommended the foreign soldiers' taverns, apparently as places to pick up men.[52] The informant who lived in the Union of South Africa, apparently a white man, helpfully explained where to cruise in Johannesburg (the streets around the post office), Durban (the Public Gardens in the city center), and Cape Town (there were no bars or restaurants in that city that homosexuals favored, but there was a movie theater that had that reputation, and gay men also met at the main public square, which is today called the Grand Parade).[53] In Tunis, one had to go to the baths in the evening, when they were reserved for men. When it came to the Arabs, Hirschfeld had trouble sticking to his universalism, no doubt because of the strong trope among white Europeans of male homosexuality in North Africa. "Homosexuality blooms quite abundantly" in the baths, he wrote, and "among the Arabs, true homosexuality is not infrequent and bisexuality is common." Often in the reception area one would find good-looking men of various ages sitting in a row, offering their services at massage.[54]

A close friend of Hirschfeld's was a homosexual who fled Europe for the greater sexual freedom of the empire. He was Richard Kandt, a friend from secondary school (*Gymnasium*) who went on to be the chief resident administrator of Rwanda under German control. To the young Hirschfeld, Kandt had been a fellow Jew in a mostly Christian town. The two remained close until Kandt, serving in the German forces in the First World War, died in a gas attack. Kandt was homosexual. He may have been an early boyfriend of Hirschfeld's. The last time Hirschfeld saw him, Kandt said that if he made it through the war, he was going to turn all of his energies to helping Hirschfeld's homosexual emancipation movement.[55] Years before the First World War, Kandt left Germany for Africa after a bad run-in with a vicious blackmailer. Hirschfeld and the Scientific Humanitarian Committee helped him deal with the blackmailer; they often extended such help to men in Kandt's situation. Gay men were frequently blackmailed in those days. Kandt fled from the blackmailer to the colonies. In his writings, Kandt was notably moderate in his anti-Black racism. He wrote that Black Africans were not immoral and that European morality could not be applied to their customs, a point that he may or may not have believed was true for sex acts. Kandt later moved back to Germany, where he socialized in a circle of homosexual men that included Johann Albrecht, the president of the German Colonial Society (Die Deutsche Kolonialgesellschaft).[56] It may be the case that gay men were overrepresented in the colonial civil service, either in general or only in German East Africa (today Burundi, Rwanda, a portion of Tanzania, and a portion of Mozambique). In that colony, where Kandt found happiness, a gay sex scandal reached to the highest echelons of the colonial regime. (It was not a colony inured to the violence that characterized colonialism. Between 1905 and 1907, German forces there brutally suppressed the Maji Maji Revolt.[57]) From 1907 to 1916, a number of colonial officials were accused of sodomy with colonized men and with other white men, though Kandt does not seem to have been involved. The accused included the colony's governor, who was said to have had sex with, among other people, a person identified in the archive as a cross-dressing Arab sex worker.[58]

   The case against the governor of German East Africa demonstrates something crucial: what white Europeans may have considered sexual freedom could easily be in fact sexual violence. The principal accusation against the governor was that he had had sex with an African man who worked in his house as a servant. The reports of their encounters, which came from third parties who appear to have spied on them, sounded like rape. Other servants in the house seem to have thought it was rape. The African man in question may have as well; given the dramatic power differential between him and the governor it would have been very difficult for him to dodge the encounters. Underscoring the difficulty of avoiding the governor's advances (which may in fact have been assaults) was the fact that a judge later convicted the two white Germans who complained on behalf of the servant of defaming the governor, writing that in "a territory where the rule of the white race over the subject colored race is based on authority," such defamation was a particularly serious crime. In other cases in German East Africa, African men accused European men of rape directly. There was no specific law in the German penal code against same-sex rape, so all of these accusations took the form of claims that the sodomy law had been broken. The normal state of affairs was for African servants to sleep in the houses of the white Europeans for whom they worked, which seems to have put them at risk. As Heike Schmidt notes, it was not only men but women and children as well who were vulnerable to the sexual violence of colonizers.[59]

Though men produced much of the discourse about homoeroticism and imperialism, white European women, too, imagined queer adventures in the colonies. In 1932 a Berlin lesbian magazine ran a very rare instance of this, a short story called "Morocco [Marokko]." In it, a white German woman reads travel literature and is captivated by descriptions of "the nomadic Arabs."[60] She learns that "among them there are extraordinarily beautiful people" who like to engage in mysterious practices of love. Though the story does not specify what exactly these mysterious practices are, readers no doubt assumed they were homoerotic. In this period Europeans spilled much ink on what they took to be the rampant homoeroticism of North Africans.[61]

Hirschfeld reported that same-sex sex was "a frequent occurrence" among Christian as well as Muslim women in French North Africa and that female Moroccan fortune-tellers were reputed to pick up women by offering to read their fortunes in exchange for lesbian sex.[62] Homoeroticism, he wrote, proliferated among "the Arabs."[63] Indeed, his "uniform face … of homosexuality" shakes a bit when he considers Arabs – he struggles to fully depart from the long-standing white European view that they were prone to male homosexuality.

The protagonist of the short story "Morocco" books passage on a cruise to North Africa. Almost immediately upon disembarking in Morocco, she meets a mysterious and alluring woman. Without much provocation, the woman declares in Spanish: "'Beautiful blond, since I saw you, I have been smitten [im Liebesrausch].'" The lovers lack a common language. During their affair, which fills the twelve days before the protagonist's ship returns for her, they do not talk much about the circumstances of their lives. But the protagonist also seems to lack any interest in discussing the political situation in colonial Morocco or in seeing the relationship become anything more complex than a whirlwind fling. The "euphoria" (Rauschzustand) that consumes her leaves her little space for curiosity about her surroundings. She has no plans to stay in Morocco, and she informs the reader that her lover, Benorina, is "so rooted to the soil of her homeland" that she would not be happy in Germany. So the German woman sails away, filled with nostalgia for the fantasy she has lived.

In this story, race is a physical difference, although not an unimportant one; the protagonist admires Benorina's brown skin and Benorina appreciates the protagonist's blondness. But it is seemingly due to culture, not race, that Benorina is so forward with a German stranger. The story relies on the presumption that North Africa is a particularly queer place where a traveler might indeed be picked up by a beautiful, uninhibited woman as soon as she got off the boat.

In 1925, a transvestite magazine printed a short story about empire. The magazine, *The Transvestite* (*Der Transvestit*), was one of several that catered to transvestites, for the most part trans women, running work for and by them. It and similar magazines were put out by homosexual emancipationist publishers in Germany from the mid-1920s until the Nazis took power in 1933. The story is about a trans woman who finally, after many years of hidden suffering, embraces her feminine nature and finds happiness. This white German woman's transformative moment comes as she (literally) submerges herself in colonial India.[64]

The story takes the form of a brief memoir by "H.W. Burg." Assigned male at birth, Burg suffers as a child, but then as an adult she gets a job on a scientific expedition to India. One evening the Europeans of the expedition and their "native attendants" camp near a village, by a spring renowned for its holy healing powers. Sitting alone by the tents, Burg reflects on "the feminine" within her and suddenly gets an idea. She has another European buy her one of the "long cloths" that women in the village wear, telling him she wants it as a souvenir. After the other Europeans are asleep, Burg emerges from her tent and walks to the holy spring. She bathes in the waters, returns to her tent, and wraps her body in the garment of the village women. "This was the first time in my life that I robed myself in women's clothing. How a sense of wonder went through my soul. It seemed to me as if suddenly all the old wounds healed and a new strength for life flooded me." The moment marks the beginning of a happy phase of Burg's life. She returns to Germany and begins a relationship with a woman who appreciates her as a person of "female nature in a masculine shell."[65]

Rural India, rather than Germany, was the logical site for Burg to begin her transition, and it moreover made sense that it took a spring holy to the "natives" and a garment of the village women. Europeans believed that people of the supposedly less-civilized world were more accepting of gender nonconformity as well as of an individual's passage from one gender to the other. Hirschfeld and his allies frequently cited ethnographies of "primitive" civilizations to demonstrate that transvestites were valued

in those cultures.[66] He reported stories of gender transition, gender du-
alism, and androgyny in Indian literature and religion, including a tale
of a man who enters a divine grove and changes into a woman.[67]

The empire was romantic, erotic. Edward Said writes that to nineteenth-
and twentieth-century Europeans, "the Orient was a place where one
could look for sexual experience unobtainable in Europe."[68] Europeans entertained a host of erotic images of the inhabitants not just of
North Africa but also of Sub-Saharan Africa, Asia, North America, and
the Pacific, from the threatening, hypersexual Black African man to the
welcoming, sexually available Tahitian woman.[69] Matt Matsuda argues
that the French understood their imperial project in the Pacific as an act
of love (erotic love, in some times and places) and that love displaced
French awareness of the exploitative dynamics of empire.[70] As other
studies have noted, people who felt homoerotic desires also had amo-
rous investments in empire that perpetuated empire.[71]

Yet the eroticism of empire had a particular importance for homosexual emancipationists, as well as for transvestites; this has not, to date,
been recognized by historians. Early homosexual and transvestite activists fashioned a world in which empire held the key to gender and sexual
liberation, both in the colonies and back in Europe.[72] Empire was also
the place to find crucial knowledge, knowledge that would liberate them
in Europe, when anthropology showed that homosexuality and gender
transition were natural. Empire was at the heart of early gay politics. It
was an empire of queer love.

Empire was also at the heart of early trans politics, at least in Hirschfeld's
extremely influential work.[73] It was probably not by accident that trans
activists of the 1920s appropriated an imperialist rallying cry, claiming,
"We too have a right to a place in the sun."[74] The reference is to a famous
1897 speech in which the German foreign minister declared his nation's
right to an overseas empire, which he called "a place in the sun."

The politics of the "happy Sodom" overseas were imperialist.[75] It
was not the case that the sexual cultures of Zanzibar, the Dutch Indies,
and Peking were simply more tolerant of homoeroticism. It was not
the case that, as Hirschfeld and his male informants asserted, in these
places male-male sex was less taboo than it was in Europe. The assertion relied on overstating the degree of repression in Europe as well as
in understating the degree of repression elsewhere. At the same time
that Hirschfeld's informants were paying for sex on Java and in Peking,
lots of working-class German and American men who did not consider
themselves homosexual were also casually selling sex to men.[76] Germans
could be, and were, tried for sodomy in Germany's colonies.[77]

It was rather the colonial state of affairs that made the colonies spaces of sexual freedom for white Europeans, perhaps largely for middle-class and elite Europeans – Hirschfeld's interlocutors were almost all bureaucrats. Political and economic power made it possible for the Europeans to forget the politics of colonization and to blithely assume that "fun," as Hirschfeld's Dutch informant put it, or sudden love, as in the case of Benorina, were the only salient factors motivating people living under colonial rule when they embarked on relationships with Europeans.[78] Yet it was power that made it possible for the governor of a colony to oblige a colonized man who worked for him to have sex.

In *The Homosexuality of Men and Women,* Hirschfeld is very interested in evidence from the colonies, but he is not interested in imperialism. He is, as Heike Bauer puts it, oblivious to the violence and injustice of empire.[79] The book exhaustively chronicles homosexuality in the European colonies. Yet it has few – if any – discussion of the violent politics underlying the relationships between Europeans and the people they purported to rule.[80]

Moreover, in his notion of "civilization," Hirschfeld departed from anticolonial thinkers. In his day, many people living under colonial rule did think their nations needed to Westernize to survive. Li probably thought so; he embraced Westernization. Like many others, he did not embrace foreign rule. Well before the 1920s, anticolonial thinkers had begun to push back on the notion of "civilization" and the politics of domination that it supposedly justified.[81] By the 1950s, influenced by the work of Aimé Césaire and Frantz Fanon, most opponents of empire rejected the idea that some cultures were superior to others or more civilized.

The Hirschfeld who is oblivious to imperialism, however, is not the Hirschfeld of the world journey. The author of *The Homosexuality of Men and Women* is not the man who would, years later, look on with shock as a policeman beat a coolie in Shanghai. It is not the man who would travel with Li through China and beyond, denouncing empire everywhere he went. Shanghai helped to change this, or at least, by the time Hirschfeld wrote about Shanghai, his thinking had changed drastically, and anti-imperialism had moved to the heart of his homosexual politics.

3 Hirschfeld and Li Shiu Tong Meet: Feminism and Queer Attraction at the China United Apartments

International Settlement, Shanghai, May 1931

Li Shiu Tong was a twenty-four-year-old medical student in Shanghai in 1931 when he heard that the German sexologist Magnus Hirschfeld was coming to give public lectures.[1] How Li learned about the lectures I do not know. Perhaps from the newspapers. Shanghai's English-language press reported the May 2 arrival of "the world's foremost authority on sexual psychology."[2] Even in his early twenties, Li was already a well-heeled would-be cosmopolitan, enrolled at one of the best English-language universities in glittering Shanghai, and he had already taken a particular interest in sexology.

Born on January 9, 1907, in the British colony Hong Kong, Li was the son of a rich and influential businessman.[3] His father was a British colonial subject and justice of the peace.[4] As was the custom, he had several wives and a large household.[5] Li's father was one among the rising Chinese bourgeois who were beginning to dominate sectors of Hong Kong's economy despite racial discrimination against them by the white British.[6] He believed in the power of Westernization: he sent his son to an English preparatory school, paving the way for Li to attend university in English.[7] The China of Li's young adulthood was a place of political insecurity. When he was small, the Qing dynasty fell. The following decades saw struggle between nationalism and communism under the looming shadows of European and Japanese imperialism.

When it came time for university, Li chose to study medicine at St. John's in Shanghai. That city was arguably China's most important, among the world's largest ports and a center of banking. St. John's in those days had grown beyond its missionary origins to become a mostly secular, English-language university known for educating the new business class and for preparing elite students to continue their studies abroad. It had a well-respected program in Western medicine. It specialized in grooming its students to network with foreigners; after graduation many went into the diplomatic service or business, or went abroad to study. St. John's had a culture that matched American collegiate life in many ways, with grudge soccer matches against rival schools, an English-language student newspaper, glee club concerts, and a Shakespeare Club. The goal was not to prepare upper-middle-class students to take on central roles in Republican China. It was, rather, to make them into elites in a transnational network.[8] This suited Li. He wanted to see the world. He also, perhaps, wanted to get away from his parents, away from the heterosexual obligations, the pressure to marry.

St. John's, and the Westernization it represented, irked Chinese nationalists, who called it cultural imperialism.[9] Communists hated it, too. Shanghai in the 1930s was a center of leftist student organizing, with young communist women agitating on behalf of rural China and doing shocking things such as evading arranged marriages (which were still standard) and even unabashedly getting divorced.[10] That, however, happened at other universities, not at St. John's. Li was no communist, and enamored as he was by Westernization, he was not a nationalist on the same model, though he was a foe of imperialism. Nor was Li religious: he laughed to himself as he went along with the Christian trappings at St. John's, such as the rousing choruses of "Onward, Christian Soldiers."[11]

Li was a diligent, ambitious student. He had a steely determination once he had set upon a path he had chosen for himself. He dressed impeccably, showing off his wealth, whether in a Western suit and tie or in a changshan. He was not much of a drinker, but he was charming and funny and kind and had lots of friends, one assumes. He danced a lot in his days in Shanghai. He recalled later that everyone drank whiskey.[12] Sometimes, surely, he and his chums would go out to the dance halls and movie theaters and department stores of Shanghai's International Settlement, a city-within-a-city that was under foreign control.[13]

Li had been seduced by a new Chinese modernity and he met it in the International Settlement. The International Settlement was a multinational colony run by a council of foreigners – Brits and Americans, as well as other Europeans and Japanese. Despite International Settlement laws that imposed all sorts of racial discrimination on Chinese people, most of the more than one million residents of the Settlement were Chinese. Some were migrants from rural villages living in tenements without electricity or running water. Others were college-educated, Westernized residents of the art deco apartment buildings. In the International Settlement and beyond, the rising Chinese bourgeoisie created a hybrid Chinese-Western modernity, embracing the "modern" as synonymous with "the West" and yet working to undermine the power hierarchies of imperialism. The men wore Western-style suits. The young women sported bobbed hair and makeup, smoked cigarettes, and wore trousers and blouses or capes over trendy long gowns. They walked along the Bund, the Settlement's showpiece promenade along the Huangpu River, which was lined with neoclassical buildings reminiscent of central London. The American trade commissioner in Shanghai, a white feminist who discreetly had a female partner, described the view of the Bund from a boat on the river as "a solid skyline of modern skyscrapers towering from eight to twenty stories high." The modern was Western, in this view, and at the heart of it was Shanghai. Li was, one can I think be certain, thrilled to be part of it.[14]

A city of 3.5 million, Shanghai in 1931 surely had its queer scenes as well. Perhaps Li knew those, knew at which clubs or street corners one could linger to meet another man. In the student world of Shanghai, there were same-sex affairs, tolerated in some circles, as a sensational murder case involving two women revealed the following year.[15]

Shanghai's modern glitter had a darker side. Foreign rule in the International Settlement surely angered Li. Though Chinese residents paid 55 percent of tax revenues, they could not enter the International Settlement's public parks until 1928, when the Municipal Council relented and replaced the outright racial ban with a small fee for entry, to prevent the parks from being overrun by (assumedly Chinese) lower-class persons.[16] Independent of any state, the Municipal Council ran its own volunteer army and police force, which was notorious for having shot and killed four students at an anti-imperialist demonstration in 1925, probably before Li moved to Shanghai.

Hirschfeld's first lecture was to a club of Chinese feminists at the swank China United Apartments, a modern, towering new building in the International Settlement where sophisticated Chinese people as well as white foreigners lived – it was home to not a few single white women.[17] In the fact that Hirschfeld would speak there, surely Li saw no contradiction – sexology, too, was modern, and perhaps liberating. At St. John's, Li had thrown himself into reading sexology. Unlike what Hirschfeld found in medical school decades before, there was lots to read, Chinese sexology as well as books by Europeans. Hirschfeld, ever convinced that sexology was thoroughly European, later reported Li reading only Europeans: Havelock Ellis in particular, but also Iwan Bloch, Freud, and others.[18] German sexology, particularly on homosexuality, had been influential in China, and in Japan, well before Hirschfeld arrived.[19] Republican China was also home to a vibrant sexological literature, about homosexuality and other matters, that Li probably read.[20] Though Li had not read Hirschfeld, whose work was not translated into English or Chinese, he had seen his work discussed by others.[21] Li knew who he was.

Arriving at the China United Apartments, Hirschfeld was welcomed by Mrs. Frank C.Z. Ma, president of the Chinese Women's Club, with whom he subsequently struck up a friendship.[22] Ma was thrilled to have Hirschfeld speak to the club, proud that they were hosting the first talk in Shanghai by this "distinguished German psychologist," as she put it later in the press.[23] To her, Hirschfeld stood for a modern, Western, scientific approach to the condition of women. (The press may not have wanted to print his actual disciplinary title, "sexologist.") Mrs. Ma and the other club members were fashionable, modern women, educated and wealthy.[24] Ma oversaw an annual charity ball that raised money for a hospital, for the YWCA, and for the education of young working-class women. Shanghai was a center of women's organizing in China and of the feminist press.[25] The Chinese Women's Club also maintained ties to the foreign women of the International Settlement. The foreign women had their own women's groups, and they could be domineering.[26]

Probably no more than thirty people were there for this lecture, most of them Chinese women involved in the club, a few men, and at least one white woman, who was dressed in a mannish style. Later, Hirschfeld included a photograph of the event in *World Journey*, though unfortunately Li is not in the picture (see figure 4). Hirschfeld gave one of his standard talks, beginning (in English) with what must have been a rather dry history of sexology. There is a photograph of him lecturing in *World Journey* (see figure 3). Then he launched into his point-by-point program for sex reform. Marriage and divorce ought to be secular. Modern societies needed birth control and public education about eugenics. Prostitution ought to be abolished, venereal disease prevented, and sex education made available to children and adolescents. Men and women ought to have "the same economic, political, and sexual rights."[27]

On homosexuality, that ultra-scandalous topic, Hirschfeld held to his old line: science would lead to justice. A newspaper report showed him being somewhat vague: he was for "a saner handling of criminal cases based on sexual acts." Ancient restrictions on sex ought to be abolished in "modern society."[28] My suspicion is that he was even more forthright, but the reporter did not want to print what he said. After all, the American doctor who introduced him at an early lecture in New York City praised Hirschfeld as a sexologist with expertise across the range of human sexuality, from heredity to hormones, and yet at the same time singled him out as an expert on homosexuality and a spokesman for homosexuals, a "father to the stepchildren of nature," as the doctor put it, invoking an older sympathetic term for homosexuals.[29] If Hirschfeld did not demur in the United States, home to millions of prudes, I see no reason he would tiptoe around the subject of homosexuality in Shanghai.[30] Later, Li would translate as Hirschfeld met the Minister of Health of the Kuomintang government in Nanjing to discuss prostitution, birth control, and homosexuality.[31] Another report in the Shanghai press from days before Hirschfeld's first lecture gives this summary of Hirschfeld's views: He was for a "rational attitude toward sexually abnormal persons and especially homo-sexuals." The only real sex crimes were those that "infringe on other person's sexual rights. Sexual acts between responsible adults undertaken by mutual consent" should be "the private concern of those adults."[32] In any event, even if Li did not hear Hirschfeld defend homosexuality very explicitly at that first lecture, Hirschfeld had done so in the press in Shanghai already, and one assumes Li had read that. Li's memories of Hirschfeld's lectures were that he spoke on homosexuality. Li wrote decades later, "His lecture[s] [were] about human sexual variation[,] particularly on homosexuality[,] a still ignorant and controversial topic."[33]

Hence, that May afternoon the twenty-four-year-old Li Shiu Tong sat among a small group of fashionable feminists and probably heard Hirschfeld defend homosexuals. Surely that defense touched his heart, since he himself had queer feelings.[34] Most of the other sexologists whom he had read had not defended homosexuality in such unequivocal terms.

When Hirschfeld finished his lecture, Li made his way through the small crowd and introduced himself. Likely the first thought in his mind was to make a professional connection with Hirschfeld. Li was ambitious. In the month following this meeting, it became apparent that Li wanted to be a sexologist himself and wanted to study in Europe, and he may have had that intention even before he met Hirschfeld.

Meeting Li for the first time, Hirschfeld was, I suspect, formal at first but then flirty, particularly if they could speak without anyone else overhearing. The aging sexologist probably tried to charm the handsome young stranger. Perhaps he asked Li to show him around Shanghai; Hirschfeld loved it when locals took him on city tours, particularly of places that had to do with his research, like red-light districts and cruising spots.

True, the Hirschfeld of his many books is a dry, monotonous man of science, and press reports of his lectures make it seem they were much the same. He could also be dismissive of people he deemed underlings and even overbearing – by middle age he was well convinced of his own world historic importance.[35] But he had a vibrant athleticism to him, even in his sixties. "Gregarious and full of energy," was how a Greek newspaper reporter described him at the end of the world journey in 1932.[36] The British feminist and sex reformer Dora Russell remembered Hirschfeld at the London convention of the World League for Sexual Reform in 1929. He was, she wrote, "a short, very active man dashing about from person to person, eager and enthusiastic (as I was myself). He had wild greying hair as suits such a professor." At one point Hirschfeld told Russell, who was translating for him, that she was the most beautiful thing happening at the convention.[37]

He was a flirt. Heinz Liehr, a young man in Berlin at the time, recalled seeing Hirschfeld arrive at a party with two men in tow, "with two statuesque [statuarent] types ... athletes, but well dressed, and that was also the evening when he patted me [tätschelte mich] and said that I had become an attractive young man. Well, by that time I already knew what was up with him and that he liked men." Hirschfeld particularly liked younger men, Liehr said, if they were "stable, broad types," and he had a weakness for working-class types like sanitation workers who did garbage collection, as well as an (apparently unrelated) preference for men with large feet. (This was, however, nothing like Li.) Hirschfeld was a masculine guy, Liehr avowed, not at all feminine; the gossip about him being campy or feminine was wrong. Hirschfeld had a "sonorous, masculine voice," he recalled.[38]

Günter Maeder, another young man who worked at the Institute for Sexual Science, remembered that he and Hirschfeld went together on night walks through the Tiergarten, Berlin's central park, which was close to the Institute, to see the "boys" who sold sex there. Hirschfeld, Maeder recalled, "had a good look" at some of them, "here and there," though of course as a public figure, Hirschfeld had to be careful of his reputation.[39] The Institute was a place of science, but it also seems to have occasionally hosted evening soirees – Rolf Italiaander, who was fifteen at the time, recalled meeting Hirschfeld at a ball at the Institute in 1928.[40]

Hirschfeld was adventurous. His descriptions of his world journey are full of mirth, wonder, and delight at all that he saw and did, and though he does complain, he does so infrequently. Flying from Java he sent the pilot a note asking if he could sit up in the cabin with him, to have a better view. The pilot agreed and Hirschfeld clambered up.[41] Hirschfeld and Li's ship from Hong Kong, the Dutch liner Tjinegara, made a day stop in the port of Makassar, on the island of Celebes (Sulawesi). Most of the first-class passengers drove off to see a waterfall, but Hirschfeld and Li walked through the city, then took a bumpy two-wheeled cart ride to the bayside home of a rich Chinese man, perhaps someone Li's family knew. In the afternoon they went swimming. Later, at dinner, the ship's doctor asked if Hirschfeld hadn't been worried about the sharks and crocodiles known to infest that bay, and Hirschfeld laughed off the danger – he hadn't known about them, and they had not hurt him, proving the old adage.[42]

Pompous at times, and always rumpled, he could also be self-deprecating and funny, sometimes having a laugh at his own expense.[43] One night in Benares (Varanasi), India, Hirschfeld was on his way back to his quarters after a lecture, riding in a two-wheeled cart drawn by a pony. The cart, he wrote, "tipped over backwards because of my weight and pulled the horse up, so that it stood up like a circus horse." He reported that he fell into the "soft dung and morass that covered a large part of Benares" (Hirschfeld disliked the city) and that it was only "with many difficulties that horse, wagon, and myself were righted again."[44]

There was, in short, much to like about Hirschfeld, even for a rich, much younger man.

At that first meeting, Li made Hirschfeld a very generous offer that defined their relationship for its duration and transformed both of their lives. Hirschfeld wrote later: "He offered himself to me, after my first lecture in Shanghai, as a 'companion' and 'protector,' to take care of me and help me wherever I might want to travel in China, in particular to stand by my side as a Chinese interpreter."[45] (In his account of the meeting, Hirschfeld used the English words for "companion" and "protector," which is why they are in quotations. Li made his offer in English.) This was written later, when they were living together in Central Europe and Li had become his great love. The queer possibilities of "he offered himself to me" would not have been lost on some readers, though most would not have noted them.

Li proved to be as good as his word. He became Hirschfeld's protector. In Agra, India, one night they arrived back at their hotel late, having spent the day seeing the Taj Mahal. The hotel room was full of the buzzing of mosquitoes. Malaria. Li rushed out into the city to buy smoke sticks, ointment, and spray. By the time he got back to the hotel room it was too late. Hirschfeld already had more than forty bites. His symptoms began a week later, with a high fever.[46] Hirschfeld had recurrent malaria for the rest of his life. Li nursed him through several flares, such as in 1932, when the malaria came back during the WLSR congress in Czechoslovakia. Hirschfeld wrote of this episode that his "mainstay" was "Tao Li" (a nickname of Li's, by which he was called by Hirschfeld and those in his circle).[47]

Li was Hirschfeld's guy Friday as well, his game and versatile assistant in all things, his personal secretary. Just in those first weeks, Li helped him travel around China to give thirty-five lectures on sexology in sixty-three days, with almost daily coverage in the press.[48] Hirschfeld gave a radio lecture in Hong Kong, on a very hot day and standing next to an enormous block of ice. By radio he thought he reached many hundreds of thousands of people, bringing them news of the important science of sexology for the first time.[49] Li helped him book hotels. He was out in the crowd for every lecture, operating the slides that went with Hirschfeld's talks. In Peking, people arrived hours before Hirschfeld's lecture at a university to get good spots, and by the time Hirschfeld took the stage, the crowd was tightly packed and overflowing into adjacent courtyards. "Tao Li had the worst trouble keeping himself and his slide projector upright in the crush of the crowd."[50]

For the next two years, they would speak every day.[51] Together they traveled thousands of miles, by ship, by automobile, occasionally by animal-drawn cart, and by train. Hirschfeld flattered himself that he got to know Li "as only seldom a European has gotten to know a Chinese person's life story [*Lebensschicksal*] and views of the world [*Lebensanschauungen*]."[52]

Li wrote about their meeting too, decades later. He does not really describe the moment that they met, or his offer to be Hirschfeld's assistant, but writes, "After I assisted him through China he offered a scholarship to study medicine in Germany and to continue to assist him around the world to investigate human sexual behavior. My qualification was that he needed a hard-working medical student who would live a long life to continue his work. He thoroughly searched my work habits and was told that my grandparents lived up to around ninety years of age. I jumped at the offer."[53] Li's unpublished fragment of a book about Hirschfeld, written most likely in the 1980s, entirely omits any romantic relationship between them. Li had professional reasons to join the world tour.[54]

Hirschfeld quickly decided that Li was the successor he had long sought, the bright student who could take over his life's work, the young man who would not betray him, unlike those others back in Berlin. What would it have meant for Li to be Hirschfeld's successor? It would have meant not only continuing the sexologist's intellectual work but also taking over the large institutions Hirschfeld built after *Sappho and Socrates*. Had the plan worked, the leader of sexology in Europe would have been a young Chinese man. It was a tall order for a medical student, to say the least, and a fantastical plan on Hirschfeld's part. Yet about a month after they met, they had already decided that Li would go with Hirschfeld to study in Berlin. Hirschfeld spoke about the plan in an interview in early June.[55] Li's account has it that Hirschfeld chose him because he was a hardworking medical student and because he would have a long life – a calculated decision about how to transmit one's ideas past the end of one's own mortal season.

On his first day in Shanghai, before he met Li, Hirschfeld left his hotel and took a rickshaw ride along the Bund, the International Settlement's grand riverside promenade. His attention was caught by an "old, dignified-looking" man walking with a younger man, "both in long blue Chinese coats." They were holding dainty cages wherein rested songbirds. They were taking their pet birds for a walk, "just as we in Europe do with our dogs." Hirschfeld saw something in the pair's manner that spoke of loyalty. They symbolized the temperament of the Chinese, to him – balanced, gentle, loyal. This was a racialized perspective. The entire population of China had these traits, he seemed to think.[56]

For Hirschfeld China was an ideal place to find a successor because loyalty, especially in relationships between older and younger men, was an affect that obsessed Hirschfeld, and he thought it was a racial trait of Chinese people. Loyalty had been in the front of his mind over the previous year as he battled the coup against him back in Berlin. The young man he blamed for forcing him out of the Scientific Humanitarian Committee, Richard Linsert, had been a protégé, but now Hirschfeld saw he had been "a viper in my breast."[57] It was a personal as well as professional betrayal, as were those of other men in the Scientific Humanitarian Committee who took Linsert's side.[58] But well before Linsert proved untrue, Hirschfeld already associated "loyalty" with an erotic relationship between himself and a younger man. In January 1929, Hirschfeld wrote out one of many versions of his last will and testament in his journal, singling out as heirs his lover Giese and a second man because "they have proven themselves as the most loyal and the most bound to me."[59] Hirschfeld inscribed one of the volumes of *Sexology* for another young man: "For Günter Maeder, in gratitude and friendship ... and faithfulness is no empty phrase."[60] Maeder may have had an affair with Hirschfeld.[61]

When Hirschfeld wrote about the two men and their songbirds on the Bund in Shanghai, surely he was thinking of himself and Li. In his description of the scene, Hirschfeld floats no theories as to the relationship between the two men, leaving open the possibility of queerness. When he marks their bond as one of "loyalty" and goes on to use them as an example of the loyal character of all Chinese people, he touches on a place of deep vulnerability for himself. By the time Hirschfeld published this, Li had offered the kind of profound loyalty Hirschfeld had long sought, in a way Hirschfeld thought was typical of his "race." In Patna, India, in October 1931, traveling in Li's company, he wrote in his journal,

> One of the greatest gains [*Gewinne*] of my trip was Tao Li, a young Chinese from a distinguished house, who has accompanied me for five months. His noble character, his intelligence, his stalwart loyalty [*Treue*] and devotedness makes the journey far easier for me. At his father's request he will study medicine and sexology in Germany. I think that in him I have found the long-sought student whom I can mold in my own image.[62]

Li was the "long-sought student." Hirschfeld could mold him in his own image. In a way, Li assuaged the fears of death that had plagued Hirschfeld since at least the world journey's beginning. Hirschfeld would die, but Li, molded in his image, would carry on the work.

Many queer European men came to China because they thought Chinese men feminine, more available, more complaint than men back home and because they thought China was a less sexually repressive place. Hirschfeld is something of an outlier though. He does not exactly share these common views. He certainly thought Li pliant, perhaps subservient, certainly capable of being "mold[ed]," and all of that was racialized; a severe view of Hirschfeld's attitudes would liken them to how white Europeans in the colonies viewed their Asian "houseboys," but a houseboy would never be an intellectual heir.[63] In any event, Hirschfeld did not think that China had more homosexuals than any other country. The percentage of homosexuals in any population of humans, or in any species for that matter, was constant: 3 percent.[64] China was less civilized – on a path to higher civilization, with people like Li leading the way, but still not so civilized as Europe. Therefore, it was more tolerant, not only of homosexuality but of a relaxed approach to sex in general.[65] He noticed that members of the Chinese Women's Club handled questions about sexuality with "more naturalness, freedom and grace" than did white English members of a women's group in Hong Kong that he lectured to some weeks later.[66]

Hirschfeld pushed back, gently, against the prevailing white European sexualized racialization of Chinese men, which put them down as effeminate or otherwise less masculine. He seems skeptical of that idea, discussing possible evidence for their femininity but also discussing the counterarguments that Chinese experts were making – less body hair, for example, was not a sign of being feminine but a sign of being more evolved, farther from hair-covered animals.[67] He then, however, recounts a story of a supposed folk illness, the "disappearing penis" disease, which he claims terrifies Chinese people – a man's penis can suddenly shrivel up into his body.[68] Hirschfeld does not think the penises are really shriveling up; he thinks Chinese people think that they are. The story seems like a coy play on the trope of the emasculated Chinese man, a strong trope in Hirschfeld's world.[69] Yet elsewhere he breaks with that trope, specifically when thinking of queer men. Among Chinese homosexuals, there were "relatively few who are strongly feminine, the majority give the impression of slight femininity or seem entirely virile."[70] This makes Chinese homosexual men seem practically butch, since to Hirschfeld, homosexual men in general leaned feminine. The definitional characteristics of male homosexuals included that "they behave negatively towards the opposite sex and positively towards the same sex, and they give off an impression of femininity."[71] Given how well established and strong was the idea that Chinese men were feminine, Hirschfeld's views seem a startling break with received wisdom, disappearing penises notwithstanding. It was not racialized femininity that drew him to Li. It was another supposedly racial trait: loyalty, together with Li's youth and scholasticism. Through Li, Hirschfeld could live on after his death.

This was, however, not what they told Li's family, and this speaks to another reason Li perhaps had for leaving China. The night before Li and Hirschfeld sailed for Manila, Li's father gave a farewell dinner in Hong Kong. Li had asked his father's permission to go to Europe with Hirschfeld to study sexology, and his banker father had agreed. Hirschfeld wrote later, "he entrusted his son to me."[72] Li's father told Hirschfeld that he hoped his son would become the Magnus Hirschfeld of China.[73] The idea was that Li would study with Hirschfeld and then return. Hirschfeld and Li told the same story to a reporter, too: Li, the reporter wrote, was going to study at Hirschfeld's Institute and would return after a few years abroad "with the hope of duplicating in China some of the work done by Dr. Hirschfeld in Europe."[74] There was some fiction here. Li did not have to leave China to be a sexologist. Republican China was home to its own sexologists already.[75] And Li does not seem to have planned to come back. He went back in the winter of 1933, while Hirschfeld was in exile in France, and returned after a struggle – his family, Hirschfeld wrote in his journal, did not want Li to leave again.[76]

Li's conflict with his family was possibly about marriage. There is a great amount of detail in *World Journey* about arranged marriages and the impossibility, for homosexual men, of avoiding them. Most men in China were married by twenty-two to a first wife picked by their parents, Hirschfeld reported.[77] Li was twenty-four. China had its share of single people; a few women even lived in female-female pairs.[78] It was harder for men. Homosexual Chinese men were "almost all married."[79] Hirschfeld was against this. He often urged against forcing homosexuals to get married, in part for eugenic reasons (more on this later).[80] Li remained unmarried throughout his long life.

In Shanghai, at the outset of their relationship, Hirschfeld and Li's time together was stamped by imperialism. Hirschfeld's journey around the world with Li by his side would be defined by the connection he perceived between two scenes of Shanghai that stuck in his mind. The first was the two men in blue and their songbirds, which stood for the fidelity, possibly erotic, between an older man and a younger one. The second scene occurred on the same day that Hirschfeld saw those two men. It showed the grave injustice of the oppression visited by Europeans on the Chinese and other people living under colonial rule.

Riding in a rickshaw on the Bund, Hirschfeld saw a traffic policeman in the employ of the International Settlement's Municipal Council beat another rickshaw driver. The traffic cop was probably a Sikh from British India. The Settlement had recruited Sikh men from the Punjab for many decades, copying a pattern that prevailed throughout Britain's colonies. Sikh men, enticed by relatively high wages, traveled the circuits of empire serving as police from Canada to Hong Kong. They served in the Settlement's Shanghai Municipal Police, which Settlement officials saw as an army of colonial occupation tasked with facing down internal threats, such as unruly lower-class Chinese people. To many Chinese Shanghai residents, the Sikh police were infamous for brutality. This reputation stemmed from racism; white British and Chinese police were not any less violent. The reputation for brutality was also thanks to the fact that the Sikh policemen's particular job was often to direct traffic. In the Settlement's extremely narrow byways, streetcars and motor cars crushed together with a thicket of rickshaws – 3,000 rickshaws per square mile. Sikh officers, given the impossible task of imposing order on chaos, were highly visible symbols of foreign rule. Their traffic instructions were often ignored, and it was not unknown for them to pummel offending rickshaw drivers with their black-and-white signaling batons.[81]

This was what Hirschfeld witnessed. The "rubber club of a foreign policeman whistled down on a rickshaw coolie," who had, Hirschfeld guessed, made some insignificant traffic infraction. Hirschfeld watched blow after blow fall, horrified. "The agent of a foreign government only stopped yelling at the coolie and beating him when the frightened Chinese 'kowtowed,' touching his head to the ground." Hirschfeld was "filled with sympathy" for the rickshaw driver, "this enslaved, tortured human creature [*menschliche Kreatur*]."[82]

Hirschfeld saw in this incident the naked violence of imperialism and feared that it would spur the Chinese, in turn, to violence. He thought of the Boxer Rebellion and the quotidian violence he witnessed in Shanghai, where "at many street crossings … one sees wire barricades, guarded by policemen, ready at any moment to bar the way to the Chinese." It was the lightning before "a perhaps no longer so distant global storm," a worldwide war against imperialism, and he dreaded it.[83] He was prescient: tens of millions would die in the struggle against imperialism and the violence that followed the collapse of imperial regimes, and they would die in some of the places where he traveled on his world journey – China, Indonesia, South Asia.

The two scenes of the Bund – the two men, perhaps discreet lovers, and the imperial police officer beating the Chinese man – had much to do with gay rights. Early gay rights was defined by the first scene, that is, by the possibility of same-sex love in the world beyond Europe. It stumbled over what, if anything, to do about the second scene. Yet in Li's company, Hirschfeld came up with an answer. The next chapter shows how.

4 The Fight against Sexual Oppression Is a Fight against Empire

Jawaharlal Nehru's House, Allahabad, India, October 1931

One hot day in October 1931, a train pulled up to the station in Allah-abad (Prayagraj), India. Onto the platform stepped Li and Hirschfeld. It had been a three-hour ride from Varanasi, where they had spent five days. Hirschfeld had given two lectures, to a club of professors at the university and to a medical association. Now Hirschfeld was suffering from the heat, which he tolerated poorly. As he advanced down the station platform he was probably limping. A few days before, he had been left with a bruised and aching leg after the incident in which the pony cart tipped over.[1] Li, one imagines, dealt with the luggage.

Despite the sweltering weather and the pain in his leg, Hirschfeld was thrilled to see the man who met their train: Allahabad's most famous resident, Jawaharlal Nehru.[2] Nehru, then a leader of the movement to free South Asia from British rule, would later be India's first prime minister. In him, Hirschfeld recognized a comrade – a fellow fighter for oppressed peoples. They had met years before, probably at a 1927 anticolonial conference in Brussels.[3] In the 1920s, Berlin was home to lots of anticolonial communist and more moderate leftists and was a center for expatriate anticolonialists like Nehru.[4] He probably saw Hirschfeld as a well-connected leftist who could use his influence back in Europe to support Indian nationalism. Hirschfeld more than agreed with Nehru's view of an anticolonial Germany. Moreover, he thought he had something else in common with Nehru. Just as Nehru fought for freedom for South Asia, Hirschfeld saw himself as a fighter for an unjustly oppressed minority, a diasporic people spread all over the world: homosexuals.

Nehru brought Hirschfeld and Li to the family mansion, where they met his wife Kamala Nehru, his sister Krishna Nehru, and, as Hirschfeld put it later, "his charming, perhaps fifteen-year-old daughter," who was also a future prime minister of India: Indira Gandhi.[5] As an adult in the 1970s, she would turn out to share with Hirschfeld, by then long dead, a belief in the necessity of forced sterilization, though their visions of it were vastly different.[6]

All the talk that night was of the independence movement. They were joined by the independence leader Syed Mahmud, who had already gone to hear Hirschfeld lecture earlier on in his tour of India.[7] Like Li, Nehru (who was in his forties at the time) had been raised by a father who believed in Westernization and had sent him to English schools.[8] Hirschfeld was wholeheartedly behind Indian independence. "For fifty years I have been a supporter of India's independence ... I find it one of the greatest political injustices in all of the world that one of the oldest civilized countries [*Kulturländer*], a country that has been and still is a source of wisdom for all of humanity, is not free to rule itself."[9]

The world journey with Li inspired Hirschfeld to weld his theory of homosexuality to a strong denunciation of empire. This was an abrupt change. He became a real opponent of empire, though he still had ideas we would call racist, and he still held a decidedly chauvinistic view of European civilization. I suspect that his travels with Li had something to do with Hirschfeld's far-better-informed take on imperialism in his later work, though I cannot say for sure. This is important in gay history. White gay politics has all too often refrained from such a broad vision. Yet, despite his very real racism (see subsequent chapters), the thinker who did the most to originate gay politics had an anti-imperial vision of what queer freedom was, or at least he did that night in Nehru's house.

Hirschfeld went from oblivious to empire to full-throated opposition. Recent scholarship has called him an abettor of empire; I argued as much in chapter 2.[10] Yet he changed his mind. Why? The change began before the world journey. There is a (relatively brief) anticolonial passage in *Sexology* II, published in 1928, which contains many of the anticolonial ideas he expressed later, suggesting that even before he met Li, by the late 1920s he had a lot more to say against empire than he had when he wrote *The Homosexuality of Men and Women*. In the passage in *Sexology* II Hirschfeld specifically mentions the Brussels conference, which must have helped to change his views.[11] Nevertheless, Hirschfeld's single major anticolonial work is the memoir of his travels with Li, *World Journey*. During the world tour, Hirschfeld hobnobbed with luminaries of anticolonial movements in India, China, Egypt, and the Philippines. Some – like Nehru – he had met before his trip. But he had written little or nothing about them before. In *World Journey* he wrote, "What we think about the holding of slaves, future generations will think about the holding of colonies."[12] The British might say that chaos would ensue if they got out, claiming that their colonial possessions – India, Palestine, and elsewhere – were "not yet mature enough to govern" themselves. He had no time for that idea. "As far back as I can think – and among us in Europe too – the idea that a people is 'not yet mature enough' to direct its own fate is always repeated as a justification for a small group of either indigenous or foreign rulers to suppress the rights and liberties of the great masses."[13]

Through much of his career, colonial civil servants had been his friends, collaborators, and informants. On the world tour, he loathed colonial civil servants, particularly the British and Dutch. Now, he constructed his own identity in opposition to them. He describes the chauvinism of the imperialists, at times dispassionately, at times in a critical tone. The overall effect is to make them out to be racist buffoons.[14] *World Journey* denies empire barely a shred of legitimacy. Sure, in Indonesia the Dutch had improved public health, though not nearly enough: infant mortality was high, so was illiteracy, and sanitation was abysmal in the poverty-stricken native quarters of colonial towns.[15] There was guerrilla warfare going on against the Dutch, too, he told his readers.[16] His point was that he was not like these imperialists. He was not racist; he drew no color line and never supported anyone else drawing one.[17] He got to know "natives" by spending time with them. This is in part a self-romance, surely, but there is also truth to it. Hirschfeld did spend a lot of time with non-European elites. For example, he includes a photograph of himself in *World Journey* with Javanese elites in Semarang, men (many in Western suits) as well as women, this at a time when white people in the Dutch colony often kept entirely to their all-white clubs.[18] He met white Europeans and Americans in China who had lived for decades in their set-apart districts and their clubs, avoiding "the Chinese streets, which smell evil to them, the Chinese bars and theaters, that are too noisy for them," and "the Chinese people," who are too foreign and "deep" for them.[19] They knew nothing about China. He knew far more than these other myopic white people, even if he did not claim to fully understand China.[20] He stayed in Chinese hotels as much as he could, to get to know the country better.[21] This was easier to do, he reported, because he was traveling with an English-speaking Chinese companion, Li.[22] I assume Li made all the hotel arrangements. Yet Hirschfeld could not sleep in the hotels. They were to him a ruckus of men playing mah-jongg, drinking, laughing, sending for female prostitutes, calling for the boys in the corridors – waiters and servants – until the small hours of the morning. He sent one of his "room boys" to tell the people in the next room that "an old gentleman who does not feel well wants to sleep," but to no avail.[23]

Hirschfeld's anti-imperialism had an odd pro-German dimension. As he toured the world, Hirschfeld believed that Germany was a sort of special friend to decolonizing peoples. Stripped of its own colonies in the First World War, it had been vanquished by the very powers – especially the British but also the French and Americans – that oppressed and exploited the Chinese, the Egyptians, the South Asians, and others.[24] He likened the foreign concessions in China, the zones within the country where by treaty foreigners ruled, such as Shanghai's International District, to the post–World War I occupation of parts of Western Germany by the Entente, which his German readers would almost universally recognize as a grave injustice.[25] He minimized the horrors of Germany's empire (it had an abysmal record of colonial violence). Hirschfeld never mentions that, and he calls Germany's pre-1918 overseas empire "minimal," which it was not.[26] With Germany's colonies gone, Hirschfeld, ever the patriot, was freed up to blast empire. He remained a German patriot even into the final years of his life, in exile, though Nazism sorely tested his love of country and though he was also – often, not always – a pacifist.[27] He met with non-Europeans wherever he went, and in every country he spoke before non-European audiences, but he also spent a good deal of time with expatriates, particularly Germans.

For all of his talk against imperialism, at times Hirschfeld seemed to voice some chauvinism about "civilization," such as when he reflected how the United States in the Philippines, the Dutch in Indonesia, and the English in Asia and Africa had made "very impressive" advances, particularly road-building, sanitation, and agriculture.[28] He moreover often predicated his calls for self-rule on the argument that local elites were worthy and modernized, the implication being if they were not worthy, they ought not to rule.[29]

At the same time, he saw the hollowness of the civilizing mission. Imperialists had often done a bad job of spreading civilization: the European colonial project was wrapped in hypocrisy.[30] The world beyond Europe could attain the advantages of European technology and science without imperialism. Japan's example showed what the relationships between "the whites and those of other colors [*die Andersfarbigen*]" ought to be like.[31]

Yet, with respect to some colonized people, he retained the obliviousness to violence that Heike Bauer locates in his earlier work. He had a disturbing vision of "extinction" for some people. Peoples whom he terms "prehistoric tribes [*Stämme*]," like the Ainu of Japan and Native North Americans, seemed to him "destined to a more or less rapid extinction as soon as what we call civilization encroaches upon them."[32] Hirschfeld thus endorsed an essentially genocidal view of "races ... destined" to die out of their own accord – at the same time, many of the people in question were under sustained attack by settler colonial states.

He nevertheless had three main theoretical critiques of empire. The first, and the most prominent in his thought, was that it was unjust oppression. The second was that imperialism would spark global war as people rose up to throw off their colonizers.[33] He saw something "elemental" in anticolonial violence; it was like an explosion under pressure, a natural rising against violent foreigners.[34] Empire was unnatural. This was his third charge against it. Here, he created a direct tie to his advocacy for sex reform. Repressive laws and norms about sexuality violated the natural order. So did colonialism.

Though this idea of a broad struggle against oppression is exciting in the context of gay history, and is moreover a major departure from much of Hirschfeld's other work, the way that he put it together was not always all that inspiring. In one version, he leaned on a well-traveled, racist notion about how "the races" belonged, or did not, in various climates. Hirschfeld thought that whites in the tropics could never acclimatize; they were "not viable" there.[35] White women especially could not handle it.[36] He described the Europeans in tropical colonies like Indonesia sliding into laziness and stupidity, soaking themselves in whiskey sodas, downing narcotics, and complaining of "tropical frenzy" when their real problem was born of subjecting their "heat-weakened bodies" to an excess of alcohol.[37] When white men and women had children together in the tropics, the children were stunted. "Often the 'pure-blooded' family has already died out by the third generation."[38] (When white Europeans married non-whites in the colonies, their "mixed" children were much fitter, he thought – more on this in chapter 9.)[39] Nature had clearly given Asia and Africa to "the colored peoples" (*den farbigen Völkern*).[40] "The European peoples [*Völker*] should not claim that they rightfully own lands to which they have no biological entitlement ... I am speaking here not as a politician, but rather as a natural scientist."[41] Habituation to climate meant a biological entitlement. Racists often posited differential acclimatization. One finds a similar idea about migration, climate, and race in Immanuel Kant, whom Hirschfeld had read, as well as elsewhere.[42] For example, white Canadian leaders invoked it to explain why only white people ought to migrate to Canada.[43]

Hirschfeld believed in "race" as such (more on this in chapter 6). Though he believed racial difference was mostly meaningless, he did not think it was entirely meaningless. The ability to stand heat was one meaningful difference among the races. It meant that nature never intended colonialism. He thus had a racist argument against empire: it was against the natural racial order. As he traveled, heat often bothered him, sometimes badly. His complaints about the heat were a quiet proof of his whiteness.

He, however, saw a second way in which empire was unnatural, and it is perhaps more inspiring: people had an innate desire for freedom. In *World Journey*, Egypt is the scene of many anti-imperial musings. One chapter is entitled "Egypt for Egyptians." The British had granted Egypt formal independence in 1922, but rather than leave the country, they shifted to an informal mode, influence without responsibility, which was their preference anyway.[44] Britain retained significant power in the country and kept troops there until the 1950s. The British high commissioner interfered in Egyptian affairs at will and without concern for Egypt's supposed sovereignty or for its democratic political system.[45] In the course of a passage about the British in Egypt, Hirschfeld paused and addressed his reader, who, he thought, perhaps might be wondering what Hirschfeld's opinions about "high politics," that is about imperialism, had to do with his proper subject, "the love lives of peoples [*Völker*]." The answer, he wrote, was

> More than you think. There is a desire for freedom that is biologically conditioned and deeply rooted in body-soul [*Körperseele*], and it stretches first of all to the person's individuality, then directly to "sex [*Geschlecht*]," [that is] to the impact of a person's sexuality [*die geschlechtliche Auswirkung einer Person*], as embodied by the family, and then, thirdly, to the nation.[46]

In this passage he uses some awkward language, language that does not exactly match terms he uses elsewhere and that is not entirely clear: "'sex,' [that is] … the impact of a person's sexuality, as embodied by the family." One wonders if by this he means sexual reproduction and heterosexual sex, not homosexuality. However, in his eugenic theory of homosexuality, same-sex desire did benefit families, precisely because it was non-reproductive (see chapter 9). My suspicion is that his intention is to include homosexuality here and that his meaning is that "a desire for freedom that is biologically conditioned and deeply rooted in body-soul" extended to one's individual self, to one's sexual expression, and to the nation to which one belonged. In all of these realms – the individual, the sexual, and the national – a person naturally and rightly wanted to be free. The freedom one sought was in its essence the same in all three realms. This idea comes up elsewhere in *World Journey*, on the walk with the unnamed Filipino student in Manila. To quote again what Hirschfeld wrote that the student said: "You are an advocate for the idea that the natural rights of individuals and of peoples should not be violated, so perhaps you can raise your voice for us Filipinos too."[47]

Thus, by the end of his life, Hirschfeld had made a remarkable transition to an (admittedly flawed) decolonial homosexual politics. He embraced the struggle against empire as fundamentally related to the struggle for sexual freedom. He told his readers that it was "particularly easy for a sexologist" to grasp "the psychological background" of anticolonialism because the sexologist "draws analogies and sees … the natural right to self-determination" and the "encroachment on personal freedom."[48] Like Egyptians living under British encroachment, homosexuals were suffering a violation of their natural right to self-determination. A sexologist, familiar with sexual oppression, intrinsically understood political repression when he saw it. Hirschfeld declared himself against both kinds of oppression and supposed they were in fact not so different.

At the outset of gay rights, it was possible to think of gay rights as a broad struggle for justice, with the freedom of European homosexuals intimately connected to that of other groups (including homosexuals and non-homosexuals) suffering unjust oppression. Hirschfeld saw how anti-imperialism and homosexual liberation were branches of the same struggle.

This was a transformation in his thought, and it came late in his life. Why so late? Decades before, Edward Carpenter, the British socialist and homosexual, had made much the same point, as Leela Gandhi notes, blaming toxic hypermasculinity for the oppression of homosexuals and for empire.[49] Hirschfeld knew Carpenter's work. It took him a long time to reach the same conclusion. What changed though? Why 1931?

For one thing, Hirschfeld saw the horror of empire in person. On his visit at the University of Calcutta, he spent time with the art historian Stella Kramrisch, an Austrian by birth who was a professor there – the only female professor at the university, according to Hirschfeld.[50] They went to see a performance by the poet Rabindranath Tagore, whom Hirschfeld had met the day before. When they arrived they found the lecture hall filled with distressed, angry students who were demanding that the performance be canceled to observe "a moment of national bereavement," as Hirschfeld put it, because, in his words, "two political prisoners, fighters for India's freedom," had that afternoon been summarily shot at a prison near Calcutta.[51] He and Kramrisch left the lecture hall, and she took him to see a festival at a temple instead. On his way home that evening, Hirschfeld came upon a political funeral being held for the two men shot at the prison. Twelve people, their arms stretched above their heads, held the corpses of the two prisoners aloft, so that everyone could see them. The dead men still wore their prison clothes. Behind the corpses walked, he estimated, 100,000 people. Hirschfeld returned to his hotel. From a window, he watched the funeral parade. The people marched in a profound silence; only very occasionally, someone would break the silence with a "wild exclamation," he wrote. As the corpses passed the hotel, the people carrying them stretched to hold them up even higher, to make sure they were seen by the foreigners in the hotel who were looking out of the windows and watching from the balconies. This demonstration against the English struck Hirschfeld as all the more powerful because, he assumed, it was spontaneous, unplanned. "Unhappy India!" he wrote.[52]

In Hong Kong, a European merchant "told me with a laugh" that a "sedan-chair coolie (by the sweat of their brows they carry the people who live on the heights up hill and down dale)" had told the merchant that he, the sedan-chair coolie, wished that instead he had been born a rich Englishman's dog because "'They have it good.'" Hirschfeld reported saying in response to the merchant: "'How can you laugh about that? ... That's not funny, that's a tragic story.'"[53] The pity he felt and the fellow humanity had their paternalistic notes, and their limits. He nevertheless felt them keenly.

Yet why then? He had already seen imperialism's and racism's violences, years before, when as a young man he traveled in the United States and Morocco. Hirschfeld wrote *World Journey* in exile, as racism waxed in Germany. His views of racism changed as that happened; he felt it more acutely as something that endangered his own life. Yet there are signs in *World Journey* that it was China that changed his mind.

Hirschfeld seems to have voiced anti-imperialism and homosexual liberation together for the first time just a few days before he and Li sailed from Shanghai to Hong Kong in early June 1931. They had met about a month before and had been touring cities together, including Nanking and Tianjin, and had then come back to Shanghai to sail for southern China. Hirschfeld gave an interview to a reporter for the English-language Shanghai newspaper the *China Press* on the deck of the tender as he and Li rode out through Shanghai harbor to the *Empress of Canada*. Hirschfeld told the reporter that "foreigners in China are guests of the country and not its masters. As such, a more modest attitude on their part toward the people and their ways would better become them."[54]

In this interview, Hirschfeld himself credits his time spent with Li in China with helping him to see the injustice of foreign incursion. He said, in the words of the reporter, "his experiences during the last several weeks he spent in Shanghai and North China convinced him that the general attitude of the foreigners towards the Chinese, as he found it, was not best calculated to foster mutual regard."[55] Hirschfeld went on to blast foreign encroachment on Chinese sovereignty: "The existence of foreign-controlled areas in various Chinese cities ... seems not right to me." Here someone, probably the reporter, interjected. The reporter wrote, "He [Hirschfeld] was told that the Chinese people do not consider it right either." Hirschfeld went on: "I hope soon the Chinese people will run their own country without foreign interference." He then subtly linked the question of whether the Chinese ought to rule themselves to the question of homosexual emancipation:

> I hope … that in adapting modern knowledge to the needs of the people, the Chinese leaders will not make the mistake that has been made in other … countries of placing too many prohibitions and inhibitions upon the natural impulse of the people. Where too many laws exist to make people conform to a mould, the people become nervous … they cannot be themselves and their natures rebel. The result is an undermining of their health and happiness. I can sum up my meaning in one sentence: Do not legislate too much on how people shall think, what they should not know, and what they should not do.

He may very well have had political freedoms aside from sexuality in mind here. Moreover, this is not quite the fully articulated point that one finds in *World Journey*, where empire is unnatural and so is the oppression of homosexuals. One, however, perhaps sees him moving toward that. Oppressed sexual minorities "rebel," a political term for opposition to an unjust regime such as empire, under the strain of "prohibitions upon the natural impulse." Moreover, empire is heinous, and one speaks of that in the same interview in which one – quietly, subtly – advances sexual freedom.

Li did not discuss empire in his surviving unpublished writings.[56] In *World Journey*, Hirschfeld attributes no political views to Li. He does, however, write a lot about what "Chinese students" think about empire. I assume that that usually, if not always, meant Li as well as perhaps others, though Hirschfeld does not seem to have spent much time with any other Chinese students. Hirschfeld wrote:

> One has only to see the warships of the foreign powers provokingly lying at anchor on the Yangtse River before Nanking, and on the Pearl River outside Canton. One need only know that no fewer than forty-five Chinese cities are occupied by the English, French, Italians and Japanese as "concessions," to understand that many politically minded Chinese (notably the student youth of China) still see hope for the future in the great plan of Dr. Sun Yat Sen – an alliance of China, Russia, and Germany as a massive bulwark against the rest of the capitalist world.[57]

It is hard to know what to make of this passage. Sun Yat-sen's postmortem meaning in 1931 varied depending on who you talked to; he was embraced by people on the right as well as by people on the non-communist left. The dream of an anti-capitalist Chinese-Russian-German alliance was, in 1931, an unlikely one. Nevertheless, the suggestion here is of a left-of-center take on Sun Yat-sen, an affinity for the non-communist left, and perhaps for communism given the fact that Bolshevik Russia was included in the vision. Li was, apparently, feeling more like a radical Shanghai student at that point than like the son of a rich Hong Kong banker. And he was no fan of foreign encroachment. Hirschfeld summarizes Sun's program as the overthrow of the Manchus, the founding of a democratic republic, and the reorganization of the Chinese state along socialist lines.[58] This sounds like democratic socialism, and to Hirschfeld, a moderate leftist who backed the German Social Democrats, it sounded good.

Did Li share Hirschfeld's views about China's need to adopt European technological progress? Perhaps he did. At the time, many decolonial thinkers who were themselves colonial subjects shared this idea, though increasingly decolonial thinkers were critical of the idea of progress. Li believed in Westernization.

In *World Journey*, Hirschfeld portrays imperialism as personal to him because of his experiences alongside Li. He includes accounts of trouble he and Li had to illustrate the injustice of imperialism: the incident in Manila Bay and the one in China where he and "a student" were thrown out of a club. I assume that he had many conversations with Li about Chinese politics. Li must have figured into his newfound, passionate opposition to colonialism. This was a change to that world historic theory of homosexuality, a late-breaking and a profound one.

He makes the point in *World Journey* in a passage about "Chinese students," his relationships with them, and racism. Chinese students embraced him, he wrote, for the most part not because he was an important German scholar but because they saw that "I spoke not as a European to Asians, not as an expert to the unlearned, or an elder to youth, but solely as a human being to other human beings, and as someone who is fundamentally on the side of the oppressed, no matter if that oppression is founded on reasons of nation, race, religion, society, or sexuality."[59] Thinking no doubt of Li, of his warm relationship with the Chinese student he knew best, Hirschfeld was inspired to connect the oppression of sexual minorities and that of the Chinese. Li, and other Chinese students, saw him as a foe of oppression in general, including oppression based on race and on sexuality. That was why "Chinese students" received him so warmly. This was a new self-conception for Hirschfeld and one that here he seems to link to Li – the Hirschfeld who was a heroic opponent of oppressions sexual, national, racial, and otherwise was the Hirschfeld whom Li embraced in China. This was a broad politics. The sexual minority's freedom was one with the freedom of the oppressed majority, the Chinese living under foreign encroachment.

In Nehru's house that evening in 1931, the hour grew late, the talk of anti-imperialism died down, and Hirschfeld and Li took their leave of their hosts and made ready for bed. Hirschfeld had been given the room that Mahatma Gandhi was in the habit of using when he visited Nehru's house. He proudly reported this in *World Journey*. He did not, however, record where Li slept.[60]

Some in the household may have sensed the love relationship between the older and younger man. Probably no one spoke of it. Certainly neither Hirschfeld nor Li would have spoken of it. To be queer companions, for these two, meant to be utterly discreet, utterly tacit.

My supposition is that people in the Nehru household may have wondered but that they nevertheless probably assumed Li and Hirschfeld were student/assistant and professor, nothing more. Hirschfeld never publicly identified himself as a homosexual.[61] He was rumored to be one; who knows if anyone in the house that night had heard these rumors. (Li's father, enthusiastic about his son becoming the Magnus Hirschfeld of China, seems not to have known of them.) Hirschfeld never revealed his sexuality to anyone but close friends, and even then, he could be quite secretive. For example, a close colleague of Hirschfeld's in the World League for Sexual Reform took many years to realize that Hirschfeld was homosexual and that he was in a relationship with Karl Giese.[62] Surely Hirschfeld and Li slept separately that night.

As many scholars have noted, decolonial movements often seized on heterosexual masculinity because it was denied to colonized men by the colonizers; this made the fight against empire a "profoundly heteronormative project," to quote Leela Gandhi.[63] Some Indian nationalists in this period moved in this direction, accusing the West of importing homosexuality (regardless of a very long history of same-sex love in South Asian countries prior to imperialism).[64] Yet did that necessarily have to be the path, and were there nationalist leaders who might go a different route? Leela Gandhi notes that Mahatma Gandhi had ties to late-Victorian British radicals, Edward Carpenter among them, and that Gandhi's thinking on sexuality is not aggressively heteronormative and masculinist.[65] Mahatma Gandhi did not applaud male-male eroticism, but neither did he blame the British for it, and he urged his readers not to indulge in "sitting in judgement upon others" and rather to purify themselves – he wanted everyone to practice celibacy, even married couples.[66] His views, however, were quite far from homosexual emancipation.

Jawaharlal Nehru does not appear to have written much about homosexuality. He knew at least one other prominent man besides Hirschfeld who had affairs with men, the poet Josh Malihabadi; Malihabadi also slept with women.[67] Nehru's government never repealed the section of the penal code, left over from the British, that criminalized male-male sex. But he favored at least one progressive position on sex that Hirschfeld shared: divorce by mutual consent.[68]

Nehru thought Gandhi's injunction to celibacy for everyone was "unnatural and shocking."[69] Sexual restraint was fine, but celibacy was just sexual repression, and it would cause "neurosis."[70] Nehru wrote of his own sex life, "I presume I am a normal individual and sex has played its part in my life, but it has not obsessed me or diverted me from my other activities. It has been a subordinate part."[71] He thought Gandhi's antipathy to sex was an overreaction against "the deluge of literature on sexology that is descending on us in these days," that is, in the 1930s.[72] At the same time, Nehru was no moralist, and he did not entirely discount the pleasures of marital intimacy.[73] Nehru had no problem with straight sex, and he had no problem admitting as much in print or referring to his own sex life, though he did not like to go on and on about sex in excruciating detail. From Nehru's perspective, Hirschfeld's lectures probably were too much talk of sex in public. But his friendship with Hirschfeld seems to indicate that Nehru, at least in 1931, did not have deep objections to sexology or to the view that homosexuality ought to be legal.

Perhaps homosexual emancipation, antiracism, and the fight against imperialism could all be the same struggle. Yet the legacy of Hirschfeld's theory pushed away from that coalitional politics, not toward it.

5 Was the Homosexual White? Analogy and the Making of the Sexual Minority

When Hirschfeld and other nineteenth-century defenders of homosexuals set out to abolish sodomy laws, the first thing they had to do was explain what same-sex desire was. If it was not a sin, as Christianity taught, and it was not a pathology, as psychiatrists and other exponents of secularism and science believed, then what was it? Hirschfeld made history in 1896 when he claimed it was a natural, non-pathological, biological condition. But he and others went beyond that, in a crucial way. They also argued that homosexuals were a "class of humans [*Menschenklasse*]," by which they meant a group bounded by a meaningful division, in the same way that groups of humans were bounded by economics, race, religion, sex, and other such factors.[1] While he was not the first to claim that same-sex-loving men were a "class" in this sense, Hirschfeld and his allies did more than anyone else to make them one.[2]

When this new class came forward, the course of gay politics was set for the next 150 years. It was set in such a way that it immediately became difficult to have a broad movement like what Hirschfeld envisioned on his world journey. In the last years of his career, traveling around the world with Li, then living in exile, Hirschfeld stumbled toward a vision of a broad movement. But in a way it was already too late. Many decades before, analogy had entered homosexual politics, in particular the analogy between the class of homosexuals and classes of people defined by racialization. It existed right at the start of gay politics and it suffused Hirschfeld's work. After he died, it was this analogy that lived on, not his rousing anti-imperial rhetoric.

The lives of nineteenth-century Europeans were organized around the division of groups of people into classes – socioeconomic class and other castes, chiefly race, gender, religion, nationality, and ethnicity. With the decline of absolute monarchy and the rise of liberalism, those classes had in some ways become more salient, while medieval models of caste, based for example in guild membership, had declined. Given how salient such caste divisions were, it is no surprise that same-sex-desiring men would begin to think of themselves in this way. They moreover lived in a moment when the unjust treatment of classes was under attack. The French Revolution had liberated people from the irrational bonds of caste, such as the Jews. Nineteenth-century liberalism demanded an end to class privileges for the aristocracy. A growing women's movement was decrying sex discrimination. Powerful socialist movements sought freedom for the working class.

In addition, Hirschfeld's biological model had an irritating flaw. In biology, something that is unusual is generally pathological. This was particularly true prior to the disability rights movement of the late twentieth century. Hirschfeld struggled with this. In his early work, he likened homosexuality to conditions such as "cleft palate" and "congenital umbilical hernia."[3] Many of his homosexual readers loathed these arguments. They were keen on respectability, a characteristic often denied in their day to people with disabilities.[4] The language of "class" (here I mean that term broadly construed, denoting caste divisions, not socioeconomic class specifically; most often, the homosexual analogy was not to socioeconomic class) was a way out of this bind, a way to describe what homosexuality was and to keep it biological, to keep it invested in a powerful medical discourse while avoiding ties to disability.

For many readers this story will bring up another more familiar one, the story of how nineteenth-century psychiatry created homosexuality. It was told most famously by Michel Foucault. In his version, the creation of homosexuality is a collaborative affair that defies common assumptions about how power works.[5] Foucault was not wrong. Psychiatrists talked to homosexuals.[6] They were their patients and sometimes their clients. Psychiatrists testified as expert witnesses for the defense in sodomy cases. Indeed, psychiatry defined homosexuality. But – and this is missing from Foucault's account – before all that happened, there was already a slightly different identitarian model of same-sex desire. As Hössli wrote in the 1830s, homosexuals were a class, a subset of the population with distinguishing, shared characteristics.[7] Moreover, as Marlon Ross asks, what does it mean that by the time the homosexual became a species, according to Foucault, race had already become a central marker of difference?[8]

Analogy is a mode of argument that posits a resemblance in one consequential quality between two essentially unlike objects.[9] Robert Tobin has shown that the first defenders of the nascent concept that came to be called "homosexuality" used analogy to explain that it defined a class of people. They were analogizing to Jews and to other unjustly persecuted groups, like witches.[10] The analogies worked by drawing a reader's attention to how homosexuals made up a bounded, socially relevant group, as well as to how they suffered unjust victimization. Especially authors writing in support of homosexual emancipation liked to show how the persecution of homosexuals was similar to persecutions that most people now agreed had violated Enlightenment rationality, secularism, and modern science. Abuses of Jews and witches were prime examples.

As the twentieth century dawned, a certain species of analogy became more and more dominant in homosexual emancipationist thought. These were analogies to race, ethnicity, or nation – the claim that homosexuals were a "people." These grew more common than other analogies, such as those to witches.[11] "We inverts … are a people [*Volk*] who have been unscrupulously enslaved," wrote an author in a small homosexual magazine who went by "Kurt from Leipzig" in 1923. Yet despite that, "we have a Fatherland where we are citizens: it is the great spiritual Fatherland of our love for our friends [*Freundesliebe*]."[12] Here, "inverts" sound like a diasporic nation, one that even has a "Fatherland," albeit a spiritual rather than territorial one. Kurt from Leipzig must have been influenced by the rhetoric about the destiny and fatherland of the German people (*Volk*) that one heard on the far right in Germany in 1923. Indeed, these queer analogies to nation and diaspora came into being thanks to the international politics of the post–World War I moment.

In the 1920s, across Europe, everyone was talking about the rights of "peoples" and "nations." That fact was not lost on a new generation of activists who joined the homosexual emancipation movement in wake of the First World War.[13] Many of them wanted to toss out medical language. These activists made clever use of the discourses of self-determination and nationalism that played such central roles in the First World War's dénouement. Another author in the German homosexual press around the same time called for homosexuals of all nations to organize an international body, a "world league of homoerotics," that would inspire and protect them.[14] He was doubtless modeling that plan on the new League of Nations. These analogies gave rise to perhaps the most famous queer analogy, the concept of a "sexual minority." Though initially historians thought this analogy came out of the United States and developed after the Second World War, one finds it in Germany stamped by the aftermath of the First World War. Historians to date have traced the concept of "sexual minority" to the American Donald Webster Cory (a pseudonym of Edward Sagarin) writing after 1945. But it seems he probably drew it from Hirschfeld; Cory read Hirschfeld and was influenced by him.[15]

The phrase "sexual minority" seems to have been coined by Kurt Hiller. He is not well remembered today, but he was an important ally of Hirschfeld's for much of the 1910s and 1920s and a leader of German homosexual emancipation.[16] Hiller was a journalist, an intellectual, and a colleague of Hirschfeld's in the Scientific Humanitarian Committee. His political work stretched far beyond homosexual emancipation, and though he was for the most part a non-communist leftist, his views were radically eclectic, running from pacifism to anti-democratic elitism and qualified praise of Mussolini, yet always adhering to a classically liberal defense of the right of a person to do with their own body as they saw fit, so long as no one else was injured.[17] As early as 1913, he wrote that homosexuals and Jews were both "minorities."[18] However, it was after the First World War that he really grasped the power of the concept of a "sexual minority."

Following World War I, Europe rang with talk of the rights of national and ethnic minorities, and power players moved to protect those rights. Toward the war's end, all the major belligerents promised (for self-interested reasons) to aid in the self-determination of various nationalities living in multinational empires or under colonial regimes. This fueled expectations that the peace conference in Paris would establish a just world order and liberate oppressed peoples.[19] The actual settlement fell notoriously short of those hopes.[20] Yet the postwar settlement did create international legal protections for ethnic and national minorities in some countries. The victorious Allies forced eight central, southern, and eastern European states to sign minority protection treaties to be enforced by the new League of Nations. They guaranteed toleration and equality to these countries' minorities, which were defined as people who differed from the majority "race, language, and religion."[21] The protected minorities included Jews and national or ethnic minorities, such as Germans in the newly reconstituted Poland.[22] Though enforcement of these treaties varied, the claim that minorities within nation-states deserved protection continued to be a useful lever in international affairs, as various constituencies – including the German government – advocated for protections for minorities.[23]

Hiller saw an opening. As he wrote in 1918, "protection for minorities is a principle that has a lot of support today." He had ideas for domestic politics, for one thing. He wanted homosexuals to copy strategies used by national minorities in Germany, specifically Danes, Alsatians, Poles, and Lithuanians.[24] They had banded together with Sorbs and Friesians to form a group, the Federation of National Minorities in Germany (Verband der nationalen Minderheiten in Deutschland), to fight discrimination.[25] That group worked with the Union of Poles in Germany (Związek Polaków w Niemczech/Bund der Polen in Deutschland), which helped Polish candidates run for public office.[26] National minority groups like

Lithuanians and Poles in Germany were an important model for homosexuals. "Inverts," Hiller wrote, using a synonym for homosexuals, needed their own political party, too, though that idea never got off the ground.[27] The language was what transferred most successfully, though homosexual emancipation did also adapt itself in other ways to mass democracy in Germany after the First World War.[28]

In 1921, at the first international congress of the World League for Sexual Reform, which was held in Berlin, Hiller gave a speech called "Law and Sexual Minorities."[29] In it he argued that homosexuals and others with sexual tastes different from those of most people were "sexual minorities."[30] He included sadists, masochists, and people who desired sex with animals – these made up different "sexual minorities" from that of homosexuals. So long as no one was injured, consensual sex between adults was not justifiably a crime, he told his audience: "The human rights of even the smallest minority" had to be respected by law. "This principle is recognized everywhere in the world, at least theoretically, with respect to *national* minorities; not everyone is convinced that its ethical sense demands that it be applied to *sexual* minorities." Yet it ought to be. The sexual minority that was most unfairly persecuted, he said, were men who had sex with men. "Their liberation is a pressing humanitarian and liberal necessity of our time." He ended the speech with a rousing analogy, one that stuck. A German kaiser had once called antisemitism the scourge of the nineteenth century, Hiller said, referring to the then crown prince's denunciation of antisemitism in the 1880s.[31]

> But when were the Jews in Germany ever as persecuted as the homoerotics? ["Homoerotic" was Hiller's preferred substitute term for "homosexual."] Does the penal code contain an exceptional law against the racial minority like the infamous exceptional law against the sexual minority? The shame of the century is homophobia [*Antihomoerotismus*]; the shame of the century is Paragraph 175. [Paragraph 175 was Germany's sodomy law.][32]

Here, Jews were a "racial minority" and homosexuals a "sexual minority." The persecution of Jews had been unjustified; the persecution of homosexuals was worse. Other activists used these ideas, too.[33] They spread. A Polish author wrote in 1931 that he had only recently heard the term "sexual minority" and that he thought it had first been used at a sexology convention.[34]

The men who created the concept of a sexual minority were writing at the outset of what would become international human rights jurisprudence, which emerged following the eventual failure of the minority rights system of the interwar period.[35] Hiller made the case in another speech at a World League for Sexual Reform meeting, this one in Copenhagen in 1928:

> An age in which concern for national minorities is so extraordinarily keen
> and active must find the courage to protect a minority which, to be sure, is
> not an ethnic one, but which can be found in all states, and is especially de-
> serving of protection, since there is no state in the world where they are the
> majority and with which they, like the national minorities, could identify.
> International minority rights, which are slowly taking shape, should defend
> not only the national, the racial and the religious minorities, but also the
> psycho-biological, the sexual minorities, so long as they are harmless.[36]

The argument that persecuting homosexuals violated their human rights
turned out to be a powerful tool in the hands of gay activists. It began in German homosexual emancipation. As Leila Rupp and David Churchill have
shown, after 1945 European and American groups looked to the precedent
of Hirschfeld and Hiller's Scientific Humanitarian Committee and cast homosexuals as a minority group, spinning human rights discourse in their
favor.[37] Today, human rights language is often invoked in queer politics.[38]

Increasingly, the analogy was between sex and race. One sees this in Hiller's 1921 speech: Jews, a racial minority, are analogous to homosexuals, a
sexual minority. By the 1920s, it was not uncommon for German Jewish
thinkers to assume, as Hiller did in that passage, that Jews were a race,
though they by no means endorsed the antisemitic vision of Jews as an evil
race bent on world domination.[39] In the same speech, Hiller elaborated.
People were different, "not only with respect to racial-somatic and char-
acterological aspects, but also with respect to sexual aspects." There were
differences in "skin color, eye color, hair color, in skull form, face and body
shape, in language, style, taste, temperament, talent, moral character, and
moreover also in the direction of the drive for love [*des Liebestriebes*]."[40] The
"direction" of one's desire, or "sexual orientation" as it would come to be
called, could be understood by analogizing to race. Same-sex desire, like
racial characteristics, was a natural feature of humans, and variety did not
necessarily mean pathology. In 1913, Hiller had written of homosexuality
as a sort of racialization, rather than just an analogous condition: "What
I ask of the homosexual is self-affirmation. I want him to have the feeling
that his particular race [*Rasse*] is of full value, I want him to dispense with
all of the stupid assumptions about how he is inferior by birth."[41] Homosexual politics would rely on Hiller's analogy for a long time to come.

    For Hiller, and for others, the analogies to race were a way to get away
from the creeping overlap with disability in Hirschfeld's biological model.

In the same 1921 speech in which he gave an early and clear sense of the phrase "sexual minority," Hiller went on at length about how it mattered little whether homosexuality was an inborn condition or not. The important thing was that it was deeply rooted in a person's nature, unchangeable. "Was Goethe's genius inborn?" he asked, and how would we ever be able to tell? Like the growth of artistic genius, the development of the direction of the sexual drive happened thanks to the push and pull of things internal and innate as well as things that were external to a person. Probably it was refreshing for homosexuals who had grown up hearing that they were, at best, mentally ill to hear this relatively young man (Hiller was in his thirties at the time) implicitly liken same-sex desire to Goethe's genius. Increasingly, German homosexual emancipationists did not want to talk so much about what biological science might reveal about homosexuality's root. This was one reason that younger men wrestled control of the Scientific Humanitarian Committee away from Hirschfeld.[42] Hiller was in that group of rebels. Hirschfeld did not blame him as much as he did some of the others. Hiller was not quite in his right mind, Hirschfeld thought; he was in love with the young communist who led the cabal, Richard Linsert.[43]

At the same time, "sexual minority" and "biological homosexual" were not necessarily two distinct models entirely at odds – one could use the minority model and a biological discourse as well, as many, including Hirschfeld, did.

What did racism mean to Hiller? He wrote comparatively little about "the races" so it is hard to pin him down on whether they existed in a hierarchy. In any event, he did not categorically reject the idea that, as he put it, "one race is superior to another (e.g., possibly the whites superior to the Mongols or both to the negroes)," though he termed the concept of racial superiority "very questionable."[44] On antisemitism, that particular variety of racism, he was stronger in his views. In 1921, he, and probably the overwhelming majority of German Jews, thought antisemitism a vestige of an earlier age, destined to die out.

Analogy works by emphasizing one particular correspondence between two otherwise unlike things. The implication is that aside from the correspondence that the analogy highlights, the things are not alike and are distinct rather than always already co-constitutive.[45] In Hiller's analogy, the sexual minority faces anti-homosexual oppression, while the racial minority faces racism. This can imply that members of the sexual minority do not face racism.

Hiller never claimed that homosexuals were white by definition. Indeed, he cannot have thought that they were. Members of his intellectual circle, including Hirschfeld, spent many years amassing of a giant mountain of evidence that showed homosexuality existing around the globe, including among people of various races. Hiller's own life story demonstrated that a person could be Jewish and homosexual at the same time, though he very well may have considered Jews a white race (see chapter 8). Yet regardless of Hiller's intentions, his analogy can easily function in such a way that members of the sexual minority are implicitly unmarked by race.[46]

Being unmarked by race made the homosexual white.[47] Many scholars have argued that deracialization implies whiteness. "Whiteness – in its refusal to be named and its refusal to be seen – represents itself as *the* universal and unmarked standard, a ubiquitous norm from which all else and all others are viewed as a regrettable deviation," writes David Eng.[48] Indeed, the "unmarked, unnamed status" of whiteness is an effect of racism.[49] It was white subjects who were able to perceive themselves as not having a race.[50] This made white people the default type of human: "As long as white people are not racially seen and named, they/we function as the human norm. Other people are raced, we are just people."[51] The default homosexual was assumedly white, too. Thus, what analogies like Hiller's, which have enjoyed a very long and robust life in gay rights in many countries, often did was to, in Jasbir Puar's words, "relieve[] mainstream gays, lesbians and queers from any accountability to antiracist agendas, produce[] whiteness as a queer norm (and straightness as a racial norm), and foster[] anti-intersectional analyses that posit sexual identity as 'like' or 'parallel to' race."[52]

A second serious problem for antiracism lies in a particular form of the race/homosexuality analogy. Some authors who analogize between homosexuality and race assert that race is "biologically identifiable" because they want to claim that homosexuality is as well.[53] Yet for more than a century, one of antiracism's core insights has been that race is not a biological fact but is rather a social designation based on superficial physical characteristics and fictitious science.[54]

Hiller's analogy troubles antiracist queer politics in other ways, too. The analogy's real concern is with the second element, not the first. Hiller and company offered analogies to racial "minorities" not to protest their oppression but to use their oppression to protest the plight of (white) homosexuals, who are portrayed as a separate group in separate, though similar, circumstances.[55] Another problem is that, in fact, the oppression of people belonging to racialized minority groups in Germany (be they queer or not) in the 1920s was in many respects distinctly *unlike* the oppression of queer people who were racialized as white.[56]

One could write much more about these and other analogy troubles. There is a substantial scholarship on the problems of analogies between race and racism and gender and sexuality – I have only detailed some of the concerns raised by this literature.[57] White second-wave feminism famously suffered from the same troubles.[58] The point is, analogies like Hiller's make it difficult to articulate a subject position as both a homosexual and a member of a group that is persecuted through racialization.

Members of the sexual minority were unmarked by race. This tacitly made them members of the dominant racial group. It put people who were not unmarked by race into a discursively fraught position within homosexual emancipationist thought.

In the aftermath of the First World War, activists used analogies to racial, national, and ethnic groups to build a discourse of homosexuals as a sexual minority. This way of thinking about homosexuals proved to be powerful. "Sexual minority" is now a standard term. It positions queers within human rights discourse. Major gay rights victories have been won by convincing the mainstream that homosexuals are an oppressed class of persons. Activists and allies often analogize to race.[59] My point is that this analogy, which, as others have argued, can be detrimental to queer antiracism, is woven far more deeply into gay politics than we might have thought. It existed at the very outset of gay politics. It came into being as the category homosexual came into being and helped to form it.

Analogy's erasure of queer people of color troubled queer activism across the twentieth century, in Berlin and elsewhere.[60] To take just one example, in the 1960s in the majority-Black city of Washington, DC, a small and almost entirely white gay rights organization sincerely condemned anti-Black racism. At the same time, it deployed the analogy between the sexual minority and racial minorities, at times claiming, just like Hiller did, that the sexual minority had it worse than African Americans. Kent Peacock writes that those statements were "inevitably read to mean that the two groups were entirely separate, that blacks could not be part of the homosexual community, and that homosexuals could not be black."[61] The gay rights group remained overwhelmingly white; the assumed subject of its politics stayed white, too. Queer Black people in DC had to form their own organizations. Robert Tobin, who has a far less pessimistic reading of all this than I do, argues that queer movements "built upon" the success of antiracist movements.[62] "Building upon" can, however, be narrated as a parasitic relationship.[63] It does not mean white queer movements helped antiracist movements, nor that they made antiracism a part of their queer politics rather than leaving people of color (including queer people of color) to fight racism alone.[64]

6 Magnus Hirschfeld's Theory of the Races

Magnus Hirschfeld hated racism. Yet read what he wrote about "the races" and you will encounter what seems like, well, racism. Take this passage about race and brain size from *Sexology* I, published years before Hirschfeld met Li in Shanghai. (A clarifying preliminary note: Hirschfeld thought that brain size was a mark of intellectual capacity; it is not.) Here is the passage: "The weights of the brains of the primitive peoples remain considerably less than those of the cultural peoples." But this was not a static relationship. As "the culture declines ... skull capacity will be reduced." The good news was that it worked in reverse. Some peoples' brains had been stunted by the simplicity of the culture in which they lived. That could change. Moreover, women were not doomed to permanent inferiority to men; if they exercised their brains – as if brains were muscles – they could catch up. Take, he wrote, (white) women and Black American men and women. "The female brain ... has within it a considerable possibility to increase in capacity; after all, even the brains of the American negros have experienced a rapidly accelerated development since the abolition of slavery."[1]

Given his thoughts on brain weight, you might be surprised to find that Hirschfeld has a posthumous reputation as an important antiracist. His book *Racism* (1938), which came out in English several years after he died, was for a time listed in the *Oxford English Dictionary* as the earliest use of the term "racism" in the English language.[2] A much earlier use was subsequently found: the earliest use of the term according to the *OED* now is 1903. The equivalent term in German, *Rassismus*, was also in use before 1938.[3] Nevertheless, Hirschfeld still gets credit for being an early adopter of the term.[4] Some authors even mistakenly credit him with inventing the critique of scientific racism, a critique that dates at least to Anténor Firmin's 1885 *Equality of the Human Races*.[5]

He is quite quotable as an antiracist, too. In *Sexology* II he declares the "equality of all of the races of man," dismissing the influential French scientific racist Arthur de Gobineau's argument for racial inequality.[6] At the end of *Racism*, Hirschfeld concludes that "soberly contemplated, all the premises of racial fanaticism are, as we have been able to prove in the present study, based upon errors, misunderstandings, and untenable hypothesis."[7] He calls racism "the teachings of false prophets."[8] These quotes and others like them reassured the scholars who rediscovered Hirschfeld in the 1980s. They and the younger historians of sexuality who followed them – myself included – generally took him at his word and described him as antiracist.[9] Yet new scholarship has shown that even as Hirschfeld critiqued race and empire, his thinking remained indebted to racism and to imperialism.[10] And how could Hirschfeld be an antiracist if he thought brain capacity varied according to race?

My starting point is this: Hirschfeld had a theory of "the races." Almost none of the scholarship on him notes this, and there is no single exhaustive account of his theory beyond his own work.[11] Yet he had an elaborate, coherent theory, laid out across several publications, most centrally in what he considered "my greatest life's work," the multivolume *Sexology*.[12] Here's why this is important: His theory of the races was not incidental to his theory of homosexuality. It was, rather, central to it. The two theories buttressed each other. Since Hirschfeld has come back into public memory, no one has noted this.

Hirschfeld's theory of the races was, oddly, both a critique of racism and, at the same time, an example of it. By the standards prevailing in Hirschfeld's day in some circles, much of what he wrote on "the races" was indeed antiracist. There is a much broader definition of what constitutes "racism" though. It is "the belief in the inherent superiority of one race over all others and thereby the right to dominance," in Audre Lorde's words.[13] It is the belief that "races," however you define them, exist and have group attributes, and that one's own race is superior.[14] In Hirschfeld's day, lots of antiracists worked from this much more expansive sense of the problem. It was what James Weldon Johnson described in 1928 as "race prejudice," the trouble white Americans had in deciding "whether the Negro was a human being" and whether Black Americans ought to be citizens. It was white America's image of Black Americans as "a moribund people sinking into a slough of ignorance, poverty, and decay in the very midst of our civilization" and of "the Negro" as "a beggar at the gate of the nation, waiting to be thrown the crumbs of civilization."[15] The "Negro problem," as Johnson and many others noted, was not some group characteristic of Black people that was keeping them down. The problem was white racism. Here Johnson makes no distinction between those whites who are anti-Black because they believe in scientific racism or those who, like Hirschfeld, were anti-Black thanks to a slightly different story about what races were and why white races were superior. Neither should we. On his world tour Hirschfeld met Johnson, who was a celebrated Black author and leader of the NAACP (National Association for the Advancement of Colored People). Hirschfeld, however, seems not to have read him; he does not cite him. He made a dismissive, racist note about Johnson in his journal.[16]

This chapter is the first complete gloss of Hirschfeld's theory of the races. Readers will decide for themselves what to make of it, but there is no doubt that it is important in queer history: the person who invented "homosexuality" backed it up with a kind of racism. Moreover, his theory of the races was intimately woven together with his theory of homosexuality: racial difference and the fact that homosexuality existed across it were important proofs of his model of the modern homosexual.

The best way to approach Hirschfeld's theory of the races is to begin with what was probably the most formative influence on this thinking: the liberal school of German anthropology. The liberal school were anthropologists who were active from the 1870s to the First World War and who dismissed scientific racism. Rudolf Virchow – physician, professor, anthropologist, and politician – led the subfield until his death in 1902.[17] Hirschfeld studied under Virchow.[18] Virchow was also a public advocate for striking Germany's sodomy law, as I discussed in chapter 1. He had joined nine other professors at Berlin University in 1869 to call, unsuccessfully, for the decriminalization of male-male sex.[19] Hirschfeld greatly admired him, referring approvingly to Virchow in his own work on the races.[20]

Virchow believed that humanity was divided into races. However, he insisted that these were nothing more than relatively superficial anatomical varieties caused by environment. Race, in his view, had no bearing on psychology, mental aptitude, national identity, or culture. Virchow dismissed polygenesis – that is, the theory that different races had sprung from separate origin points. Humans were a single unified species.

Nevertheless, Virchow and other liberal anthropologists believed there were "races." They spent lots of time and energy trying to scientifically verify the existence of "races," which to them meant descent groups that shared superficial physical traits. Virchow was a pacifist and a loud critic of antisemitism who thought Germany should not acquire an empire overseas. Yet he spent his anthropological career measuring skulls and noting hair, skin, and eye color in an effort to delineate the physical types of mankind.[21] He and other anthropologists in his circle such as Felix von Luschan amassed collections of body parts of colonized people, having them shipped to Berlin, where thousands of skulls and other body parts were eventually housed at the Berlin Museum of Natural History.[22] Virchow's work and that of other liberal anthropologists had a tendency to elide physical traits with mental and moral traits.[23] After Virchow's generation, German anthropology moved away from his insistence that race was nothing but physical variation.[24] Virchow and other liberal anthropologists also believed that various groups of people were culturally superior to others. This was not hereditary or innate group superiority, and it was not caused by race.[25] Yet they saw a hierarchy of subgroups within the human population.

Hirschfeld's thinking on race was very close to what Virchow and other liberal anthropologists of his day taught. To begin his discussion of race in *Sexology* II, Hirschfeld offers a definition of "race," albeit a convoluted one (emphasis in original):

> At the outset, in order to clarify our point of view on the racial question (which we will explain in more detail below), the following should be noted: If by race we mean an aggregation of physical, mental and sexual characteristics, which inhere in a [population] subgroup and are passed down and act as unchangeable distinguishing characteristics, it should not be denied that there are such characteristics (although many things that are taken to be such characteristics are only superficial, are caused by mimicry, and are due to a particular milieu, not to a particular hereditary constitution). *We however dispute that the characteristics of race should be taken as signs of a person's worth. There are no good or bad races or peoples; rather, within every race there are people with good or bad (handsome or ugly, beneficial or detrimental) characteristics. Only the individual physical, mental, and sexual characteristics (in connection with family descent) are relevant to heredity, to the choice of partners in love relationships [Liebeswahl], and also to breeding for the improvement [Höherzüchtung] of the human race.*[26]

To parse this: for Hirschfeld, there are "races." They are population subgroups. They are distinguished by "physical, mental and sexual characteristics." At least some of these characteristics are hereditary, "unchangeable." However, most group traits are not. They are neither hereditable nor permanent. They are, rather, caused by "mimicry" or "milieu" – the two principal forces that shaped the shared characteristics of population subgroups that Hirschfeld termed "races." By "milieu" he meant environment. By "mimicry" he meant a human tendency to conform to the people around you, to "assume an aspect which makes [a person] inconspicuous."[27] One saw this tendency in the ways in which norms and customs shaped behavior.[28] The natural tendency to mimic could even shape a person's mannerisms.[29]

Environment was, to him, the other big influence on the races. It, too, shaped bodies.

> When exposed to sunlight the colouring of plants and animals is intensified, but when sunlight is cut off it fades ... Human beings ... [are] usually taller in the north than in the south. Obviously this is associated with the later maturity of the reproductive organs in northern climes, growth in the length of the long bones ceasing at or soon after puberty. Northerners, therefore, are usually taller and slimmer than southerners.

There were many exceptions to the rule about height and girth, he allowed, as "other endocrine glands" influenced growth.[30] Elsewhere, he wrote that immigrants to the United States gradually took on facial features that were like "the almost extinct Indian aborigines," probably not because of an "admixture of Red Indian blood" but because "the terrestrial and atmospheric environment are inducing in the immigrant germ-plasm mutations akin to those impressed upon Red Indian germplasm long before Columbus set sail."[31] Environment shaped the races.

Beyond mimicry and environment, Hirschfeld left a small space for a third type of racial characteristic: permanent characteristics passed from parent to child. Skin color, for example. He approvingly quoted the following statement, which he attributed to Ernst Vohsen, who was a leading advocate of Germany's imperial project in Africa: "Only in tint of skin does the Negro differ from the European."[32] To Hirschfeld, as it was to his teacher Virchow, skin color was a superficial physical difference, not a sign of underlying, hereditary, and constitutional differences in intelligence.

Though Hirschfeld believed in races and though racial groups had common characteristics, those group characteristics were, to him, useless for making judgments of worth and value. He dismissed them no matter their cause, be it mimicry, environment, or heredity. I'll requote the passage from above to clarify:

> We however dispute that the characteristics of race should be taken as signs of a person's worth. There are no good or bad races or peoples; rather, within every race there are people with good or bad (handsome or ugly, beneficial or detrimental) characteristics. Only the individual physical, mental, and sexual characteristics (in connection with family descent) are relevant to heredity, to the choice of partners in love relationships [*Liebeswahl*], and also to breeding for the improvement [*Höherzüchtung*] of the human race.[33]

Note how Hirschfeld concludes a passage about how there is no hierarchy of races by bringing us to eugenics. Heredity *does* matter, and it makes for unequal capabilities – more on this later. Nevertheless, race is not a good barometer of inequality. Within each race, individuals vary. There are no better or worse races.

What may not be so obvious to us today is that to many of Hirschfeld's contemporaries, his theory of "the races" was a resounding rejection of racism. Antiracism, too, has a history. To Hirschfeld and many others, to be an antiracist meant to reject a specific theory of race, that of scientific racism. The influential scientific racists of Hirschfeld's era, such as the English-born German Houston Stewart Chamberlain and the Frenchman de Gobineau, believed that subgroups of the human population, "races," shared many inherited, unalterable traits and that these traits were important, defining of persons, not at all superficial. There was a natural hierarchy of races, with the "Nordic" race at the top.[34] These thinkers and their followers believed in "the cultural superiority of the Nordic race," as Hirschfeld put it in his disapproving gloss of them.[35] Some also backed polygenesis.

Hence, what Hirschfeld meant by "racism" was scientific racism, the belief in polygenesis, or alternatively in "racial aristocracy," as he put it, that is, a biological hierarchy of races.[36] When he called himself an antiracist, he meant that he rejected these two concepts. Which he did. He repeatedly disputed polygenesis.[37] He also avowed that there was no inherently superior race. I made this point above, but here are more examples. He approvingly quoted Felix von Luschan, Virchow's most prominent successor in the liberal tradition of anthropology: "'There is no such thing as an essentially inferior human type'; or again, 'There are no savages, but only peoples whose civilization differs from our own.'"[38] Great human achievement, he wrote, was not limited to a particular body size, hair color, eye color, nose shape, or race. "It is not the race that determines a person; rather, it is the individual's character and his or her sexual type."[39]

Hirschfeld at times openly doubted whether there really were "races," by his definition. He observed that racial classifications were "uncertain and shaky" because nature produced gradations, not clear divisions.[40] There were not pure races – all were a mix of some kind. Despite these moments of skepticism, he held to the view that there were such things as "races." He did not stop using the word "race" or use it only surrounded by quotation marks, as he mused about doing in his final word on the subject, the 1938 *Racism*.[41]

As shorthand for the "races," he usually had a limited, schematic palate of skin shades in mind. "Behind the barred windows of their miserable cages" in Singapore's Malay Street brothels he saw "brown and black, yellow and white girls."[42] This color scheme was a trope of scientific racism. Hirschfeld was aware of one of its shortcomings: he noted that skin color varied widely among various people of various races.[43] Yet he used the color scheme himself to denote the races as he understood them to exist. He also at times had a binary division between white/not white. He used the word "colored" to denote people who were not white. For example, he wrote that members of the KKK in the United States persecuted "colored [*farbige*], Jewish, and also Roman Catholic fellow-citizens."[44] (Note here that Jews are implicitly white; more on this in chapter 8.) He also used the term "negro [*Neger*]" to describe Black people regardless of where on the globe he met them.[45]

Antiracism, to Hirschfeld, meant rejecting polygenesis and rejecting the idea of inherent, biologically ordained racial superiority. What it did not necessarily mean was asserting that non-whites were the equals of whites.

This is a profoundly counterintuitive idea for contemporary readers of Hirschfeld, myself included. He characterizes his own views as "antiracist."[46] What he meant by that, however, was that he did not endorse scientific racism. He did think some groups of people had superior cultures. Progress was a universal path along which different groups of humans advanced at different paces, arriving at different "level[s] of civilization."[47] This was a very old idea, one that had become central in anthropology as well as in global imperial politics well before Hirschfeld reached adulthood.[48] Echoing a stock metaphor of the scientific racists whom he criticized, Hirschfeld wrote about a set path of progress, much like the path a child takes from infancy to adulthood: "Agreed that there are peoples and races at varying levels of development: some that appear childlike when contrasted with their more advanced, more adult brethren; and there are others which produce in us the impression that they are senile – but the former is no more an index of inferiority than the latter is of superiority."[49]

By "inferiority" and "superiority," he meant that the adultness of one group or childlikeness of another was not due to biological group differences. None of this was because of innate, heritable characteristics. Thus, his view of a hierarchy of societies was not, to him, racist. Some races had gotten lucky, thanks to accidents of history and environment. They had moved more quickly along the path of civilization, but all groups were equally capable of moving along that path. His tour of the world gave him lots of chances to test this theory, and he found it sound. He had examined, he wrote, whether the "coloured races ... can justly be regarded as endowed with less capacity for a high civilization than are Whites."[50] They could not – that is, they were just as capable of civilization. He approvingly quoted Humboldt: There were no inherently superior races; rather there were "more highly cultured stocks, that have been ennobled by a fortunate spiritual environment; but there are no stocks intrinsically nobler than the rest."[51] White races had advanced more quickly up the ladder of civilization. But capacities were equal. He drew this idea from liberal anthropologists, who argued that groups of people (they might very well be racially heterogeneous groups) went forward along a standard path of progress at uneven rates. They attributed the speeds at which groups advanced to beneficial circumstances in the local environment and in a group's position in trade networks – that is, to history and geography. In the words of von Luschan, "Favourable circumstances and surroundings, especially a good environment, a favourable geographical position, trade and traffic," had "caused one group to advance more quickly than another, while some groups have remained in a very primitive state of development."[52] Von Luschan nevertheless warned against underrating "the danger to civilised nations" posed "by the immigration of coarser or less refined elements."[53] Hirschfeld knew von Luschan's work well and drew on it.[54]

Hirschfeld put a lot of stock in technology. Whites had no advantages in other areas, such as law, social customs, or morality.[55] This idea was common to anthropological narratives and to imperialist thinking: there was a set path of technological achievement along which humans traveled. Some were bogged down in spots that the more advanced peoples had passed in earlier historical epochs.[56]

In Hirschfeld's view, whiteness, Europeanness, and technological or civilizational advance were all indelibly welded together, even though they were not bound together by biological predetermination. To him, "white" denoted a group or set of groups of people defined by a superficial physical marker, white skin color. Whiteness was a physical condition. European colonialism was a bad idea, he argued, because white races lacked the physical capacity to thrive in the tropics.[57] Moreover, whiteness of skin coincided with the category "European." In Hirschfeld's work, "Europeans" are white by default.[58] Black Europeans or other Europeans of color are just not "European" to him: he almost never mentions them.[59] "Civilization" is the provenance of whites, that is, of Europeans, though again, not because scientific racism was correct. He wrote, "The difference between the natural peoples [*Naturvölkern*] and the cultural peoples [*Kulturvölkern*], between the coloreds [*Farbigen*] and the whites is not at all as great as it first appears."[60] This is a statement against racism, but it also includes racism: the "primitives" or "natural peoples" are "colored," and "culture" or civilization is the possession of "whites."

In a nutshell, Hirschfeld's theory of the races was this: Races existed. They were, for the most part, only superficially defined by hereditary biological characteristics like skin color. They were meaningfully defined by shared history and geography. Some races were more civilized than others. White skin and Europeanness and civilization all coincided. Brown, Black, or yellow skin, primitiveness, and non-Europeanness coincided as well. These coincidences between race and civilization were not caused by biology, however, and in that claim lay Hirschfeld's antiracism. He was an antiracist, in his view, because he blamed group differences on history and geography and he believed things could change. The Chinese, for example, were just as capable of civilization as were whites. They merely needed to catch up.

Hirschfeld retained these views throughout his world journey, even as he grew far more passionate about the injustice of empire, and even as he came to see a fundamental connection between anticolonialism and homosexual emancipation. His theory of "the races" did not, it seems, change much. Hirschfeld thought of himself and Li as members of two different races, himself white (more on this in chapter 8) and Li a member of a yellow race. This meant virtually nothing, however. Li was an exceptionally talented person, in part by virtue of birth. The first thing Hirschfeld tells readers about Li in *World Journey* is that the younger man was from "one of the most distinguished families" in China.[61] Moreover, the Chinese had, in Hirschfeld's view, little to make up in comparison to the West. The Chinese were not among the "primitive races" such as the "pigmy peoples" in Sumatra and New Guinea, who "make their homes in tree nests and generally live like animals."[62] China had had its own great civilization. Li and he might have a few physical differences, but these were meaningless. If Li tolerated the heat better than Hirschfeld did, Hirschfeld probably thought that was because of race. What was most different between him and Li was civilization, not race, and that could change. With Li as his student, Hirschfeld would help to bring modern science to China.

Hirschfeld's theory of the races was well in line with a moderate, liberal critique of racism elaborated in the period prior to the Second World War. Franz Boas, who also trained with Virchow and who is remembered as a major antiracist today, had views very like Hirschfeld's.[63] Hirschfeld was on well-trodden ground in calling himself an antiracist. However, he had contemporaries, such as James Weldon Johnson, who went much further in their critiques of racism. One could both emphatically reject scientific racism and remain a racist oneself.

The idea that there are "races," and that racial divisions are significant and meaningful, is apparent throughout the more than one hundred pages Hirschfeld published about homosexuality around the globe.

There are many examples of this in chapter 2; allow me to requote one: "Beyond question, the sexual type conquers the racial type."[64] If "the racial type" were not a major distinguisher of people, it would not be worth mentioning that the sexual type conquered it. Showing this conquest would not be a convincing proof of the model of homosexuality. Heike Bauer makes the crucial point that in Hirschfeld's work, "the first claims for homosexual rights were largely built over, rather than against, the racism of the time."[65] Bauer finds Hirschfeld's critique of racism in *Racism* anemic. In that book he fails to really apprehend what racism was and how it affected people, and he spent little time on it, she writes, moving quickly to his main interest, the naturalness of homosexuality.[66] I agree. I would add that it is not only that he built his theory over the racism of his day, eliding it. He also built it *on* the racism of his day. His theory of "the races," which included some racism, supports his theory of homosexuality.

7 Tea with Langston Hughes: Hirschfeld's Anti-Blackness and Queer Black New York

Manhattan, Winter of 1930

On December 29, 1930, the poet Langston Hughes went for afternoon tea at the apartment of his friend, writer and photographer Carl Van Vechten.[1] Hughes was twenty-seven years old. He was already a sought-after young poet, one of the leading figures in a circle of artists and intellectuals in Harlem who had set out to create a new Black cultural movement, which they and others would later call the Harlem Renaissance.[2] Yet that cold day, Hughes was not well. The tyrannical white Manhattanite who had been bankrolling his living expenses had just thrown him off, leaving him broke, furious, and shaken. He had resigned himself to move in with his mother in Cleveland. The stress was intense; he was afflicted by stomach pains.[3] One expects that the habitually guarded Hughes hid all this at the tea that day.

At Van Vechten's, Hughes found himself in an eclectic group of men. All had been invited for tea, though some may have been drinking cocktails, knowing Van Vechten's boozy habits. One was a friend of Hughes's: James Weldon Johnson. Johnson was an elder statesman, a leader of the NAACP. He was also a celebrated novelist and lyricist. Johnson was much older than Hughes and married. He was a member of the senior generation of Black intellectuals and political leaders and a major backer of the Black arts movement.[4] He and his wife often had the young Hughes over for dinner. The other guests were white. At least two were queer. The white guests were the occultist journalist (and notorious cannibal) W.B. Seabrook, the composer Aaron Copland, and George Sylvester Viereck. Copland was discreetly queer, as was Viereck.[5] Also arriving at Van Vechten's a half hour late was an energetic, self-important, but charming German doctor in his sixties. He was temporarily in New York City giving lectures about sex. Van Vechten had gone to see one about a week before, at the Labor Temple. It was three hours long, with slides. Apparently inspired, Van Vechten had then arranged the tea.

Why Langston Hughes and James Weldon Johnson would want to have tea with Magnus Hirschfeld is somewhat mysterious, but surely it had something to do with an interest in homosexuality. That is not to say that either Johnson or Hughes was homosexual, but both had enough queer friends that one can see why they might be interested. Van Vechten was one. He had discreet affairs with men, and he was rather open about it among his friends, though not in his public life. He was also happily married to a woman.[6] Johnson is not often suspected of having been queer.[7] Hughes, on the other hand, often is, though whether or not he was ever intimate with men, he did have affairs with women.[8] Hughes never married. Johnson and Hughes belonged to a circle of Black artists and intellectuals that included men who were queer: Alain Locke, Coun-tee Cullen, Richard Bruce Nugent, Wallace Thurman, Claude McKay.[9] That circle also included women: Nella Larsen, who thematized queer desire between women in one of her novels, and Zora Neale Hurston, whose fiction told of Black female heterosexuality emancipated from bourgeoisie conventions.[10] People in Hughes's circle were well aware of German-language sexual science – Nugent read Krafft-Ebing on homo-sexuality – and of Germany's special position as the home of male same-sex love, which Locke wrote about in a flirty letter to Hughes.[11]

Yet according to Hirschfeld's journal, he had no interesting talks over tea that winter day with either Johnson or Hughes. Hirschfeld seems not to have considered the two Black men to be worthy intellectual in-terlocutors. He could not extend his antiracism to Black people without running up against deep conflicts within himself. Veronika Fuechtner writes, "Blackness clearly seems to present the limit of Hirschfeld's uni-versalist vision."[12] This persistent, egregious flaw in Hirschfeld's antira-cism was unremarked-upon by scholars for decades.

This chapter is the first exhaustive look at what Hirschfeld wrote about Black people. I have sought to collect as much of it as I could. Much of it is about Black Americans. Why Black Americans and not Black Germans, one might well ask. Berlin was home to more Black Germans than any other city.[13] Hirschfeld even had ties to a white group that supported the Black German struggle against racism.[14] Black America, not Black Ger-many, is in the foreground here because, to my knowledge, Hirschfeld never wrote anything at all about Black Germans. Their fight against rac-ism did not interest him. He casually assumed Europeans were white, as I argued in chapter 6. There is, however, a long, rich tradition of activism by Black Germans and other Germans of color, including in the early 1930s.[15]

My goal here is to show conclusively, and in a vivid enough portrait that it cannot be ignored, how Hirschfeld's antiracism failed Black people, including Black people who had queer affairs and who were, like him, fighting to create queer worlds.

A few years before he met Hirschfeld, Langston Hughes had been part of an avant-garde challenge to the politics of Black respectability that reigned among Harlem's elite. In 1926, he, Nugent, Hurston, Thurman, and Aaron Douglas published the short-lived magazine *FIRE!!* It featured Nugent's explicitly homoerotic short story "Smoke, Lillies and Jade," in which a character named "Langston" is seen in the company of a lovely boy. The queerness of Nugent's story was part of the magazine's larger goal of telling the truth. Hughes and the others wanted to get out from under the older generation of Black leaders and their project of "racial uplift," based on the assumption that the success of the Black middle class would erode white racism.[16] The older establishment – people like Johnson, W.E.B. Du Bois, and Locke – wanted to flaunt Black artistic genius in order to win over whites. Hughes in 1926 wanted none of this. He wrote, "We younger Negro artists who create now intend to express our individual dark-skinned selves without fear or shame. If white people are pleased we are glad. If they are not, it doesn't matter. We know we are beautiful. And ugly too … If colored people are pleased we are glad. If they are not, their displeasure doesn't matter either."[17] The magazine was a challenge to white heteropatriarchy and Black respectability at the same time. It did not last long. Harlem's powers-that-be castigated Nugent for "Smoke, Lillies and Jade."[18] Open admissions of queer desires among Black men would be used by whites to denigrate the Black race, or so many people believed.[19] Thus, racism put a heavy pressure on Black people with queer desires.[20] In the years after *FIRE!!* magazine went bankrupt, an important Harlem clergyman railed against homosexuality, and Du Bois fired the business manager of the NAACP's flagship magazine *The Crisis* after he was arrested in a sting on gay sex.[21] Nugent refused to hide his queerness, but his friends went a different way, falling into line. The poet Countee Cullen's very brief marriage to Du Bois's daughter Yolanda Du Bois, in 1928, was a capitulation to Du Bois's vision of successful Black heterosexuality.[22] Hughes, for his part, went on to construct a public persona that was not radical and that perhaps hid his queerness (though who knows for sure what he felt).[23] In the 1950s, he and Copland both testified before the McCarthy commission.

Hirschfeld labored against a similar, though not identical, pressure not to confirm the antisemitic trope of the homosexual Jewish conspiracy seeking to emasculate the "Aryan" race that haunted the pages of right-wing German propaganda. His strategy, however, was not that of *FIRE!!*, not to confront racialized heterosexuality in public, but rather to fight racism and to fight homophobia separately, by less confrontational means – through education, and science, and relatively dispassionate public advocacy. Yet, at the same time, one can see how Hughes and his friends could perhaps have made use of Hirschfeld's argument that homosexuality existed to the same degree in all races and that there was nothing inherently wrong with it. In 1931, Hirschfeld made a pronouncement about Black heterosexuality being no more lascivious than white heterosexuality, and the Black establishment applauded. It came in a newspaper article about his visit to a Harlem dance hall that ran in the Black press on the East Coast.[24] In the article, Hirschfeld spoke against the well-worn racist characterization of Black people as hypersexual – in fact, whites were sluttier, he said. "Whites More Sexy in Dancing than Negroes, Scientist Thinks," ran the headline. Perhaps at tea, Hughes and Hirschfeld spoke about how homosexuality factored in to the racialized sexualization of Black people, with Hirschfeld asserting that "the sexual type conquers the racial type," an idea that is not completely divorced from racism, I argued earlier, but that Hughes could have made use of to argue that the condemnation of *FIRE!!* was misplaced: queer Black fiction did not endanger the struggle against racism, since homosexuality was natural and was just as common among whites.

Yet Hirschfeld's account of his meeting with Hughes says nothing about Black sexual politics. In his journal, Hirschfeld mentioned the tea in a numbered list of "highlights and main events" of his time in the United States:

> 29. Get-together with Karl v. Vechten, a very original, appealing [*anziehend*] personality. Visited Harlem. Went to tea at v. Vechten's with the negro poets Johnson and Langston.
> 30. Studies of the black race.[25]

Hirschfeld might have learned something from Hughes and Johnson, but he did not. Rather, to him it was anthropological field research. Unlike the white Van Vechten, who in Hirschfeld's journal gets a description, Hughes and Johnson are reduced to racial specimens. He seems not to have understood who Johnson was – he was a poet but also a politician. This seems odd given Hirschfeld's interest in anticolonial politics elsewhere in the world, such as in India. Johnson did not register as a leader of his people in a struggle against injustice, a New York Nehru, though he was. Harlem's arts scene depended on the white downtowners who came uptown and spent money, but those whites saw Harlem through a racist prism, and their fascination with Black art grew out of a racial fascination that nauseated Black Harlemites. Hughes wrote later in his autobiography that white visitors who came to Harlem to see Black culture regarded Black Harlemites as "amusing animals in a zoo."[26] As much seems to be true of Hirschfeld.

"Negros," to Hirschfeld, were a racial group that included Black Americans, Black Africans, and indigenous Australians.[27] He did not believe in
the present intellectual equality of most whites and most "Negros." He
thought many Black people suffered from intellectual stunting caused
by historical circumstances, as discussed in chapter 6, though he also
thought that they could and would overcome this. Before he embarked
on his world journey, he wrote:

> In America and Africa I have attempted to independently get a sense of the
> inner life of the coloreds and became even more convinced on the grounds
> of that impartial examination, that the colored people are probably in many
> cases more primitive (less developed, more childlike) than we are, but are
> also often more sophisticated, and that their objective worth, their capacity
> for culture, is in no way lower than that of the white peoples. Different does
> not mean inferior.[28]

There might be exceptional Black people – such as Langston Hughes
and James Weldon Johnson, perhaps. But many Black people were "less
developed." He wrote elsewhere that slavery had stunted the brains of
African Americans (I referred to this quote in the previous chapter as
well) but that they were catching up: "The female brain … has within it a
considerable possibility to increase in capacity; after all, even the brains
of the American negros have experienced a rapidly accelerated development since the abolition of slavery."[29]

The word "even" is telling in that quotation. Hirschfeld often betrayed
the sense that among the "races," it was Black people who really needed
serious mental improvement. There was hope for the (white) female
brain if "even" the (assumedly female and male) Black brain was getting
stronger. There is much denigration of Black people as a "race" in these
passages, even if there is hesitation, equivocation, and an endorsement
of a vision of racial equality.

Elsewhere he hinted that race did make a meaningful difference, albeit
a slight one. This is an important addendum to his theory of the races
discussed in the previous chapter, and one that I suspect underpinned
some of this thinking about Black people. It was "apparent," he wrote,

> that in their desires for food and drink, health and love, exercise and sleep,
> rest and exaltation – desires that are based in physical and emotional qual-
> ities – people are 99% the same, and that even the one percent of differ-
> ence is largely constitutional-individual rather than racial [*und daß selbst die
> einprozentige Verschiedenheit noch in höherem Grade konstitutionell-individuell als
> durch rassische Übereinstimmung bedingt ist*], as it is the case that among all

peoples [*Völkern*] there are three classes: the average, the above-average, and the below-average (plus and minus variations), and above all, judgment of worth can be based on the individual person, not on the race.[30]

This is, for the most part, a statement of racial equality. It allows, however, for a sliver of meaningful racial difference, of biological inequality. This sliver of difference seems to have come up for him most often when he thought about Blackness.

When describing Black people, at times Hirschfeld fixated on skin color to the exclusion of all else. He met the South African leader of the African National Congress J.T. Gumede, whom he describes as "a deep black jurist." He writes not much else about Gumede except that having dinner with him offered Hirschfeld more evidence for his view, quoted above, that although whites were often more mature than people of color, they were also often less sophisticated, and anyway people had equal capacities regardless of race.[31] Gumede is, however, reduced to his complexion. This is a dehumanizing view.

Black New Yorkers are not only reduced to their skin color in Hirschfeld's work. Sometimes they are food. In New York City, Hirschfeld was fascinated by the presence of Black people. "In New York alone there are well over 100,000 negros, from the deepest black to the shade of Viennese coffee to the lightest mélange, indeed to the color of milk – of those, one can barely notice their dark ancestry. In particular when they have their hair straightened, which is often the case."[32]

In the United States, the "theme of the Black body as food is massively present," writes Kyla Wazana Tompkins, and it encodes "all the ambivalence and terrible violence of American racial politics."[33] For whites, these images are a means of consolidating whiteness, though a messy one – the Black subjects in the fantasies "fight back, and bite back, both in the white imaginary and in domestic manuals and novels produced by Black authors."[34] Tompkins notes that the disturbing theme of Black people as food seems to aim toward "a compromise between white America's twinned emotions – desire and fear – nothing will do but to actually internalize and obliterate Blackness."[35] Hirschfeld need not have picked up this cultural logic in the US. In his day, Europe was saturated with imagery about the edibleness of Black people, about how they were like other consumables.[36] Here there is a dehumanization and commodification of Black bodies, as well as the white eater's lust for violence – cannibalism, a particular violence – against the Black body. Even decades after Hirschfeld died, in the 1980s and 1990s, Black Germans were forced to advocate against this sort of racist advertising for products such as soda and candy, which to some was so profoundly dehumanizing that, in the words of Helga Emde, who grew up in postwar Germany being taunted with the racialized names of popular candies like "Negro Kiss" by her white peers, "I felt unworthy of existence."[37]

Hirschfeld embraces this vile theme. It is a telling moment if one wants to know what Blackness meant to him. He does not frequently compare human skin shades to food. To my knowledge, this description of Black New Yorkers is the only such instance. He moreover picked a food he loved, coffee, which occupied his first waking thoughts each morning and was a pleasant part of each afternoon.[38] Tompkins observes that the trope of the edible Black body can encode a white desire for intimacy, though a dominating, ultimately obliterating intimacy, and that one can read this craving of intimacy as anxiously erotic, too.[39]

Yet Hirschfeld's theme of Black people as food takes a curious twist. He writes his own body into the trope. The passage continues: "The other day [on the subway] as I sat between two black beauties clad in the highest fashions as they did their lipstick, trying to make themselves even more beautiful, and I felt like a piece of ham sandwiched between two pieces of bread."[40] He makes himself into a piece of ham. Ham is not kosher. Ham is also pink, a color associated with the skin tone of people deemed white. Hirschfeld was aware of the association between the racial status white and a skin tone of pinkness, or a "ruddy white" skin color, as he puts it.[41] In making himself into ham, Hirschfeld figures himself as white and a non-Jew, or as a secular Jew for whom dietary laws meant nothing. At the same time, the metaphor betrays an anxiety about his whiteness. He figures two Black women as food and himself as food in their presence. This is unusual. Generally, in this trope, white bodies eat Black bodies, or white bodies watch Black bodies getting eaten.[42] A slice of ham cannot eat anyone. Does Hirschfeld's metaphor refer to something he knew well, that his Jewishness threw his whiteness into question for many racists? As ham he symbolically is not a Jew, but he is an ambivalent thing nevertheless, a white food, when whites are not usually the food. It is as if in metaphor he tries to make himself white, but he cannot and gets only part of the way there, making himself white but a food, not an eater. Yet, in a familiar rhetorical move, it is through aggression against Black people that he achieves whiteness at all; it is by sitting between two Black women, and then denigrating them, that he can make himself white, albeit not white enough.[43]

The sandwich scene perhaps betrays sexual anxiety, too. As Tompkins shows is often the case in this trope, these edible Black subjects are not going to go down easily. The two unnamed women are active agents here, "sandwich[ing]" Hirschfeld, turning him into food along with them. Hirschfeld wrote the sandwich scene in a letter to close associates. Perhaps part of the joke to his readers – surely he meant the scene to be funny – was about being a covertly queer man assaulted by the beauty of Black women. Sexology was full of images of Black female sexuality as aggressive, hypersexual, and masculinized. Hirschfeld knew these tropes, though he does not recycle them himself in his very brief comments on the homosexuality of Black women.[44]

Whatever else the sandwich scene reveals, it shows that Hirschfeld had a dehumanizing view of Black women.

Yet Hirschfeld considered himself someone who loved Black people. That self-impression came back to him in a moment that was freighted with strong emotion and a sense of destiny, when he was sailing alone to Japan from Hawaii in March 1931 and writing to his lover, Karl Giese, to explain why he was not coming back to Berlin. Hirschfeld feared he would not see Giese again, but he was determined to circumnavigate the globe, alone, despite bad health and an obsessive fear of death. He had been hospitalized for a day in Chicago with high blood sugar.[45] Doctors had cautioned him that he might succumb to diabetes if he kept traveling.[46] He did not like the thought of dying alone in a foreign country or on a ship with strangers.[47] Yet he decided to risk it.

If Hirschfeld wrote Giese a letter about this momentous choice, which he probably did, that letter is lost. What we have is an entry he wrote in his journal. That little book was several things at once: a last will and testament, a set of notes for a book he planned to write (this became *World Journey*), and instructions for his heirs as to how to carry on after his death. A lot of what he wrote in the journal were posthumous instructions for Giese and for another man who worked as an administrator at the Institute in Berlin.[48]

Sailing to Japan, Hirschfeld used the journal to plan for the solitary death on the journey that he feared, to control it as much as he could. He wrote out a simple will, giving instructions for what to do with his body if he was found dead, maybe in a hotel, or if he died in a hospital abroad. If he succumbed at sea he wanted his body committed to the ocean, which he loved. If on land, he should be cremated and his ashes sent back to Berlin and scattered at the Institute. All of his possessions, with the exception of useless things like clothing, should be sent back to the Institute, to Giese.[49] This would have included the notebook itself. Thus, though he believed he was writing for Giese, he thought others might read what he wrote. The journal was both private and public at once. This is probably why in the notebook he is so circumspect about his sexuality, never overtly suggesting he is anything but a heterosexual bachelor. Save for one journal entry about Li penned at the very end of his life, he is extremely discreet about his queer loves. Such behavior was standard at the time for a person like Hirschfeld.[50]

In the oddly public space of the journal, he tried to explain to Giese why he had decided to sail west, away from him, not back east across the Atlantic. Here is what he wrote:

> I am no *homo familiaris* (family man, in the usual sense); certainly there are some in Germany with whom I am close, people who I would want with me in my hour of death, people I would miss terribly, people whose hand I would want to hold in my own.

Here, Hirschfeld wrote in later: "one in particular!" He went on,

> but I surely belong more to those whose love and affection belongs more to mankind, to all people, rather than to individuals; I am an enthusiast of mankind, I am someone who, purely physiologically and biopsychologically, is not made for a family, for a wife and children, and also in my ability to love, I was not built for only one other person, but rather I was made for the whole, for all peoples [*Völker*], *all* people.[51]

This is a gesture toward a heterosexual self, doubtless with an eye on his public persona. Here he is also telling Giese that their love is superseded by his love for humanity. He goes on to illustrate the power of this love for humanity by listing all of the differences among people that his love leaps over. The first such difference he lists is race: "I love not only the whites rather the Blacks and the yellows just as well – the blonds as well as the brunettes [*Dunklen*]." He loves Christians and Buddhists as well as Jews and Muslims. He loves women as well as men, "the good as well as the bad, the rich as well as the poor," and continues to list differences of various sorts – intellectual, national, professional, and others. The list is long. It ends with people who live in castles and fine villas, whom he loves just as well as those who live in attic and basement apartments. "I love them all."[52]

When Hirschfeld sought a way to show how powerful his love of humanity was, the first example he thought of was that he loved across the color line, and in particular the line between white and Black. That he offers his ability to cross it as proof of the strength of his love demonstrates how profound the color line was to him, even if he could cross it and called himself its enemy. Blackness signaled a radical alterity. To love across the divide between white and Black was a strong love indeed.

Yet Hirschfeld *saw* people who were Black and queer and trans. He put them in his books. Moreover, he did not invoke the very well-established ideas in scientific writing on sexuality that Black people differed fundamentally from white people.[53] Rather, homosexuality's essential nature and frequency were constant, among all peoples. Black people were queer, just like other people. "Already among the original Indian peoples Uranianism [homosexuality] was known, and … among the many peoples which are mixed together in the great American melting pot, not one is without homosexuals, from the Yankees and the Germans to the Negros and the Chinese."[54] Hirschfeld toured San Quentin prison in Northern California and several other prisons in the United States, which at the time was building prisons and would by the century's end incarcerate more people than any other country on earth. At San Quentin, "I also saw hundreds of homosexuals – a third of them negros – who are isolated from the other prisoners and work in the prison laundry. Many were in women's clothing and were very feminine, in particular the blacks."[55] He spoke with them, then complained to prison officials about them, apparently about their work conditions, or about how they were isolated – he wrote later he complained on their behalf but does not say about what exactly. Possibly he objected to the fact that they were in prison at all (some for simple homosexuality, perhaps; California had a law against sodomy). His note here that Black prisoners were more feminine is such an unusual departure from his universalism that one wonders if it was in fact the case that some of these Black Americans were more feminine than their white comrades.

When he was a newly minted doctor traveling the US in 1893–4, Hirschfeld met a Black trans woman in Chicago.[56] He briefly reports the meeting as he is in the midst of a very unusual digression from his core theory. In this passage about Chicago, he argues that the homosexuality of "transvestites" *does* vary according to national borders – most, if not all, "American transvestites are homosexual."[57] On Clark Street in Chicago, he recalled, "I was introduced to a Negro girl, within whom a male prostitute was hiding. On the other hand, two other transvestites from San Francisco and New York who I got to know were heterosexual."[58] He marks the woman from Chicago as Black and does not mention the race of the New Yorker or the San Franciscan – this meant they were white. The Blackness of the Chicago sex worker is worth noting, to him, while white is a default that can go without saying. Even so, the case of the woman from Chicago is, to his mind, just as valid a piece of evidence as are the cases of the two assumedly white transvestites. Race makes no meaningful difference in transvestitism (though here nationality does).

Hirschfeld opposed the racism of white Americans. Segregation on train cars, the contempt of whites for Blacks, and the racist penal system, which meted out death penalties to Black men convicted of raping white women while white men convicted of raping Black women got fines – all of these things were signs to Hirschfeld that the United States was not "a sanely ordered society."[59] He denounced them. The sentencing for rape he termed "abominable injustices."[60]

Nevertheless, as Bauer notes, Hirschfeld is often quiet about white racism.[61] He just does not write much about it. When Hirschfeld considered what he disliked most about the United States, it was not racism but Prohibition, as Herzer points out.[62] He did report one racist incident in the US – a white supremacist attack on himself. While he lectured to "an overflow crowd" in Chicago, "young people (almost certainly Ku-Klux-Klan people or German Hitler followers, who also exist in American in small groups) slashed the tires of our car."[63]

Moreover, Hirschfeld's attacks on white racism often feed into somewhat racist ideas. In a passage in *Racism*, he denounces racism but does so in the course of a larger argument that is not about the injustice of racism but rather is about why "the offspring of mixed marriages" seem inferior. They are not biologically inferior, he explains, but they act inferior because white racism has given them an "inferiority complex."[64] He defends people against white racism here but ends up emphasizing that they do indeed seem inferior to whites. The whites and their racist violence fade into the background, and the reader sees in the foreground an image of people of color who feel and seem inferior, though not biologically inferior. In the interview he gave about his trip to a Harlem dance hall, he disputes the racist characterization of Black people as hypersexual but eventually claims that white men and women who date Black men and women are "thrilled by the sense of being subjugated by the more savage passions, the more dynamic life urge of a primitive race."[65] (Some Black thinkers at the time celebrated primitivism, but they saw it as a critique of white culture, which Hirschfeld did not.)[66] If Black Americans could not dance out their anger about their oppression, they would get violent, he said. His thoughts lead one away from the injustice of white racism and toward a vision of Black people as primitive – if unfairly subjugated – and violent. This is a critique of racism that winds up in more racism.

His thoughts took a similar meandering course when white American racism against Asian Americans and Asians caught his attention, which it almost never did. Asians opposed the United States' racist immigration laws, he observed, and this might someday inspire them to wage "a war of extermination against the Whites" living in Asia.[67] A critique of racism, but an oddly sideways one. It both makes Asians seem like the violent parties and seems to concede that Asians are fundamentally of Asia, not of the United States.

Indigenous people in the United States were, to Hirschfeld, a unitary, dying race, "the almost extinct Indian aboriginies [*sic*]."[68] He saw "Indian settlements" on the prairies.[69] He visited the Grand Canyon and "Indian reservations" on February 5, 1931. Possibly he met members of the Navajo, Kaibab, Havasupai, Hualapai, or Hopi nations. They do not seem to have registered to him as victims of colonialism.

Years later, however, Hirschfeld wrote an entry in his journal that did express profound horror at anti-Black racism in America. It was Easter 1933. He was in exile, living with Li in Switzerland. He was reflecting on the April 1, 1933, Nazi-orchestrated boycott of Jewish businesses in Germany. Since the boycott, he wrote,

> the humiliation and debasement of the Jews grows by leaps and bounds day to day and is today almost worse than that of the negros in America. For a freedom-loving person of Jewish descent it seems to me that life in Germany, if one is not utterly forced into it, is a moral impossibility. I have personally resigned myself to the idea of never seeing Germany, my homeland, again, as much as I suffer from it emotionally.[70]

Hirschfeld knew about white racism in the United States; he could not have penned this comparison had he not. He implies that racism is so bad in the US that Black Americans would be well advised to go into exile, which some did. His own plight, and that of his family members back in Germany, brought the plight of Black Americans to mind. This sounds like empathy. Looking on from exile as a racist regime like that of the United States went to work in Germany, he concluded that he could never go back. He would eventually advise German Jews to flee their country.[71] The destruction of his status as a member of the favored race and his subjugation to fascist racism gave him more empathy, though at the same time, white racism in the US here figures as a comparative to make a point that is not about Black and white Americans but about "Aryan" Germans and German Jews.

Compared to his longwinded, impassioned denunciation of colonialism in *World Journey*, these scattered comments stick out as lackluster. It is as if the racial politics of the United States did not strike him as profoundly troubling. They were troubling, to be sure, but perhaps, in his mind, they were somewhat excused by the (sociological) inferiority of people who were not "white."

In the 1920s and 1930s, William Pickens was one of the most popular Black speakers in the United States.[72] Born in 1881 to former slaves, Pickens grew up in Arkansas, where his parents toiled and sacrificed to send him to school. He was an excellent student and went to Yale, then into an academic career, and then into the NAACP leadership.

Hirschfeld met Pickens and heard him speak, most likely in Berlin in 1927.[73] Pickens liked Germany. This was not an uncommon sentiment among Black elites in those years. Traveling in Europe, Black Americans like W.E.B. Du Bois and Alain Locke found white Europeans less racist than white Americans.[74] Du Bois had enrolled at Berlin University (now Humboldt) the year that Hirschfeld finished his medical studies at that institution, and when Du Bois matriculated, Rudolf Virchow, whose theory of the races was so important to Hirschfeld, was serving as the university's rector. He officially welcomed Du Bois to the university.[75] Pickens was in Germany four times between 1913 and 1932.[76] The meeting between Hirschfeld and Pickens is a vivid example of how Hirschfeld passed over an antiracist discourse that was right in front of him (that of Pickens), preferring, rather, his own far less radical, and racist, antiracism. It also demonstrates his attitude toward Black intellectuals, whom he almost never cited or quoted.

In Pickens's early career, around 1900, his thoughts on race and civilization were not all that different from Hirschfeld's in the 1930s. Yet well before he met Hirschfeld, Pickens's views had changed. By 1918, he blamed racism, not race, for differences between American whites and Blacks. Hirschfeld saw these differences as cultural or civilizational. But Pickens wrote about how racist education systems, labor practices, and judicial systems – that is, "a caste system" – forced African Americans into "the triple chains of ignorance, semi-serfdom and poverty."[77] Savageness, he wrote, was to be found in the white racists themselves, not in those they foolishly oppressed: "To fix the status of a human soul on earth according to the physical group in which it was born, is the gang spirit of the savage which protects its own members and outlaws all others."[78] This is a profound difference from Hirschfeld. Though both men thought education could alleviate ignorance, and though they agreed that despite how people vary in their intellectual abilities, such variations do not run along racial lines, to Pickens, Black "ignorance" was created by white oppression and violence.[79] Pickens writes nothing of differential brain sizes or of savageness versus civilization. African American thinkers often celebrated African civilizations in Egypt and Ethiopia.[80] Though Hirschfeld discusses glorious past civilizations in South Asia, China, and Egypt as a critique of racism, he does not seem to consider Egyptians Black. He never writes about the glorious past of Black Africa.

Hirschfeld wrote about his meeting with Pickens and Pickens's speech on racism, briefly. What he had to say about the American is typical of Hirschfeld's rambling style and of his at times internally contradictory ideas. It also typifies his attitude toward Black intellectuals. He notes his acquaintance with Pickens, "the highly intelligent North American negro professor," in the course of a statement about his impressions of "colored peoples [*Völker*]"; he has met many people of color, he states.[81] He met prisoners of war in German camps during the First World War. He mentions Gumede, the leader of the African National Congress, in a quote I discussed above. Hirschfeld's assertion of firsthand knowledge of these Black people, and specifically of Pickens's intelligence, is the direct setup for another statement I quoted above, which I offer again here in the interest of clarity: "In America and Africa I have attempted to independently get a sense of the inner life of the coloreds ... the colored people are probably in many cases more primitive (less developed, more childlike) than we are, but are also often more sophisticated, and ... their objective worth, their capacity for culture, is in no way lower than that of the white peoples. Different does not mean worse."[82] Hirschfeld then goes on to very briefly say something about Pickens's speech in Berlin, which was, apparently, on "the situation of the North American Negro" and was, according to Hirschfeld, about the fact that "race struggle is class struggle." Rather than elaborating on what Pickens meant, he swiftly moves to the idea that the struggle between races is really a struggle about land. Startlingly, he then includes a lengthy quotation from the anthropologist Friedrich Ratzel, who originated the term "Lebensraum," which had become a central part of the Nazi worldview by the time Hirschfeld wrote this passage.[83] This is an example of Hirschfeld's somewhat disorganized thinking, or perhaps of his strategy of defeating enemies by turning their quotations against them, or both. It is not a tacit endorsement of Nazism. His thoughts on a fundamental human struggle for land are fleeting: he does not repeat the notion in other passages in his work where he discusses the races. To return to my point: the passage on Pickens does not take up Pickens's ideas. Rather, it turns Pickens into a piece of evidence for Hirschfeld's own theory of race. So much for Pickens's speech – we get only a very glancing reference to what it may have been about, a reference cut short as Ratzel is dragged onstage instead. This imperviousness to the ideas of Black thinkers was on display in Hirschfeld's meeting with Hughes and Johnson, too. Hirschfeld was well aware of a more critical antiracism, such as that voiced by Black American thinkers. He rejected their ideas in favor of his own.

Black Africans were primitive, in Hirschfeld's view.[84] They were isolated from the rest of the globe: "Africa remains a world unto itself," Egypt excepted.[85] Hirschfeld traveled to Morocco and Algeria as a young man, then to Egypt on the world tour.[86] He never went to a Black African country. On the train to Cairo, Hirschfeld met a British colonial official who was returning home from a fifteen-year posting in the British colony of Sudan.[87] The British man described how his government's imposition of clothing on people accustomed to nudity had, in Hirschfeld's words, stimulated the "childish fantasies" of the Sudanese, who now grew greedy, lascivious, and violent as an unintended result.[88] However, Hirschfeld reported that the Black residents of Egypt whom he saw were not prone to vice, certainly no more so than the debauched whites.[89]

As a guest at an Egyptian wedding, Hirschfeld encountered a Black man from Sudan who was working as a servant. The man was the life of the party, making many droll remarks that got lots of laughs. He also danced a "belly dance" in women's clothing, a dance that was, to Hirschfeld, "as grotesque as it was graceful, as one so often finds is the case with the blacks."[90]

Hirschfeld had connections to the Black freedom struggle, particularly in the United States, and was a proponent of decolonization, a struggle fought by Black people against the American empire and other imperial powers around the world. He had many opportunities to adopt a politics that was more inclusive of Black people and of other people of color. Yet his writing on Black people is dehumanizing, racist. This is despite the fact that he considered himself an antiracist. He tried to defend Black people from racism. Yet he was capable of naked racism against Black people, too.

What does this mean for queer history? One of the main theorists of homosexuality, who helped create the deracialized homosexual subject, possessed an unyielding anti-Black racism, despite being an opponent of racism as he defined it. This is in part why his aspirations to combine antiracism and queer politics fell short. His published remarks about Black women and men are disturbing. They ought to make it impossible to celebrate him as a queer hero.

8 Making Jews White

Tel Aviv, Palestine, Winter of 1932

Hirschfeld and Li arrived in Palestine by train from Egypt on the morning of February 14, 1932. Chaim Berlin, a Tel Aviv doctor who had studied at Hirschfeld's Institute, met them at the train station in Ludd and drove Hirschfeld and Li to the city, through orange groves, past an agricultural school for Jews, and past Sarona, a colony established by a German Protestant sect called the Templers in the 1870s, in what was then Ottoman Palestine, about a decade before the first wave of Jewish immigration from Romania and the Russian Empire arrived.[1] They reached Tel Aviv's wide thoroughfare Allenby Street and drove to the end, where the San Remo Hotel looked out on the Mediterranean.[2] They would spend five weeks in Palestine. Among the places Hirschfeld rested in his wanderings around the world, he would come to find that "there was no country that I found it harder to leave than Palestine."[3]

In between his lectures in Tel Aviv, which he gave in German while a local colleague stood next to him and translated into Hebrew, Hirschfeld liked to walk out from the hotel to the gorgeous white beach.[4] He went in Li's company, I feel safe in assuming. Tel Aviv's planners had modeled the city on European spa cities like the one in which Hirschfeld had grown up.[5] He and Li "tarried" at the beach, gazing at the lively scene of hundreds of February bathers, "swimmers of both sexes, tanned athletes male and female … cheerfully crowding between vast rows of beach chairs [*Strandkörben*]."[6] Adding to the "scenic appeal" of all those bronzed bodies, if in an odd way, were the trains of camels making their way up the coast carrying loads of oranges.[7] "Looking to the horizon, the eye is captivated" by the city of Jaffa jutting out into the sea, Hirschfeld recalled when he wrote about it years later.[8] That beach was, in those days, raising some fears in Tel Aviv about sexual immorality. Rabbis complained about coed bathing and nudity. There were men's and women's sections of beaches, and a 1926 law banned naked swimming, but the city did not enforce the rules.[9] One of the big complaints was that everyone wanted the first Hebrew city's beaches to be civilized and European, and this meant propriety. A European traveler might decide the Land of Israel was neither European nor civilized if they got to the beach and saw naked cavorting and flirting.[10] The rabbis need not have worried about one European traveler. Hirschfeld decided just the opposite.

Those tanned, athletic bodies: what Hirschfeld saw on the lovely beach of white Mediterranean sand was a vigorous and white race, a civilized and European people. It was a heterogeneous, mixed race, to be sure, and yet a white one. Jews were white. He was a Jew by descent, and therefore he was white, too.

This chapter argues that Hirschfeld sought, subtly, to sure up the whiteness of Jews. This was part of a larger project that Jewish thinkers undertook in his day, a self-protective project to defend Jewish whiteness, which had been relatively well established prior to the 1870s. Here I depart from the findings of other Hirschfeld scholars.[11] I argue that he was, quite reasonably, pursuing two strategies for combating antisemitism at once. He claimed scientific racism was bunk science. At the same time, he retained a concept of "race" and put himself in the safest category.

Hirschfeld scholars have not noted that Hirschfeld believed Jews to be white. It ought not to be surprising, however, that in 1932 a Jewish thinker considered Jews a white race. From the nineteenth century well into the twentieth, many Jewish thinkers did.[12] Non-Jews, too, asserted that Jews were a white race. In nineteenth-century America, most white Americans thought American Jews were members of a distinct, white race, and as American Jews integrated more and more into the white middle class, their white status was even more secure.[13] (Scientific racism generally held that there were multiple "races" in the category "white.")[14] Racist discourse that made Jews white often "continued to devalue" Black people, Leonard Rogoff notes.[15] For example, take the work of the Dillingham Commission. It was set up as the US federal government's fact-finding body on immigration, and it played a major role in that country's harsh immigration restrictions in the 1920s, which included a literacy test, a ban on Asian immigrants, and a restrictive national quota system that would later help keep out Jews who were trying to flee Hitler's Europe.[16] Among its many publications, the commission produced the 1911 *Dictionary of the Races or Peoples*.[17] Its entry on Jews was something of a pastiche of ideas. Jews had a "Semitic origin" but were now "more truly European" than anything else, and were, indeed, "Aryan."[18] The *Dictionary* asserted that

the "Negro" belonged "to the lowest division of mankind from an evolutionary standpoint."[19]

There was another view about Jews, of course. From the 1870s, on
both sides of the Atlantic, people argued the contrary: that Jews were
not white.[20] Antisemites claimed Jews were a dangerous, non-European,
and enemy race, distinct from "Aryans." By 1932, in the United States, as
antisemitism went mainstream, lots of white thinkers were writing omi-
nously about how American Jews were racially distinct from whites and
were a problem.[21]

Nevertheless, in the days when the Nazis were a laughable German
fringe party – that is, before 1930 – the notion that merely calling Jews a
"race" was a dangerous form of anti-Jewish prejudice had not occurred
to many people. This changed dramatically after the global rise of antisemitism in the 1930s and the Holocaust.[22] Yet even in 1932, the year
prior to Hitler's appointment as chancellor of Germany, many Jewish
thinkers considered Jews a white race.[23] Hirschfeld did not come up with
that idea and he was by no means out on a limb.

Why does it matter that Hirschfeld made Jews a white race? For one
thing, it bears on the question of what sort of thinker he was, that is,
a self-described antiracist who used whiteness in self-defense. Yet what
also interests me here is what the whiteness of Jews means for the conceptual model of homosexuality that Hirschfeld did so much to create. For him and many others, the emancipation struggle of Western
European Jews was a model for homosexual emancipation. The Jewish
"racial minority" was the foremost model for the "sexual minority." That
is, it was an unjustly oppressed *white* race that served as the model for
the sexual minority, the homosexual. This speaks, I think, to the limits
of empathy implied by what we might call the foundational analogy of
mainstream gay politics. Not only did analogy implicitly make the homosexual white, as I argued in chapter 5, it also implicitly enacted limits
to solidarity across the color line by calling on homosexuals to model
their struggle on that of a white people, not on the struggles of other
"racial minorities," struggles which, in 1931, looked a lot less successful
than that of Jews.

One day Hirschfeld, and Li I assume, stopped by a Tel Aviv kindergarten and watched the children. Hirschfeld did not write down why he
went to see a kindergarten; on the world tour he did not usually visit
children's schools. He enjoyed taking walks through cities. Perhaps he
and Li happened upon the kindergarten by chance while out for a walk.
They stopped to carefully count the children. For Hirschfeld, it was a
chance to gather evidence of Jewish whiteness, even Nordic-ness.

One sees, especially among the children, a strikingly large number of blonds and individuals with blue eyes; in one kindergarten I counted thirty-two light-haired children out of fifty-four – that is more than fifty percent.

Not pure races, but rather mixed races, are the biological norm [*sind eine biologische Selbstverständlichkeit*]. How could there be "pure" races among the white races? Take into account that each individual comes from a line of ancestors stretching back through father and mother and spanning thousands, perhaps even hundreds of thousands of generations. How pronounced must the mixture of genes be over so long a period![24]

In all of his work on race, Hirschfeld argues that pure races do not exist. This did not mean he didn't believe in the existence of races at all though. Most authors on race held that there were multiple races within the big color categories.[25] There were a number of white races. This is what he means when he writes that there was not purity among the white races, using Jews as an example. To say a race was impure or that all races were mixtures was not necessarily to call the whiteness of Jews into question. The kindergarten class was an example of a group of heterogeneous but nevertheless "white" children. In another moment, writing about the United States, Hirschfeld set Jews (and Catholics) apart from "colored" people, listing the victims of the KKK as: "colored [*farbige*], Jewish, and also Roman Catholic" people.[26] That is, Jews and Catholics were white, he assumed.

This contradicted the antisemitism of Hirschfeld's day but fit in well with scientific racism and anthropology. Often, scientific texts on the races counted Jews as a single race and as a non-white, non-European race, and antisemitism uniformly did so, often claiming the Jews were an Asian or Middle Eastern race.[27] At the same time, in a lot of scientific racism – an older body of thought than the secular antisemitism that originated in the 1870s – Jews were a white race.[28] The nineteenth-century Frenchman de Gobineau, an influential thinker in the field of scientific racism whose work the Nazis read avidly, has Jews as a unitary, non-European race within the "Semitic" group of races, which is distinct from the group of "Caucasian" races, which includes the "Aryan" race.[29] Yet in de Gobineau, the "Semitic" races are within the category "white," though they are inferior to other white races such as those in the Caucasian group.[30] White supremacists in the antebellum southern United States believed Jews were racially white.[31] Often only some Jews – Ashkenazi Jews – counted as white, while Sephardic Jews and other groups of Jews did not.[32] Hirschfeld seems to consider members of the diaspora of Baghdadi Jews to racially Jewish, and white, because he makes no comment as to race when he meets them.[33] Yet he does not consider all who are Jews by religion to be Jews by race. He distinguishes a Jewish woman from South Asia, with whom he chatted in Bombay (Mumbai), as "colored" and as a "black" Jew. She and people like her are, he explains, most likely Indian by race; they descend from converts to Judaism.[34]

At the kindergarten that day, one imagines Hirschfeld felt satisfied in finding confirmation of what he already knew: Jews were white. He had done a similar informal study in the 1920s in Germany, in a courtroom where an antisemite was on trial for a political murder and a number of the reporters and lawyers at the trial were Jews. The features of the supposed "Aryan" physical type, like blond hair, were more common among the Jews in the courtroom – lawyers and reporters – than among the antisemites and their supporters, he found.[35]

Tel Aviv was "quite remarkable," Hirschfeld thought, because with its 50,000 residents it was at the time the world's only "completely Jewish city."[36] From the political elite to the working class, from the police officers to the chimney sweeps, everyone was a Jew. What was also remarkable was that he never would have guessed. Had he not seen newspapers in Hebrew, or noticed how all the shops shut on Saturdays, he could not have said he was in a city of Jews. He seldom saw anyone with the facial characteristics commonly attributed to Jews.

> Only very occasionally, and far less often as in say Karlsbad or Marienbad [two Czechoslovakian spa towns Hirschfeld liked to visit], one sees the [Hermann] Struck character studies [*sieht man die "Struck'schen" Charakterköpfe*] or the oriental beauties whom Sichel painted in my youth. Also the so-called "Jewish nose," supposedly an Aramaic-Arab characteristic, is hardly more common than the snub-nose. What predominates are noses of the "western" or "northern" form (to use Günther's nomenclature) – and moreover the shape of the lips, the hair, and the eyes, the hands and feet, all of those hardly deviate from the average European type.[37]

Nathaniel Sichel was a German orientalist painter known for his portraits of women; he was Jewish and some of his work depicted Jewish women.[38] Hermann Struck was a Jewish graphic artist known for character studies of Berlin Jews.[39] Hans F.K. Günther was a leading antisemitic race theorist who joined the Nazi Party the same year Hirschfeld visited Tel Aviv. Günther argued that Jews were not European.[40] He would later become Nazi Germany's "most prominent and widely cited expert on race," according to Alan Steinweis.[41] Hirschfeld's citation of Günther in this passage is subversive. He uses Günther's own racial categories to show that the Nazis were wrong: Jews *were* European. You could tell by their noses.

In Hirschfeld's worldview, as I discussed earlier, to be white meant to be European or of European descent and to be civilized. Jews were. They had helped to create European culture. When God granted the Ten Commandments to Moses, he laid "the foundation of European morals to this day."[42] Hirschfeld noted that the questions about sexuality and medicine he fielded from Jews in Palestine were essentially the same as the questions he got in European countries.[43] He shot down antisemitic assertations about homosexuality being more or less common in the Jewish race – like other racial differences, that between Jews and others had no effect on homosexuality, which was universal.[44]

Take as another example of the whiteness of Jews in Hirschfeld's thinking a passage from *Racism*, published years after his death and only ever in an English translation by the left-wing eugenicists Eden and Cedar Paul.[45] Hirschfeld sets out to dispute the idea that there is a pure white race. He brings in Günther, who, he explains, is on a futile mission to distinguish the subgroup of whites who are "Nordic." He refers to the pictures of people chosen to typify the Nordic race in Günther's book. Then, Hirschfeld shows just how ridiculous such labeling is:

> In this connection I will mention an incident reported to me as throwing some light on the alleged trustworthiness of the objective differentiae which are supposed to characterize race. A Jewish student was fluttering the pages of Hans Günther's *Rassenkunde des deutschen Volkes* [*Racial Science of the German Race*]. Pulling himself up with a jerk, he exclaimed: "How in thunder did Cousin Selma's portrait find its way into this gallery?" Only when someone looking over his shoulder pointed to the description, which in this case was unadulterated "Nordic," was he satisfied that it was no more than a deceptively close resemblance.[46]

It is easy to read Hirschfeld's point in this passage as being that Günther's race science is bunk because Jews match his definition of the "Nordic" and are in fact, of course, not Nordic, being Jews. However, that is not what Hirschfeld meant. The story about Cousin Selma is evidence for the argument that there are multiple white races, and in fact whites are a mixture and defy attempts to differentiate among them: the whole passage bears the heading "The Racial Composition of Ninety-Nine Per Cent of Whites Remains an Enigma." Hirschfeld's point is that white is white, and Jews are white. One white woman, the unnamed one in Günther's picture, looks very much like another, Selma, though the fervent antisemite Günther would be loath to admit that.

Hirschfeld was a secular person. He was nevertheless, in his own mind, "a person of Jewish descent," as he put it in an entry in his journal in April 1933.[47] He was considered a Jew by probably most of the people who encountered him. He knew that. Yet he also considered himself racially Jewish and therefore white.[48]

Despite having been raised by parents who were very involved in the Jewish community in their city and who assumedly gave their children religious upbringings, Hirschfeld almost never wrote about himself as a Jew.[49] He marked the passage of the year by the Christian calendar, often noting in his journal when he was writing on a Christian holiday.[50] When he had occasion to write about a Jewish holiday in his journal, which he did in November 1931 as he referred to news reports of attacks by Nazis on German Jews leaving Rosh Hashanah services, he called the holiday "the Jewish New Year" rather than by its Hebrew name.[51] He was a thoroughly secular individual who blamed religion, foremost Christianity, for sexual oppression and wanted to be buried without any clergy present, yet he – like many assimilated German Jews – nonetheless loved Christmas and celebrated it each year.[52] He was in Alexandria, Egypt, in 1931 with Li on Christmas Eve. (Li was not Christian.)[53] He took Li out to a sailors' bar that styled itself after a Bavarian beer hall so that they could see a Christmas tree.[54]

When he and Li left Tel Aviv and sailed back to Europe, they did not go back to Berlin. Instead, out of fear of the Nazis, whose influence in Germany was growing day by day, Hirschfeld went immediately into exile. He would never again set foot in Berlin. This caused him agony and confusion. It drove him to grapple with his Jewishness and his Germanness. In May 1932, he wrote, "The questions: where do you belong? What are you really? [These questions] give me no peace. I formulate this question: Are you a German, a Jew, or a citizen of the world? and my answer is, 'world citizen,' or 'all three.'"[55] This was something of a move back toward a Jewish identity, but a secular one that did not take precedence over his cosmopolitanism. Nevertheless, for most of his life, and quite independent of Nazism, he remained convinced that he belonged to the Jewish race – he was physically, by descent, a Jew, and therefore white.

In Palestine, Hirschfeld and Li were once again traveling in a British colony. Hirschfeld did not forget all he had learned about empire. The region had been ruled by the Ottoman Empire until the First World War; the peace settlement at Paris put it officially under British authority.[56] He had little to say about the British in Palestine. This was something of a contrast to his denunciations of their imperial doings in Egypt and wherever else he encountered them. The British were at the time largely friendly to the Zionists, supporting Jewish immigration and promising some kind of Jewish sovereignty, though they were mealymouthed about what exactly.[57]

Palestinian Arabs rejected British rule and Zionism.[58] Hirschfeld was not entirely closed off to the Palestinian Arab criticism of Zionism as a colonial project, reporting it at some length and warning that the Arabs posed a threat to Zionism.[59] He did not agree that Zionism was itself a colonial project. He supported Zionism, though he thought Jewish immigration to the United States and assimilation there an equally sound plan.[60] (It was the latter, immigration to the US, that Hirschfeld eventually recommended to his own family.)[61] Hirschfeld hoped that diplomacy could solve the conflict in Palestine; violence never would.[62] Or did Hirschfeld quietly think Zionism was indeed a sort of colonial project, but one to which he did not object? He wrote, approvingly, that Tel Aviv was a Jewish "'place in the sun'" – that phrase being a decades-old watchword for empire in Germany.[63] He presented the phrase in quotation marks, I assume to show he was thinking of its connotations, which were imperial.[64]

If Jews were white, in Hirschfeld's thinking, then the foundational analogy that created homosexuality likened homosexuals to the members of an oppressed white race. As I argued in chapter 5, thinkers in the homosexual emancipation movement like Hirschfeld and Kurt Hiller (another secular German Jew) used an analogy between Jews and homosexuals to explain what homosexuality was.[65] One activist, for example, wrote in the 1920s that Germany's sodomy law "causes us to wear the signs of shame as conspicuously as the Jews did in times gone by,"[66] a reference to the distinguishing badges that Jews were required by law to wear on their clothing in many medieval cities. Hiller wrote, "The homosexual problem bears a striking resemblance to the Jewish problem. Here are two minorities that are scattered throughout all of the peoples of the world, and that have been subjugated [geknechtet] for hundreds of years."[67] He went on to enumerate other similarities: though a diverse group, Jews were united by a "mystical brotherhood," just as homosexuals were. Both Jews and homosexuals were hated "by the ruling race." For the most part, both Jews and homosexuals lacked pride, although at the same time, "in an understandable reaction against the brutality of persecution, they are prone to excessive over-valuation of their own type."[68] As examples for this last point, he offered Zionists, cabbalists (Neokabbalisten) in Palestine, and the German homosexual emancipationist Benedict Friedländer, who argued that same-sex love was superior to all other forms of love.[69]

Hirschfeld, too, likened the struggle of homosexuals to that of Jews. He made this point in a 1919 film that he co-wrote and in which he played himself. The film, Different from the Others (Anders als die Andern), advocated the repeal of Germany's sodomy law and was the first film in history to portray homosexuals in a positive light.[70] In it, Hirschfeld comforts the young lover of a man who has just taken his own life because he has been convicted of sodomy. The surviving lover is considering suicide himself. Hirschfeld urges the young man to live instead and to dedicate his life to the fight against the sodomy law. He tells him, "This is the life task I assign you. Just as Zola struggled on behalf of one man who innocently languished in prison, what matters now is to restore honor and justice to the many thousands before us, with us, and after us."[71] The reference is to the notorious wrongful conviction for treason of a French army officer, the Dreyfus Affair, which set off a national reckoning about antisemitism in France between 1894 and 1906. Hirschfeld likened Émile Zola's campaign to overturn the railroading of the innocent Jew, Captain Alfred Dreyfus, to the struggle on behalf of innocent homosexual men unjustly convicted under the sodomy law.

Hirschfeld saw a specific commonality between the fight against antisemitism and the fight against the persecution of homosexuals: both were battles to overcome irrational, unscientific prejudice. Both were just causes that could triumph, he reasoned, when secularism, science, and modernity also triumphed.

The campaign waged by European Jews for civic equality from the late eighteenth through the nineteenth century began to style itself "Jewish Emancipation" in the 1840s.[72] (This name must have influenced the choice of "homosexual emancipation" as a moniker for the later homosexual movement.) German Jews, including Hirschfeld's father, insisted that they were not an alien nation but rather "German citizens of the Jewish faith."[73] By the turn of the twentieth century, Jewish Emancipation had brought equal rights and full citizenship to Western European Jews. It also brought them assimilation, integration into the wider Christian society, and growing toleration by the Christian majority. In the German lands, national unification in 1871 did away with the patchwork of legal discrimination that state and religious authorities had inflicted on Jews since the Middle Ages. With its roots in the Enlightenment belief in the power of human rationality, Jewish Emancipation had been part of a broader movement to weaken religious authority and to build modern, secular states in which individuals rather than corporate bodies of subjects were imagined as the fundamental unit.[74] Medieval restrictions on Jews and prejudices against them, such as the claim that they had murdered Christ, were, to advocates of Emancipation, "vestiges of ancient barbarisms ... doomed to fall before the liberating onslaught of reason," as the historian Donald Niewyk puts it.[75]

As a young man, Hirschfeld had lived through a wave of antisemitism in Germany and had seen it defeated by science, or so he believed. This was the antisemitism of the 1870s and 1880s, a movement led by now-forgotten men like Adolf Stöcker, Heinrich von Treitschke, and Eugen Dühring. That wave of antisemitism died down, Hirschfeld wrote, when the then crown prince spoke out against it and when the anthropologists Rudolf Virchow and Felix von Luschan knocked down Dühring's racial theories.[76]

Just as science had defeated antisemitism, he thought, it would defeat prejudices against homosexuals. He wrote:

> Once, the zealots of the Christian Church burned heretics, Jews and witches in the name of God, and almost all men persecuted science in God's name … so now they are still hounding innocents whom they claim are guilty, driving hundreds of them into suicide … chasing them through the darkness of lunacy.[77]

The persecution of Jews had been religious and irrational, motivated by the same maniac zeal that animated the church's bloody pursuit of witches and heretics and its opposition to science. Enlightenment reason and secularism had finally brought an end to those persecutions. But irrationalism, religion, and superstition were still persecuting homosexuals. Reason – and particularly biological science – would stop them once again.

In his many publications, Hirschfeld doggedly and repetitively made the point that "biological research has shown that same-sex love complies with certain natural laws, just as other kinds of love does."[78] Homosexual emancipation was, for him, "the battle of modern science against superstition and ignorance of nature," and its purpose was to prove "that same-sex attraction [*gleichgeschlechtliches Fühlen*] is no vice."[79] Rather, homosexuals (and transvestites) were "actualizing their natural inclinations" and were being unfairly punished by the law and persecuted by society.[80] Hirschfeld insisted that that would change only when people realized the truth. He hoped that *The Homosexuality of Men and Women*, his meticulous defense of the biological, non-pathological nature of homosexuality that ran to more than 1,000 pages, would help. He wrote on the book's final page:

> Heterosexuals who read this book and who had previously had an outdated, prejudiced view will unlearn that opinion and will realize, for better or worse, that each day that state and society, family and individual persist in their old prejudice against homosexual men and women – a prejudice that is based on ignorance – an injustice is done, one that has only few parallels in human history.[81]

This faith in the power of science to convince the general public of the injustice of the persecution of homosexuals was very much like the Enlightenment confidence in reason that animated Jewish Emancipation and inspired its supporters to identify anti-Jewish prejudice as irrational, counterproductive, atavistic superstition. They had insisted that Jews were worthy, useful citizens. Echoing these strategies, Hirschfeld approvingly quoted the sexologist Richard von Krafft-Ebing's view that many homosexuals were "useful and respectable citizens."[82] Scientific Humanitarian Committee petitions asserted that among homosexuals were "men and women of the greatest intellectual prominence."[83] Hirschfeld told a crowd of thousands gathered to hear him speak in Leipzig in the early 1920s that homosexuals "are human beings with a physical disposition that is naturally directed" to same-sex desires and acts, and that "their persecution is of the same kind as the persecution of people of different faiths [*Andersgläubiger*] in past centuries. The times call for tolerance in this area just as they call for religious toleration."[84]

In Germany in the first decades of the twentieth century, antisemitism was not a thing of the past. Hirschfeld knew that as well as anyone. In 1920, he was attacked in the streets of Munich and beaten unconscious by antisemitic thugs who abhorred his advocacy on behalf of homosexuals.[85] Hirschfeld was a favorite target of the Nazis well before they took power.[86] Thanks in part to the relative openness of specialties in sexology and venereal disease (dermatology) to Jews within the medical profession, many of the leading progressive sexologists were Jews.[87] Antisemites blamed progressive sexual politics, and homosexual emancipation in particular, on Jews. Yet, in the 1920s, a German Jew had many reasons to believe that Jewish Emancipation had succeeded. Legal discrimination was now many decades in the past. Major political parties opposed antisemitism. Jewish citizens held high positions in government and civil service as well as in important industries and cultural institutions. Reason was the weapon that had freed the Jews. It would free homosexuals too, and it would eventually defeat antisemitism altogether. Hirschfeld denounced contemporary antisemitism, such as that of the Nazi Party, and all racism as unscientific.[88] Attacking the methodology of scientific racism, he argued that the measuring of skulls was scientifically flawed, and science had proven that blood did not carry hereditary material.[89] While in exile, he proposed that an international committee of scientists be convened to objectively test the hypotheses of scientific racism, which would, he believed, be found wanting.[90] By the 1920s, other homosexual emancipationists, including Hiller and some of the men who produced the gay magazine *Friendship*, had grown frustrated with Hirschfeld's strategy of relying solely on science to sway public opinion and to persuade politicians to repeal the sodomy law.[91] But Hirschfeld remained committed to this strategy until the end of his life. What he understood as the successful example of Jewish Emancipation most likely helped to confirm his faith that, in the final analysis, homosexuals were like Jews because reason would free them.

Antisemitism was the racism of some whites *against other whites*, according to Hirschfeld's thinking. It was the racism of civilized white Europeans against other civilized white Europeans. He thought all racism was based on bunk science. Yet he thought whiteness, civilization, and European-ness all lined up. He believed there were meaningful distinctions among racial groups that might not reduce to biological race but that were nevertheless real. Jews were, I suppose, an attractive partner in the analogy for Hirschfeld because they were so unfairly and irrationally subjected to racism. Racism against them was the most ridiculous sort of racism. They were white and civilized, after all.

One day in Palestine, Hirschfeld and Li visited a kibbutz, Beth Alfa, which had been founded by migrants from Poland in the 1920s. Interested as he often was in the whiteness of Jews, Hirschfeld marveled at how "most of the pioneers" he met there looked far more "Aryan than semitic."[92] Racialization directed at his beloved Li caught his attention too, though it worked in the opposite direction, making Li an outsider while, in a sense, the whiteness of the residents of the kibbutz made them, to Hirschfeld, insiders, civilized Europeans. The residents of the kibbutz greeted him and Li warmly, he recalled, and were fascinated by his race. Especially the children would not leave Li's side, because "they have never seen a Chinese person in the flesh [*lebendigen Chinesen*] before."[93] He does not record how Li might have felt about being greeted as a racial specimen.

Hirschfeld's model of "the homosexual" has a hidden legacy: a link to the defense of Jewish whiteness. I think it is important to keep it in view. The analogies between the sexual minority and racial minorities were not an effort to build solidarity between white European homosexuals and people of color, such as the African American homosexuals Hirschfeld met on his tour of the US or, for that matter, his queer Chinese student/secretary/assistant.

Figure 8. Otto Scherer, the expat professor who explained to Hirschfeld how eugenics, not racism, ought to be used to direct human reproduction, with his wife and children, assumedly at his home on the day Li and Hirschfeld visited. Philippines, 1932. (From *World Journey*)

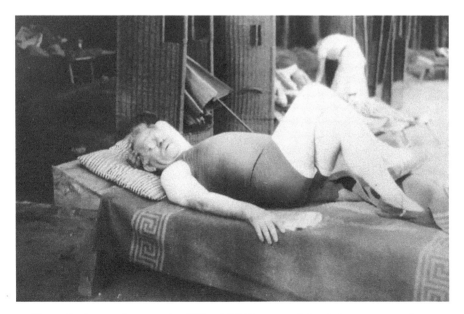

Figure 9. A rare photograph of Hirschfeld in a casual, feminine moment, also from the Reiss papers. Probably at a beach in France during the exile. (MHG)

Figure 10. The 1933 *Voilà* magazine cover photo. (Jean-Nickolaus Tretter Collection, University of Minnesota)

Figure 11. Li and Karl Giese on the grounds of the Institute for Sexual Science, Berlin, 1932, from Hirschfeld's exile guest book/scrapbook. (Deutsches Literaturarchiv Marbach)

Figure 12. Hirschfeld and Li walking together in Vichy, 1934, from Hirschfeld's exile guest book/scrapbook. (Deutsches Literaturarchiv Marbach)

Figure 13. Two photos of Li that were in his papers. They appear to be passport photos or similar; the earlier one appears to have been used in Swiss official paperwork. (MHG)

9 Magnus Hirschfeld's Queer Eugenics

Berlin, Germany; Manila, Philippines; Pasadena, California, United States; and Bondowoso, East Java, Indonesia

For most of his adult life, Hirschfeld maintained a private medical practice in Berlin, in addition to his many other projects. One of his patients was a woman in her early twenties. Her story, as briefly recorded by him, is worth hearing if one wants to know Hirschfeld's position on eugenics.

Hirschfeld did not publish the patient's name. Her parents brought her to see him. She hailed from what he calls a "very good southern German family."[1] The only thing about her as a person that shines through the dim view of her saturating his brief account is that she liked to visit fairs and carnivals. Apparently, she met men at them. When Hirschfeld examined her, she had already been pregnant four times. The men were otherwise complete strangers to her, or at least that was the story. Hirschfeld published this case in 1930, when birth control could be difficult to come by and abortion was illegal.[2]

Hirschfeld diagnosed the woman as "feebleminded" and hypersexual. Despite how laughable it sounds today, "feeblemindedness" (*Schwachsinn*) was a bona fide psychiatric diagnosis at time. It was an intellectual disability. People who were "feebleminded" were, supposedly, relatively close to normal, capable of many things – they might be able to live a normal life in a rural village, for example, but be out of their depth in a big city.[3] They had a mild form of mental impairment. It made them incapable of judgment about morality. Feebleminded women, the psychiatric literature claimed, had powerful sexual desires and lacked inhibitions. Many were prostitutes.[4] Tens of thousands of people in many countries were forced into sterilization operations because they were diagnosis as "feebleminded."

The woman's parents were at their wits' end. Their daughter was a scandal. Here was a young woman from an important family cavorting in a public place, having sex outside of marriage, and getting pregnant. They could not control her. She knew how to evade their supervision.

Pregnancy outside of marriage carried a heavy stigma, particularly for an important family. There was a stigma attached to abortion as well, and legal, not to mention physical, risk.

Hirschfeld recommended castration. He writes, "She was severely fee-bleminded, hyper-erotic and she was castrated [*kastriert*] and since then no longer 'runs away'; they keep her busy with light house and garden work, which she performs slowly but neatly."[5] It is disconcerting to see the term "castration" applied to a woman, but in 1930, the science of cas-tration versus sterilization was still rather fuzzy. As Hirschfeld himself de-fined the terms, sterilization meant the destruction of a person's capacity to reproduce, and castration meant the destruction or diminishment of the sexual drive.[6] Sterilization destroyed the body's capacity to become pregnant, but it left the sex drive intact and perhaps could even increase it. Castration destroyed not only the ability to bear children but the de-sire to have sex. The sex drive could only be destroyed by removing the gonads, he wrote.[7] In this young woman's case, we can hope that the surgery was just an ovariectomy, not a hysterectomy plus an ovariectomy, but either way, it was not an easy or safe surgery in the decades before an-tibiotics. Hirschfeld did not perform it himself; he was not a surgeon. He probably referred the family to a surgeon. Sterilization (including vasec-tomy) and castration were technically illegal in Germany at the time, but doctors seem to have often performed the surgeries quietly, and even doctors who publicly discussed doing so were not prosecuted.[8]

Hirschfeld's south German patient may have been disabled by today's standards. She may not have been. Historians have identified many cases of people designated "feebleminded" because they did things that disa-bled as well as non-disabled people do, such as live in a messy house or have sex with more than one partner.[9] To give an example that typifies many other cases: a 1948 report on North Carolina noted that bureaucrats working in the state's sterilization program considered a suspect person's "using a hotel room for immoral purposes" to be evidence of feeblemind-edness and believed that sexual misbehavior in and of itself was grounds for compulsory sterilization.[10] No matter how today's standards of disabil-ity would have applied to this person, her forced sterilization was wrong. Hirschfeld does not say specifically whether this patient consented to the operation, but he uses her case as an example to illustrate the very few cases in which he recommends surgery without the patient's consent. I think it is safe to assume that, at the very least, the surgery was not her idea.

Magnus Hirschfeld's enthusiasm for eugenics was not a minor, fleeting thing. It was at the heart of his vision of a better world. It was not for nothing that one of the associations he helped to found was called the

Medical Society for Sexology and Eugenics (Ärztliche Gesellschaft für Sexualwissenschaft und Eugenik), or that the international congresses of the World League for Sexual Reform regularly hosted discussions of eugenics, or that the WLSR officially supported it.[11] On his tour of the world, he talked about eugenics in his lectures. Over the course of a long career, Hirschfeld found little time for his own research. He did, however, find time to research the eugenics of transvestitism, homosexuality, and other "intersexual" conditions.[12] Eugenics, the science of human heredity, belonged to the field of sexology. As eugenics advanced as a science of its own, it would probably "form the epicenter of sexology," in his words.[13]

For almost forty years, scholars who have grappled with Hirschfeld's thought and legacy have had to puzzle out what to make of his eugenics. Historians have fought long and hard over whether it is important or not.[14] Around the turn of the twenty-first century, a consensus opinion emerged: it held that it was not all that important.[15] A key to this consensus was the fact that, as Andreas Seeck put it in a 2004 essay, "Hirschfeld did not connect eugenics with racism."[16] Another oft-repeated point was that among the many, many supporters of eugenics, Hirschfeld stood out as a left-of-center advocate of voluntarism. He promoted education; he was not, for the most part, an advocate of compulsory sterilization.[17] This second idea is now so entrenched that two leading Hirschfeld scholars have gone so far recently as to assert that Hirschfeld was *only* in favor of voluntary eugenics.[18]

The purpose of this chapter is to argue that we ought to revisit that consensus.[19] Not only is it based in errors, but it misses just how central eugenics was to Hirschfeld's thinking, how important it was to his antiracism and to his struggle for homosexual liberation. Hirschfeld thought eugenics worked in favor of gay rights. He sought a queer eugenics, that is, a eugenics that would justify some queer erotics, even as it sought to suppress other queer erotics. "Eugenics … is a science of invaluable worth," Hirschfeld wrote, and it was at the heart of the fight for freedom.[20] Rather than unscientific racial prejudices, eugenics ought to be used to distinguish fit from unfit humans, for the good of humanity. When it came time to write a dedication for his memoir of his world journey, Hirschfeld dedicated it not to his traveling companion Li but to eugenics.[21]

What is perhaps most shocking – and forgotten – about eugenics is how popular it was, and in such diverse political circles, for so long. From the nineteenth century into the 1950s, at least, people around the world thought that a long list of mental, physical, and moral traits were passed from one generation to the next in a simple and easily understood way, just like the Austrian monk Gregor Mendel's experiments had shown characteristics of pea plant pods, wrinkly or smooth, passing in a relatively simple fashion from one generation to the next. By managing this transmission for entire populations, humanity's future could be improved. Chronic social ills could be cured. Francis Galton, who coined "eugenics" in 1883, was an English gentleman of the Victorian age, a scientist and a polymath. He believed in Charles Darwin's theory of evolution. (Darwin happened to be his cousin.) Galton moreover saw no reason to let evolution take its course without the guidance of a human hand. Humans ought to direct their own evolution for the better, maximizing fit offspring.[22] Eugenics was, as Daylanne English puts it, "the science of breeding better humans."[23] Perhaps not incidentally, Galton also had some antisemitic views.[24] Nevertheless, Hirschfeld, Galton's cousin Charles Darwin, and – between the last third of the nineteenth century and, say, the middle of the twentieth – millions of other people around the world thought this was a great idea.[25]

The best-remembered tool of the eugenicists was forced sterilization. Most US states had eugenic sterilization laws well into the twentieth century. Sterilization programs in the US and Canada were run by white elites who forced tens of thousands of poor white people as well as a disproportionate number of Native people, Black people, and Latino/a people to undergo sterilization surgeries.[26] Germany only passed a eugenic sterilization law after the Nazis took power, but then it quickly made up for lost time and surpassed the United States in forced sterilizations, targeting Black Germans as well as hundreds of thousands of disabled white Germans, people who qualified as members of the "Aryan" race but were thought to carry hereditary "defects." Prior to the Nazi state's very aggressive program, the US led the world in eugenic sterilization.

Eugenicists, however, did not only seek to sterilize people. They thought there were lots of other ways to get people to have more high-quality babies and fewer inferior ones. These included birth control, welfare assistance for pregnant women, eugenic marriage counseling, bans on the immigration of people with disabilities, and the involuntary incarceration of intellectually disabled people in single-sex institutions, so that they could not reproduce.

Eugenics is remembered as a far-right scheme. We easily call to mind the Nazis, or Paul Popenoe, the mainstay of California's aggressive, racist sterilization program. But there was nothing intrinsically far right about eugenics. It was quite versatile. People of many different political stripes embraced versions of it. Frank Dikötter writes, "Eugenics belonged to the political vocabulary of virtually every significant modernizing force between the two world wars."[27] It was also global, counting adherents beyond Europe and the United States, including in Brazil, China, and Japan.[28]

Was eugenics racist? Most of the time, yes. But not all the time. It wasn't *necessarily* racist. You could want to improve the hereditary stock of humanity regardless of race, as Hirschfeld did.[29] Support for eugenics was common in Germany's Social Democratic circles, where Hirschfeld moved, as was opposition to imperialism and rejection of right-wing theories of the "Aryan" race.[30] As one swings one's gaze from the far right to the moderate left (communists on the far left were generally critical of eugenics), the shape and character of eugenic ideas shift drastically. Someone on the far right might favor aggressive sterilization of supposedly inferior whites and people of color, while Social Democrats in Germany for example often expounded the eugenic virtues of marriage counseling and birth control. Most of the louder advocates of eugenics also believed in scientific racism and combined the two visions of the world, and those are the people best remembered today. However, some left-of-center people liked eugenics and rejected racism: W.E.B. Du Bois for example.[31] Hirschfeld is another example. In fact, he thought eugenics had to be antiracist in order to work.

During their brief time in Manila, Hirschfeld (and Li, I assume) met a white man with an unusual marital history. Otto Scherer was an expatriate German and a professor at the University of Manila. He had not been back to Germany for fifty years, but he struck Hirschfeld as so thoroughly German that he could have stepped off the ship yesterday. He had thinning white hair and a neat white moustache and reminded Hirschfeld of Bismarck. (A photograph that either Li or Hirschfeld took of him and his family appeared in *World Journey*; see figure 8.) Scherer was around Hirschfeld's age and they got along. The professor invited Hirschfeld to his villa. I presume Li went too. They relaxed in the heat, Hirschfeld probably sweating in the often-rumpled white suit he sported in tropical climates, and Scherer in a crisp white shirt and pants and a tie without a jacket. Hirschfeld, being Hirschfeld, wanted to talk about the professor's marriages. He had had three (non-concurrent). The first was to a Malayan woman. Then he married a Javanese or Japanese woman (Hirschfeld was unclear on which). Then he wed a Malaysian Filipino. Scherer's children were at the villa that day, and Hirschfeld sized them up. They were "all well-built mixed-bloods [*Mischlinge*]." One of Scherer's sons was twenty and had the "tall stature of his father and the brown hair color of his mother." Another son was one of Manila's most sought-after lawyers.[32]

Hirschfeld asked Scherer what he thought of "the problem of mixed marriages."[33] Well, Scherer responded, actually it was useless to talk about the racial composition of a marriage. It was not race that determined a marriage's success – that is, the fitness of offspring. It was the fitness of the partners. "My wives were all from better families, well-bred and well-mannered. That is why the mixture came out well."[34] Sure, he went on, the children of some racially mixed marriages were inferior. But it was, ironically, racism that caused this, not race mixing. Often, mixed marriages were between women of the lower classes and white European men who were mavericks within their own social class, because only European misfits were willing to step across the color line. The result was below-average children. When humans did away with racism, they would finally have a clear path to better marriages, that is, eugenically successful marriages. Scherer explained,

> It is only the individual's heredity, not the individual's membership in a race [*Stammeszugehörigkeit*], that has eugenic significance. As misconceptions disappear, natural selection (in the sense of Darwin's work and Galton's) will result in the ripening of better fruit than what we formerly got when we were in the shadows of evil ideas.[35]

Professor Scherer's impromptu speech summed up Hirschfeld's own views quite well.

Hirschfeld was a self-described antiracist eugenicist, and moreover a very moderate and left-of-center eugenicist. He wanted to take race out of the equation. Race science was an irrational fiction based in emotion; it polluted the true science of eugenics.[36] He approvingly quoted the American geneticist and eugenics-backer H.J. Muller:

> In regard to really important characteristics, the natural differences between the races pale into insignificance besides the natural differences between individuals – so much so that an impartial science of genetic improvement could not afford to take the former into account ... Thus we see that only the eugenics of the new society, freed of the traditions of caste, of slavery, and of colonialism, can be a thorough-going and a true eugenics.[37]

One could chuck racial categories and still improve the human population, and this was what Hirschfeld wanted. Individuals varied. People were more or less strong, more or less clever, more or less happy. They tended either to be romantic and emotional or objective and intellectual.[38] Human excellence, though not determined by race, was indeed real; it was partially biological and hereditary and it was unchanging: "It is not the racial type that is decisive, but rather, the individual and sexual type that is decisive in terms of a person. A great individual can appear anywhere and at any time ... what is necessary is only a good mixture of genes."[39] Genius ran in families, partly because of heredity.[40] He had been lucky to have two parents of good hereditary stock; others were not so lucky.[41] People naturally preferred more beautiful and more intelligent partners – no one wanted to marry the "crippled" or the offspring of convicts or madmen, and there was sound reasoning behind this general preference: it was working toward "the perfection of the human race."[42] Evolution was real; why shouldn't humans direct evolution for the better?[43] If they did, social ills could be cured – male prostitution, for example.[44]

We remember Hirschfeld as a force for justice, but his vision of justice was stamped by the biological determinism of the late nineteenth century. Enlightenment thinkers such as Rousseau and the French revolutionaries all championed equality. As worthy as that goal was, it was based in bad science. "The premise that individuals are equal in nature and in capacities was proven wrong in the nineteenth century by natural science." Hirschfeld was for equality and freedom, insofar as it was possible to achieve them given natural human inequality. He still wanted equal rights and democracy, with a small qualification: all adult women and men ought to have the vote, with the exception of "the mentally stultified."[45]

It is true that the eugenic programs Hirschfeld really liked were voluntary programs. He also believed in public education. If people learned about eugenics, he thought, they would apply it to themselves, for example by choosing not to have children if a counselor explained that they carried bad hereditary material. He did lots of public outreach about eugenics himself, in his lectures and publications. He supported a Weimar Republic effort led by left-of-center, sex-reform-minded people to set up hundreds of marriage counseling clinics all over Germany; some of the clinics did eugenic counseling. One was housed in the Institute for Sexual Science. Hirschfeld thought the clinics were a very good start. In a paper for the 1929 WLSR meeting in London, he described an idea for a matchmaking service that would operate by mail, matching men and women based on sexual, physical, and mental factors, as well as eugenic criteria. The decision about whether or not to marry would of course be up to the people in question.[46]

Hirschfeld was very skeptical about forcing people to go along with eugenics. In *Sexology* III, he goes through a long list of proposed eugenic programs and gives his thoughts on them. He spends a lot of ink there mulling marriage bans or sex bans. Though he did not like the idea of banning certain eugenically unfit people from marrying or having sex, he made a few exceptions. The children of very young parents tended to have hereditary defects, thus he favored banning sex for young people – under eighteen for men and under sixteen for women.[47] He wanted bans on the unions of close relatives, for eugenic reasons. He also wanted restrictions on people who had infectious illnesses that damaged hereditary material (he does not specify which, but he was possibly thinking of syphilis).[48] But any other marriage or sex ban was scientifically unfounded. He seemed open to laws requiring certificates of health prior to marriage, so long as the choice to marry or not remained voluntary.[49]

He did not, however, have a principled objection to compulsory eugenics or, specifically, to forced sterilization. His concern was that the science was just not there yet, in most cases, though not in all cases. There were a few cases in which it was obvious that sterilization would stop the transmission of hereditary defects: cases like that of the "feeble-minded" women discussed above and cases involving alcoholism, which Hirschfeld and many others believed caused heritable damage. Sterilization was nothing more than the application of a principle that every gardener followed – one had to pull out the weeds. Yet it was not time to jump on board with an ambitious plan for mass sterilization. Human reproduction was a lot more complicated than animal reproduction; scientists did not understand human hereditary all that well yet. Large compulsory sterilization programs like those in the United States, or even more ambitious plans to sterilize hundreds of thousands of people, were impractical, he thought.[50]

When the Nazis passed a eugenic sterilization law in 1933, Hirschfeld, then in exile, raised essentially the same objections to it – it was too ambitious, too vaguely crafted, too tainted by racism, and too reliant on junk science. Norway's law was much better, he wrote.[51] As was true for other left-of-center reformers, the problem with the German sterilization law was in the execution, not in the very fact of forced eugenic sterilization per se.[52]

Traveling through the United States by train and automobile in 1930 and 1931, Hirschfeld had the chance to see the country that he would later call, with justification, "the mother land of the sterilization movement."[53] The United States was then in the midst of the world's most ambitious effort to surgically sterilize "unfit" people without their consent. (The number of victims of these programs is estimated at over 60,000 people – Nazi Germany's eugenic sterilization law would later far outstrip that.)[54] The United States also had federal eugenic immigration restrictions. Hirschfeld criticized them; he was also critical of the US's racist immigration laws.[55] Yet many of the states Hirschfeld visited had sterilization laws, such as Arizona, New York, New Jersey, Michigan, and Wisconsin.[56] When he got to California, Hirschfeld reached what was then arguably the global epicenter of eugenic sterilization. He reported to friends back home:

> I studied the problem of qualitative birth control at the source, in Pasadena (California), when I visited Gosney and Popenoe at the Human Betterment Foundation. They are at the vanguard of the work of improving humanity by sterilizing unfit men and women (in particular feebleminded people). Here, too, I was greeted like an old friend [*Bekannter*], "whose work we have studied for 25 years," as Paul Popenoe wrote in my travel book.[57]

Founded in 1928 on the fortune of citrus grower Ezra S. Gosney, the Human Betterment Foundation's mission was to expand eugenic sterilizations in California. Gosney and Popenoe coauthored a book called *Sterilization for Human Betterment* (1929).[58] The 1933 Nazi sterilization law was modeled on American laws, including California's, and through the 1930s the Human Betterment Foundation maintained strong ties to the right-wing German eugenicists who were thriving under the Nazi state, as well as to powerful people in California, such as the owner of the *Los Angeles Times*.[59] By 1979, California had sterilized over 20,000 people, many of them patients in state hospitals and asylums.[60] Popenoe, who together with Gosney greeted Hirschfeld "like an old friend" and flattered him about having read his work, was one of the American sterilization movement's leading advocates; in the 1950s, he would reinvent himself as the man behind the "Can This Marriage Be Saved?" column in *Ladies' Home Journal*.[61]

Given that one of the major apologies for Hirschfeld is that he was not a racist sterilization zealot like Popenoe, let's take a look at how they differed. Not only did Popenoe favor a very ambitious program of eugenic sterilization; he was also a fanatical white supremacist. "The Negro race differs greatly from the white race, mentally as well as physically, and … in many respects it may be said to be inferior, when tested by the requirements of modern civilization and progress," he and his coauthor, a professor at the University of Pittsburgh, wrote in their influential 1918 textbook on eugenics.[62] In California, eugenicists like Popenoe and Gosney went after Mexican Americans in particular.[63] The textbook repeats, in detail, the major tropes of scientific racism, such as that Black people were gregarious but hapless, with powerful, poorly inhibited "sexual impulses" but a lack of "that aggressive competitiveness which has been responsible for so much of the achievement of the Nordic race."[64] The book inveighs against interracial marriage – many American states banned such marriages prior to 1967 – as well as interracial sex and the immigration of South and East Asians. Popenoe's book also disparaged Jews.[65]

If Hirschfeld, who hated exactly this sort of racism, objected when they met, Popenoe had an answer. Germans might speak out for racial equality, but this was only because they lacked "race experience."[66] They changed their tunes when they went to their own colonies (stripped from them after the First World War) or to the southern United States and saw societies where Black people were a large slice of the population.[67]

Despite their differences, Popenoe and Hirschfeld shared common ground. Both doubted the intellectual abilities of women: Popenoe's textbook frankly informed students that women were by nature the intellectual inferiors of men.[68] Both wanted to sterilize the "feebleminded." Hirschfeld, however, thought there were a lot less "feebleminded" people in need of sterilization. They were so few, in fact, that the government need not get involved. He seems to have wanted to leave the decision about whether to sterilize a "feebleminded" woman without her consent up to her doctor. He wrote, "This is in no way to deny that there are cases of feeblemindedness in which there is indeed a pressing indication in favor of sterilization. But on the whole, these are extremely exceptional cases, and moreover they can be appropriately treated without a sterilization law."[69] Simply give physicians like himself free rein; that was what was needed. A large part of the sterilization abuse in the United States and elsewhere has, historically, been carried out quietly and informally by doctors acting on their own without the consent of their patients, not only through the formalized sterilization bureaucracies. This kind of quiet, doctor-directed forced sterilization is very difficult for historians to chronicle since it leaves few traces in government archives.

Though Hirschfeld did not support racism like that of Popenoe, his chummy familiarity with the Californian suggests that Hirschfeld's anti-racism was not all that profound. Moreover, his obvious pleasure in his visit to the Human Betterment Foundation suggests that he and these right-wing Americans had enough common ground when it came to eugenics that they got along without much of a hitch, despite Popenoe's antisemitism.

California was not only about eugenics for Hirschfeld. He saw Hollywood. He visited Albert Einstein, who was then at CalTech.[70] Einstein was a public supporter of homosexual emancipation.[71] But Hirschfeld did not encounter eugenics only in Pasadena. One day he visited San Quentin penitentiary north of San Francisco. There he met the famous labor activist Tom Mooney – a political prisoner, Hirschfeld thought – and they talked about "sex starvation," that is, the fact that prisoners had no opportunities for (heterosexual) sex, an issue that had gotten lots of attention in Germany.[72] At San Quentin, Hirschfeld also saw Black and white homosexual prisoners, including people he described as men in women's clothing (see chapter 7). His visit was a big deal: on his tour of the prison he was escorted by the superintendent himself and by the prison doctor, Leo Stanley.[73]

Dr. Stanley of San Quentin was a man who, like Popenoe, had many interests in common with Hirschfeld but who fell in with the right wing of eugenics, not the left wing where Hirschfeld fit in. Stanley pressured over 600 prisoners to undergo quasi-legal vasectomies.[74] He also did medical experiments on prisoners. He was particularly taken with the famous rejuvenation experiments of Vienna's Eugene Steinach, whose work also influenced Hirschfeld.[75] Copying Steinach, Stanley implanted material from the testicles of a dead man into a living man. He got the testicular material from men executed at the prison.[76] Stanley took a dim view of homosexuality and pressured homosexual prisoners to be sterilized.[77] Though even Gosney of the Human Betterment Foundation considered Stanley overly zealous, Stanley and Hirschfeld probably found lots to discuss.[78] Hirschfeld seems not to have worried at all about the hundreds of coerced vasectomies. If he did have concerns, he made no mention of them in what he wrote later about the prison tour.

Eugenics, that truly dismal science, was closer to the center of Hirschfeld's worldview than we have let ourselves admit. He only wanted compulsory sterilization in a few exceptional cases. But does it matter that it was only a few people? Moreover, why would Hirschfeld's clear separation of eugenics from racism logically lead us to drop the subject, to conclude that there is nothing to see here? The violence of eugenics targeted people because of their disabilities and their gender as well as because of how they were racialized.[79] Magnus Hirschfeld really was in favor of *eugenics*, with all that that word means – a plan at the scale of population, a biological hierarchy of the value of individual people, a view toward influencing millions of individual choices about reproduction in order to improve the population over time, and a violent rejection of disability together with a dream of eradicating it in the future. He did want to use coercion to prevent some people from reproducing, even though his willingness to do so was far, far more limited than that of a typical right-of-center eugenicist like his chum Paul Popenoe.

In what ways was Hirschfeld's eugenics queer? First, in the sense that it victimized queer people. In what to us seems an odd, disturbing twist of logic (though it was no twist of logic to Hirschfeld and many of his contemporaries), some of the people Hirschfeld saw a reason to sterilize were queer people, by my definition of "queer." That is, they were people who got into trouble because they had non-normative, consensual, adult sex. He wanted to sterilize those people not only for strictly eugenic reasons, with an eye on future generations. He wanted to sterilize them *in part to stop their queer behavior in the here and now.* This depended on a fuzzy understanding of what sterilization (or castration) did to a person's sex drive, an imperfect understanding that was widespread at the time. For example, the Swiss literature on eugenics around 1910 held that sterilization put a stop to masturbation; one sees such confusion in the Dutch literature as well.[80] The American state of Oregon had men castrated to stop their same-sex erotic behavior.[81] Another key idea here was that disability and queerness were inextricably linked: one's sexual misbehaviors could be signs of one's eugenic unfitness. "Feebleminded" people could not control their urges, for example. Sterilization could stop masturbation. In 1925, school and medical officials in Germany had a nine-year-old boy sterilized to stop him from masturbating at school and encouraging his fellow pupils to masturbate.[82] The official who oversaw the boy's sterilization was Heinrich Boeters, a doctor who made a name for himself in Germany in the 1920s as the single loudest proponent of passing a national eugenic sterilization law modeled on laws in the United States.[83] Boeters, on his own initiative, sterilized 150 people – most or all without consent – and announced the sterilizations after the fact. This caused a public outcry and Boeters lost his job. Prior to the Nazi takeover, eugenic sterilization was deeply controversial in Germany, though by the late Weimar period a modest sterilization law was probably in the offing. Hirschfeld thought Boeters was far too ambitious. He however defended him. He thought Boeters had done Germany a service by raising the issue.[84]

Female heterosexual promiscuity seems to have made Hirschfeld apprehensive not just for future generations but for the here and now as well. In his discussion of the sterilization of the woman who liked carnivals, Hirschfeld makes the point that he only favors surgery without the patient's consent in special cases, and the examples he gives are those are of unmarried young women who had repeatedly been pregnant. The first is the woman who liked carnivals. The second is an "unmarried single feebleminded girl that Boeters reports – she gave birth to eight children, all of whom had 'no father' and all of whom were more or less mentally defective [blödsinnig]. I have seen similar cases repeatedly in my sexual-medical practice [Sexualpraxis]," he wrote, calling these "very difficult cases … when the persons in question are so mentally stultified that they are incapable of being in control of themselves."[85] He also called for a eugenic approach to the supposed problems of women selling sex to men and of men selling sex to other men.[86] He never says that he wants to prevent offspring *and* to stop the behavior. I assume that he did want to stop the behavior, did value the way sterilization worked in the here-and-now, given that many people assumed that the operations prevented offspring and changed behavior and given his obvious satisfaction in how the problematic behavior had changed following the operation in the case of the woman who liked carnivals. Even if he did, here he is targeting people because of their queer behavior, even when, as with male sex workers, the bad sex they are having is not reproductive. These inclinations were entirely in keeping with Hirschfeld's sexual politics, which emphasized respectability, at times at the expense of sex workers and others who could not adhere to public standards of conduct. These views are also well in line with moderate-left Weimar-era sex politics in Germany, which fought for sexual freedoms for respectable middle-class people while simultaneously trying to lock up disreputable working-class people such as men and women who sold sex in public places.[87]

Hirschfeld spent much of his life fighting for "sexual freedom," as he put it.[88] By "freedom" he meant something very particular. He did not mean the abolition of all bourgeoisie norms or the liberation of all who suffered under them. This is an important corrective to his rousing, if alarmingly bio-deterministic, claim that humans have a biological need for freedom and thus will shrug off the chains of imperialism, as well as those of heteronormativity. Even for gay sex (think male-male sex work), his intent was not to toss *all* bourgeoisie sexual conventions out the window.

Hirschfeld's eugenics were queer in a second way, too: he thought homosexuals were a force for eugenic good. On Java, Hirschfeld and Li trekked to Bondowoso, a relatively remote town, to visit Lucien von Römer, a Dutch doctor and researcher on homosexuality who had studied with Hirschfeld decades before. They spent a lovely day with him, his wife, his young son, and a mysterious visitor. Hirschfeld saw von Römer as one of the people who had proved that eugenics was good for homosexual liberation, and vice versa. In Hirschfeld's day, this was not a popular idea. Though eugenic sterilization programs did not use homosexuality in and of itself as a criteria, lots of the scientists who wrote about heredity and homosexuality claimed that inferior hereditary material caused homosexuality, and people who had same-sex sex could be caught up in eugenic programs.[89] But Hirschfeld believed that he, von Römer, and another colleague had discovered the flaw in this science. From 1901 to 1903 Hirschfeld, a Berlin neurologist named Ernst Burchard, and von Römer, who was then a student of Hirschfeld's and a member of the Scientific Humanitarian Committee, did a study of degeneration and abnormalities of the sexual drive.[90] They became convinced that homosexuality and other abnormal sexualities were not themselves symptoms of degeneration but rather were a natural means of preventing the spread of degeneration to successive generations.[91] Homosexuals were born into families with bad heredity material and acted as evolutionary dead ends, absorbing the bad material. Since homosexuals were naturally disposed not to have children, they never passed on bad hereditary material.[92] Homosexuals were thus a force for eugenic good.

Hirschfeld went on to do his own informal research on this. In 1927, the Fifth International Congress for Hereditary Science took place in Berlin, and he gave a paper.[93] The paper drew on his experience in determining the sex of people who had a condition called "hermaphroditism" (*Zwittertum*).[94] In private practice, he had been called in to consult in forty-four cases in which a patient had this condition. Most of the time Hirschfeld was called in because the patient had been given the wrong sex assignment – that is, the patient had been assigned male at birth, for example, but was in fact closer to female, doctors had decided. He considered these patients to be members of a subcategory within a category he called "intersexuality" (*Intersexualität*). "Intersexual variations" meant these conditions: "hermaphroditism, androgyny, transvestitism, metatrophism, and homosexuality."[95] The medicine of "hermaphroditism" in the late nineteenth and early twentieth centuries was confused, if one judges by contemporary standards. Some of the people defined as having "hermaphroditism" most likely had one of a variety of conditions that today are known as intersex. Some may have been trans individuals living as their self-confirmed sex. In any event, Hirschfeld noticed that a large number of the "hermaphroditic" patients he had seen – seventeen – were the products of marriages between close relatives.[96] Four of those were marriages between siblings. With respect to all of the conditions in the category of "intersexual" people, one often found incestuous marriages in the parental generation, or close relative marriages, he noted. Here, he assumed, one saw how forms of "intersexuality," including homosexuality and transvestitism, stopped bad hereditary material that had come into the family tree thanks to incestuous marriage. Homosexuality was not itself a defect. It was, rather, quite possibly nature's way of stopping degeneration. Nature intended homosexuals to be non-procreative so that homosexuals would "bleed off some of the current that would otherwise lead to degeneration, acting like the asexual blossoms of plants," Hirschfeld wrote in *The Homosexuality of Men and Women*, quoting von Römer and attributing the theory to him.[97]

Pressuring homosexuals into opposite-sex marriages, therefore, was a terrible idea, a violation of nature's intent. In Hirschfeld's day, doctors often proposed heterosexual marriage as a way to cure a person's homosexual feelings.[98] Racists and eugenicists often banned or tried to ban certain marriages on racial or eugenic grounds. Most of those bans made no sense, he wrote. One of the few that did make sense to him was a ban on the marriage of a homosexual person to a "sexually normal" person, though Hirschfeld stopped short of actually calling for such a ban.[99] Even for a homosexual to have "sex with a person of the other sex" was a dangerous thing, "eugenically speaking," and a threat to future "healthy generations."[100]

He was responding to a world in which, as he was all too well aware, many queer men and women married, some before they realized they were queer.[101] Though these marriages could be miserable, some people worked things out. Carl Van Vechten was happily married to a woman for many years while he had affairs with men on the side. The English sexologist Havelock Ellis was straight but married to a queer woman.[102] Hirschfeld insisted that the way forward was for homosexuals to remain unmarried. The modern homosexual would recognize him or herself as such and be single for life, having discreet same-sex relationships.

He was adamant that homosexuals not reproduce. To him this insight was part of homosexual emancipation. In Egypt he wrangled with the minister of health, Dr. Mohammed Shahin Pascha, who thought homosexuality was a disease that ought to be treated by doctors, not criminalized. Pascha believed in homosexual "seduction," broadly defined: he feared that Hirschfeld was increasing the instance of homosexuality by arguing in public that it was harmless. Hirschfeld, in typical fashion, stuck to his guns. Based on his vast experience with cases of homosexuality, he told Pascha,

> there is no way to medically cure homosexuality, and for the same reason, there is no way to artificially propagate it through seduction. Also, in view of a healthy future generation, from a eugenic standpoint sex between a homosexual and a person of the other sex involves more risks than does sex between two homosexuals.[103]

Lucien von Römer's tragically unappreciated contribution to science, Hirschfeld thought, was that he had theorized this final part. As a young scholar in Amsterdam around 1900, von Römer had been a brilliant researcher, Hirschfeld wrote.[104] His dissertation on homosexuality, which made the case for homosexuality as a eugenically beneficial and natural force, was rejected by the supervising faculty at his university, however, merely because it was on a sexological subject. Sex was so taboo that even to study it was impermissible; German-speaking scholarly circles at the time were unusually open in that respect, but not so the Dutch.[105]

The young von Römer "never in his life got over this rejection."[106] He moved into another career, securing a job as a colonial doctor, and left Europe. He was part of a wave of Dutch professionals – doctors, teachers, and others – who moved to colonial Indonesia around this time; they came for the good salaries and the luxury they could obtain in the colony.[107] Only in the colonies, for example, could these middle-class people afford a cook and a "house boy."[108] In Indonesia, von Römer married a white French woman and had a son, a son who by virtue of his white status qualified as a colonial elite, eligible for higher education while the vast majority of Indonesians and Chinese, who were classified legally as colonial subjects rather than citizens, were not.[109] At the time, Dutch rule in Indonesia was becoming more intense.[110] There had been rebellions in western Java and Sumatra in 1926 and 1927, which the Dutch put down with arrests, executions, and the internment of almost 5,000 people in a prison camp on Irian Jaya (New Guinea).[111]

Yet von Römer's scientific view of the world hampered his second career in colonial Indonesia. He was not racist enough to do well in the Dutch civil service. He thought Indonesians just as capable of cultural development as white Europeans.[112] This opinion kept him from being promoted, Hirschfeld reported, and he spent his career in remote backwaters like Bondowoso.[113]

The reunion of Hirschfeld and his former student was a happy one. "The days I spent in quiet, beautiful Bondowoso in von Römer's home – the home of a scholar – were filled with magical charm." Aside from the servants it was an intimate gathering, "a small circle" of only von Römer, his wife, his son Djayo, Li, Hirschfeld, and an additional guest – a friend of von Römer's from Sumatra, a Malaysian man named Mansoer. They ate meals together and talked. Mrs. von Römer played the piano. The mood, Hirschfeld recalled, was "luscious" and "panhumanistic," by which he seems to have meant racially diverse and antiracist. I assume in this house Li and Hirschfeld could be more open about their relationship than they would in most places, such as in Nehru's house.[114]

One wonders who among that contented company was queer. Was von Römer? His early membership in the Scientific Humanitarian Committee and his career-ending choice to write his dissertation on sexuality, including homosexuality, makes me wonder if he was. A very few (and maybe none) of the men who staked their careers on homosexual emancipation in the early twentieth century were not themselves queer, because it took an overriding interest to take such a risk and usually that was a self-interest. Many of those men married and had children. Who was Mansoer? A visiting friend, or something more? If von Römer thought himself a homosexual, why did he have a child, given his theories about degeneration? Ever aware of such things, Hirschfeld seems have decided that Djayo was eugenically fit, because he calls him "handsome" and "clever."[115] Perhaps von Römer was not homosexual; or perhaps he had had a child despite his theory.

Von Römer brought Hirschfeld into his library and took down a copy of his rejected dissertation. It was probably the world's sole copy. That unpublished book was so important, Hirschfeld thought. It ought to be on the shelves of "all of the major libraries of the world," but thanks to unscientific prejudice, it languished here in a remote corner of the Dutch empire. Speaking of the dissertation, von Römer remarked that perhaps it would be a "valuable heritage [*Erbstück*]" for his son.[116] That is, a dissertation that showed, among other things I assume, that homosexuals were like the asexual blossoms of plants was among the good hereditary things the doctor – possibly himself queer – would pass to his son. Whatever exactly was the elaborate interplay of theory, conviction, desire, politics, and love – romantic and paternal – in the life of this Dutch doctor on Java, I cannot say. To Hirschfeld, von Römer was a tragically thwarted advocate of antiracism, eugenics, and homosexual emancipation.

In eugenics, Hirschfeld saw hope for homosexual liberation. In this he worked against an anti-queer discourse that prevailed across the twentieth century. It denigrated queers as anti-child and anti-future. He did not, however, work against that discourse in the way that early twenty-first-century queer theory wanted to do, that is by embracing it.[117] Rather, he slotted homosexuals neatly into a eugenic worldview, making them definitively non-reproductive and yet pro-child and pro-future. It was a worldview that moreover opposed racism, or so he believed. Eugenics and biological inequity were at the center of his vision of a better world, for queers and for everyone.

10 "And What about Women?"

"And what about women?" the reporters on the ship in Manila Bay in 1931 asked Hirschfeld, as if half the human population was an afterthought, though one seemingly uttered with breathless anticipation.[1] The ancillary manner in which the reporters posed the woman question happened to coincide with the way Hirschfeld saw the world. Women are missing from "homosexuality" as he defined it – or rather, he includes them in it, but it's an uncomfortable fit.[2] The model leaves no space for an analysis of sexism or of how racialized gender worked in concert with anti-homosexual animus. While women of color are pushed aside by the implicit whiteness of "the homosexual," even in Hirschfeld's day elite white European women did not fit well under its mantle and often did not make much use of it. Hirschfeld noticed this. He wrote in *Racism* that he was once serving as an expert witness in a court case and the judge asked a witness if she was homosexual. She said she was a lesbian, not a homosexual, because she thought "homosexual" only applied to men. Many people shared that misinterpretation, Hirschfeld wrote.[3]

Was it a misinterpretation? Hirschfeld thought so. He argued that "homosexuality" was uniform across the divide between male and female, just as he argued it effortlessly crossed divisions of race and civilization.[4] At the same time, he admitted that female homosexuality was opaque to him. There just was not good data. He had statistics based on painstaking documentation of male homosexuality, but it was possible they did not apply to women. He concluded, however, that female-female desire must be just as common, though far less public and therefore harder to perceive.[5] Another way to put this is that he had not bothered to really study female homosexuality. As many other authors have noted, he had little to say about homosexual women, and the male-dominated science of sexology often ignored them.[6] Women were an afterthought in Hirschfeld's work on homosexuality. He would write pages and pages about male homosexuality in various parts of the globe, then put in a paragraph about how female homosexuality, too, was common, just as common, the less-interesting mirror image of male homosexuality.[7]

The sciences were all but closed to women in Hirschfeld's lifetime. The sex reform movement was more open, but there was, as the radical leftist feminist Helene Stöcker pointed out at the 1930 conference of the WLSR, a problem with the "masculine" approach taken by men in the field of sex research.[8] Female researchers worked to rectify it.[9] It was not easy for them – women taking an interest in sexual matters risked their reputations in a way that men did not, and moreover, their male colleagues largely dismissed them, preferring to see women as research subjects, not intellectual collaborators.[10] Women had more luck in psychoanalysis than in sexology – by the 1930s the two had developed into distinct and rival fields.[11] Hirschfeld almost never cites female sexologists.[12] As his biographer Charlotte Wolff, herself queer and a sexologist, notes, Hirschfeld argued in print on several occasions that generally, men were smarter than women (he meant white men and white women).[13]

At the same time, he did chronicle the lives of queer women. Not many other authors did. For example, here is a story of people who may have been butch lesbians or trans men in Tianjin, China, in 1931. Li and Hirschfeld took a short trip to see that city. They were welcomed at the train station by "Dr. R.," a German who was perhaps a holdover from the German mini-colony (or concession) that had existed in the city prior to the First World War. There were still Japanese, English, and French concessions, districts where the foreign powers were legally sovereign, similar to Shanghai's International District (with the difference being that these zones in Tianjin were ruled by foreign states, not by a council of expatriates that was independent of any nation-state, as was the unique situation in Shanghai). Dr. R. took them on a tour in his car. He was quite genial, but the talk got to politics and Li and Hirschfeld learned that the doctor was the sole official member of the Nazi Party in Tianjin. From the doctor's car they saw museums, the Catholic mission, and the foreign concessions. Evening found them touring sailors' and soldiers' bars, perhaps hobnobbing, as they seem to have done happily with some sailors in Peking in 1931 (figure 5). Around the world in the 1930s, sailors, "young and manly, unattached and unconstrained by conventional morality," at least in the queer imaginary, were often involved in queer urban subcultures.[14] Li and Hirschfeld also peeked in on bordellos where Korean, Russian, Japanese, and Chinese women sold sex. This was Hirschfeld and Li's world tour, after all: they had to see the city's sex district. (Hirschfeld probably did that in most places he visited. It was his research. Later, in his own travels after Hirschfeld's death, Li may have emulated this method.) Then, they went to play mini golf. Li was probably good at mini golf – he was a sporting type, a good swimmer and driver. To Hirschfeld, mini golf was as American as jazz. It was at the mini golf course that they saw the lesbians (or trans men). Among the other golfers were "rakish Chinese women in men's clothing" who were courting women.[15]

Yet almost all of Hirschfeld's close professional contacts were male. Women often gave talks at the WLSR's Congresses, but the Scientific Humanitarian Committee was an almost universally all-male affair.[16] All the doctors and scientists who had offices at the Institute for Sexual Science were male. He hoped at one point that a female scientist who had ties to Margaret Sanger, Sidonie Fürst Chiavacci, would join the Institute, but she did not.[17] Historians have given him credit for collaborations with other prominent women, but I doubt that any of these were substantial. He listed women, including Sanger and the Soviet sex radical Aleksandra Kollontai, on his letterhead as leading members of the World League for Sexual Reform. As far as I can tell, that was for show, to make the group look bigger and more important (Sanger and Kollontai were famous), not to make it look more gender-diverse, which would not have been a concern at the time. Neither Kollontai nor Sanger were substantially involved in the WLSR, if they were involved at all.[18] Sanger apparently visited the Institute on a 1920 trip to Berlin and met Hirschfeld several times, including later in New York during his world tour, and he visited some of her clinics in the United States.[19] She, however, did not want to be involved with his WLSR or to have him closely involved with her international campaign for birth control because of his homosexuality, and possibly because he was Jewish, as I discussed earlier.[20] She wrote in a 1928 letter to a colleague that Hirschfeld had asked her to be on the WLSR's International Committee and she had said no – she did not want a visible tie to a known homosexual.[21] Sanger was nevertheless listed as a member of the International Committee in 1928 and was on the letterhead in 1930.[22] Did she change her mind, or did Hirschfeld just throw her name on there anyway, figuring she would never know? I suspect the latter. In any event, Sanger had nothing to do with the WLSR or Hirschfeld's other projects.

Historians sometimes give Hirschfeld feminist credit for a partnership with Helene Stöcker, the leftist Berliner and radical feminist, but I suspect that that professional connection did not run very deep, though Stöcker did work in the WLSR – she gave a paper at the group's 1928 conference. At least in the 1920s and 1930s, Stöcker and Hirschfeld were fellow travelers who nominally supported each other's causes. Hirschfeld sometimes contributed to Stöcker's journal. Hirschfeld was also listed as a founding member of what came to be Stöcker's radical feminist group, and Stöcker is named as a chairperson of Hirschfeld's WhK.[23] I suspect this was more for appearances than because either played a real leadership role in the other's group, or at least that seems to have been the case in the period I have examined, which is post-1918. See Hirschfeld's cursory statement about Stöcker in his history of homosexual emancipation – he puts her name in a list of famous women he has met and has nothing else to say about her.[24] He did however write that Stöcker was mentally superior to the average man, while most women were not.[25]

Hirschfeld's social world appears to have been nearly entirely male as well. Women were peripheral, aside from being patients, such as the woman he recommended for forced sterilization on account of her unladylike behavior. In his daily life he had little to do with women aside from his sisters and his housekeeper.

At the same time, Hirschfeld supported women's rights, explicitly so, and criticized misogyny.[26] The equality of men and women was the first plank in the WLSR's platform, and that organization had prominent female members.[27] Feminists saw him as an ally. Many decades after he died, Dora Russell lauded his dedication to "the complete equality of men and women."[28] He also had a very progressive theory of sexual difference for his day, arguing that every individual was a unique mixture of male and female characteristics and that "every person is first and foremost a person, and only secondarily a male person or a female person."[29] In *World Journey*, he writes about this. He also writes about feminists he met on his tour and women's groups he spoke to, such as the feminists in Shanghai on the day he met Li. As Heike Bauer shows, however, he almost never quotes these feminists.[30] He has his less inspiring moments as well, such as in a passage Bauer discusses, when he comments on the good looks of female students and professors in Delhi and not much else.[31] "It was a delightful sight," he found, to look out at the audience of female faculty and students at the Lady Hardinge Medical College for women in Delhi, one of the only institutions in India where a woman could get a medical degree, and to see the large lecture hall "filled with good-looking female students in their Indian costumes, who followed my lecture intently." He was a bit disturbed that many of them were knitting as they listened, he admitted.[32] Women are not intellectual interlocutors, in his world.

Hirschfeld also pulled up short of entirely breaking with patriarchy. This will sound familiar; it is very like his thinking on "the races." Despite his rousing statements about gender being a continuum, he kept associating some characteristics with women and others with men. Most women, he wrote, were childish, reproductive, practical, while most men were more active and given to abstract thought.[33] This distinction was exactly what a lot of theorists of sexual difference thought at the time – women were irrational and emotional, men rational. Helene Stöcker and many others were articulating a far more robust feminism, and he ignored it. (Stöcker's position on homosexuality was actually not as liberatory as was Hirschfeld's, though she opposed the sodomy law.)[34] Around 1900 a critic, Martha Asmus, published against this part of Hirschfeld's theory, calling on him to give up on the idea that there were such things as intrinsically, or usually, male or female characteristics (even if he argued that everyone was on a continuum and that some men had many feminine characteristics).[35] He did not give those ideas up. He went on to argue in *The Transvestites* (1910) that women probably did not have the abilities required to author masterworks of art or science, not because they were oppressed but because they just did not have the brainpower.[36] One cannot but think of the passage of his about how the brains of African Americans (men and women) and (white) women were all stunted.[37] Hirschfeld's defenders might call this a "misstep," to quote Herzer, and remind us of his more inspiring statements about gender equality.[38] But Hirschfeld did not think everyone was born equal.[39] He believed that sex was a physical and hormonal difference between people that determined character.[40] Moreover, if it is you the reader being condemned as inferior for all intents and purposes – for example, because you are a South Asian woman – you tend not to overlook such statements and rather to put the book down and to seek help elsewhere. If Hirschfeld was a feminist, he was a bad feminist.

What is more important than Hirschfeld's bad feminism is the bad feminism of "the homosexual" as a conceptual model. The model makes sexism a separate issue from the troubles facing people with queer desires. Yet sexism was not a separate issue. Women who wanted to be with other women were in a profoundly different position than were men who wanted to be with other men.[41] To consider white European women and men only, well past the 1930s, sexism worked so profoundly to open up opportunities for queer men and to shut them down for queer women that it would have been hard to have a joint political movement. As terrible as sodomy laws were, into the 1930s women faced something similar that is never discussed in male homosexual emancipationists thought: unless they inherited wealth or joined a convent, many could not avoid marriage to men and the obligation to have sex with one's husband, a legal obligation backed by the full force of the state. The 1970s were just the beginning of the end of legal marital rape – not until the early 1990s was it illegal for a husband to force his wife to have sex in all parts of the United States.[42] This was literal compulsory heterosexuality.[43] Histories of queer women have shown how, in other respects, women and men were not at all in similar positions.[44] Bauer, drawing on Adrianne Rich, makes the same point in a masterful analysis of Hirschfeld's myopic thoughts on lesbian suicide. Incredibly, he was not able to see why queer women might take their lives, since they were not oppressed by the sodomy law as men were.[45]

I don't think it ought to be any wonder that Hirschfeld's theories have not been taken up by lesbian feminism. When Hirschfeld was rediscovered by activist gay Berlin university students in the 1970s, female gay activist students quickly broke off and formed their own group because they thought there was no way to have solidarity with the gay male students who were interested in Hirschfeld and inspired by his theories. This is according to Herzer, who was one of those male students and later became a major Hirschfeld scholar. In his biography of Hirschfeld, he tells this story, that the lesbian activists saw all men as the oppressors and rejected solidarity with gay men, refusing to see that gay men were oppressed as well; they turned away from Hirschfeld and toward lesbian feminist writers, though, Herzer notes, Hirschfeld did think gender was a continuum, like they did.[46] I would add that Hirschfeld offers little to lesbian feminism. He did not think gender was socially constructed; he thought it was essential, and though he had gender as a continuum, he tied certain traits to an essential femininity. He was not, as he is sometimes called in Magnus Hirschfeld studies, a precursor to social constructionism.

Moreover, for people assigned female at birth, he is an off-putting read. There is lots in Hirschfeld that telegraphs his sexist disinterest or paternalism against white women, his racist sexism against women of color, and his occasional misogyny – as one sees in his letter about women's shipboard antics on the voyage to New York that I quoted at the beginning of chapter 1, for example. The women he watched on the ship looked to him like caricatures, one a "tart," one a "mummy" (as in ancient Egypt). The dressed-up women were "a true orgy of narcissism, exhibitionism and fetishism," while the men in their tuxes rouse Hirschfeld to no commentary at all.[47]

Thinking about queerness without thinking about sexism made little practical or intellectual sense to lesbian feminists. One can see why.

Some ten years after students at Berlin's Freie Universität (FU) began to rediscover Hirschfeld, Black German feminists in Berlin, some of them queer, found inspiration in the American poet Audre Lorde, who taught at the FU and visited Berlin on and off from 1984 to 1992, forming close ties with German lesbian activists.[48] One of Lorde's students at the FU in a seminar on African American literature was Katharina

Oguntoye, who found Lorde's teaching transforming and inspiring, particularly in the ways Lorde confronted and analyzed racism.[49] Oguntoye went on to publish one of the first academic histories of Afro-Germans and to work in Black and feminist activist groups.[50]

Audre Lorde's fight was against racism, sexism, imperialism, and homophobia all at once. Tiffany Florvil writes that during a seminar at the FU in 1984, "Lorde remarked, 'As I say as a 49 year old Black feminist lesbian socialist mother of two, including a boy, there is always something wrong with me, there is always some group of people who define me as wrong. It is very encouraging, I learn a lot about myself and my identities that way.'"[51] Lorde learned, and taught, a lot about systems of oppression, too. She wrote in 1978 that racism, sexism, heterosexism, and homophobia all "stem from the same root – the inability to recognize or tolerate the notion of difference as a beneficial and dynamic human force, and one which is enriching rather than threatening to the defined self."[52]

Lorde and Hirschfeld have a tenuous connection beyond having both been happy and queer in Berlin. Both knew Langston Hughes, who went out of his way to help Lorde early in her career.[53] In 1964, Hughes published Lorde's poems in an anthology. (Incidentally, she thought he was queer.)[54] Lorde grew up in Harlem in the decades after Hirschfeld came to town and would go on to be an important Black lesbian feminist, not only in the United States but in Germany too.[55] To my knowledge, she never cites Hirschfeld. Her thoughts on queerness differ markedly from his. His theory is not all that useful to people for whom the fight against queer oppression is always already a fight against sexism and racism.

11 The Exile

Athens to Nice, 1932–1935

On March 17, 1932, Li and Hirschfeld reached Europe, arriving in Athens, most likely by ship.[1] When Li joined the world tour in Shanghai the year before, both men expected they would end the journey in Berlin, where Li would become a sexologist, completing his medical degree at the university and working under Hirschfeld's tutelage at the Institute for Sexual Science. Instead, Greece began years of insecurity and frustration, as European sexology crumbled under the pressure of the rising far right and Hirschfeld dodged anti-homosexual animus and homicidal antisemitism (see map 2).

The story of the exile has been told before, but never from Li's perspective. Hirschfeld seems to have been closer to Li than to anyone else during those years, and Li's choices speak to his devotion to his mentor. Yet the relationship, and Hirschfeld's dying wish, put Li into a bind.

In Athens they were met by Karl Giese, the man who had been Hirschfeld's lover for some fifteen years.[2] One hopes that Hirschfeld had already told Giese about his relationship with Li by letter. Probably the meeting did not go as badly as one might imagine. It was not a monogamous relationship, Hirschfeld and Giese's.[3]

Though Giese is often called Hirschfeld's partner (so is Li), neither was a "partner" to Hirschfeld in today's sense of the term. The relationships had a different shape. Giese and Hirschfeld lived together, discreetly, for years. Giese looked after "Papa," as he called him.[4] Hirschfeld also saw himself as a father figure to Li. Li's father "entrusted his son to me."[5] The pattern was a teacher-pupil or father-son relationship, not a marriage. The much younger Giese was Hirschfeld's heir and, at least in theory, his student (it is unclear to what extent he studied with Hirschfeld and he does not seem to have been at work on a degree). Giese was not, however, an intellectual or professional equal. He was never a player in sexual politics in Germany or in the sex reform movement abroad. He worked at the Institute, but not as a scientist.

The Giese-Hirschfeld relationship may have been sexless, with Giese having affairs on the side. Biographers of Hirschfeld tend to think this possible.[6] I think it more likely that Hirschfeld and Giese both had affairs outside of the relationship, with the other's consent. There are too many hints that Hirschfeld liked to flirt with younger men. Before Hirschfeld left on his world journey, he seems to perhaps have been having a second affair with another man who worked at the Institute as his personal attendant, Franz Wimmer.[7] One can tell from Hirschfeld's journal that Giese was jealous of Wimmer – though it is not clear why he was jealous – and that his jealousy frustrated Hirschfeld.[8] Giese himself had another erotic partner, according to one account.[9] People in the world of leftist sex reform (notably Dora Russell) were advocates of non-monogamous heterosexual marriages.

Happily for Hirschfeld, the two younger men and "heirs" seem to have gotten along. In his journal, Hirschfeld never complains of tension between them like what apparently existed between Giese and Wimmer. Giese wrote of Li in a letter a few months after Hirschfeld died, "he is very nice and chummy to me."[10] For his part, Li could be so polite, charming, and nonconfrontational that he could probably get along with just about anyone.[11] Or perhaps not. "Aunt Magnesia has once again arranged for glorious nuisance [*Unfug*] in Paris," a snarky acquaintance of Hirschfeld's gossiped in a letter to friends, using an insulting Hirschfeld nickname. "He's living now with both flames (Tao and Karlchen). And the best part is, both of them are soooo jealous about the old geezer. Now if that's not true love?!"[12] I suspect this letter writer was just having a nasty laugh at the expense of the three men; they seem to have gotten along remarkably well.

In Athens, even if the meeting of the two "students" was a success, other things did not go as planned. For what appears to be the first time in any city on the world tour, the local press attacked Hirschfeld. It was a menace he already feared – the growing power of antisemitic political rhetoric in Europe. He spoke to a medical society a few days after he and Li arrived. The audience included everyone who was anyone on the local scientific scene.[13] Shortly after that first lecture, a far-right daily newspaper went after him.[14] Hirschfeld was a "supposed Professor, who has degraded science to the lowest point," and smart observers knew "what strange kinds of depravity are hidden under the transparent veil of the so-called sexual science and the Institute for sexual research, established by this 'Professor' in Berlin."[15] Distinguished people defended

Hirschfeld in another newspaper: "All Greek scientists who have studied in Europe know the value of the famous Institute for Sexual Science."[16] The president of a medical society called Hirschfeld "one of the most distinguished contemporary scientists and researchers on the issues of sexology."[17] One gets a sense of the strength of his reputation here, as well as of its weaknesses. The far-right paper hit back with an editorial that called Hirschfeld's work, specifically his advocacy for homosexual emancipation, "Jewish propaganda" intended to "shake one of the pillars of Christian morality."[18] Hirschfeld thought it was Germans who had stirred this up, German antisemites reaching into Greece, perhaps Nazis.[19]

He and Li soon went on to Vienna, but antisemites went after him in the press there too.[20] What was worse: in Vienna he got letters threatening to kill him, apparently from antisemites back in Germany.[21] He was frightened. Even the previous winter, he had foreseen the Nazi takeover that was to come in January 1933, and friends had been warning him since 1931 not to return to Berlin.[22] Hirschfeld was unusual in this respect, a special target of the fascists. Most German Jews did not try to leave the country until after the Nazis took power, and even then, at first most decided to stay, expecting Hitler to be out of office in a few years.[23] No doubt Hirschfeld was thinking of the attack he had suffered at the hands of antisemites years before. Many decades after Hirschfeld died, Li wrote of that attack, of how the antisemites tried to slit Hirschfeld's throat and he sustained a severe wound on the back of his neck; perhaps Hirschfeld told Li about this during the exile, and perhaps Li saw the scar on his neck.[24]

One wonders if Hirschfeld was getting death threats in 1932 because in May of that year, a top Nazi, Ernst Röhm, was outed. Decades earlier, Hirschfeld had been called in during a libel trial involving accusations of homosexuality against a top advisor to the kaiser and had publicly testified that the man in question was indeed a homosexual, causing much uproar. Did Nazis fear he would do something similar about Röhm, who indeed belonged to one of the homosexual emancipation groups (though not Hirschfeld's)? There were moreover rumors that Hirschfeld's Institute held incriminating evidence about homosexual Nazis. Li thought as much. He wrote, "Dr. Hirschfeld' Institute of Sexual Science had the record of sexual type of the Nazi leaders his secretaries destroyed all the records in fear of implication which death to them one day Hitler order to burn all the books and papers in the Institute publicly in a bonfire."[25] Li was not the only person close to Hirschfeld who believed there were incriminating papers about Nazis at the Institute. I am not sure there really were. The Nazis did burn the Institute's archive, but they were not in a hurry; it was months after they took power that they sacked the Institute. What is certain is that Hirschfeld had long been a favorite stalking horse of the far right. In April 1932, staying in a hotel in Vienna, Hirschfeld wrote to Harry Benjamin that he would not go to Germany at present, what with its thirteen million Hitler backers.[26] (Sadly, that was a considerable understatement of Hitler's popularity at the time.)[27]

But Hirschfeld was not sure where to go. For about a year, he and Li moved from hotel to rental to hotel, from Vienna to Zurich to Ascona, Switzerland, on the shores of Lake Maggiore, where he stayed at the storied Monte Verità, a hilltop complex founded at the turn of the century as a vegetarian, nudist, socialist artist colony; in the 1930s it was a hotel.[28] Their time there and in Zurich seems to have held happy memories. Hirschfeld gradually resigned himself to never going back to Germany, but Li was there with him; perhaps he was a comfort.[29] In Hirschfeld's scrapbook/guest book, a record of his exile, there is a page devoted to him and Li in Switzerland. "Memories of Easter in Switzerland … 1933 in our cottage in Ascona," reads a caption on a photograph of Hirschfeld and Li together on a balcony with a view out onto the lake. In a second picture, captioned "1933 under clouds on the Zürichberg," Li is alone on a hilltop, assumedly the one named in the caption, which is just east of Zurich. Written in English on the photograph is this sentence: "I wish I could see our home from the top of this mountain but Alas! I see nothing but clouds."[30] The language about "our cottage" and "our home" suggests mutual love and a sense of having made a home together. The mixture of German and English on the page also speaks to their particular relationship – they probably mostly spoke English together, though Li's German got better and better.

Hirschfeld was writing *World Journey of a Sexologist*. He knew, I assume, that it would make money. He worked steadily, often in Li's company.[31] He also took many side trips, such as to the Czechoslovakian spa towns of Karlovy Vary (Karlsbad) and Marianske Lazne (Marienbad). For some months, Li and Hirschfeld were together in Zurich, with Hirschfeld at work on his "travel book" while Li helped.[32] Werner Vordtriede, who was then a student at the University of Zurich and later a friend of Li's, remembered that Li and Hirschfeld had customary places in the university library, where they worked side by side, with Li acting as Hirschfeld's "secretary."[33] Li may have been attending classes in Zurich as well. Hirschfeld intended to work out a plan for Li's future once *World Journey* was finished.[34]

Around this time, Li finally got to Berlin, to the Institute. He went without Hirschfeld. There is no surviving record of the trip save for a photograph. It is of Li and Giese on the Institute's grounds, side by side and smiling, probably taken sometime in 1932. Li is holding a little dog in the photograph. He must have gotten a dog when they reached Europe. He had also bought a car. He must have driven to Berlin with the animal. In his guest book/scrapbook, Hirschfeld has the following caption written under the photograph: "Karl G. and Tao L. in front of our Berlin Institute" (figure 11).[35] Around this time, Li enrolled at the University of Vienna, to study medicine.[36] In his unpublished manuscript, he sketches a happy student life there. He got to know a professor, he hung out at cafes, and he even chatted with Freud about "Chinese dogs" – Freud had one, Li writes.[37] (Freud had Chow Chows.) This does not match Hirschfeld's journal entries, which show Hirschfeld mostly living in Switzerland in 1932–3; they must have spent time apart.

The 1932–3 wanderings in central Europe held out the chance, to Li, that his ambitions could be fulfilled after all. Though Hirschfeld was in a bad spot, he was still among the world's leading sexologists, he was still at work, and Li could do his medical studies in Vienna, or perhaps in Zurich. There was a high point in September 1932 when Li gave a paper with Hirschfeld at the Congress of the World League for Sexual Reform in Brno, Czechoslovakia.[38] To give a joint paper with the WLSR's president was prestigious for Li. He must have been pleased.

To my knowledge no copy of their paper survives, but according to a report on the Congress, the paper was noteworthy as the first extensive discussion of "research on intersexuality [*Intersexualitätsforschung*]," and the two men argued that with regard to both homosexuality and intersexuality, both "disposition and environment [*Anlage und Lage*]" were important. Both conditions, they argued, were in need of "liberation for those affected from severe and antiquated laws."[39] In his other work Hirschfeld used the term "intersexual variations [*intersexuelle Varianten*]" to mean the "large number of sexual types who fall on a range between the extremes of fully masculine [*Vollmännern*] and fully feminine [*Vollweibern*]. In that range one finds a great diversity of hybrids with male and female characteristics."[40] Elsewhere he writes that the category includes "hermaphroditism, androgyny, transvestitism, metatrophism, and homosexuality."[41] So Li and Hirschfeld's paper, in what seems a curious turn, separates "intersexuality" from "homosexuality," whereas in Hirschfeld's earlier work, intersexuality contained homosexuality. It is not clear what this meant, and sadly the paper is gone, but it seems possible that their paper distinguishes what we might call gender fluidity or what we might call transness from homosexuality – something Hirschfeld had already done, crucially, in his 1910 book *Transvestites*. The importance of "environment," I assume, was not about the source of same-sex desire – surely in this paper, Hirschfeld was not breaking with his biological model, the core of his entire career; in his subsequent work (his last book, *Racism*) he did not. Li, however, eventually did. In his unpublished manuscript, Li also held that transness was important; perhaps that interest was reflected in this paper. The old sexologist and the young one had written something together.

There is a photograph of Li and Hirschfeld in Brno, in Hirschfeld's hotel room. (It is reproduced here as figure 1.) The photographer was Edward Elkan, a doctor from Hamburg who had given a paper on orgasm at the conference. Elkan, who was Jewish, would soon have to flee Germany. In the photograph, Li and Hirschfeld are sitting on a sofa together. Hirschfeld was already ill with the malaria flare that would cut his time in Brno short, it seems – Elkan reported (erroneously) that he was near death. Writing decades later, Elkan seems to have known Hirschfeld had a relationship with Giese, but he did not know that Hirschfeld and Li were intimates and did not remember Li's name. He wrote on the back of the photograph that Li was "a visiting Chinese doctor."[42] Hirschfeld and Elkan were just as much visitors in Czechoslovakia as was Li; Elkan, I assume, read Li's being Chinese as disqualifying him from belonging in Europe, as many white Europeans did. Yet Elkan also did Li a favor after the fact – Li was not yet a doctor in reality.

Having their picture taken, Li and Hirschfeld both seem happy in the company of the other. Their bodies are inclined toward each other, though they are not touching. Hirschfeld is looking at Li. Li is looking off, beyond Hirschfeld, smiling a somewhat tentative smile. Hirschfeld's body seems relaxed; Li's less so. Is Hirschfeld content and confident in his love for his student, while Li is conflicted, looking off to something beyond his teacher? Was Li worried about Hirschfeld's health?[43]

The bright moment at the Congress, with Li a junior sexologist and Hirschfeld the gray eminence, did not last. The malaria flare that came upon Hirschfeld there was bad: high fevers, things Hirschfeld termed "heart attacks."[44] They left to get him treated in Vienna. Li drove him, I assume. Li was Hirschfeld's main caregiver through this illness, as he had been on the world journey; Hirschfeld wrote in his journal about this malarial spell, "mainstay: Tao Li."[45] Hirschfeld was very sick that winter.[46] He kept working on the travel book and finished it in Zurich in 1933.[47] More and more, he did not feel safe where he was. He digested the horrible news from Germany – the Nazi takeover, the colleagues, like Max Hodann and Kurt Hiller, now thrown into concentration camps, the Institute's future bleak.[48] Friends warned him to put more distance between himself and the fascists. One person sounding a warning may have been the feminist Helene Stöcker, who escaped to Switzerland and seems to have gone to see him; she and Hirschfeld both feared for their imprisoned colleagues Hodann and Hiller.[49] Back in Germany, Hirschfeld's sisters were thrown out of their house.[50] Their fates were grim, though both outlived Hirschfeld: one, Recha Tobias, was deported from Berlin to Theresienstadt, where she died in 1942, a victim of the Holocaust, as were other family members.[51]

With Hitler in power as of January 1933, to Hirschfeld all of German-speaking Europe felt unsafe.[52] A harrowing moment came in the spring of 1933, when he went to see a movie and, apparently on the newsreel before the main feature, he saw footage of Nazi students in Berlin looting the Institute. Then, the newsreel showed the Nazis holding a public burning of his library and a bust of himself. He sat in the dark theater "under the deepest psychic shock."[53] Not long after, he learned the Berlin police had shut the Institute and seized his bank accounts, and that one of the Institute's main administrators had joined the Nazis.[54]

Li describes a death threat, then panicked flight together from Vienna in a taxi, with Hirschfeld hidden, lying on the car's floor.[55] This may be fiction (see chapter 12) or not. It dovetails with another thing that did happen: Li and Giese snuck Hirschfeld across the border from Zurich into France in May 1933. Hirschfeld's passport had expired and he had well-grounded fears that German authorities would refuse to renew it; this made it necessary to sneak him into France.[56] Hirschfeld does not explain how they did this, but it seems like Giese and Li drove him to the border in Li's car, then he got out of the car and a Swiss friend brought him over, bypassing border control somehow, and then Li, whose passport was good, met him with the car again in Strasbourg. "Then Tao drove me to Paris," Hirschfeld wrote in his journal.[57]

Paris offered hope. Hirschfeld made a deal with a French publisher to bring out several of his books in French, with the books excerpted at the same time in the publisher's two popular magazines, one of which was *Voilà*, which ran a splashy multi-issue feature on Hirschfeld in the summer of 1933. *Voilà* put a portrait of him and Li on its cover (figure 10). The book contract put him on better financial footing.[58] The French were friendly, he wrote to Harry Benjamin – they were going to republish the books of his that the Germans had burned.[59] He thought he might be safe in France.[60] He went about re-founding his Institute there, announcing in the spring of 1934 that he had done so, dubbing the new iteration the Institut des Sciences Sexologiques.[61] He took Li to London in fall 1933 for a few days and hobnobbed with his fellow queer, Jewish sexologist Norman Haire, and other members of the WLSR.[62]

To Li, however, even with a French Institute, Paris was an interruption. "It was difficult for me to use my third foreign language to study medicine," he wrote in his unpublished manuscript.[63] To enroll at a French university he also would have needed to first retake his BA in French, which would have forced him to earn a French high school certificate: it was not a real option.[64] With Hirschfeld in Paris, he went home to China to see his family, on an epic journey by train via Moscow.[65] He was gone for about three months.[66] He came back by ship, to Venice, in February 1934, and Hirschfeld met him there. "10 days in magical Venice," the older man wrote.[67] Hirschfeld went back to France, and Li seems to have gone with him, abandoning, for now, his ambitions to go to medical school. Li had had a horrible time leaving his family in Hong Kong on this second occasion. They did not want him to go back to Europe. I assume he had explained to them that Hirschfeld, the famous scientist with whom he was supposed to train, was now struggling in exile, his Institute destroyed, but that he would finish medical school at a European university nevertheless. Hirschfeld wrote that Li was in "severe conflict" with his family because he had left to return to Europe and that as a result "he does not want to part from me."[68] Li's decision to come back when he could very well have gone back to Shanghai and finished up his studies there probably demonstrates what he felt for Hirschfeld; it also shows his determination to live in Europe.

Then, in summer 1934, the Paris rebuilding, too, came crashing down, when the police caught Karl Giese having sex in a bathhouse. He was convicted of public indecency (*outrage public à la pudeur*), sent to prison for three months, and then kicked out of the country.[69] Those events must have been a devastating blow to Giese and to those around him, including Hirschfeld, and Li as well. They had to move again. Hirschfeld wrote later that he left Paris because of what had befallen Giese, for which he in no way blamed his lover; it was "an unlucky circumstance," it was "horrible … the most acute injustice"; three months in prison for "a meaningless trifle … after Karl was expelled … I would not stay in Paris any longer."[70] It was also a blow to Hirschfeld's reputation and may have compromised his new Institute in Paris and his collaborations there, though it did not jeopardize his book contract. To be publicly associated with someone with such a conviction on their record could affect one's own reputation. It surely did not help that some months before, a prominent German sex researcher had denounced Hirschfeld to French colleagues, claiming Hirschfeld had fled Germany because he was wanted there for moral crimes.[71] Driven from Berlin by a fascist animosity born of fury about queerness and "racial enemies," Hirschfeld had now been driven from Paris by the French state's policing of homosexuality, ostensibly irrespective of "race." Li wrote later that "Paris was again not safe for him[;] we went to Nice where he died."[72]

December 1934 found Hirschfeld at the Hotel Mediterranean in Nice. There, he faced the last major choice of his life. He sat in the winter light in the hotel suite he was happily sharing with Li, rooms that looked out on the gorgeous sea, which lifted his spirits, and he laid it all out in a very long journal entry. He had reached "the beginning of the last chapter of my life."[73] He liked Nice, the ocean, the sun, and the friends he had there. Nice probably had a queer scene; it had one after the Second World War.[74] His financial situation was improved thanks to the contract to publish his books in French.[75] But should he stay? Giese was now banned from France, and Hirschfeld was reconciled to seeing him only infrequently, at least for the time being, or so he wrote.[76] But Hirschfeld worried about his own chances of getting a long-term visa in France. He had been on month-to-month visas.[77] And then there was Li. Hirschfeld wrote in his journal:

> My Chinese student and friend T.L. … does not want to part from me; his return journey from China to Europe brought him into severe conflict with his family – they did not want to let him leave. Also I am highly reluctant to do without his true devotion and his for the most part very charming company (which however is not seldom disrupted by quite temperamental, nearly hysterical petulance). On the whole, I could not have a more beloved, sunnier, more helpful person around me. On the other side of the matter, I think (and he thinks himself) that an exam for him in France would be extremely difficult because of the language. He inclines toward America, to Columbia or Harvard University, and very much wants to have me with him (even at his own cost). I have trepidation about deciding for the USA – the tempo there, etc. Next year all will be decided: Nice or New York. Time will tell [*Qui vivra vera*].[78]

He was in love with Li. He loved Giese too, surely, but it was Li whom he now felt he could perhaps not live without. They were, however, at a serious impasse. Li could study in German or English, but not French. Hirschfeld could not live near a German-speaking university. Li had an idea – they could all go to America; he would pay for Hirschfeld to come with him. America might not be a bad place for Giese either, Hirschfeld thought, and maybe not such a bad place for himself.

Hirschfeld had been thinking of emigrating to the United States for some time. He had first tried to arrange a second lecture tour there, but that did not work out, in part because almost no lecture tour managers in the US would agree to represent such a taboo-breaking speaker.[79] (This is a fascinating piece of evidence that I am not sure how to read: Had attitudes changed so drastically in the US since his first tour? Had his reputation suffered in the US in the meantime? Was it rather that the first time, he had no tour manager but himself and his friends, thus he had not had to deal with this problem before? I do not know.) Nevertheless, before Giese's arrest, Hirschfeld wrote to Harry Benjamin and proposed that he join Benjamin's medical practice as a partner. He hoped to be in the US in the fall of 1934; he could lecture here and there and see about getting his books out in English.[80] Benjamin must have been taken aback. He had a warm relationship with Hirschfeld but not a close one, and often Hirschfeld ignored his suggestions and squelched his initiatives in the World League for Sexual Reform.[81] Benjamin demurred on Hirschfeld's proposal to take over half of his medical practice, reminding Hirschfeld that his medical license was no good in the United States. Come to the States, he told him, but plan to make money doing lectures and occasional medical consultations, for which one did not need a license.[82] Hirschfeld wrote that indeed he would. He wanted to be "where I can feel *homelike* in my old days, where I can live restful and peaceful in a spiritual way, especially where I can work and where I have the impression that I am welcome," and France was not that place.[83] He wrote this on June 3, 1934; it is not clear whether this was before or after Giese's arrest, but it seems to probably have been written in the aftermath of that disaster because he told Benjamin, "I have the idea to bring with me as secretary Karl Giese, who has worked in our Institute nearly twenty years and knows very well the material etc. which I will bring with me."[84] Though Hirschfeld always asked after Benjamin's wife, Gretchen, in his letters, and Benjamin sent on greetings from her, this was the first mention in their correspondence of Giese. Discretion was the rule for same-sex affairs, even with a fellow leftist sex reformer like Benjamin.

America seemed possible, in any event. Li wanted to study in New York or Boston. Hirschfeld had enough income from his books to live, and he could bring Giese.[85] Li, who had substantial resources, was even offering to bankroll the transatlantic move.

Yet finally, Hirschfeld decided against the United States. He felt too old and sick to undertake such a change, he suggested in a letter to his nephew.[86] One wonders what would have happened had the three men left for the United States together in the fall of 1934, as Hirschfeld told Benjamin he probably would. It might have saved Giese's life. In 1938, he died by suicide in Brno.[87]

The final and very brief entry in Hirschfeld's journal is dated February 8, 1935, about three months before he died. The decision, he wrote, was for Europe, not America – Nice, not New York. He had rented a spacious place in Nice on the Promenade des Anglais, a five-bedroom apartment with a view of the sea. He did not know if he had chosen correctly, but he was glad to have his own apartment again. The difficulty of what to tell Li remained, but maybe he could study in France after all. Hirschfeld, apparently sensing the end – though he had been sensing the end for years and had written many wills – concludes the entry noting that he had written a will and left it with a lawyer in Nice.[88]

With the move to the United States called off, Li enrolled at the University of Zurich for the spring semester to study medicine, business, and finance.[89] He left Nice in his car on March 29, 1935.[90] Recalling the whole series of events and Hirschfeld's choice many years later, Li simply wrote that he could not resume his medical studies in French and Hirschfeld was afraid to live in Zurich, so close to Germany. "I took him to live in Nice and I returned to Zurich."[91] Li's words, "I took him," suggest that by this time Hirschfeld was quite frail and that Li saw himself as a caregiver.

Li had devoted several years of his life to Hirschfeld and to Hirschfeld's career. He had broken off medical school at St. John's and joined the world journey in the expectation that he would become a student at the Institute in Berlin. The Institute was no more, and its prospects of rising again in France were dim now. Whatever Li felt for Hirschfeld, the relationship had always been grounded on Li's ambitions and Hirschfeld's power to help him achieve them. Quite openly so – Hirschfeld was frank about this in *World Journey* and in the press when they left China. Finally, now, Li would leave Hirschfeld and try to build his own career anew, in Zurich, at a German-language university, when he had begun his studies in English, no easy feat. In the novel that was eventually written about Li in Zurich, the character based on Li is hampered in his medical studies by having to work in German.[92] Li had wanted to study at Harvard, in English, but Hirschfeld would not leave Europe. Li's departure for Zurich was a break, a shift in the relationship, an admission of the sad reality that Hirschfeld no longer had the power to make Li's career. Li was striking out on his own, trying to have a career of his own, to escape the wreckage of Hirschfeld's Institute. Yet he had not gone to the United States. He was staying relatively close, close enough that he could come to Nice often, though it was a long and difficult drive from Zurich to Nice, through the Alps, then down the coast.

In a letter to Norman Haire in London, Hirschfeld put a sunny face on the move to Nice – Karl had had "difficulties" in Paris, but the Riviera was lovely, a good place to land, except "the only distressing thing is … soon Tao is going to leave to finish up his medical studies in Switzerland." At least, he went on, he had gotten Li well situated, and the young man was close enough to come back to Nice during university breaks.[93] The day after Li left, Hirschfeld penned a darker letter to another friend: "We had to part with heavy hearts" and now here Hirschfeld was, "sitting on the rubble of my life's work." Then he found some hopeful words. He was no helpless old man. He was filled with the desire to work. He would rebuild his life.[94]

With Li away it was not so easy. Hirschfeld had a bad spell one night in April 1935 – dizziness, heart pains, loss of consciousness. A cook and Hirschfeld's handsome new secretary had rooms in the large apart-ment, but that night they did not hear his cries for help. In his letter reporting this to Li, he implored him not to come back to Nice. He was feeling better, Hirschfeld assured him, and he wanted his student to focus on his medical studies. The letter is, however, wretched enough that Li must have felt conflicted and guilty for not coming back. The semester was "only three months, only perhaps for you, but for me like three hundred months," Hirschfeld wrote. He concluded near the let-ter's end, "Once again best wishes for the next three months till we can see each other again and many thanks for everything, what you have done for me in the last four years."[95] He wanted him to come back from Zurich, though he told him not to. It is not clear if Li came back, but it seems he did not.

A few weeks later, in the afternoon on May 14, 1935, Hirschfeld died. Despite his spotty health, no one expected him to die that day. It was his sixty-seventh birthday. Li had not come back for it; there is no record in the archive as to why. As deaths go, Hirschfeld had a good one. He was in fine spirits in the morning, opening birthday mail.[96] Then he seems to have gone out to lunch in a restaurant with his visiting nephew, of whom he was quite fond, and with the young man who had taken Li's position as his secretary. When they were on the way home, Hirschfeld said he felt dizzy. He reached the garden of his apartment and collapsed. His stunned companions found that he had gone unconscious. He never woke up. The cause of death is unknown.[97]

Li got the news in Zurich, probably by telegram, and arrived a few days later. Giese somehow got a two-week visa to re-enter France and came back in a rush, by motorcycle, train, and airplane. He arrived suffering from pneumonia but took part in the cremation and funeral anyway. Because of the bathhouse case, Giese dared not overstay the visa he had been lucky to get at all.[98]

The man Li had followed from Shanghai, the man he had pledged to assist, his teacher, the man he had cared for and whose work he had supported for years and whose health he had worried over, the man who loved him passionately, the man he had only recently left to go to uni-versity, was gone.

Hirschfeld's will made Li and Giese heirs, of a particular sort. "The main purpose" of his will, he wrote in it, was "to secure and as the case may be to promote my *intellectual* legacy [*Erbe*] contained in my life's work in science, and in particular in sexology, beyond my death [*mein persönliches Ende*], as I have no heirs of my body [*Leibeserben*]. The *personal* bearers and executors [*Träger und Verwalter*] of this inheritance [*Erbschaft*] are my students."[99] They were, above all, intellectual and professional heirs, standing in, in his mind, for the sons he did not have. The will stipulated repeatedly that they must use the resources he was leaving them to advance his intellectual project, sexology. They could not use it for living expenses.

In his will, Hirschfeld elevated one frame of his relationship with Li and with Giese over another. All along to him they had both been "heirs" – sons of a sort, professional and intellectual successors who would carry on his work after his death. They had also been lovers. That erotic world was coeval for Hirschfeld, and apparently for Li and Giese, with paternalism and mentorship. This was a queer kinship. The will, however, stripped away some of the many dimensions of the relationships. It made the relationships all intellectual. The money must be spent for sexology. It was to carry on Hirschfeld's work, advance Hirschfeld's ideas, his "intellectual legacy." Li did not need his living expenses covered, but Giese desperately did. He borrowed money from Li when he left Nice after the funeral.[100] The will could not publicly acknowledge the love affairs – to do so would have only hurt Li and Giese. But perhaps it could have left them some freedom to make their own lives and to spin their own theories after Hirschfeld passed.

Li and Giese were both badly equipped to carry on Hirschfeld's intellectual work. But Li and Giese it would be. "Papa" had alienated or dismissed every possible qualified successor. He could have picked someone in the World League for Sexual Reform, like Norman Haire, or Harry Benjamin, but he did not. Germany's domestic homosexual emancipation movement was in ruins at the time thanks to the Nazis, but anyhow, Hirschfeld had broken with many of those involved and considered those who were still his allies unfitting successors. Instead, he named his two lovers. Neither had the right credentials. It was a myopic decision born of profound self-regard. He wanted no deviation from his ideas, and so he shied away from naming a successor who was his professional equal. He wanted someone molded by himself and in his own image. This had been his intention for years.[101]

"Tao is rather panicky," wrote Giese to a friend. "Apart from the personal loss, the responsibilities that Papa has sort of imposed [*quasi auferlegt*] on him are a bit oppressive in light of his youth … It is an inheritance just as honorable as it is obligatory, obligatory to the greatest possible extent, such that Tao does not even know whether he should accept it."[102] The older man had proved a demanding lover: at his death, he had named Li as the person who would carry on the whole project of sexology, while in the meantime, sexology was being destroyed by the fascists. Was Li up to the task? Did he want it?

Li did finally accept the inheritance, thereby symbolically accepting the duty to carry on Hirschfeld's work. He was twenty-seven or twenty-eight at the time. He did not yet have a medical degree. He had given one conference paper, with his mentor, and had published nothing of his own. The entire discipline of sexology was crumbling – Germany had been a key fulcrum for the whole intellectual project. What is more, many sexologists would not take him seriously as Hirschfeld's intellectual heir, what with his youth, his lack of credentials, and the prevailing white racism of the time. Kurt Hiller probably never met Li in person but thought of him as nothing more than "the very young Chinese student."[103] One wonders if Li said yes to Hirschfeld's dying request out of love, or duty, or guilt that he had not been there at the end, or all of these. Carrying out Hirschfeld's plan would be hard, and yet Li, whose subsequent adventures took him from Zurich to the United States to Hong Kong to Vancouver, would pull it off, in his own way.

12 Li Shiu Tong's Queer Masculinities

Hotel Baur au Lac, Zurich, Late 1930s

One evening late in the 1930s, Li Shiu Tong could be found at the posh Hotel Baur au Lac, in Zurich. Perhaps he was sitting in the garden, as he surely sometimes did, beyond the lights that spilled from the hotel's colonnade, looking out at the lake. He was probably impeccably turned out as usual, maybe in a pale gray suit with a pastel tie.[1] Perhaps he had brought along his little pet dog and was holding the creature in his lap as he sat, smoking, with a lemonade in front of him.[2] Hirschfeld was dead. Not long after he had passed, Li's father died. Now Li was a student at the University of Zurich, studying medicine. I do not know the year, but say it was 1937 or 1938. Li had defied his family and refused to go back to China. Then Japan had invaded. If it was 1938, Shanghai had fallen to the Japanese; some years later, they would take Hong Kong from the British garrison.

Why had he come to the Baur au Lac that night? Perhaps he had come with friends. He had friends at the university, though perhaps no close ones. Aside from one other man, Li was the only Chinese student in a student body so white that simply being Chinese made him a sort of celebrity, a figure of mystery and occasional mockery to his fellow students, many of whom had internalized prevailing tropes about the romantically inscrutable Far East. He was, however, not unpopular. Self-effacing, empathetic, and funny, he had chums to eat with in the student union. He lived in a rented flat and kept small pets – in succession, he had miniature parrots, a monkey, a little dog, and a Siamese cat. He was in the habit of taking the parrots out for "an airing," a walk in the courtyard of his apartment, just as Hirschfeld saw the two men on the Bund in Shanghai doing years before.[3] Li did not like to drink or carouse. If he was with friends that night, they sat at a little table in the garden, in red chairs, in relative darkness beyond the lights of the hotel's arcade, where they could perhaps hear the hotel's little orchestra playing a medley of Wagner.[4]

Or perhaps Li had come alone. It seems like discreetly queer men favored the garden of the Hotel Baur au Lac.[5] That night at the hotel, Li met one, a wealthy and well-known English writer of popular novels, Robert Smythe Hichens.[6] Like Hirschfeld, Hichens was successful and famous, and like Hirschfeld, he was much older – over seventy the night he met Li, who was then in his late twenties or early thirties. Unlike Hirschfeld, Hichens was rather conservative on sexual-political questions, abhorring what he apparently took to be "decadent" displays of queerness, favoring a discretion far deeper than what Hirschfeld had had, and even perhaps allowing himself no more than celibate male-male love.[7]

Hichens was taken with Li, enchanted by his story of the world tour. So taken was he that he modeled the main character of his next novel on the young medical student. Li, for his part, must have liked famous older men, because he and Hichens struck up a friendship. The novel Hichens wrote about Li is one of the few records of Li's life after Hirschfeld. The other, more important record is Li's unpublished, unfinished book, improbably rescued from a garbage bin in Vancouver in the 1990s.

Li was racialized and at times exploited by some of the men around him – by Hirschfeld, who perhaps asked too much of him, and by Hichens, who may have been a lover, and whose portrait of Li in the novel is a racist caricature. Yet the sketchy archival record about Li that survives shows a very different person: not a victim but a self-made, discreetly queer sexologist who was well aware of the exploitative racialized power dynamics around him and quite capable of making those work for him, insofar as that was possible. By his own lights, he embarked on a decades-long sexological research project and fulfilled his terrible promise to the dead Hirschfeld, the promise he made when he accepted the terms of the will. Li was Hirschfeld's heir, and he remained faithful, though not in all things. He defied his mentor in the end, rejecting some of his core ideas and floating his own theory.

In this chapter and the following one, I read Li's archive to show how Li became a sexologist and also how he defied the sexualized racism and imperialism around him with his queer Chinese European Canadian masculinities. This speaks to Li's agency, but I think we would do well to go beyond recognizing the agency of this extremely wealthy cosmopolitan.[8] Rather, my point is that though we know so little of Li's life after 1935, from the surviving papers it is clear that Li lived a life on his own terms, and we can get a glimpse of what those terms were.

The trouble is, the Li archive is made up of just two books, and they are such flagrantly terrible historical sources, running roughshod over the history profession's rules for evidence, so roughshod that a historian has to consider whether they can be used to tell Li's story at all. Yet queer archives, or straight archives one seeks to use to write queer history, are often "bad" according to these same rules, because people want to hide traces of queerness, or they think its traces unimportant and throw them in the trash; queer historians often end up having to find ways to work with rule-breaking sources.[9] No one has used Hichens's novel, which probably not ironically bears the title *That Which Is Hidden*, to write about Li's life. When I began to read it, I quickly decided that neither would I. The novel is dripping with racism. None of the characters in it are explicitly queer. There is a character based on Hirschfeld, for example, but he is a straight Christian Austrian psychologist – Hirschfeld's scandalous professional identity and his Jewishness are scrubbed away. We are no longer in the radical leftist circles of sex reform in the 1930s, but rather in a conservative expat British world of fervent male bonding and suppressed desire. The novel is moreover about Li, but not by him. Thus, according to professional norms, one can read it to say something about Hichens but not to say anything about Li. All the more so given Hichens's obvious play to the assumed racism of his presumedly white readership.

Li's own book and his notes for it raise a different set of problems. Li's manuscript, penned in Vancouver late in his life, seems to show signs of dementia or psychosis or both. It is fragmented and very short. It contains fantastic stories about aliens, Hitler, and the possible homosexuality of Winston Churchill. If Li's manuscript is out of touch with reality, how can a historian read it to say something about Li's life?

Are the troubles in the Li archive resolvable? What is Li's story, and what does it mean for the canonical history of homosexuality of which Hirschfeld is a star?

In Zurich and beyond, Li Shiu Tong went about fulfilling the terms of Hirschfeld's will as he had gone about being Hirschfeld's student when the German sexologist was alive – that is, by working diligently and by, moreover, "working" some discreetly queer Chinese European masculinities. One sees this in *That Which Is Hidden*. Apprehending Li's queer masculinity makes the novel (a flagrantly bad historical source) useful, indeed makes it a part of Li's archive, and redeems the novel as a vivid portrait of him in the years after Hirschfeld passed.

Hichens, not well remembered today, was a very successful popular novelist. In the 1890s in London, he was an acquaintance of Oscar Wilde, known for having "rather ungenerously parodied" him in an 1894 novel.[10] By the late 1930s, the well-off Hichens had been living in exile on the Riviera for a long time. He was probably one of those British men who fled abroad because England cracked down on male-male sex in the 1890s; he left the country around then.[11] Hichens's novels were not frankly queer, but some invited queer readings, which many readers picked up on apparently – between the wars, a covert queer hangout in Baltimore was named after one of Hichens's best-selling books, an orientalist fantasy entitled *The Garden of Allah*.[12] Hichens traveled in queer circles and had social ties to Hirschfeld; Hichens, however, reports that he met Li in the garden of the Baur au Lac, assumedly after Hirschfeld passed.[13] The subsequent novel, *That Which Is Hidden*, is a too-long psychological thriller set in the homes of monied expat Brits in Nice and Cannes and at the University of Zurich, where most of the characters are students. One of the students is Kho Ling, the former pupil and private secretary of a famous, recently deceased Austrian psychologist. Hichens wrote in his memoir that for this novel he

> required a minute study of a Chinese character. I asked Li Shiu Tong whether I might try to draw him, and he gave me permission to do so. He exists in my book. Anyone who knew him could recognize him there, with his curious unusual intuition, his apparently quite natural faculty of penetrating below the surface of things, his love of small birds and animals, his knowledge of the Far East, his innate delicacy when dealing with others, so characteristically Chinese, his power of reserve, and his persistence when walking in a route he has traced out for himself … Li read the book when it was finished, and was quite satisfied with my presentation of him in circumstances devised entirely by me, but in which he acted as he acknowledged that he would have acted had Fate cast him as the chief performer in so tragic a drama. In the opening of the book, which is at Nice on the French Riviera, I have described a tomb which Li actually erected to the memory of a friend of his long since dead, and which can be seen by anyone who visits the great cemetery of La Cocarde on the hill above Nice.[14]

(Indeed, Li put up a beautiful tomb for Hirschfeld.)

If one is unwilling to take Hichens's word that the character Kho Ling is Li, here is what Li wrote in his unpublished manuscript: "Robert Hichens, after working with me on *That Which Is Hidden*, published by Doubleday in 1937, wanted to write a long novel with me. We just began preparation of the book I had to leave because I received news that the Nazis tried to get me."[15] Li worked with Hichens on *That Which Is Hidden* and then they began a second novel, as a joint project. This suggests, I submit, that we read *That Which Is Hidden* as a book authored by Hichens but with input from Li; Hichens "worked with me" on it, Li writes. At the same time, Li's name is not on the cover; the project was under Hichens's control. The second book, just begun when Li had to leave Zurich (more later on the Nazis threatening him), is, I think, the book that Li decided to write on his own in Vancouver in the 1980s – details on that later. In *That Which Is Hidden* there is a portrait of Li's life after Hirschfeld, and such portraits are very hard to come by.

The book is about a rich young Englishman, Mark. When the novel opens, Mark is living in Nice with his mother and father. His father is dying, apparently from diabetes, though he takes insulin, administered each day by a distinguished doctor, Sir Chesney. Mark meets Kho, who is a medical student in Zurich but has come back to Nice to visit the grave of his teacher, the famous psychologist. Mark tells Kho about his father. Kho suspects Sir Chesney is to blame for the father's illness. Then, the father dies. Mark goes off to study in Zurich, where he pals around with Kho and meets a German, Max. Mark is platonically (or not) smitten with Max. Meanwhile, back on the Riviera, Sir Chesney seduces Mark's widowed mother. Alarmed when they learn of the impending nuptials of the doctor and the widow, Mark, Kho, and Max return to France. Kho, brave and alone, drives to Sir Chesney's mansion one night and heroically confronts him. Kho challenges the doctor with the facts: he murdered Mark's father by intentionally botching the insulin injections, administering overdoses on purpose, so that he could seduce Mark's mother. His crime revealed, the villainous doctor takes his own life. The mother is rescued, and Max, now the main point-of-view character, is left in awe of Kho, whom he had formerly mocked and belittled.

The trouble is the novel is racist. Here are some highlights, or rather lowlights. Much of the plot depends on how the Li character is a mysterious Chinese man, with the mysteriousness being a racial trait. This is much discussed by the other characters, all of whom are white and many of whom muse about how Kho is unfathomable and totally alien, thanks to racialization: "There was something baffling in Kho Ling ... Perhaps it was his Chineseness, the great difference existing between him and anyone born and brought up in the Western world."[16] Hichens has endless fun with the Li character's accent in English and with his overt politeness. A drunken Kho Ling drives away in his little car in the following scene: "His good-bye was hilarious ... Kho Ling, at the wheel of his car, waved a fluttering farewell with his little hand and cried out, 'Thank you for a velly gland evening! Whiskey and soda is velly stlengthening and refleshing. Everly one dlinks it in Shanghai. Switzerland is a velly nice countly.'"[17] Behind his back, Kho's friends laugh about his accent and tell themselves he is not as smart as they are.[18] There is a subplot about how the Li character becomes more "Chinese" when he drinks alcohol and about how he cannot hold his alcohol.[19] The Li character is also feminine, though his gender is rather subtly drawn given the strong racialization in the white European mind of East Asian men as feminine. Kho "had tiny hands … was amazingly slight … there was something exceptionally neat and even delicate in his movements and gestures."[20] The white characters leave all the hard work of justice in the novel to Kho – at first, they do not believe him that the doctor is the murderer and feel he is too prejudicial in his judgment of Sir Chesney (never mind the endless prejudicial judging of Kho because he is Chinese!) Then, finally convinced, they put it on Kho to stop the doctor from marrying Mark's mother.

A final racialized plot point: Kho never gets the boy (though ostensibly no one does, the novel would otherwise be overtly queer). Looking at recent Hollywood movies, Celine Parreñas Shimizu notes the persistent relegation of male Asian American characters to asexuality or celibacy.[21] Richard Fung describes how in 1960s TV shows like *I Spy*, "if you had non-white characters, you either had to find them 'one of their kind' or else make the character celibate."[22] This same kind of racialized narrative seems to unfold in the Hichens novel. Aside from Kho, no one else in the novel is not white, with the exception of a second Chinese student in Zurich whom the reader never actually sees or meets. In the novel's queer romantic subplot (which is extremely subtle but quite clear to a reader attuned to such things), the Li character is dismissed as a romantic partner for any of the other major male characters. Kho has a strong initial connection with Mark, but then Mark moves on to Max.

Why did Li like this novel? Hichens writes that he did approve of it, though we do not have to believe Hichens. Yet Li himself wrote that he worked on this book with Hichens, and Li kept a copy of the book until the end of his life.[23] He appears to have treasured the novel. Surely one reason is that the Li character is the novel's hero. The story is also shot through with accurate details about the parts of his life that are otherwise documented. It does indeed seem to be a sort of portrait of him. Amid the racism, one gets flashes of Li's student days in Hong Kong and Shanghai and his travels with Hirschfeld. A small example – Kho Ling mentions that on the world journey, he won a donkey race in Egypt. This must have been a very happy memory for him and for Hirschfeld because it is also mentioned in *World Journey*, where Hirschfeld writes that Li surprised everyone and won the donkey race, and Hirschfeld was the only person who had bet on him, so Hirschfeld netted quite a sum.[24] Hirschfeld's death in Nice, with Li away in Zurich, is realistically sketched in the novel as well, as is Hirschfeld's grave in Nice, though the Hirschfeld character is not a dead-on portrait of the German sexologist. There are many other examples. If you know the story of the world journey, the novel makes for uncanny reading.

What to make of depictions of Li that Li endorsed and that also trade in racialized stereotypes? Hichens's novel would be one example. Another is the 1933 *Voilà* magazine spread on Li and Hirschfeld. The French magazine put Li on its cover in a patterned changshan, the long tunic that was a common fashion in China, where it was not coded as feminine (figure 10). Li did wear a changshan sometimes, though much less in Europe than on the world journey, judging from surviving photos.[25] On the magazine cover Li is beautiful; he may even be wearing makeup. The cover was intended to sell magazines and probably did. To white French eyes in 1933, here was an exotic, mysterious, feminine Chinese man. In the article inside, Li appears briefly: He is "a young Chinese, slim and elegant … a young sexologist studying at the University of Vienna. He joined Doctor Hirschfeld in Shanghai and assisted him with all of the piety that a Chinese disciple has for his master." Li is racialized and exploited here. Yet he was very fond of this magazine cover. He kept several copies in his papers until he died.

A place to begin is in the recognition of the racism that was all around Li as he made a life in Europe. How could Li respond to the racialized sexualization of himself? Could he make those power structures somehow work for him, would they destroy him, or was there a path in between? Considering depictions of Asian American women in film, Shimizu argues that Asian American women cannot but respond to these hypersexual images; rather than ignoring or rejecting them, Asian American women engage with them, not by accepting them but by working "against and with" them.[26] Though she is writing about Asian Americans in a later time period, Shimizu's ideas seem to apply here. Richard Fung, David Eng, Tan Hoang Nguyen, and others make the point that resorting to normative straight masculinity in the face of feminizing racialized tropes is not a response that does much to help a queer man such as Li.[27] As an alternative path, Nguyen draws on José Muñoz's concept of disidentification, quoting him: "Identifying with bottomhood becomes a matter of disidentification with it, whereby the gay Asian American male subject 'neither opts to assimilate within such a structure nor strictly opposes it; rather, disidentification is a strategy that works on and against dominant ideology.'"[28] These are useful ideas with which to think about Li's queer masculinities and femininities.

At times while in Europe, Li intentionally played on racialized tropes, in the service of his own ends, without accepting those tropes. He *worked* the tropes. I suspect he was proud of that and took some pleasure in it. He saw the benefit in it, which was to establish his own fame and career. This is apparent in the novel as well as the *Voilà* spread. In both novel and magazine, he is queer, feminine, exotic, and mysterious. His performance of these racialized tropes of gender and sexuality serves his ends: Li is Hirschfeld's star student who is carrying on his genius.[29] By apprehending the murderer in the novel, he proves that he is becoming a sexologist (or, in the novel, psychologist) in his own right.

One sees this working of racialized tropes in the scene where the Li character confronts the murderer. To get to this point, more than 600 pages in, the character has endured lots of racism. Yet in this scene, some of the racism (though certainly not all) gets turned on its head. Even before the confrontation scene, the reader knows that in their racialized dismissals of him, the white characters have underestimated the Li character. Those white characters are already realizing that themselves.[30] In the climactic scene, the murdering doctor seeks to deploy racism as well as homophobia against the Li character, and it fails.

Kho arrives at Sir Chesney's mansion at nine o'clock at night, dressed "soberly smart. Always very neat, he looked if possible even neater than usual in a black jacket suit, black shoes and socks, a broad black silk tie, snow-white collar and cuffs." He is in a Western suit, and a very sober one, as if for a funeral. Sir Chesney, who is not sure why Kho has come to see him, brings Kho to his library, where they get to talking about Kho's teacher, the dead psychologist Ellendorf. As they talk, Sir Chesney recalls that he saw Kho, the "Chinese pupil" with an "Oriental face," for the first time on the cover of a magazine. (The magazine's name is not *Voilà* and Hichens does not describe the photo, but surely the reference, which some readers would get, is to the *Voilà* cover.) Sir Chesney, anxious about what Kho might want from him, finds solace in racism by recalling the magazine cover: though Kho has dressed in a suit for the evening, Sir Chesney dresses him mentally in a changshan, as the exotic, feminine, young Chinese assistant. Sir Chesney decides that though Ellendorf was a genius, one cannot transmit genius to a student. Kho is "impotent": if he has come to accuse Sir Chesney of murder, he cannot succeed, Sir Chesney thinks. "Impotent! Impotent! He's impotent to do me any harm. He can't! He can't! I've only to stand firm, to show I'm not afraid of him." Here, Sir Chesney tries to neutralize the threat Kho poses to him by enacting, to borrow Eng's term, racial castration, assuring himself that Kho is no genius but is rather "impotent," the flaccid Chinese man who cannot overcome Sir Chesney if he will only "stand firm," the erect white Brit.[31] Kho finally gives voice to his accusation: "I ask you not to mally her because I know you killed her husband."[32] In the face of the truth, Sir Chesney resorts to homophobia, too. He disparages Kho, claiming he has cooked up the accusation because Kho has a "perverted imagination," a mind "perverted" by his time on the world tour with Ellendorf, who studied "sexual perverts."[33]

The Hirschfeld character, who at the novel's outset is a psychologist who studies criminals, here is revealed to have studied homosexuals and, moreover, to have corrupted his student.

Kho, remaining calm, says it is not he who is sick in mind, it is Sir Chesney. The reader knows Kho is correct. Sir Chesney, who has grown belligerent, regains some poise ("this little Chinese wasn't going to undo all the tortuous and secret work") and tries to intimidate him: Kho is insane, he says, he ought to be committed. "Now please go away … you ought not to be at large. You ought to be secluded in a maison de sante." Kho, who has remained quietly determined throughout, responds, "Verlly well! … I will go. But tomorrow I shall go to the villa and I shall tell Mr. Mark's mother the tluth, that you killed her husband. And I shall tell her exactly how you did it. When I have done that my conscience will be quite clear." Sir Chesney quickly sees that this is his undoing: Kho has "a will of steel"; he is not "impotent" after all. The scene ends with Sir Chesney asking Kho for time to think. The doctor considers his options for a day, then takes his own life, making his death appear to be a swimming accident. Thus, the slurs Sir Chesney voiced in the confrontation scene – that of Kho as incapable of the genius of his teacher, that of him as unable to follow in his footsteps, and moreover the related racialization of Kho as the exotic feminine non-intellectual pupil of a white man who corrupted him with homosexuality – these are defeated along with the murdering doctor himself, who had sought to enact a racial castration of Kho. By the end of the novel, the other characters recognize Kho's heroic intelligence, though they still view him through racist tropes. The novel ends with the American student Enid, who is the ostensible straight love interest of Max, praising Kho in a racialized way: He is "first-rate Chinese jade," she declares.[34]

White racism persists. But the Li character has beaten the accusation of perversion and has brought down the murdering British doctor, even as the murderer resorted to racial castration and tried to weaponize the *Voilà* cover photo against him. Kho turns racism against the racist: in the end, the murderer's underestimation of the Li character helps to defeat him. The Li character has what he wants: he is recognized as the worthy successor of the Hirschfeld character, a genius in his own right, and a profoundly ethical one. He is the novel's most heroic and brave character. He has succeeded even as the other white characters in the novel obsessively racialize him. One sees this in a dinner party scene prior to the novel's climax, as Kho tells a funny story about life in Shanghai. Max reflects on Kho's "vivacious gaiety," how he is "very much at home in this company of Europeans," and realizes "that this small Chinese was quite definitely the centre piece of the company. Upon all of them his influence had descended. Their minds were attending to him."[35] Racism persists, but Kho is powerful and respected.

Like many people, Li could shift his gender performance in order to be read in various ways according to codes of race, class, and gender. While living in Europe, he most often affected a performance that was more conventionally masculine by European standards – the Western suit, very carefully done, as when Kho arrives at Sir Chesney's mansion, though that's a special occasion; Li seems to have often favored a less somber and less conservative look, such as a gray suit with some color in the tie or pocket square. One sees this in the many photographs of Hirschfeld's exile. Li suits up very well, emphasizing his wealth and his slight, lithe body (Li and Hirschfeld were both relatively small of stature). The Li character has a stylish car, a red Austin in the novel, and sometimes Li affects tastefully flashy sartorial touches, such as a pink carnation in his buttonhole, a beret, or wingtip shoes.[36] Perhaps Li was sometimes, in informal settings, feminine. In his apartment in Vancouver, Li kept such an image, a beautiful drawing of his young self, among his papers (figure 2). In a rare description of Li, which I quoted earlier in another context, Hirschfeld wrote in his journal that Li's devotion and charm were "not seldom disrupted by quite temperamental, nearly hysterical petulance." At this point in their lives, Hirschfeld was sick, in exile, and refusing to move to the United States, where Li wanted to go, perhaps in part because he thought Hirschfeld would be safer there, which was true. Li had good reasons to be upset, and Hirschfeld's description minimizes them. Of note, however, is the gendered language Hirschfeld chose. "Temperamental" and "hysterical" make Li sound girlish. The white European view of Chinese men gendered them feminine. Perhaps here Hirschfeld succumbed to that trope, of which he was elsewhere critical (see chapter 3). Or perhaps both the racist trope and Li's own authentic gender expression were in play. In any event, Li was also much beloved by Hirschfeld, who followed the remark about his petulance with this: "On the whole, I could not have a more beloved, sunnier, more helpful person around me."[37]

Hirschfeld too seems to have at times been playfully feminine, as (possibly) in the posing of his legs in the photograph of him and "phallic stones" in Central Java, which may have been taken by Li – Hirschfeld told the *Voilà* reporter that Li took 1,200 photographs on the world journey; I hence assume most of the photos of the journey are Li's work.[38] (See figure 7.) Hirschfeld is certainly striking a feminine pose in the photograph of him on an unidentified beach, perhaps in France during the exile (figure 9).[39]

Both men, however, had another gender presentation for professional life. There, Li was an utterly formal, conventionally masculine, up-and-coming scientist. To be masculine was to be rational, intellectual; femininity signaled the opposite – thus, Sir Chesney links the Li character's supposed lack of acumen to his femininity. One sees Li's professional self in a photo in the exile scrapbook/guest book, which someone (probably Hirschfeld) captioned "with colleagues from England, Holland and China in Paris." One picture is of Norman Haire, Hirschfeld, and Li, who is dressed quite like he appears in figure 12, with the addition (in the photo with Haire) of a waistcoat and white pocket square.[40] Li is Hirschfeld's colleague here, and this was far more common than the image on the *Voilà* cover, where he is Hirschfeld's mysterious and (to some viewers) erotically alluring assistant.

Yet was the beautiful young assistant queer himself? One can read *That Which Is Hidden* as categorically straight – Max, Kho, and Mark, not to mention a number of minor characters, including two disagreeable spinster expats who travel as a couple, are not explicitly marked as anything but good friends, and indeed by the novel's end it seems like Max will get together with Enid, and Mark is not in the least bit dismayed.[41] (Hichens himself had moved in with his married protégé and friend, that man's wife, and their baby and had lived with them for many years. Around the time Hichens met Li, the threesome had a house near Zurich.)[42] In 1940, the year the novel came out in the United States, just about any legal jurisdiction in the world would have banned the book had it depicted a queer relationship explicitly and in positive terms. Hichens was working within those parameters. Behind a straight façade, the novel invites a queer reading, to those who pick up on its signals, and it does so intentionally. To give one example: much of the novel's first half is in Mark's point of view, as he moons over Max, who spends a summer tutoring him in German and living with him and his mother in their mansion. In one scene, Mark bids his mother good night and turns to go into Max's bedroom:

> The horns were calling in the depths of the Forest of Life. And what romance there was in their distant voices – romance irresistible! … He turned to go into Max's bedroom. Mark found Max, already nearly undressed leaning with his bare arms on the window sill of his bedroom and gazing out into the night. He turned his head, with its tumbled brown hair, as Mark came in.[43]

The make-out scene a contemporary reader may expect to follow does not. What does follow is, however, coded as queer – the two young men have a conversation, including about the wisdom of the ancient Greeks (a nod to European male queer subcultures in which ancient Greece held enormous import, being a time and place that accepted some forms of male-male eroticism). Then Mark and Max "parted for the night merrily," and Mark is, explicitly, "alone in his bedroom."[44] Hichens's unspoken point here may be an argument in favor of queer chastity, something he seems to explore in other things he wrote.[45] There is, however, here and in many other spots in the novel a space for a reader who wants a queer sex scene to sketch one in. This sort of reading was common to queer readers at the time and in the decades that followed.[46] Hichens signals in favor of queer reading in general by repeating the words "queer" and "gay," which by 1940 already had well-established homoerotic connotations, though they also had other, straight connotations that were the prevailing ones, and thus straight readers might not pick up on the cues.[47] Indeed the novel seems to have a queer politics, in that it makes a very subtle comment on improper queers contrasted with the heroic "gay" character of Kho. The spinster women are bad queers, figures of fun. The word "queer," as well as apparent queer men lurking in the shadows of the Riviera checking out Max, are associated with sickness and "over-civilization."[48] "Gay" seems in contrast to only have a positive connotation, and it is often used to describe the Li character.

Taken together with what else we know of Li, the way that the novel marks the Li character as "gay" makes me more certain that he was queer, though it seems that by the novel's logic, "gay" means homoerotic but honorable and not sexual, whereas "queer" means improper, excessive same-sex desire. "Kho Ling drove up in his little car, smartly dressed in a pale grey suit, with a flesh-coloured tie, a pink carnation in his buttonhole and a grey hat with a flexible brim placed slightly sideways on his head. Opening the door he almost skipped out of the car, smiling and looking so gay in a happy Chinese manner."[49] Kho's apartment building's interior court is "grassy and gay."[50] If Kho is gay, nevertheless he was not intimate with his teacher. It is the murderer who is the primary voice of that accusation; other characters entertain it but decide they are wrong. All that Kho says of his beloved and revered teacher is that he was his beloved and revered teacher. He describes himself as "my Teacher's chief pupil, who had lived with him for years … and been told all his secrets."[51] In another passage, Kho says, "He was a great man, a scientist, and I loved him velly much. He was my Teacher."[52]

To Hichens, what may be going on here is the idealization of intense and romantic male-male relationships that are chaste and very, very discreet. From Li's perspective, however, I think we can at least say that Li was comfortable being represented in this novel by a character who is coded as gay. Yet, even as Kho is marked as gay and seems to have a flirtation with Mark at the novel's outset – they appear about to fall into an intense friendship like the one Mark later has with Max – the novel denies that the Hirschfeld character corrupted the Li character and seems to deny that they were lovers. Li apparently was happy with that as well.

Reading with an eye on how Li himself negotiated racialization, a portrait emerges in the novel of Li's life in Zurich that shows a very hardworking young man determined to become a doctor and utterly faithful to the legacy of his teacher. He is also a very clever young man, charming and concerned for the well-being of others. This was, I submit, what Li wanted other people to see in him, at least at this point in his life, and I have in this book occasionally drawn details from the novel that are not confirmed by other historical sources, chiefly in chapter 3 and in this chapter.

Here, then, is what life was like for Li after Hirschfeld: At first, he was lonely in Zurich. He was very busy with his studies, but he felt "desolation" inside. Everyone liked him, he spoke German fluently by now, but since the death of his teacher and that of his father "he had withdrawn into himself, had cultivated a habit of reserve." In the novel, Kho breaks his isolation when he becomes friends with Mark, the young Englishman – perhaps in real life, Li was lonely till he met Hichens, the old Englishman. His aloneness in Zurich is compounded by the way that Swiss people treated him. Kho does not want to go back to China now that his father is dead, but the Swiss do not understand him. "Sometimes he felt suspended between two worlds as if he belonged to neither." It is "an ugly feeling." Perhaps in real life Li was mostly friends with other foreigner students, as is the case for the character in the novel. On a usual day, Kho works with a student group on his studies, he takes French lessons and fencing lessons, and he plays chess for fun at the student union (he was good at chess). Occasionally he went to the cinema. "He filled up his life as much as he could." Though rich, Kho deplores idle rich men. His motto is "work or dai [die]." When he is done with medical school, which he finds challenging, not the least because he is taking his courses in a foreign language, he will go back to China and practice, Kho tells Mark as he sips a lemonade in the Baur au Lac garden one evening.[53]

There are yawning gaps in the Li archive. After the novel ends, the story of his life is hard to follow. He was in Zurich on and off for almost two decades.[54] He left in 1940 for America, probably in part because of the war. He enrolled at Harvard University in the Graduate School of Arts and Sciences, studying there until 1944.[55] To my knowledge, he never became a doctor. He also seems to have spent some of the Second World War, perhaps 1944–5, living in Washington, DC, possibly working at an embassy.[56] Li went back to Zurich in 1945 and lived there until 1960, when he moved to Hong Kong.[57] In 1969, while he was living in

Hong Kong, Li took a cruise on the *President Cleveland*, a newer ship with the same name as the ship that he and Hirschfeld had sailed on from Hong Kong to Manila more than thirty years before, on the first voyage of their life together. On the 1969 cruise, Li went deep-sea fishing. I do not know if he was alone or not. Li saved a souvenir from the cruise in his papers.[58]

Li left Hong Kong in 1974, settling in Vancouver. By now his passport photograph was that of an older man (figure 13). He was part of a wave of middle-class and wealthy emigrants from Hong Kong to Canada around that time. Though earlier Canada had had an outright ban on immigration from China (1923–47), in the 1970s Canada's new points immigration system made it easier for educated Chinese professionals to resettle there. The wave grew in the 1980s, when it became clear Hong Kong would revert from British to Chinese rule. The 1960s in Hong Kong were marked by leftist violence by supporters of the PRC (People's Republic of China). The uncertainty of Hong Kong's future, higher standards of living in Canada, the US, and Australia, and doubtless the specter of mass violence under Mao's PRC prompted many to leave.[59]

In Zurich, when he was a young man, Li planned to carry on Hirschfeld's work. Yet did he? Recent searches in English, German, Mandarin, and Cantonese turned up no papers or books by Li Shiu Tong.

13 Li Shiu Tong's Defiant Sexology

Vancouver, British Columbia, 1974–1993

On October 5, 1993, Li Shiu Tong died at the St. Paul hospital in down-town Vancouver, British Columbia. He was eighty-six years old. He had lived in Canada for almost twenty years. Li had family in Vancouver. A younger brother must have been with him in the hospital; he signed the death certificate. Li had an apartment in a modern building downtown, up the street from a YMCA and not far from the St. Paul hospital. He seems to have lived alone. It fell on Li's younger brother to decide what to do with the belongings in Li's apartment.[1]

There were books, some old, many with dedications to Li written on their inside covers or first pages. There were suitcases and papers and photographs. There were, I assume, Li's clothing and shoes. Months went by. Then, in the spring, some of those things ended up in the gar-bage bins at Li's building.

A neighbor stopped and looked through the objects in the garbage. He noticed some things that looked antique, things he thought might be valuable or important. There was an old German passport from the 1930s, black-and-white photographs, papers, a little journal filled with a scrawling hand, a few letters, many copies of a French magazine called *Voilà*, and a plain cardboard box about the size of a small cake box. One assumes the neighbor opened the little cardboard box. Inside was a white plaster cast of an old man's face. It was Hirschfeld's death mask. Someone had made the cast after he died in Nice in 1935. Li had kept the death mask all these years.[2]

The neighbor took some of Li's belongings out of the garbage. He put the smaller things in a leather suitcase that had also been Li's and had been in the bins; it bore a label that read "Made in Hong Kong." He brought the suitcase back to his apartment. The neighbor seems to have realized that Hirschfeld was somewhat famous. He posted a notice about his find on the nascent internet, in a newsgroup.[3]

Eight years went by. Then, thousands of miles away in Berlin, one of the world's foremost Hirschfeld scholars, Ralf Dose, typed Magnus Hirschfeld's name into a search engine, as he often did. What was different this time was that he accidentally set the search for newsgroups, not web pages. Li's neighbor's post came up. Dose must have been frantic with hope and then, as he read the date on the post, with anguish. So much time had passed. Would the neighbor have kept the stuff for eight years? The email on the newsgroup post was dead, but Dose found Li's former neighbor by searching an odd turn of phrase the neighbor had used in his newsgroup signature. The neighbor had moved to Toronto. But he still had the suitcase. Dose flew to Canada to get it. He went to Vancouver on that trip, too, and met Li's younger brother, who had saved Li's books. The brother did not tell Dose much about Li's life. Li's brother thought the books were important. Li had told his brother that he risked his life to save them from Hitler's Germany – that is, from the book burning that destroyed Hirschfeld's library and archive in Berlin. But it was not the books that were important. It was the old papers and photographs.[4]

Among the treasures in the suitcase was Hirschfeld's journal, which I have often used as a source in this book. There was another treasure there as well, a treasure that almost no one has written about: Li's book.[5]

Li seems to have started on the book in the 1980s, in Vancouver, because he refers to his fifty years of research on sexuality after Hirschfeld's death.[6] The manuscript is fragmentary, just sixteen typed pages; there are also cryptic notes for the book, made by hand on loose-leaf paper in a red plastic three-ring binder. The book was far from finished when Li died. It is possible that there were other parts of the book that the neighbor did not rescue and that ended up in a Vancouver landfill, as he does not seem to have necessarily pulled all of Li's things from the garbage. There may have been other papers as well. Li also had a career and a family – brothers, nieces and nephews, others – and, one supposes, many other things in his life that were important.

The manuscript and notes, which are in English, are fantastic – and repetitious, disjointed, and cryptic (what does "to 3 bi / 70-?" mean?).[7] They break the history profession's evidentiary norms in a way that is very different from the problems with *That Which Is Hidden*, the Robert Smythe Hichens novel that depicts Li. That is, they raise the question as to whether Li was so out of touch with what actually had transpired in his life when he wrote them that we ought not use them to conclude anything about events prior to the 1980s. For example, a theme in Li's book is the Nazi regime's effort to find out if Winston Churchill was a homosexual. The narration seems at times paranoid, and moreover to be reporting things that Li could not have witnessed, things that may involve extraterrestrial beings: "The Aliens also spied on Hitler. They paid attention to all the habits of the daily life of Hitler. They could find the slightest homosexual nature."[8]

Yet when one takes the manuscript and notes on their own terms, when one "just reads" or "reads along the grain," not against it – that is, when one reads as Li intended one to read, when one takes what Li writes that he means to do with the book and lets that stated goal frame one's reading – one sees the meaning in it.[9] On the first page of the three-ring binder there is a working title: "The Institute of S. Science in Berlin/ Long introduction/Story (mixed with science) the whole book."[10] The unfinished book must thus be an account of sexological research (the science) mixed with a story, that is, with fiction. It is the second book Li planned to write with Hichens before he left Zurich. The book was, I submit, planned as a work of sexology plus a psychological thriller like *That Which Is Hidden*, with a much more exciting plot about Nazis, espionage, and sexual blackmail.[11] "Make the introduction as a short story," Li wrote in his notes.[12] He also wrote, "It was the advice of Hichens the writer this book in a novel form after he ha[d] written [T]hat [W]hich is Hidden. [A] novel about Hirschfeld" and "I write in a fictional form taking the advice of Robert Hichens ... about my travel with – ." Li's text breaks off here but one assumes he means "with Hirschfeld."[13] The fantastic in this unfinished book is fiction.

The first page of Li's manuscript reads just like a historical novel about Hirschfeld. It is a firsthand account of a torchlit Nazi march. One assumes it is meant to be the marches just after Hitler took power. Li puts himself in the crowd, a Chinese medical student watching in horror, who then turns away, brings Dr. Hirschfeld "straight to the airport," and flies with him to safety in Zurich.[14] This sort of happened, but not this way – Li helped smuggle Hirschfeld across a border, but not that one and not by plane. (Elsewhere in the manuscript is a similar story of flight from Vienna in a taxi.) Li penned a gripping opening for his book, a fictional one for a popular audience, but not one entirely divorced from what happened in his life, very like *That Which Is Hidden*. The perception of paranoia in Li's text is doubtless heightened by the fact that it is fiction about Nazis, with sex and secrets thrown in, a mix that for contemporary readers can easily veer into the realm of supermarket tabloids. Li, however, was writing about his direct experience with actual Nazis, as well as with sex and secrets. He has, it seems, spun an old rumor about the Institute for Sexual Science into a compelling plot.

Here is the plot: After Hirschfeld's death, while Li was living in Zurich and working with Hichens on *That Which Is Hidden,* someone warned him that Nazi agents were in the city trying to find him. The agents wanted to get him because they were after lost records from the Institute in Berlin, records about "the sexual behaviors of foreign patients." Hirschfeld's other assistants had burned the records, but Nazi agents had gone after them anyway, assumedly intending to wrest the information out of them one way or another, and in fear, the assistants had killed themselves. (Here Li depicts, in fiction, Giese's death by suicide.) Li heeded the warning. He escaped from Zurich with his life and with Hirschfeld's books, saving them from destruction. What the German agents really wanted went well beyond traces of Nazi homosexuality that might have been in the Institute's archives. They wanted to find out if Churchill, Roosevelt, or de Gaulle were homosexual. "The strategy" was "blackmailing on homosexual and bisexual," that is, the German government planned sexual blackmail of enemy leaders. The other side tried the same thing, and here Li's aliens become legible. He frequently misspells; "aliens" is a misspelling of "allies," as in the Second World War.[15] The Allies sent agents to find out if Hitler was homosexual. In fact, Hirschfeld thought Hitler was not a homosexual but rather was a boot fetishist, Li wrote. That is the gist of the fictional plot. Li repeats it with a bit of variation several times in the sixteen pages.[16] What is going on here is that Li is spinning a novel out of the events of his life. My guess is that this is rather far from what really happened. There probably were no agents in Zurich seeking sexual secrets. It does, however, make for a good story.

The other part of Li's book seems to be a presentation of his sexological research. It is interspersed with the novel in a way that at first glance makes the whole manuscript seem out of touch with reality. Yet the book and the notes are, indeed, easily reclaimed as usable sources when one acknowledges the fictionalization. The notes in particular are repetitive and perplexing, but they are notes. Even in them, one sees themes. Even if Li, in his seventies or eighties, had some dementia when he was working on this project (the repetition is striking, as are the broken-off phrases and the unconventional spellings by a person who grew up going to English schools and studied for years at English-language universities), the manuscript and notes are quite comprehensible. Themes are clear, particularly if one knows the story of the world journey. Here is Li, picking up the history of sexology where it left off when Hirschfeld died in Nice: "I have continued his research as [a] full time occupation until now, I travel almost every country in the world from Siberia to South Africa, Asia, North America, except Australia and South America

[and] study most people except the Eskimo and Australian native."[17] Hirschfeld's decades of research plus Li's added up to an entire century of sexological research, Li notes with apparent pride.[18]

Li traveled around the world studying sexuality for decades. Hirschfeld's method while he was on the world journey went something like this: arrive in a city, meet a local, get word on where sex work happens (and, one assumes, on where the queer scenes are), go there, observe. Meet local experts, learn about local sexual norms. Record all this. Draw conclusions. Li probably did something similar. He wrote, "Sexual research is a dangerous and difficult work. I had to know the countries, law religion and moral [customs ?] and their languages. In fifty three years I had no difficulty. Being travel with Dr. Hirschfeld in his world lecture tour I learned the trade, in four years."[19] Li was known in his family as "a great traveler," as his brother told him in a 1975 letter.[20] Li himself writes that he went to far-flung places, always making notes on sexual customs. One wishes terribly for details; the manuscript gives almost none, save for a little note: "Swim in Washington/fieldwork/theory."[21] Was he living in Washington, DC, during the war, doing "fieldwork" at a swimming club or a beach? Had Li been in apartheid-era Cape Town making notes? What city in (assumedly) Soviet Siberia did he visit? Did Li have a job that required him to travel, a day job that gave him time in the evenings to conduct his research? Perhaps not – he writes that his fieldwork was a "full time occupation."[22]

Hirschfeld chose him for this, he writes. Hirschfeld came to Shanghai, Li acted as his assistant in China, and then,

> he offered a scholarship to study medicine in Germany and to continue to assist him around the world to investigate human sexual behavior. My qualification was that he needed a hard working medical student who would live a long life to continue his work. He thoroughly watch[ed] my work habit[s] and was told that my grandparents lived up to about ninety years of age. I jumped [at] the offer.[23]

That is, before they sailed for Manila, Hirschfeld told Li his plan to groom him as his successor – eerily, long life was a qualification. Li agreed, or at least he jumped at the chance of a scholarship to study in Berlin.

Li entirely leaves out their love affair. This, I think, forces us to ask seriously if there was a love affair. Hirschfeld loved Li. But he had power over Li; Li was his student, whose career depended on him. Perhaps he unwittingly (or not) forced Li to undertake what for Li was just a semblance of an affair. Perhaps the relationship was an exploitative, abusive one.

This is a question that I cannot entirely resolve; I do not have enough evidence of what Li thought. My strong suspicion, however, is that the relationship was not exploitative or abusive and that Li did love Hirschfeld when they were together. Hirschfeld's late journal entry, where he writes, "he does not want to part from me," is telling. What is more telling is Li's relative power and autonomy from Hirschfeld. Li was very wealthy. He could have left. He could have had a fine career with a degree from St. John's or from a school in the United States. Yet he kept living with Hirschfeld even when it increasingly seemed their connection was no longer professionally advantageous. The fact that Li kept Hirschfeld's death mask and papers his entire life, and that he wrote the beginnings of a book showing himself carrying on Hirschfeld's work, also speaks to this.

Nothing survives in which Li wrote that he loved Hirschfeld. One reason for the "badness" of archives of queerness, one reason for their inability to yield proper proof, is how "queerness is often transmitted covertly," writes José Muñoz. "This has everything to do with the fact that leaving too much of a trace has often meant that the queer subject has left herself open for attack."[24] Yet there are many photographs of Li and Hirschfeld together in the scrapbook/guest book Hirschfeld kept during the exile.[25] In many of the photos they are subtly touching, such as in two where they walk side by side on a street in Vichy (figure 12). Hirschfeld is disheveled and tie-less, Li impeccable. In the first of these pictures, Hirschfeld appears to be offering his arm to Li. In the second, Li has taken his arm; he is grasping Hirschfeld's elbow as they walk together.[26] In another set of photos, Hirschfeld has his arm through Li's.[27] Hirschfeld pasted a childhood photo of Li in the scrapbook/guest book, captioned "my student T.L. [Tao Li]."[28] In group photographs, Hirschfeld and Li are usually next to one another.[29] In none of these many photographs does Li look uncomfortable. It is apparent from the archive that Hirschfeld loved him; there is no doubt Li knew this. Judging by Li's body language in these photographs, together with all of the rest that we know about his life, I would think that Li felt something similar. Li left the love affair out of his book and allowed Hichens to write it out of the novel, for propriety's sake. Hirschfeld had certainly been a model of this in both his books and his unpublished papers.

And what was Li's sexology? In some respects, his work is Hirschfeldian; in others, not at all. The successor was his own theorist.

Like Hirschfeld, he saw gender as a gradation: "No man is absolute [one] hundred percent male and no woman is [one] hundred percent female. Nature never jumps."[30] Li asserts that some sexualities (he thinks there are about fourteen distinct sexualities, including homosexuality) are "minorities" but that they are "natural."[31] He is strongly in favor of decriminalizing homosexuality, particularly in the United States, where it remained criminal for a decade after he died.

Yet he broke with Hirschfeld's model of homosexuality: "A homosexual is not born but made."[32] Young children bond with people who show them deep affection, and this shapes the child's sexual development – boys who bond early with male figures grow up to be homosexual, and vice versa for girls. Environment shapes sexuality – boot fetishism does not occur among "tropical people," he writes, assumedly because people in tropical climates do not wear boots.[33] Li also thought that homosexuality and other variations from the heterosexual norm were "new human types," that "nature has created ... to cope with [the] danger of over-population instead of famine war and disease."[34] This is close to Hirschfeld's idea that homosexuality was a natural check on degeneration. Indeed, here one perhaps sees the post-1945 shift in eugenic thinking from concern about degeneration to concern about overpopulation. But Hirschfeld would not have liked the idea that homosexuality was new or increasing; he rather insisted it was as static across time as it was across race. Li thought the fluidity he saw was a new development that occurred after Hirschfeld's passing.[35] Li wrote that normal and abnormal were social distinctions, and they might change over time: "The abnormal someday may [view] themselves as the majority. Then the now-normal would become abnormal."[36] Things were changing even quicker now, evolution was at work, sexuality was ever more complicated, so much so that he felt, "the more I study the less I know."[37] He thought that the main engine behind rapid change was nature's effort to evolve more and more non-reproductive sexualities to combat overpopulation.[38]

Li also broke with Hirschfeld about queers having children. He writes in favor of allowing same-sex couples to adopt "orphans," asserting that "nature has created a new species of mankind, society must change accordingly."[39] By the time Li wrote this, openly queer couples raising children together was unusual but was nevertheless definitely happening in Canada. He called for "house husbands" in male-male relationships, who would take care of the children.[40] This is a significant departure from Hirschfeld's commitment to queer childlessness. Li, however, remains enamored of the idea that queers are nature's means of population control (he repeats that idea often) and seems to here be allowing for parenting via adoption only. At the time it was difficult or impossible for same-sex couples to adopt in most jurisdictions; Li calls for that to change: "These kind of couple[s] are the best way to solve the problem of supporting orphans."[41]

On the question of racism, Li's work is tough to parse out. He almost never mentions race and seems to have nothing to say about colonialism. Like his mentor, Li assumed the uniformity across "races" of sexuality and gender, writing at one point that his findings are based on the study of almost all of the human races, but unlike Hirschfeld, he does not assert that this uniformity is an important proof of his theory.[42] Though he does not seem to have chucked the idea that there are "races," neither is he invested in using racial difference as proof, though he does think that for his data to be valid he has to look at all races. This differs from Hirschfeld's work. Li's work is racially representative but not invested in an assertion of the significance of race as a major divider of humans into meaningful groups, and Li does not reveal any lingering belief in hierarchies of "the races," unlike Hirschfeld. In contrast, he has not gone far from his mentor on eugenics. He has ideas about population control and homosexuality that bring Hirschfeld's ideas about degeneration into the late twentieth century.

Transness was an important topic, in part because it seems Li considered Hirschfeld to be its discoverer, but in part for its own sake. Li writes:

> transsex (transvit) which is the most interesting manki[n]d. A complex sexual of mankind. Dr. was the best authority of this subject in fact he discovered it. The behavior of transvertit put some explanation on homo sexual bisexual and even on heterosexual.[43]

He had found transness to be remarkably common: "There are more than 100% including total tranvertit and partial tranerit [*sic*] among men and women" – here it is unclear what he means but clear that he thinks transness widespread.[44] He suggests at one point in the notes that people approached him after Hirschfeld's death and asked him to certify their official permissions to "cross dress," or to live as their self-identified sex, which is quite possible and may not be fictionalization.[45] At a few places in the notes, he seems to plan to have one of the characters in the novel, "John," be a trans Jewish spy; the medical student in the novel (the Li character) will ask John for help.[46] In his notes is a sketch of a subplot where Nazi Germany uses trans agents to try to sexually entrap the Allied leadership.[47] Li and Hirschfeld's paper at the 1932 conference in Brno was apparently about transness as well, and transness comes up a good deal in the *Voilà* profile of Hirschfeld.[48] Li had made it a focus for a long time.

Li, who had lived through the sexual revolution of the 1970s, also found a much higher percentage of non-heterosexuals in the world population than Hirschfeld did: humans were 40 percent bisexual,

30 percent heterosexual, 20 percent homosexual, and 10 percent "all the others such as hermothodit, sadist, masochist, transvestite, fetist, pyalienist, exhibitionist, scopophilia, zoophilia, and etc."[49] One thing to take note of here is how Li is claiming bisexuality as a category. There had been a wave of interest in bisexuality in the 1970s, and perhaps Li had read some of the books and articles that came out then.[50] He had also read the American Alfred Kinsey, famous for arguing that attractions to both sexes were not uncommon, and planned to cite him. He has some Kinsey page numbers in his notes.[51] They seem to be pages in *Sexual Behavior in the Human Male* where Kinsey and his coauthors assert that homosexuality is not biological and that, rather, "the capacity of an individual to respond erotically to any sort of stimulus, whether it is provided by another person of the same or of the opposite sex, is basic in the species."[52] At one point Li made a note about "Agnes Wolf" – did he mean Charlotte Wolff, the Jewish German British sexologist and lesbian who wrote a major book on bisexuality and then a biography of Hirschfeld?[53]

In Hirschfeld's work, there are very few bisexuals.[54] In his day, other authors argued for bisexuality as a universal condition. He quoted one, from a book published in 1906: "All people are bisexual to a certain degree; between 'heterosexuals' and 'homosexuals' there is a gradation, not an absolute distinction ... heterosexuals are not entirely heterosexual ... [Similarly] homosexuals are not entirely homosexual but also have heterosexual feelings."[55] Hirschfeld did not agree with this. He thought the condition existed, but was rare, and that what might seem bisexuality was usually really homosexuality or heterosexuality.[56]

Yet Li seems to suggest that on the world journey, Hirschfeld had revised his view on this and had found the sexual types to exist in new percentages, those Li gives of 40/30/20/10: "This statistic was Dr. Magnus Hirschfeld's prediction in 1932 in search of sexual types around the world in which I was his assistant. And after fifty years of living and traveling in almost every country in the world except South America and Australia study all race of people except the [E]skimo and the [Australian] native I confirm the prediction."[57] Li at one point seems unsure whether he ought to publish this. He crossed out portions of this passage, striking "Dr. Magnus Hirschfeld's prediction in 1932" as well as "I confirm the prediction," yet elsewhere in the manuscript he again asserts that these statistics are the result of the world journey without crossing them out; he also repeats this in his notes.[58] I am not sure what to make of his edits beyond noting some trepidation about claiming Hirschfeld had found this about bisexuality too but had died before he could publish it, a notion that seems in conflict with what Li writes elsewhere about things having changed so much since Hirschfeld's day.

In this draft of the book, perhaps Li was as yet unsure how to present specifically the ways in which his work departed from Hirschfeld's and was testing different approaches. In any event, Li's findings are a major revision of Hirschfeld's published work, an important and clear argument for bisexuality, for sexual fluidity, and against innate sexual identity. Li wrote that almost no man or woman was heterosexual for life. "Such a person should be classified as [an] endangered species."[59]

History indelibly links Li Shiu Tong's name to that of Hirschfeld, but across his long life, the affable and charming Li surely had other love relationships. When Ralf Dose met members of Li's family almost a decade after Li's death, they recalled that Li was a solitary person, without many friends, who spent much of his time with his books and manuscripts, aside from the sports things he liked to do, such as play tennis.[60] Yet perhaps he had a social life his family did not know about; many queer people set up their lives in that way. Maybe he hung out with people in Vancouver's gay scene. Vancouver had queer Asian networks.[61] In the mid-1980s, the city was home to the groups Gay Asians and the Long Yang Social Club, and other groups were founded in the 1990s.[62] The queer Asian Canadian community fought back during the AIDS crisis, decrying the straight Asian Canadian community's sluggishness and moralizing about AIDS and providing support for Asians living with AIDS, including phone help lines in Mandarin and Cantonese.[63] I have no idea whether Li got connected to these activists. He would have been older than many of them.

    If Li went to the majority-white gay bars in Vancouver, he probably ran into some of the racist exoticization and objectification that one sees in Hichens's novel about him. Moreover, he probably faced the sort of racialization Richard Fung analyzes in his classic essay "Looking for My Penis," first published in 1991. Fung describes going to gay clubs in Toronto in the early 1980s and being stopped by the doorman because the doorman thought Fung and his friends were not queer. "I do not believe it was a question of a color barrier. Rather, my friends and I felt that the doorman was genuinely unsure about our sexual orientation. We also felt that had we been white and dressed similarly, our entrance would have been automatic."[64] Fung writes that by 1991, this might not have happened in Toronto any longer because the city by then had such a large Chinese community, but that still "there is an onus on gay Asians and other gay people of color to prove our homosexuality."[65] The shadow of the implicitly white homosexual surely shaped Li's life in Vancouver as well.

Li's book gives one the sense that he was afraid on account of the work that he did. After Hirschfeld, Li seems to have been wary of his public reputation, concerned about being connected to the controversial topic of homosexuality. Understandably so, given that he saw Hirschfeld attacked and exiled for his work. And yet, he hoped to write a book about it. He writes that he would have translated Hirschfeld into English, but Hirschfeld himself told him to wait fifty years after his death to do that. "The reason he gave," Li writes, "was that he did not want [me] to suffer from persecution as he had suffered by entering the forbidden territory in the sexual world."[66] When Li describes his decision to become Hirschfeld's student after they met in Shanghai, he writes, "I jumped [at] the offer unaware of the political trouble to associate with him. His lecture[s] [were] about human sexual variation particularly on homosexuality a still ignorant and controversial topic."[67] Concern for the costs of such work, which would have struck Li in a different way because he was Asian, may be in part why Li did not publish. Hirschfeld, too, seems to have worried that he had set out a dangerous path for Li to follow, warning him not to translate his books. The years of exile and danger weighed on both of them.

Li had, moreover, clearly despaired of sexology as a discipline and had decided to make art as well, to write fiction and sexology together. Maybe he felt similarly to what the French philosopher Michel Foucault felt. Foucault told the gay American magazine *The Advocate* in 1984,

> We have to create a gay life. To *become* ... what the gay movement needs now is much more the art of life than a science or scientific knowledge (or pseudo-scientific knowledge) of what sexuality is ... Sexuality is something that we ourselves create – it is our own creation, and much more than the discovery of a secret side of our desire.[68]

In fiction, Li could create and by creating perhaps more readily write through the intersections of racism, empire, sexuality, and gender that had shaped his life. His sketched-out plot for the novelization portion of the book does not, however, really speak to this, but rather seems, like the work of Hichens, to be seeking to entertain a popular audience. What is clear is that sexology alone, Li thought, was not going to interest the readers of the 1980s, even if he had groundbreaking findings on bisexuality to report. Moreover, the implicit subject of sexology was a white man. Yet Hirschfeld had bound him to carry on with sexology.

One wonders if the indelible whiteness of the homosexual that Hirschfeld did so much to create, and that persisted despite the glimpses of something else in *World Journey*, helped to keep Li's book unfinished and unpublished. In the 1970s and 1980s in Vancouver, would Li have been moved to advocate for an implicitly white "homosexual"? In the 1970s, not in Canada but south of the border, Asian American writers were challenging the white male canon, but they did so by backing what Tan Hoang Nguyen describes as "a very narrow conception of Asian American identity … of the ideal, authentic Asian American subject characterized as male, heterosexual, American born, and English speaking."[69] Richard Fung and others pushed back against the heterosexuality of Asian organizing. In his 1980 "Asians: Gay and Proud," Fung wrote,

> Non-white gay and lesbians face a double-edged sword: the racism of the general society as filtered into the gay community and the sometimes-vicious sexism and homophobia of our own "ethnic" communities. These two factors alone have kept us isolated. The latter has prevented many from participating fully in our own community or if we do, it enforces a secretiveness that leads to cultural schizophrenia.[70]

It was of course not only in some Chinese Canadian circles that homophobia prevailed. White Canadians were generally very invested in heterosexuality, and many (if not most) were profoundly homophobic. Moreover, white racism prevailed in Vancouver. The Asian Canadian community, and Li's family, would have been supports to Li as he faced that racism; could he risk losing their support?[71] Li could have written his queer Asian Canadian masculinity into his book; perhaps that was his intention. In the 1980s, other Canadians, such as Fung, were writing about and organizing around being queer and Asian. Yet Hirschfeld's thought left little space for that, and Hirschfeld had obligated him to carry on his legacy. Li was heir to the implicitly white homosexual. Faced with these conundrums, did he decide, finally, to put the book aside, to put his energies elsewhere?

What does Li's story mean for the canonical history of homosexuality, of which Hirschfeld is a star? Lots of things. Li was a central player in that canonical history – he was Hirschfeld's mainstay between their meeting and his death, the last four years of Hirschfeld's life. Not only was whiteness a big part of homosexual politics, but right at the center of homosexual politics was a man of color, a queer man who was Chinese, Chinese European, and Chinese Canadian. Moreover, Li's view was, eventually, that Hirschfeld's biological model of homosexuality was wrong. The young heir came up with his own theory. At the end, Li was a dissident, and on a central matter. He wrote that desire was more mutable, far more so than Hirschfeld allowed, and he claimed bisexuality as a category, arguing that it was more common than either heterosexuality or homosexuality. Close to half of the human population was bisexual, in Li's model. Desiring other men was not like being member of a "race," he thought. It was a nearly universal desire.

Conclusion: Li Shiu Tong's Berlin and Magnus Hirschfeld's America

Magnus Hirschfeld's model of the modern homosexual owes a tremendous debt to intellectual systems about "the races," Jews, empire, and disability that were swirling around the globe from the nineteenth century into the 1930s and beyond. "The homosexual" borrowed promiscuously. It drew from both sides of major intellectual conflicts of the day. It borrowed from scientific racism. It borrowed from antiracism. It hitched itself to the struggle of Jewish intellectuals to claim whiteness for Jews. It used European and American empires as a natural experiment to prove its validity, and it invited erotic fantasies of an empire of queer love. "The homosexual" drew coherence from eugenics, too. Patriarchy shaped it. Yet it also, at times, lent itself to the struggle against imperialism – Hirschfeld sometimes thought that anticolonialism and homosexual emancipation were two branches of the same crucial struggle for human freedom, that essentially you could not fight one without fighting the other, though he did not make much of that insight. Hirschfeld was racist. He harbored consistent and profound anti-Black sentiment that sometimes erupted into disturbing, racist pronouncements. Yet even he saw on occasion how obvious it was to think queer liberation together with anti-imperialism, and even he saw clearly how racism hurt queer people, such as his beloved Li. Gay politics did not have to be implicitly white, racist, or tied to eugenics.

In the end, it was the more reactionary themes that won out. The analogy that gave form to the sexual minority made the homosexual implicitly white. Though Hirschfeld and other activists knew that queer desires existed around the globe, and sometimes went around the globe themselves seeking queer love, they nevertheless built a political movement that assumed that empire and racism were separate issues from queer liberation. Almost one hundred years later, one sees these same ideas in a lot of white gay organizing in the United States, Germany, and elsewhere.[1] This left queer people who did not have the protection of whiteness, who were exposed to the violence of white racism – people like Li, though there were many forms of racism and experiences varied – in a vexed position, having to choose between queer politics that, at best, ignored racism and antiracist political movements that, at best, did nothing to advance queer freedom, at least until the end of the twentieth century.[2] What is more, all the debts to eugenics made the model of "the homosexual" exclusionary of anyone who was not deemed "fit" in body or mind. I have argued elsewhere that working-class sex workers, men and women, were not only abandoned by Hirschfeld's movement but were sacrificed in the breach in order to win rights for respectable, discreet men like Hirschfeld himself.[3] Hirschfeld's model left the majority of queers out, often in an attempt to put the people it included in a safer and more powerful position.

Why does all of this matter? Throughout this book, I have contended that Hirschfeld's model of homosexuality was hugely influential in the twentieth-century politics of sex writ large, and not only in Germany. One could see this in the 1930s, and it was thanks in part to Hirschfeld and Li's world tour. Zhou Zuoren, China's most important essayist at the time, wrote in 1934 of Hirschfeld as "the grey eminence" of global sexology and condemned the destruction of his Institute and the Nazi arrests of gay men, though Zhou did not fully endorse Hirschfeld's theory and held rather that homosexuality was a mental illness.[4] Yet the rise of fascism destroyed sexology, scattering Hirschfeld and his colleagues in exile.[5]

There is to this day an easy proof of Hirschfeld's influence: describe his model, enumerating the key points – innate, non-pathological, biological, immutable homosexuality, tied to nascent human rights discourse and the concept of a sexual minority – and whoever is listening immediately recognizes a very familiar idea. In some places, it is hegemonic. As an undergraduate instructor in relatively progressive parts of the United States in the 2010s, I often found that my students thought this was the only good explanation for queer desire and that to question it was homophobic. Yet do we really have Hirschfeld to thank for this? How could his model be so well remembered when he is not?

In 1935, when Hirschfeld died, almost no one agreed with him, save other queer activists. That state of affairs seems to have persisted into at least the 1970s. However, Hirschfeld was not forgotten.[6] Many authors, in English as well as German, discussed him and his model, if only to disparage it. Moreover, in the 1950s, following the catastrophic disruption of the Second World War, gay activists returned to Hirschfeld. His ideas seem to have been consistently present in gay activism in parts of

German-speaking Europe and in the United States from the 1950s onward. Indeed, though historians have so far thought of Hirschfeld as a figure in German history, his is a transnational story that is part of American history, too.

Beginning in the 1920s, studies of same-sex sex in US prisons – used as laboratories for the study of sexuality at the time – referenced European psychiatry and sexology and, as they did so, increasingly posited same-sex desire as an innate feature of some prisoners, "homosexuals," not a perversion to which all prisoners were susceptible.[7] They cited Hirschfeld. Among other things, authors on prison sex liked his distinction between real homosexuals and "pseudohomosexuals," people who engaged in same-sex sex only because they were in prison.[8] Hirschfeld visited several prisons in the US in 1930–1. He may have personally influenced some of these other authors. Havelock Ellis, who was influenced by Hirschfeld and had a similar model of homosexuality, was more widely read than Hirschfeld, but Hirschfeld's model was relatively widely discussed.[9]

Americans were not, however, settling into a Hirschfeldian model. Psychoanalytic models of same-sex desire, which were emphatically anti-queer, were far more influential.[10] The prevailing view was that same-sex desire was some kind of mental illness.[11]

Nevertheless, citations of Hirschfeld in the American literature on homosexuality are widespread even decades after his death.[12] Often, these books take a psychoanalytic approach, but they gloss Hirschfeld, identifying his as an older and erroneous theory.[13] "The famous German sexologist" Hirschfeld, wrote the author of the 1954 *Female Homosexuality: A Psychodynamic Study of Lesbianism*, "unfortunately … harbored the misconception that homosexuality is congenital."[14] Some of Hirschfeld's books came out in unauthorized English translations; *Female Homosexuality* cited them.[15] American authors also read German.[16] Jeannette Howard Foster wrote in her 1956 *Sex Variant Women in Literature* that Hirschfeld was a "crusader for official leniency and general tolerance on the grounds that homosexuality is inborn and therefore should not be penalized."[17] The twentieth century ushered in toleration of homosexuality, she argued, because of the spread of a model of homosexuality as innate and hereditary, for which she credited Hirschfeld, Ellis, and others.[18] The Freudian Sandor Rado wrote in a 1965 essay that Hirschfeld "engaged in a lifelong defense of homosexuals against the harshness of a medieval law."[19] An anti-queer psychiatrist and professor at Catholic University in Washington, DC, wrote that homosexuality was psychological, not biological. He went on, in a passage that gives one a sense of these conversations and the place of biological homosexuality in them, to describe how it propagates itself as a morally contagious disease ... tend[ing] to bring about more and more unfruitful unions that withdraw men and women from normal family life, the development of homes, and the procreation of children. The growth of a homosexual society in any country is a menace, more or less serious, to the welfare of the state. One cannot say that one must recognize the existence of homosexuals as a biological fact and that because all homosexuals are biologically determined they have rights of their own which society must grant.[20]

For those ideas – biological homosexuality and homosexual rights – this author writes that "Magnus Hirschfeld advocated the repeal of laws against homosexuals because homosexuality rests as a rule on deep inner constitutional disposition."[21] One can see how to a reader of such a passage, a reader seeking a pro-queer position in the midst of vitriol, Hirschfeld's biological, rights-bearing homosexual would look like a useful idea and feel like a relief.

Sex researcher Alfred Kinsey, whose model was not psychiatric, had a detailed knowledge of Hirschfeld's work. Kinsey, perhaps not incidentally, was, like Hirschfeld, in a non-monogamous relationship, though Kinsey was married to a woman. Also like Hirschfeld, Kinsey had an affair with a younger male sexologist who worked as his assistant. Kinsey shifted his research from zoology and botany to sexuality just a few years after Hirschfeld gave lectures in Detroit, Chicago, and Kansas City, not that far from Kinsey's home in Bloomington, Indiana.[22] Kinsey even knew the work of Lucien von Römer, Hirschfeld's Dutch student whom he and Li visited in East Java, though Kinsey does not mention von Römer's eugenic take on homosexuality.[23] Kinsey and his coauthors spend several pages in their groundbreaking *Sexual Behavior in the Human Male* taking Hirschfeld down. While they do, they acknowledge that Hirschfeld has been very influential, that no other study of homosexuality "has had as great influence on the thinking of clinicians" and that the "professional literature" on homosexuality rarely cites anyone but Hirschfeld and Havelock Ellis.[24] "Males do not represent two discrete populations, heterosexual and homosexual," Kinsey and his collaborators wrote. "The world is not to be divided into sheep and goats."[25] Kinsey, moreover, felt Hirschfeld's own (covert) homosexuality had tainted his work.[26] Nevertheless, Kinsey and his coauthors believed Hirschfeld was important and was widely known. Hirschfeld's ideas also traveled via Kinsey's books, and Kinsey's data on same-sex behavior basically matched Hirschfeld's.[27]

Even decades after his death, Hirschfeld was well remembered in America. In a speech to what was most likely a left-leaning sex reform group in 1969, Harry Benjamin said of Hirschfeld, "he needs no introduction as a sexologist and spokesman for the homosexual community." In the speech, Benjamin then outed Hirschfeld, something Hirschfeld himself never did.[28]

Hirschfeld's ideas lived on in American homophile literature in the 1950s. As Leila Rupp and David Churchill have shown, the precedent of Hirschfeld's Scientific Humanitarian Committee was important to many European and American homophile groups, which used minority language and drew on human rights discourse.[29] This was true of the important early US group the Mattachine Society: "The Mattachine Society holds it possible and desirable that a highly ethical homosexual culture emerge ... paralleling the emerging cultures of our fellow minorities ... the Negro, Mexican, and Jewish Peoples."[30] It was also true of Donald Webster Cory's influential 1951 *The Homosexual in America*. Written under a pseudonym, the book was a defense of homosexuality by a homosexual.[31] Cory had read Hirschfeld. He admired Hirschfeld's argument that "the prevailing social conditions and the laws which reflected them were designed to make a minority suffer without contributing anything whatsoever to society at large."[32] Cory's first chapter, "The Unrecognized Minority," begins in a familiar way: "In recent years, the world has become extremely conscious of minority problems ... one constantly hears that human rights must be granted, regardless of race, religion, color, or political creed ... Minority rights, many contend, have become the challenge of his century."[33] Touching on the plights of Jews, of Hindus and Muslims in India and Pakistan, Catholics in Northern Ireland, Protestants in Italy, and African Americans, Cory asserts, "We who are homosexual constitute a minority."[34] Cory's description of a sexual minority, which had a large impact on queer activists in the US, West Germany, and probably elsewhere, has been credited as the first iteration of that idea, but it was not.[35] He had read it in Hirschfeld, and perhaps even in Hiller.[36]

Though homophile activists like Cory kept Hirschfeld's model circulating, my guess is that it was only during the 1970s that the model began to be accepted beyond queer activist circles, in the mainstream. In the US this seems to have happened during the fight to remove homosexuality from the *Diagnostic and Statistical Manual of Mental Disorders* in the early 1970s, when activists whose model of homosexuality was basically identical to Hirschfeld's insisted that homosexuals were a "sexual minority," not mentally ill.[37]

Hirschfeld was much better known in his lifetime and after his death, even into the 1970s, than we have realized, and not only in Germany but in the United States. His ideas shaped sexual politics in a profound way.

I wonder if this book will be read as a call to "cancel" Hirschfeld – that is, as I take it, to stop reading him, to stop assigning him to others to read, and to stop writing about him. That is not my intention, and yet, what to do with him? It is true that Hirschfeld courageously fought for a better world. He did indeed help to make a world in which many people with queer desires are in far better positions than they would have been in 1931. At the same time, he does not make a very good gay hero. He has far too many violent and profoundly unjust trends in his work. I have endeavored to judge him by the standards of his own time, as well as by the standards of my time, and by the words that he himself wrote. He was not an antiracist feminist; let's stop saying that he was.[38]

Yet neither should we turn away from Hirschfeld. What I would like for those of us who read Hirschfeld, write about him, and assign him to students is that we present his theories in their totality, for what they are, without excuses, apologies, or elisions. I have endeavored to do that in this book. Indeed, this book is an argument for a much wider community of people to pay attention to him, a contention that he was more important than he often gets credit for being, a contention that the history of gay rights has a first chapter that is quite different from what most people think. Yet, as we recognize that, let's also recognize the parts of his work that we abhor and that are yet still with us. Let's stop naming things after him. Maybe some of the things named for him could be renamed. Finally, what's most important is that we examine how the parts of his work that we reject have lingered in the present, how some of us have benefited from them, how those of us who have been hurt by them have had to struggle, and that we work toward a gay politics that does not assume a white subject, promote a violently anti-disability politics, marginalize women of color and white women, fail to consistently reject imperialism, throw sex workers under the bus, wrap itself in a strict respectability, or go down any of the troubling paths that we have seen Hirschfeld tread.[39] He can, in that way, be an inspiration.[40]

Li Shiu Tong's Berlin was the Berlin of 1932. The year Li arrived in Berlin was the year before Hitler came to power. Li was there without Hirschfeld. He posed for a photograph with Karl Giese, who was still living and working at the Institute for Sexual Science, which had not yet been destroyed (figure 11). Li's Berlin was a Berlin of numbered days, a Berlin about to plunge into the abyss. It was nevertheless a real place. To say Li never was *of* Berlin is wrong – he was. The city, a destination only tentatively reached, an imagined future never lived out, shadowed his years with Hirschfeld and, indeed, the rest of his life, as he lived in Switzerland, Hong Kong, the United States, and Canada, and as he worked to live up to the charge laid on him in Hirschfeld's will, to carry on his mentor's life's work even while all that his mentor had built in Berlin, all he had hoped to leave to Li, had been destroyed by fascism. For many of those years, Li worked in German, as a student at Europe's renowned German-speaking universities in Vienna and Zurich. He has been mostly ignored by German studies; he is however a figure in a transnational (often but not only German) story of empire, exile, and the search for a better world.[41]

What sort of figure in transnational gay history is Li Shiu Tong? We know so little of his own thoughts on all of this. We are left having to read for what he thought and did through the lines of what other people wrote about him. We are left with his fragmentary manuscript, a partial book that does not answer all of the questions one would like to ask of Li. Nevertheless, I think we can say that Li was a lot more important in queer history than we have up until now acknowledged. He fashioned his own queer masculinity, he flourished in the transnational world of sexology as Hirschfeld's protégé, and with much justification he looked forward to a promising career. He gave a paper with Hirschfeld at an important conference. He worked with him on a book that attempted to articulate the struggle for sexual freedom, the struggle against racism, and the struggle against empire as the same struggle. Li's career, the path he had laid out before him, was dashed by the rise of Nazi Germany. Yet Li survived Hirschfeld's passing. He went on, pursuing his career in Zurich, collaborating with Hichens on a portrait of himself. That portrait is racist and demeaning of Li. We can attribute that racialization to Hichens. At the same time, there is in that portrait a wonderful queer masculinity in which the Li character works the exoticization and plays on the racialized white gaze of white gays in ways that, in the end, make the Li character the hero of the novel and leave the white characters who dismissed, mocked, and desexualized him in awe. Here, I would argue, Hichens's novel shows Li as he was or hoped to be, a wealthy, dapper, charming, sweet, and very smart young man making a life for himself in Zurich and making a name for himself, a man of great promise determined to take up Hirschfeld's work, to bring liberation to humanity through sexual science. Between his days as a student in Zurich and his final years in Vancouver, the archive reveals little about what Li did. Yet, at the end of his life, in his unfinished manuscript, Li portrays himself as having succeeded. There, he is the sexologist he set out to be. He has, like Hirschfeld, traveled the world, amassing data. His findings dispute his mentor's in some ways and not in others. He is an independent thinker, a mature sexologist in his own right who had despaired of his discipline and who aspired to write a book that merged

two genres, the sexological treatise and the adventure novel. Li's unfinished theory holds out what may seem like liberation. Long experience
shows that neither a universalizing nor minoritizing model necessarily
embraces justice.[42] At the same time, in Li's work there was no analogy
to a minoritized race and no place for such an analogy: queerness is
too fluid and too widespread. In other ways, Li's model was moored in
some of the biopolitics that are so troubling in Hirschfeld's work. It says
nothing about empire. Yet Li's story shows the path forged by a queer
Chinese European Canadian sexologist whose life nearly spanned the
twentieth century.

Queer male lives in the 1930s were not easy to forge. Yet Hirschfeld
and Li did so. I hope that in this book one gets a sense of the texture
of the lives they made. They were discreetly queer. This did not protect
them completely from anti-homosexual animus. Hirschfeld, an advocate
of respectability and discretion, was ironically undone in 1934 by a police
raid on a bathhouse. The precarious position of sexology as a science,
and the radical nature of his views, as well as antisemitism, kept him
outside of the academy in a moment when American academics saved
a few of their European colleagues with special visas.[43] Hirschfeld had
recourse only to a friend, Harry Benjamin, a doctor in private practice
who could do little for him.

The form the love between Hirschfeld and Li took is an important part
of queer history. They lived at a time when people organized their queer
love affairs around, rather than through, the institution of marriage.
Their love affair was no "marriage" or "partnership" but something else
entirely. Their relationship had an inventive structure (though the homoeroticism of a male-male mentorship was a very well-trodden path), a
structure that did not exclude Hirschfeld's relationship with Giese. Others they met had original arrangements too – possibly von Römer and his
wife and friend; Hichens and his friend and his friend's wife. These loves
were shrouded in discretion.[44] This was decades before gay liberationists
of the 1970s would disparage such discretion as "the closet" and urge
people to come out.

The Li-Hirschfeld connection was an important professional relationship between two sexologists. It was also a love story, one that began in
Shanghai's International Settlement, in empire. In that story, Li navigated anti-Chinese white racism and Hirschfeld navigated antisemitism.
The story had tragic moments. It had blissfully happy ones, too, surely:
Li's improbable victory in the donkey race in Egypt. The shared dream
that a young man from Hong Kong would take over all that Hirschfeld
had built and become the world's premier sexologist, leading the new
discipline into the second half of the twentieth century from his seat

at the Institute in Berlin and fighting for the freedom of homosexuals. Easter in their hilltop temporary home in a left-wing Swiss enclave. Li's return from China in 1934 and the ten days in Venice. Their swim together in the bay outside of Makassar.

In his research on sexuality around the world, Li Shiu Tong found that only 30 percent of people were heterosexual and that almost none of them could hold out forever: "Such a person should be classified as [an] endangered species," he wrote of lifelong heterosexuals. The sexual category in which most humans fell, Li found, was bisexuality. He also found that same-sex desire was not a birthright but something one came to over the course of one's life.

After Hirschfeld, science did not prove that homosexuality was innate, biological, and immutable. This is despite lots of trying and lots of funding. If you ask me, this failure tends to show that it is not. Take, for example, the 2019 Ganna et al. study of the genetics of roughly half a million cisgender white people in the UK, US, and Sweden, a study ballyhooed in the press as having squashed the theory of a single gay gene, which it did. The study also excluded people of color – here, once again, the homosexual was made white – and excluded trans people. It found that "genes contribute minimally, inconsistently and complexly to human sexual expression."[45] It also found, however, that having gay sex seemed to correlate – minimally – with genetic markers associated with the propensity to take risks. In homophobic societies, acting on one's queer desire entails taking risks. This suggest that, in fact, it is courage that has a minimal, complex, and partial genetic cause, not queerness, which is a secondary effect. The findings in favor of Hirschfeld's model were weak.[46]

It is nevertheless at times helpful to think about comparisons among systems of oppression (rather than analogies between supposed states of being), systems of oppression such as racism, sexism, and homophobia, and though it is imperative not to treat them as independent systems, I am not calling for the end to all such analytics. Even biological homosexuality itself – the assertion that queerness is innate, non-pathological, and unchanging – can nevertheless be a useful part of an antiracist, anti-imperial, and feminist queer politics. I am thinking of the day a friend came out to her family; she said her family would never have accepted her had she explained her sexuality in any other way. Though I would love to see Hirschfeld's model decline, I am all for a nimble politics that is not categorically against invoking it, in thoughtful ways that do not reproduce the exclusions to which it is so prone. Yet what is more exciting by far are the possibilities for another queer politics entirely.

Models of queer desire that do not anchor it in a biological minority admit that same-sex sex is an attractive thing, something one might fall happily into – despite the tremendous pressure not to fall into it – rather than something that one would avoid at all costs unless one was born with an insurmountable predisposition. Queerness might be something that one might choose, something that might make one's life better, an intentional and liberating expansion of the world. Katharina Oguntoye writes that over time, she experienced her coming out in Berlin in the 1980s as "a liberation, a tremendous expansion of the world as I lived in it and of the possibilities open to me."[47] Queer desire might call for the courage of one's convictions, were it not innate. It might call on one to think about how unjust the interconnected racialized, gendered social organizations of sexuality were and to try to change them.[48] For women, queerness might offer an escape from patriarchy, might mean the possibility of a more egalitarian love relationship. There are lots of good arguments for queer liberation that are not about biological homosexuality.

Ditching the biological model does not mean ditching identity. Contrary to what some queer theorists wrote in the 1990s, identity is not the problem.[49] Identity is a project of fashioning, even if the project is to make one's identity a foreordained thing, and even as the work of fashioning identity is work that always exceeds one's control.[50] Identity need not be a received scientific fact, though some people may fashion a narrative of identity that poses it as such. Doing "the fiction of identity," writes Muñoz, is tougher work for those "whose identities are formed in response to the cultural logics of heteronormativity, white supremacy, and misogyny," and it is done by more complex means – more interesting and sophisticated means.[51] Li was right, I think, that lots of queers would want to read the story of a young man like he was in the 1930s rescuing his older lover from the Nazis, finding a safe haven for the two of them, enlisting a trans spy's help, protecting secrets that could have turned the course of the Second World War, and defeating the fascists. That fiction would, I submit, feed the grand fiction of queer identity and push back against the fiction of straight identity, a fiction that is, in Muñoz's words, "accessed with relative ease" but that is also less cinematic, far more routine, less thrilling and romantic than the daring escape by plane or taxi.[52] To paraphrase Foucault and Rich, we have to become gay, whether we are born gay or not; heterosexuality is the automatic default, compulsory; Li's story of escape, his turn away from science and toward art, is a creation of queer life.[53]

Li, too, had some dark moments in his (only partially articulated) theory, eugenic moments. He wrote nothing about empire. I do not mean to make him into the intersectional theorist I hoped he was when I first learned some of his own papers had survived. Perhaps the most inspiring, to me, definitional moment for "homosexuality" in the story I have told here came at the beginning, when Hirschfeld, in Manila with Li on a morning walk with an unnamed student, talked about how sexual liberation and the struggle against imperialism were branches of the same struggle. The more important thing, I think, than figuring out what queerness is, determining what causes it, or describing it conclusively is to envision a better world, a world with more equality of resources, less racism, less antisemitism, less sexism, less trans oppression, less anti-queer animus – a more just world – and to work toward it.

The tale of Li and Hirschfeld's world journey shows something else, too. Even to such a flawed leader of queer politics as Hirschfeld, at times the struggle for queer liberation seemed intrinsically tied to other struggles against injustice, such as decolonial politics and antiracism. The grounds for a broad struggle, one that included more people, were self-evident and present at the very beginning of gay politics. In the 1930s, those who struggled for gay liberation included a young man from Hong Kong, who helped to make it possible for a progressive sexologist to go around the world promoting sexual liberation, and who went on to devote his life to a version of the project of liberation that that sexologist had bequeathed to him. A lot of the gay politics that followed Hirschfeld was implicitly white, dominated by white people who did not centrally grapple with racism as a queer problem. That political tradition betrayed Li. It betrayed the promise of gay politics to be a broad struggle against racism and empire and for sexual liberation for many people, a promise that was present at the beginning of gay politics. But it need not have been so. And it need not be so now.

Acknowledgments

Thanks to these institutions for their support: the Department of History of the University of Washington, the Walter Chapin Simpson Center for the Humanities at the University of Washington, the University of Washington Royalty Research Fund, the Keller Fund and Hanauer Fund at the Department of History of the University of Washington, the Jon Bridgman Endowed Professorship, the Stroum Center for Jewish Studies, the Tretter Collection at the University of Minnesota, and the Modern European History Research Centre, University of Oxford.

While, as one was obliged to say in older days, the errors are mine, I am grateful to these people for their help: the three peer reviewers (thank you so much for your time and your ideas, you made this book better), Stephen Shapiro of the University of Toronto Press (without whose encouragement this may not have ever been a book at all), Kate Blackmer, Barbie Halaby, Robin Studniberg, Jennifer Harris, Barb Porter, Doug Manelski, Anne Schult, Ben Klassen, Ron Dutton, Guang Yu Ren, Indrani Chatterjee, Nick Freeman, Rachel Mattson, Matt K. Matsuda, Belinda Davis, Marc Matera, Kris Alexanderson, Samantha Kahn Herrick, Norman Kutcher, Tamara Chaplin, Katie Sutton, Jennifer V. Evans, Monica Black, Anna Hájková, Richard Wetzell, Elizabeth Heineman, Radha Kumar, Amber Jamilla Musser, Glennys Young, Jordanna Bailkin, Purnima Dhavan, Josh Apfel, James Felak, Alexandra DuSablon, Arbella Bet-Shlimon, Susan Glenn, James Gregory, Liora Halperin, Ting-chieh Ou Yang, Ray Jonas, Eric W. Johnson, Hajin Jun, Tracy Maschman Morrissey, Matthew Mosca, Rachel Silberstein, Theresa Mudrock, Devin Naar, Kristin Roberts, Margaret O'Mara, Vicente Rafael, Shannon Vacek, Benjamin Schmidt, Joshua Reid, Ileana Rodriguez-Silva, Lynn M. Thomas, Sarah Zaides Rosen, Joel Thomas Walker, Adam Warren, Anand Yang, La TaSha Levy, James Lin, Noam Pianko, Becky Mandelbaum, Kathy Woodward, Adair Rounthwaite, Kathryn A.V. Schlenker, Rachel Arteaga, María Elena

García, Jenna Grant, Belinda He, Jang Wook Huh, Adrian Kane-Galbraith, Priti Ramamurthy, Christopher Teuton, Melissa Melby, Rafe Rachel Neis, Amanda Marcotte, and Weihong Bao. I was privileged to have the research assistance of Jiahui Huang, Taylor Soja, and Charles Coffland, and, moreover, the enthusiasm and sage advice of Soja and Coffland in the bleak pandemic year that saw this book's completion; thanks.

In Berlin, the Magnus Hirschfeld Gesellschaft opened its archive to me, allowed me to use images, and gave encouragement and advice. Members of the MHG may not agree with all that I wrote here, but I am in their debt: they rescued Hirschfeld and Li's history from neglect, and, once, literally from the garbage. Herzlichen Dank insbesondere an Raimund Wolfert und Ralf Dose.

Thanks to the people who taught and cared for my kid while I wrote this book. They also heroically did childcare through the COVID-19 pandemic, allowing other parents to keep working in the hospitals and labs. What is more, in the thick of the Trump "coprocracy," they taught my kid to cherish democracy, and in the wake of the terrible murders of Ahmaud Arbery, Breonna Taylor, and George Floyd, they taught my kid to fight against racism. Thanks Andrea Mosko, Jack Harrington, Meaghan Carroll, Frisian Waller, Emily Talman, Warinda Bongkotmart, Ana Peeters, Eliot Murray, and Jennifer Sorenson.

In memory of Laurence Joseph "Joe" Marhoefer (October 14, 1935–August 29, 2021). Tough-guy dad and fast runner.

RIP Bob Maher. We miss you, man.

Love and thanks to Leigh-Anne Francis, Niamh Duggan, Desireena Almoradie, Nili Shani, Erika Krech, Bonnie Whiting, Nikki Crouse, Beckett Crouse, Deb Kamen, Sarah Levin Richardson, Julie Gozan, Tom Keck, Ruby Gozan-Keck, Sasha Gozan-Keck, Barbara Marhoefer, John Marhoefer, Maria Regan, Grace Marhoefer, Jack Marhoefer, Mary Beth Gaiarin, Manu Gaiarin, Alex Gaiarin, Ben "Ben-a" Gaiarin, Melinda Maher, Joe Maher, Cia Maher, Will Maher, Molly Maher, and Maggie "swim little Maggie!" Maher. I'm not putting Tigger in my book acknowledgments. She can't read. Ditto Zigra and forget about Butch and Gilda. However, if I may, shout-out to my mom, Barbara: best mom ever. We love you.

Stephanie Clare – Je t'aime. Merci pour tout. J'espère que tu dormiras toute la nuit.

Hattie Marhoefer Clare – One time I was taking you to the zoo on a weekend (we went so much to the zoo in the years I wrote this book, and then for months it was all that was open so we went again and again and then finally you said, *Momo, I saw the hippos last week I do not want to see them again now!*) and you fell asleep in your car seat and napped in the parking lot and I sat in the driver's seat and worked on this book – I forget which part. Then you woke up and I pulled you in the wagon, probably in the rain, to see the hippos, Guadalupe and Water Lily. At first they were not there, the pool was still and dark, because they glide invisible under untroubled water – then, shock! Up burst a fierce head, gaping – fist-sized teeth! – she eyed us, us just beyond the railing. When I was finishing this book, I went to pick you up at school one afternoon and you ran out of the gate and climbed fifteen feet up a tree in the sunlight. I love you, little kid, so much I can't describe it. Sleep all night!

Seattle, Washington, July 2, 2021

Notes

Archives and Abbreviations Used in Notes

Bundesarchiv Lichterfelde
Deutsches Literaturarchiv Marbach
Haeberle-Hirschfeld Archiv für Sexualwissenschaft, Humboldt University
    Library, Berlin (HHAfS-Humboldt)
Magnus Hirschfeld Gesellschaft, Berlin (MHG)
    Li Shiu Tong Nachlass
    Sammlung Max Reiss
Geheimes Staatsarchiv Preußischer Kulturbesitz (GStAPK)
University of Sydney Library, Sydney
    Norman Haire Collection
New York Public Library Astor, Lenox and Tilden Foundations: Manuscripts
    and Archives Division
    Carl Van Vechten Papers
Wellcome Library Special Collections, London
    Charlotte Wolff Papers
    Family Planning Association Collection (E. Elkan Papers)

Introduction

1 Magnus Hirschfeld, *Die Weltreise eines Sexualforschers* (Brugg, Switzerland: Bözberg, 1933), 134. Translations into English are my own unless otherwise noted. *Die Weltreise eines Sexualforschers* was translated by O.P. Green, who took some liberties with the original: *Women East and West: Impressions of a Sex Expert* (London: William Heinemann, 1935). I have used the original German version and refer to the book as *World Journey of a Sexologist* or *World Journey*; these are my translations of Hirschfeld's original title, which is a better descriptor of the book than the title of Green's translation. On translation and sexology see Bauer, "Not a Translation but a Mutilation."

A note on the notes: With the exception of a few key texts, citations are abbreviated; full bibliographical information is in the bibliography. When possible and appropriate, all citations for a given paragraph were consolidated into a single note at the end of that paragraph.

2 Though Hirschfeld's fame is again growing in Germany, few remember his global fame or his global influence even decades after his death (on this see the conclusion).

3 Hirschfeld, *Weltreise*, 134.

4 Molnar, *American Mestizos, the Philippines, and the Malleability of Race*, 14; Winkelmann, "Dangerous Intercourse"; Chu, *Chinese and Chinese Mestizos of Manila*, 24–5, 282–3, 288–9; Abinales and Amoroso, *State and Society in the Philippines*, 64–6. Quotation at Hirschfeld, *Weltreise*, 134.

5 Ferguson, *One-Dimensional Queer*, 2.

6 Hirschfeld, *Weltreise*, 65. I am inferring somewhat here. Hirschfeld's account of this incident only says it happened to himself and "a Chinese student." I assume the student was Li. On the Munich attack see Marhoefer, *Sex and the Weimar Republic*, 4.

7 Hirschfeld, *Weltreise*, 134.

8 See Vaid, *Virtual Equality*; Vaid, *Irresistible Revolution*.

9 Most of humanity is not "white."

10 Ferguson, *One-Dimensional Queer*; Osorio, "Embodying Truth." On leftist queer radicalism see also Hobson, *Lavender and Red*.

11 See for example BLM Seattle–King County: https://blacklivesseattle.org /about (accessed July 2, 2020). On the capitalization of "Black," see Florvil, *Mobilizing Black Germany*, 184n9.

12 Hirschfeld, *Weltreise*, 135.

13 Chu, *Chinese and Chinese Mestizos of Manila*, 289–90.

14 Canaday, *Straight State*, 19–54; Hirschfeld, *Geschlechtskunde* III, 53. Li lived in the US later, and Hirschfeld seriously considered immigrating there, and neither man seems to have worried about his sexuality being an issue.

15 Vordtriede, *Das verlassene Haus*, 244–5.

16 Hirschfeld, *Weltreise*, 65.

17 Hirschfeld, *Weltreise*, 138–9. Hirschfeld identifies the university as the "University of the Philippines, *philippinische[] Staatsuniversität.*"

18 Hirschfeld, *Weltreise*, 141.

19 Hirschfeld, *Weltreise*, 141–3.

20 Hirschfeld, *Weltreise*, 142.

21 Hirschfeld, *Weltreise*, 143.

22 Hirschfeld, *Weltreise*, 59–60, 68–9, 143–5. Quotations at 60 and 68–9. On the ship's first year: Alexanderson, *Subversive Seas*, 9. On his love of the sea: Magnus Hirschfeld, *Testament, Heft II*, ed. Ralf Dose (Berlin: Hentrich and Hentrich, 2013), 118. On Li as a dinner companion: Hichens, *That Which Is Hidden*, 604. On my justifications for using this novel as a source, see chapter 12.

23 Hirschfeld, *Weltreise*, 68; on the language of "Chinese pupil" for example: Wolff, *Magnus Hirschfeld*, 429–30.

24 By "queer" I mean erotic identities and desires that were non-coercive and non-violent, involving consenting adults, and yet were stigmatized, suppressed, and considered out-of-bounds by mainstream societies in the time and place in question. See Eng, Halberstam, and Muñoz, "What's Queer About Queer Studies Now?"; Evans, "Introduction: Why Queer German History?"

25 Alexanderson, *Subversive Seas*, 119–22, 194–5.

26 Sears, *Arresting Dress*, 124–5; Fung, "Looking for My Penis." This continued through the twentieth century and into the twenty-first. See, among others, Cheung, "Woman Warrior Versus the Chinaman Pacific," 113–33; Eng, *Racial Castration*; Canaday, *Straight State*, 29; Nguyen, *View from the Bottom*, 3–6.

27 Gandhi, *Affective Communities*, 51–3.

28 See chapter 3.

29 Lim, *Brown Boys and Rice Queens*, 1–40; Eng, *Racial Castration*, 158–9, 220. See also Lowrie, *Masters and Servants*.

30 Mungello, *Western Queers in China*, 1–7. For Hirschfeld's theory as to why China was more tolerant, see chapter 3.

31 The phrase "empire of queer love" is a riff on and homage to Matsuda, *Empire of Love*, which argues that the French experienced their empire in terms of love.

32 Alexanderson, *Subversive Seas*, 4–5, 81, 86–7, 100, 117–26; Kris Alexanderson, email to the author, June 14, 2021.

33 Alexanderson, *Subversive Seas*, 107.

34 Alexanderson, *Subversive Seas*, 80–1.

35 Alexanderson, *Subversive Seas*, 72–87, 112.

36 Alexanderson, *Subversive Seas*, 81–2.

37 Alexanderson, *Subversive Seas*, 97.

38 Hirschfeld, *Weltreise*, 60, 145.

39 Alexanderson, *Subversive Seas*, 72–4. I have followed Alexanderson in the practice of not putting the word "coolie" in quotation marks, though it was a racialized term of abuse at the time. Currently it is a badge of honor for many descendants in South Asia – see *Subversive Seas*, 72n1.

40 Alexanderson, *Subversive Seas*, 112–13. See also Koven, *Slumming*.

41 Hirschfeld, *Weltreise*, 60.

42 Hirschfeld, *Weltreise*, 60. On his confidence that he had gotten to know China like few other Europeans did, partly thanks to Li, see *Weltreise*, 59, 69.

43 Alexanderson, *Subversive Seas*, 122–3.

44 "Whites More Sexy in Dancing than Negroes, Scientist Thinks," *Baltimore Afro-American*, February 14, 1931.

45 See chapter 11.

46 Duman, "Eine Minderheit unter vielen." While in this quotation Duman suggests this is new, this book contends that it was the case from the beginning of gay politics.

47 On this persistence, see, for example, how whiteness is a default assumption for the authors of a widely reported 2019 study of queerness and genetics: Clare, "Biological Sex and the 'Overrepresentation of Man.'"

48 The scholarship on intersectionality was shaped by Crenshaw, "Demarginalizing the Intersection of Race and Sex"; Crenshaw, "Mapping the Margins." For more on intersectionality see Collins and Bilge, *Intersectionality*. Though Crenshaw coined the term, the analytical practice has a much longer history in Black feminism: Collins and Bilge, *Intersectionality*, 53–69.

49 Eng, *Racial Castration*, 2.

50 Key works include Eng, *Racial Castration*; Eng and Hom, *Q&A: Queer in Asian America*; Fung, "Looking for My Penis"; Ferguson, *Aberrations in Black*; Somerville, *Queering the Color Line*; Ross, "Beyond the Closet as a Raceless Paradigm"; Mumford, *Interzones*; Perez, "You Can Have My Brown Body and Eat It, Too!"; Bravmann, *Queer Fictions of the Past*; Puar, *Terrorist Assemblages*; Decena, *Tacit Subjects*; Hochberg, "Queer Politics and the Question of Palestine/Israel"; Stein, *Measuring Manhood*; Musser, *Sensational Flesh*. See also more recent work on race and trans politics: Snorton, *Black on Both Sides*; Sears, *Arresting Dress*, especially 121–38. See also recent queer histories that center queer people of color, such as Mumford, *Not Straight, Not White*; Hartman, *Wayward Lives, Beautiful Experiments*; Capó, *Welcome to Fairyland*.

51 El-Tayeb, *European Others*; El-Tayeb, "Gays Who Cannot Properly Be Gay"; Haritaworn, *Queer Lovers and Hateful Others*; Haritaworn, "Women's Rights, Gay Rights and Anti-Muslim Racism in Europe"; Ewing, "Color Him Black"; Fuechtner, "Indians, Jews, and Sex"; Funke, "Navigating the Past"; Herrn and Taylor, "Magnus Hirschfeld's Interpretation of the Japanese *Onnagata* as Transvestites"; Boovy, "Troubling Sameness"; Egelmeers, "Universal Fetishism?"; Bauer, *Hirschfeld Archives*. A note about Bauer's wonderful book *The Hirschfeld Archives*. I am seeking to do something similar to what Bauer does there, particularly in the chapter on racism, and most of what I argue dovetails with what Bauer argues, though we cover different ground. Bauer does not treat Hirschfeld's writing on "the races" as a coherent theory (which I argue that it is), does not explore some of his most racist moments, and is not as interested in Li. My view of Hirschfeld's self-described antiracism is, at the end, more damning than Bauer's. Bauer does not argue that Hirschfeld's book about his world journey harbors a vision of a fundamentally anti-imperial gay politics that was essentially betrayed by Hirschfeld.

52 This point is now well established in European history; on gender and sexuality with respect to it, see (among many others) Stoler, *Race and the Education of Desire*; Stoler, *Carnal Knowledge and Imperial Power*; McClintock, *Imperial Leather*.

53 See, for example, Najmabadi, *Women with Mustaches and Men without Beards*;
   Rupp, *Sapphistries*; Clare, "Biological Sex and the 'Overrepresentation of
   Man.'"

54 See Fung, "Looking for My Penis"; Mumford, *Not Straight, Not White*, 70–7;
   Nash, *Black Body in Ecstasy*.

55 Hammonds, "Toward a Genealogy of Black Female Sexuality," 101.

56 This is arguably the takeaway of Somerville's widely read article and chapter on the topic, though the overarching concerns in her book are to the
   contrary. See her "Scientific Racism and the Emergence of the Homosexual Body" and *Queering the Color Line*, 37; for the broader project of that
   book with respect to this topic, which to my eye is quite a different argument, see *Queering the Color Line*, 7. Something similar seems to be going
   on with respect to historical findings in Rohy, *Anachronism and Its Others*,
   such as at ix–x, while at the same time (indeed, on the next page) Rohy argues against analogies between queerness and blackness: *Anachronism and
   Its Others*, xi. Compare my argument, especially chapters 2 and 5.

57 An example of people racialized as non-white and white queers being
   discursively constructed in very similar terms is the theme in evolutionary theory about less evolved peoples being less gender differentiated,
   which appears in the work of Havelock Ellis and others, and contrasts with
   Hirschfeld's universalist model of the homosexual. See Markowitz, "Pelvic
   Politics." This does not mean that white European power structures at the
   time treated people who were racialized as non-white (be they queer or
   not) and white queers in similar ways.

58 For a take on this in trans history see Gearhardt, "Rethinking Trans History."

59 For example, the masculinist, racist wing of the German homosexual
   emancipation movement led by Adolf Brand. On Benedict Friedlaender,
   Adolf Brand, and their intellectual tradition, see Keilson-Lauritz, *Die
   Geschichte der eigenen Geschichte*; Tobin, *Peripheral Desires*; Bruns, "Politics of
   Masculinity in the (Homo-) Sexual Discourse"; Marhoefer, *Sex and the Weimar
   Republic*, 40, 58, 158; Marhoefer, "Queer Fascism and the End of Gay History."

60 Marhoefer, *Sex and the Weimar Republic*. See also McKenna, "Safer Sex";
   Wheeler, *How Sex Became a Civil Liberty*.

61 Hirschfeld biographies and work that deals centrally with him: Herzer,
   Magnus Hirschfeld; Herzer, *Magnus Hirschfeld und seine Zeit*; Kotowski and
   Schoeps, *Der Sexualreformer Magnus Hirschfeld*; Dose, *Magnus Hirschfeld:
   Deutscher – Jude – Weltbürger*; Dose, *Magnus Hirschfeld: The Origins of the Gay
   Liberation Movement*; Mancini, *Magnus Hirschfeld and the Quest for Sexual
   Freedom*; Wolff, *Magnus Hirschfeld*; Leng, "Magnus Hirschfeld's Meanings";
   Bauer, *Hirschfeld Archives*; Mildenberger, "Per scientiam ad iustitiam?";
   Marhoefer, *Sex and the Weimar Republic*. See also the many issues of the
   Mitteilungen der Magnus-Hirschfeld-Gesellschaft, published since 1983 by the

Magnus Hirschfeld Gesellschaft; see https://magnus-hirschfeld.de
/publikationen/mitteilungen/ (accessed November 26, 2019).
Work on Li, by comparison, is limited: Dose, "In memoriam Li Shiu Tong
(1907–1993)." Hirschfeld's biographers only mention Li in passing.

62 Evans, "Introduction: Why Queer German History?," 378.

63 See, for example, Stryker, *Transgender History*.

64 On problematic gay heroes and the gay desire for heroes, see Amin, *Disturbing Attachments*.

65 One among many possible examples is Faderman, *Gay Revolution*.

66 A perhaps related point comes in Chu and Drager when they invite readers
to imagine how the field of trans studies would be upended if they would
"just speak candidly about our lives as transsexuals, the way we might talk
over dinner or text message." Chu and Drager, "After Trans Studies," 113.
Thanks to a peer reviewer for pointing this out to me.

67 For example, Chauncey, *Gay New York*. On this see also Love, *Feeling Backward*.

68 For example, Evans, *Coming of the Third Reich*, 128. Irvine seems to imply as
much: *Disorders of Desire*, 206.

69 The only other existing account of Li's work is Dose, "In memoriam."

70 Gutterman, *Her Neighbor's Wife*, 10–11.

71 I use "transgender" as well as "trans" in the sense of "transgender" described by Stryker, *Transgender History*, 1.

72 Marhoefer, *Sex and the Weimar Republic*, 59–61. On Hirschfeld in trans history
see also the work of Herrn, Meyerowitz, and Sutton, including Sutton,
Sex Between Body and Mind, 173–201.

73 Marhoefer, *Sex and the Weimar Republic*, 59–62.

74 See Chu and Drager, "After Trans Studies."

75 Robert Tobin's excellent book demonstrates some of this as well, but he
reads its significance very differently: *Peripheral Desires*.

**1 "Einstein of Sex": Magnus Hirschfeld at the End of the First Century
of Gay Rights**

1 Magnus Hirschfeld, "I. Brief. Norddeutscher Lloyd, Bremen. 19 November
1930," in *Testament*, *Heft II*, 204–5; Magnus Hirschfeld, "II. Brief. The New
Yorker, 34th Street and 8th Avenue, New York City, 25 December 1930," in *Testament*, *Heft II*, 205–6. The ship was SS *Columbus*, Norddeutscher Lloyd, built in
1922 and scuttled by her crew off the eastern coast of the United States in 1939.

2 Hirschfeld, *Weltreise*, v.

3 See Hirschfeld's reference to this in Hirschfeld to Benjamin, June 3, 1934,
in HHAfS-Humboldt. On the relationship between Hirschfeld and Benjamin see also Haeberle, "Movement of Inverts"; Benjamin, "Reminiscences";
Haeberle, "Der transatlantische Pendler."

4 Hirschfeld, *Weltreise*, vi.

5 Hirschfeld, *Testament, Heft II*, 84.

6 See Marhoefer, *Sex and the Weimar Republic*, 129–43; see also Sutton, *Sex Between Body and Mind*, 188–9.

7 Hirschfeld, *Testament, Heft II*, 56.

8 See Riese and Leunbach, *Sexual Reform Congress*. On international sexual progressivism in this period see also Herzog, *Sexuality in Europe*, 53–6.

9 I have drawn this account of Hirschfeld's expulsion from the WhK and his fight with Richard Linsert and Max Hodann from his journal: Hirschfeld, *Testament, Heft II*, 54–86. On this see also Marhoefer, *Sex and the Weimar Republic*, 129–43, which examines Linsert's motives and has a different take on them than Hirschfeld's.

10 Hirschfeld, *Testament, Heft II*, 64–6, 80, 86; quotation at 86.

11 On Karl Giese see Wolff, *Magnus Hirschfeld*, 185–7, 431; Dose, *Magnus Hirschfeld: The Origins of the Gay Liberation Movement*; Wolfert, "In Memoriam Karl Giese."

12 Dose, *Magnus Hirschfeld: The Origins of the Gay Liberation Movement*, 28.

13 See, for example, Hirschfeld, *Testament, Heft II*, 16, 82, 122, 146–8, 156. The other man was Friedrich Hauptstein, who later betrayed him.

14 Hirschfeld, "I. Brief," 204.

15 See chapter 10.

16 Hirschfeld, "I. Brief," 204.

17 Isherwood, *Christopher and His Kind*, 17.

18 "L'Amour et la Science par le Docteur Magnus Hirschfeld."

19 Hirschfeld, "II. Brief," 205.

20 Hirschfeld, "I. Brief," 205.

21 Sutton, *Sex Between Body and Mind*, 2–5.

22 For a detailed study of what sexology was and was not, see Sutton, *Sex Between Body and Mind*.

23 See Fuechtner, Haynes, and Jones, *Global History of Sexual Science*; Chiang, *After Eunuchs*.

24 Sutton, *Sex Between Body and Mind*; Leng, *Sexual Politics and Feminist Science*, 43–62. Sexology, and the science of sex more broadly, were global projects, not sole European efforts: Bauer, *Sexology and Translation*; Fuechtner, Haynes, and Jones, *Global History of Sexual Science*. Sexology initially basically encompassed psychoanalysis, which by the 1920s had broken away: Sutton, *Sex Between Body and Mind*.

25 Hirschfeld, "I. Brief," 205.

26 On his difficulties with diabetes see Wolff, *Magnus Hirschfeld*, 431; Dose, *Magnus Hirschfeld: The Origins of the Gay Liberation Movement*, 27. He seems to have controlled his diabetes with diet.

27 On Hirschfeld's letters to Benjamin about the New York lectures, see Wolff, *Magnus Hirschfeld*, 284.

28 Magnus Hirschfeld to George Sylvester Viereck, Berlin, October 22, 1930, in Hirschfeld, *Testament, Heft II*, 202–3; Hirschfeld, *Testament, Heft II*, 102n262; Herzer, *Magnus Hirschfeld und seine Zeit*, 34.

29 On Viereck's queer poetry see Mader, "Greek Mirror," 389. Two unsigned essays that discussed Hirschfeld appeared in *Current Literature*, a magazine for which Viereck wrote. "The Advent of the Male Prima Donna," *Current Literature*, November 1911, discussed "transvestitism," and Hirschfeld is glossed in an essay on Edward Carpenter: "The Conquest of Love and of Death," *Current Literature*, August 1912. I assume these were by Viereck or someone he knew; they reflect an interest in Hirschfeld's work.

30 For jumpstarting the press craze Hirschfeld also had to thank Viereck, who interviewed him at his hotel in New York for a wire service; the piece ran in many papers and boosted Hirschfeld's fame: Magnus Hirschfeld and George Sylvester Viereck, "World Famous Advocate of Sex Reform Gives His Views," *San Antonio Light*, December 7, 1930. On Viereck's interview see also Bauer, *Hirschfeld Archives*, 105–7.

31 Karla Popprová-Molínková to Sanger, September 15, 1932, in Sanger, *Selected Papers of Margaret Sanger*, 224.

32 Sutton, *Sex Between Body and Mind*, 22.

33 Agnes Smedley to Sanger, March 18, 1928, in Sanger, *Selected Papers of Margaret Sanger*, 141n5. Smedley was an American journalist expatriate and a leftist with ties to the German Communist Party: Miller, Pennybacker, and Rosenhaft, "Mother Ada Wright and the International Campaign to Free the Scottsboro Boys," 398.

34 Letter to Karl Abraham quoted in Herzer, *Magnus Hirschfeld und seine Zeit*, 65.

35 *Staatsbürger-Zeitung*, 10 August 1919, in GStAPK Hauptabteilung (HA) I. Rep. 76 VIII B Nr. 2076.

36 Berlin Polizei an Ministerium für Volkswohlfahrt Berlin, 24 July 1920, in GStAPK HA I. Rep. 76 VIII B Nr. 2076; Regierungs-Medizinalrat, 21 May 1920, in GStAPK HA I. Rep. 76 VIII B Nr. 2076.

37 Regierungs-Medizinalrat, 21 May 1920, in GStAPK HA I. Rep. 76 VIII B Nr. 2076.

38 This was Albert Moll: Crozier, "All the World's a Stage," 32–3. See also Herzer, *Magnus Hirschfeld und seine Zeit*, 65–6.

39 Hirschfeld, "II. Brief," 204.

40 Hirschfeld later credited Viereck for coming up with the line: Vyras, "Magnus Hirschfeld in Greece," 24. Viereck, at the time a friend of Harry Benjamin's, was apparently quite involved in the American leg of Hirschfeld's tour, judging by how often Hirschfeld sent greetings to him in his letters to Benjamin and by how he relied on Viereck's advice about a second tour of the US. See the Benjamin-Hirschfeld correspondence

in the HHAfS-Humboldt. He later turned out to be a Nazi. On Viereck's betrayal see in particular Benjamin to Hirschfeld, September 20, 1933, HHAfS-Humboldt.

41 Marcus, *Drama of Celebrity*.

42 "Kill Dr. M. Hirschfeld: Well-Known German Scientist Victim of a Munich Mob," *New York Times*, October 12, 1920. *Medical Record* termed him "noted German physiologist" in 1920: "News of the Week," *Medical Record* 98 (1920). For his influence in the US in this period see also "The Male Homosexual as a Social Peril," *Medical Record* 98 (1920): 821; Bauer, *Hirschfeld Archives*, 103–8.

43 Kissack, *Free Comrades*, 4, 6, 39; Bergemann, Dose, and Keilson-Lauritz, *Magnus Hirschfelds Exil-Gästebuch*, 55.

44 "Experts from Germany Will Appear in Case," *Davenport Democrat and Leader*, June 12, 1924. I assume this was a wire service story that ran in other papers too; the dateline is Berlin. In a 1957 column looking back on the case, Dorothy Thompson remembered Hirschfeld and his Institute for Sexual Science in connection with it: Thompson, "Governor Stratton Was Right." On homosexuality and Leopold and Loeb, see Fass, "Making and Remaking an Event."

45 "Experts from Germany Will Appear in Case." For other examples of Hirschfeld in the American press before the world journey, see "Sexual Reform Congress Meets in Staid England," *Atlanta Constitution*, September 9, 1945; "Quotations," *Ogden Standard-Examiner*, December 26, 1930 (I assume this came from a wire service and ran in other papers).

46 "Youthful Strength" [display ad], *Chicago Defender*, September 4, 1932. See also, for example, "Youthful Strength" [display ad], *Denton Journal*, September 17, 1932.

47 On the limits of his reputation in the United States, see the letter from the American Medical Association about how they had not heard of him: "American Medical Association Bureau of Investigation to Managing Editor … in re: 'Titus-Pearls,'" *New England Journal of Medicine*, September 8, 1932, 480.

48 For more on Hirschfeld and Titus Pearls see Bauer, *Hirschfeld Archives*, 107.

49 "Wild Sex Talk Has Not Been Helpful," *Modesto News-Herald*, March 5, 1931.

50 Hirschfeld, *Testament, Heft II*, 208.

51 Vyras, "Magnus Hirschfeld in Greece," 23.

52 Hirschfeld, *Testament, Heft II*, 98; Hirschfeld, *Weltreise*, vi, 15, 54–6; quotation in Hirschfeld, *Weltreise*, v.

53 Hirschfeld, *Von einst bis jetzt: Geschichte einer homosexuellen Bewegung 1897–1922*, ed. Manfred Herzer and James Steakley (Berlin: Rosa Winkel, 1986), 16–17.

54 Mills, *Seeing Sodomy in the Middle Ages*, 3–4, 11; Rydström, *Sinners and Citizens*, 1. Opinions on what exactly "sodomy" was varied somewhat: Ragan, "Enlightenment Confronts Homosexuality," 9; Crompton, "Myth of Lesbian Impunity"; Ruggiero, *Boundaries of Eros*, 114; Clark, *Desire*, 74.

55 Mills, *Seeing Sodomy in the Middle Ages*, 3, 91.

56 Rare, but a capital crime: Crompton, "Myth of Lesbian Impunity." On death as the punishment: Ruggiero, *Boundaries of Eros*, 110–11; Moore, *Formation of a Persecuting Society*, 88. On rare enforcement see among others Ragan, "Enlightenment Confronts Homosexuality," 10–11; Sibalis, "Regulation of Male Homosexuality," 81.

57 On sodomy and the Reformation see Puff, *Sodomy in Reformation Germany and Switzerland*.

58 Clark, *Desire*, 114; Ragan, "Enlightenment Confronts Homosexuality."

59 Ragan, "Enlightenment Confronts Homosexuality," 22; Tobin, *Peripheral Desires*, 7.

60 Hunt, "Pornography and the French Revolution," 308.

61 Sibalis, "Regulation of Male Homosexuality," 82.

62 Sibalis, "Regulation of Male Homosexuality," 83, 95.

63 Steidele, *In Männerkleidern*.

64 See Tobin, *Peripheral Desires*, 83–110; Spector, *Violent Sensations*, 91, 100.

65 Kates, "Jews into Frenchmen."

66 Hirschfeld, *Von einst bis jetzt*, 153–4.

67 On Jewish Emancipation see among others Magnus, *Jewish Emancipation in a German City*.

68 For a much more nuanced account of the developing discourse of homosexuality in this period, such as how Ulrichs responded to a discursive linking of graphic violence (including against children) with homosexuality as sensationalism and violence, see Spector, *Violent Sensations*.

69 Beachy, "German Invention of Homosexuality," 810–13; Mildenberger, ... *in der Richtung Homosexualität verdorben*.

70 *Unzucht* can be translated as "sodomy" or "fornication."

71 Schoppmann, *Nationalsozialistische Sexualpolitik und weibliche Homosexualität*, 80–1. Schoppmann argues it was a purposeful move arising from a lack of concern about lesbianism.

72 "Gutachten der wissenschaftlichen Deputation für das Medizinalwesen in Preussen vom 24. März 1869," reprinted in Krafft-Ebing, *Der Conträrsexuale vor dem Strafrichter*, 37.

73 "Gutachten der wissenschaftlichen Deputation für das Medizinalwesen in Preussen." The German parliament came close to doing something like this in 1929: Marhoefer, *Sex and the Weimar Republic*, 112–45.

74 "Gutachtliche Aeusserungen des k. k. obersten Sanitätsrathes zum Sodomieparagraph (§ 186) des österreichischen Strafgesetzentwurfes," reprinted in Krafft-Ebing, *Der Conträrsexuale vor dem Strafrichter*, 38.

75 For a much more complete account, see Spector, *Violent Sensations*.

76 See Anne Lister's diary: Whitbread, *I Know My Own Heart*, x.

77 Tobin, *Peripheral Desires*, 27.

78 Tobin, *Peripheral Desires*, 27–52. Hössli's work has been republished: Hössli, *Eros*.

79 Tobin, *Peripheral Desires*, 28.

80 On Ulrichs see Kennedy, *Life and Works of Karl Heinrich Ulrichs*; Sigusch, *Karl Heinrich Ulrichs*.

81 Tobin, *Peripheral Desires*, 24.

82 Tobin, *Peripheral Desires*, 86; Sigusch, *Geschichte der Sexualwissenschaft*, 152.

83 Beachy, "German Invention of Homosexuality," 829.

84 Quoted in Beachy, "German Invention of Homosexuality," 829.

85 Tobin, *Peripheral Desires*, 7.

86 Tobin, *Peripheral Desires*, 14; Beachy, "German Invention of Homosexuality," 804.

87 Beachy, "German Invention of Homosexuality," 820–7.

88 Beachy, "German Invention of Homosexuality," 826.

89 See also Tobin, *Peripheral Desires*, 230; Spector, *Violent Sensations*.

90 On women in Hössli see Tobin, *Peripheral Desires*, 46.

91 Leck, *Vita Sexualis*, 216.

92 Herzer, "Karl Heinrich Ulrichs und die Idee des WhK."

93 Oosterhuis, *Stepchildren of Nature*.

94 Oosterhuis, *Stepchildren of Nature*, 172; Hirschfeld, *Von einst bis jetzt*, 9.

95 Compare Beachy, *Gay Berlin*, 40; Leck, *Vita Sexualis*.

96 Hirschfeld, *Von einst bis jetzt*, 8.

97 Herzer, *Magnus Hirschfeld und seine Zeit*, 15–46, 153–7. On his doctoral thesis see Bauer, *Hirschfeld Archives*, 18–19. On his sisters see Wolfert, "Annäherungen an Franziska Mann." The spelling "Kolberg" was not in use until the early twentieth century (Herzer, *Magnus Hirschfeld und seine Zeit*, 15n6) but Hirschfeld used it later in his life; I have therefore used it.

98 Hirschfeld, *Von einst bis jetzt*, 162–3.

99 Hirschfeld, *Von einst bis jetzt*, 163. On the state of medical expertise on homosexuality in this period see Sutton, *Sex Between Body and Mind*, 64–6.

100 On epilepsy, which commentators on eugenics and public health tied to degeneration and to sexual disorder, see Marhoefer, "Among Abnormals," 122, 125, 134, 137, 142, 147, 188.

101 Hirschfeld, *Von einst bis jetzt*, 153.

102 Sutton, *Sex Between Body and Mind*, 69–70, 72.

103 Leng, *Sexual Politics and Feminist Science*, 8; Dickinson, *Sex, Freedom, and Power in Imperial Germany*, 44–7; Herzer, *Magnus Hirschfeld und seine Zeit*, 44–6.

104 Magnus Hirschfeld, *Sappho und Sokrates: Wie erklärt sich die Liebe der Männer und Frauen zu Personen des eigenen Geschlechts?* (Leipzig: Max Spohr, 1922). On his publications before this, see Herzer, *Magnus Hirschfeld und seine Zeit*, 39–40, 44–6. For the page count of the original brochure: Herzer, *Magnus Hirschfeld und seine Zeit*, 47.

105 Hirschfeld, *Von einst bis jetzt*, 48. On queer suicide see also Bauer, *Hirschfeld Archives*.

106 Hirschfeld, *Von einst bis jetzt*, 48.

107 Hirschfeld, *Von einst bis jetzt*, 50–1, 53; Bauer, *Hirschfeld Archives*, 37–56; Marhoefer, *Sex and the Weimar Republic*, 112.

108 On Hirschfeld's motives see Herzer, *Magnus Hirschfeld und seine Zeit*, 47; Bauer, *Hirschfeld Archives*, 37–56.

109 On Ellis and Symonds's book see Crozier's critical edition of it, *Sexual Inversion*; Sutton, *Sex Between Body and Mind*; Bland and Doan, *Sexology Uncensored*. Hirschfeld, like Ellis and Symonds, was reading Edward Carpenter at the time, but he does not seem to have read Ellis yet: he does not cite Ellis and Symonds, nor does he cite Ellis's 1895 article on female inversion, which appears to be Ellis's first publication on his theory of homosexuality.

110 Wolff, *Magnus Hirschfeld*, 35.

111 Hirschfeld, *Sappho und Sokrates*, 28–9.

112 Herzer, *Magnus Hirschfeld und seine Zeit*, 57; see also 38–9.

113 Wolff, *Magnus Hirschfeld*, 34.

114 Wolff, who was herself a queer Jewish sexologist, though not of Hirschfeld's generation, makes basically this point: *Magnus Hirschfeld*, 34.

115 Rupp, *Sapphistries*, 151.

116 On the global influence of German sexology see Rupp, *Sapphistries*, 149–51.

117 Hirschfeld, "Vorwort zur II. Auflage" (1902), in *Sappho und Sokrates*, unnumbered page.

118 Marhoefer, *Sex and the Weimar Republic*, 127–8.

119 Beachy, "German Invention of Homosexuality," 836.

120 Doan and Waters, "Introduction," 42; Funke, "We Cannot Be Greek Now," 151–2. For a brilliant explanation as to why the German-speaking world was the location for so much early homosexual activism, see Beachy, "German Invention of Homosexuality."

121 Hirschfeld, "Vorwort zur II. Auflage" (1902), in *Sappho und Sokrates*.

122 Hirschfeld, "Vorwort zur II. Auflage" (1902), in *Sappho und Sokrates*.

123 To be sure, moreover, the novel aspects of Hirschfeld's pamphlet are very like what one finds in Ellis and Symonds's *Sexual Inversion* – Hirschfeld did not come up with his theory in an absolute vacuum but expressed ideas that occurred to others around the same time.

124 Wolff, *Magnus Hirschfeld*, 34–5. On innate homosexuality and current science see the conclusion.

125 Cited in Beachy, "German Invention of Homosexuality," 820n83.

126 See Fuechtner, Haynes, and Jones, *Global History of Sexual Science*; Fuechtner, "Indians, Jews, and Sex."

127 Beachy, "German Invention of Homosexuality," 822, 824; Wolff, *Magnus Hirschfeld*, 37–8; Bauer, *Hirschfeld Archives*, 24; Herzer, *Magnus Hirschfeld und seine Zeit*, 69–70.

128 Herzer, *Magnus Hirschfeld und seine Zeit*, 72–3.

129 Hirschfeld, *Von einst bis jetzt*, 54; Bauer, *Hirschfeld Archives*, 24–5; von Bülow, *Deutsch-Südwestafrika*.

130 Hull, *Absolute Destruction*, 88–90.

131 See Hirschfeld, *Von einst bis jetzt*, 54.

132 Hirschfeld, *Von einst bis jetzt*, 50–1; Herzer, *Magnus Hirschfeld und seine Zeit*, 67.

133 Hirschfeld, *Von einst bis jetzt*, 52. I am skeptical. A lot of married men had affairs with men. Having a public tie to homosexual emancipation was a very radical and risky thing to do – few undertook it in the absence of a personal stake. Hirschfeld himself, who denied Spohr's homosexuality, never admitted his own homosexuality in public either.

134 Hirschfeld, *Von einst bis jetzt*, 51, 54.

135 Herzer, *Magnus Hirschfeld und seine Zeit*, 66–80.

136 Wolff, *Magnus Hirschfeld*, 43.

137 Wolff, *Magnus Hirschfeld*, 43.

138 Wolff, *Magnus Hirschfeld*, 43.

139 On his age see Herzer, *Magnus Hirschfeld und seine Zeit*, 50.

140 See, for example, the incident at the Magic Flute dance palace in 1929, when Friedrich Radszuweit's style of activism alienated an important politician: Marhoefer, *Sex and the Weimar Republic*, 132. Radszuweit publicly claimed a homosexual identity.

141 See Marhoefer, *Sex and the Weimar Republic*.

142 Steakley, *Writings of Dr. Magnus Hirschfeld*; Herzer, *Magnus Hirschfeld und seine Zeit*; Wolff, *Magnus Hirschfeld*; Bauer, *Hirschfeld Archives*; Domeier, *Eulenburg Affair*; Marhoefer, *Sex and the Weimar Republic*.

143 Tridon, *Psychoanalysis and Love*, 158.

2 The Empire of Queer Love

1 Tobin makes the same point, though he reads its significance quite differently: *Peripheral Desires*, 160–1. On this point see also Chiang, "Double Alterity and the Global History of Sexuality." Moreover, there is a large body of recent scholarship that makes a similar point with respect to European knowledge of sex broadly. See Fuechtner, Haynes, and Jones, *Global History of Sexual Science*, especially the introduction and part 1.

2 Fisher and Funke, "Let Us Leave the Hospital."

3 Hiller, "Sexualfreiheit und Proporz," 83–4.

4 Hirschfeld, *Die Homosexualität des Mannes und des Weibes*, 1026.

5 See Mühlhahn, "New Imperial Vision?"; Steinmetz, *Devil's Handwriting*.

6 On this passage see also Bauer, *Hirschfeld Archives*, 62–3.

7 Samper Vendrell, *Seduction of Youth*.

8 Hirschfeld, *Die Homosexualität des Mannes und des Weibes*, 617.

9 See Amin, *Disturbing Attachments*; Cleves, *Unspeakable*; Cleves, "From Pederasty to Pedophilia"; Fischel, "Of Polymaths and Pederasts"; Samper Vendrell, *Seduction of Youth*; Keilson-Lauritz, *Die Geschichte der eigenen Geschichte.*

10 Samper Vendrell, *Seduction of Youth.* See also Marhoefer, *Sex and the Weimar Republic.*

11 On this see Samper Vendrell, *Seduction of Youth*; Amin, *Disturbing Attachments*; Miller and Gómez Bravo, "Why We Shouldn't Cancel Foucault"; Fisher and Funke, "Age of Attraction"; Bauer, *Hirschfeld Archives*, 62–6.

12 Bauer, *Hirschfeld Archives*, 24–7.

13 Hirschfeld, *Die Homosexualität des Mannes und des Weibes*, 606.

14 Hirschfeld, *Die Homosexualität des Mannes und des Weibes*, 606.

15 Hirschfeld, *Die Homosexualität des Mannes und des Weibes*, 528. He made the same point elsewhere. See Magnus Hirschfeld, *Geschlechtskunde: Auf Grund dreißigjähriger Forschung und Erfahrung bearbeitet*, vol. 1, *Die körperseelischen Grundlagen* (Stuttgart: Julius Püttmann, 1926), 573; and Magnus Hirschfeld, *Geschlechtskunde: Auf Grund dreißigjähriger Forschung und Erfahrung bearbeitet*, vol. 2, *Folgen und Folgerungen* (Stuttgart: Julius Püttmann, 1928), 640–4.

16 Magnus Hirschfeld, *Racism*, trans. and ed. Eden and Cedar Paul (London: Victor Gollancz, 1938), 162; see also Hirschfeld, *Weltreise*, 47: "The individual sexual type far outweighs the racial type in strength and significance." See also Bauer's analysis of this quotation from *Racism* (*Hirschfeld Archives*, 16) and Bauer's larger point that in *Racism*, Hirschfeld is more interested in the plight of homosexuals than in racism and, moreover, that he obscures the fact that racism and homophobia intersect.

17 Hirschfeld, *Racism*, 120.

18 Hirschfeld, *Racism*, 116.

19 Hirschfeld, *Racism*, 110–12, 84–5; see also chapter 6.

20 Von Luschan, "Anthropological View of Race," 21–2.

21 Hirschfeld, *Die Homosexualität des Mannes und des Weibes*, 628.

22 Marhoefer, "Homosexuality and Theories of Culture," 255–8; Tobin, *Peripheral Desires*, 157–9.

23 Marhoefer, "Homosexuality and Theories of Culture," 258.

24 Hirschfeld, *Die Homosexualität des Mannes und des Weibes*, 530.

25 Hirschfeld, *Die Homosexualität des Mannes und des Weibes*, 626.

26 On Ulrichs making this argument see Hirschfeld, *Die Homosexualität des Mannes und des Weibes*, 529.

27 Richard B.C. Vogel, "Homosexuelle Neger-Stämme," *Die Freundschaft* 26 (1920).

28 Examples in the Scientific Humanitarian Committee's *Jahrbuch für sexuelle Zwischenstufen* include "Länder, die den gleichgeschlechtlichen Verkehr mehr oder weniger anerkennen," which discusses Turkey and China:

147–9; Tessmann, "Die Homosexualität bei den Negern Kameruns." In addition, see Hirschfeld, *Die Homosexualität des Mannes und des Weibes*, chapters 26–8.

29 Karsch-Haack, *Das gleichgeschlechtliche Leben der Naturvölker*. On his ties to the Scientific Humanitarian Committee, see Hirschfeld, *Die Homosexualität des Mannes und des Weibes*, 1013. See also a 1925 Scientific Humanitarian Committee letter to the government that Karsch-Haack signed: Wissenschaftlich-Humanitäres Komitee, January 29, 1925, in GStAPK I. HA Rep. 84 a. Justizministerium Nr. 8100, 320; see as well a cover letter for a Scientific Humanitarian Committee petition signed by the group's leaders, including Karsch-Haack: Wissenschaftlich-Humanitäres Komitee, "Sehr geehrter Herr!," in GStAPK I. HA Rep. 84 a. Justizministerium Nr. 8100, 324. On Karsch-Haack see also Herzer, *Magnus Hirschfeld und seine Zeit*, 161–3; Tobin, *Peripheral Desires*, 136–8, 155–9. Unlike Tobin, I am skeptical that Karsch-Haack was widely read or credited outside of homosexual emancipationist circles.

30 Karsch-Haack, *Das gleichgeschlechtliche Leben der Naturvölker*.
31 Hirschfeld, *Die Homosexualität des Mannes und des Weibes*, 554.
32 Vogel, "Homosexuelle Neger-Stämme."
33 Vogel, "Homosexuelle Neger-Stämme."
34 For a definition of "transgender," which I take to be consistent with "transness," see Stryker, "My Words to Victor Frankenstein Above the Village of Chamounix," 251–2.
35 Vogel, "Homosexuelle Neger-Stämme."
36 Hirschfeld, *Die Homosexualität des Mannes und des Weibes*, 623–4; quotation at 623.
37 Hirschfeld, *Weltreise*, 136.
38 Hirschfeld, *Weltreise*, plate 15; see also 188–9, 291.
39 Hirschfeld, *Die Homosexualität des Mannes und des Weibes*, 626.
40 Hirschfeld, *Die Homosexualität des Mannes und des Weibes*, 626.
41 Hirschfeld, *Die Homosexualität des Mannes und des Weibes*, 626.
42 Hirschfeld, *Die Homosexualität des Mannes und des Weibes*, 626.
43 Hirschfeld, *Die Homosexualität des Mannes und des Weibes*, 626.
44 Hirschfeld, *Die Homosexualität des Mannes und des Weibes*, 626.
45 Hirschfeld, *Die Homosexualität des Mannes und des Weibes*, 626.
46 Hirschfeld, *Weltreise*, 113.
47 Hirschfeld, *Weltreise*, 113.
48 "Hirschfeld Hits Foreigners Idea of Superiority: Has Faith in Future of Chinese People to Make Good," *China Press*, June 11, 1931.
49 Hirschfeld, *Weltreise*, 112.
50 Magnus Hirschfeld, *Transvestites: The Erotic Drive to Cross-Dress*, trans. Michael A. Lombardi-Nash (Amherst, NY: Prometheus Books, 1991), 255.

51 Hirschfeld, *Die Homosexualität des Mannes und des Weibes*, 606; see also 616–17; Karsch-Haack, *Das gleichgeschlechtliche Leben*, 34–5; Aldrich argues that the colonies were perceived to be, and to some extent were, a "homosexual playground": *Colonialism and Homosexuality*, 5. On how fears of male-male sex shaped colonial policy, see Stoler, *Carnal Knowledge and Imperial Power*, 2, 48.

52 Hirschfeld, *Die Homosexualität des Mannes und des Weibes*, 615.

53 Hirschfeld, *Die Homosexualität des Mannes und des Weibes*, 555, 558.

54 Hirschfeld, *Die Homosexualität des Mannes und des Weibes*, 567.

55 Hirschfeld, *Von einst bis jetzt*, 156, 160–1; Davis, *Colonialism, Antisemitism, and Germans of Jewish Descent*, 144–5.

56 Davis, *Colonialism, Antisemitism, and Germans of Jewish Descent*, 145; Hirschfeld, *Von einst bis jetzt*, 156–61.

57 Hull, *Absolute Destruction*, 3, 145–7, 155–7.

58 Schmidt, "Colonial Intimacy."

59 Schmidt, "Colonial Intimacy," 46–7, 54, 56, 59; quotation at 48. For cases in colonial Namibia that also sound like assaults, see Lorway, *Namibia's Rainbow Project*, 26–7 (Lorway argues these may not have been assaults).

60 Töppsdrill, "Marokko," *Die Freundin*, February 3, 1932.

61 Gandhi, *Affective Communities*, 51–3; Martin, "Panthers, Palms, and Desert Passions."

62 Hirschfeld, *Die Homosexualität des Mannes und des Weibes*, 569.

63 Quoted in Bauer, *Hirschfeld Archives*, 119; see also 123.

64 H.W. Burg, "Meine Weihnachten: Erinnerungen eines Transvestiten," *Der Transvestit* (in *Die Freundin*), January 1, 1925.

65 Burg, "Meine Weihnachten."

66 Hirschfeld, *Transvestites*, 245–55; Tobin, *Peripheral Desires*, 157–8.

67 Hirschfeld, *Die Homosexualität des Mannes und des Weibes*, 601–3, 641; see also Hirschfeld, *Weltreise*, 264. On Hirschfeld and India see Fuechtner, "Indians, Jews, and Sex."

68 Said, *Orientalism*, 190.

69 Said, *Orientalism*; El-Tayeb, *Schwarze Deutsche*, 149–52; Morgensen, *Spaces Between Us*.

70 Matsuda, *Empire of Love*. See also McClintock, *Imperial Leather*.

71 On queerness and European imperialism see also Aldrich, *Colonialism and Homosexuality*; Tobin, *Peripheral Desires*, 134–61.

72 Allies of Hirschfeld, such as the radical feminist Helene Stöcker, sought to do something quite similar with heterosexuality: Leng, "Culture, Difference, and Sexual Progress in Turn-of-the-Century Europe."

73 On this see also Herrn and Taylor, "Magnus Hirschfeld's Interpretation of the Japanese *Onnagata* as Transvestites."

74 Werner Kn., "Der Kampf der Transvestiten," *Die Freundin*, April 2, 1928. Sutton quotes another transvestite activist using the phrase: Sutton, "We Too Deserve a Place in the Sun," 340.

75 The phrase is Aldrich's: *Colonialism and Homosexuality*, 411.

76 Marhoefer, *Sex and the Weimar Republic*, 116–18; Chauncey, *Gay New York*, 47–98.

77 Lorway, *Namibia's Rainbow Project*, 22–7; Schmidt, "Colonial Intimacy." Hirschfeld was involved in one such case: Tobin, "Sexology in the Southwest."

78 Hirschfeld, *Die Homosexualität des Mannes und des Weibes*, 606.

79 Bauer, *Hirschfeld Archives*, 10–12; see also 23, 29–31.

80 For an example of a place where he is oblivious to violent imperial rule, see his passage on Johannesburg: Hirschfeld, *Die Homosexualität des Mannes und des Weibes*, 555–8.

81 Gandhi, "Loving Well," 94.

3 Hirschfeld and Li Shiu Tong Meet: Feminism and Queer Attraction at the China United Apartments

1 Hirschfeld, *Weltreise*, 70–1.

2 "An Eminent Psychologist: Prof. Magnus Hirschfeld in Shanghai," *North-China Herald and Supreme Court and Consular Gazette*, May 5, 1931.

3 For Li's date and place of birth see the information about him in Zurich city records: Einwohner- und Fremdenkontrolle der Stadt Zürich, Abteilung III, an Frau Dr. Claudia Schoppmann, February 16, 1993, Li Shiu Tong Nachlass, Box 1, cited hereafter as "Stadt Zürich an Schoppmann, Li Shiu Tong Nachlass, Box 1."

4 Li Kam Tong to Li Shiu Tong, undated (1975), Li Shiu Tong Nachlass. Li's father was Li Wing Kwong.

5 On family politics in this era and the *da jiazu* (big family), see Yeh, *Shanghai Splendor*, 111 and following. I found no evidence that Li was related to the Qing general Li Hung-chang as has been sometimes asserted.

6 Carroll, *Concise History of Hong Kong*, 72–6; Carroll, *Edge of Empires*.

7 Yeh, *Alienated Academy*, 67; Hichens, *That Which Is Hidden*, 318, 667.

8 Yeh, *Alienated Academy*, 65–75.

9 Yeh, *Alienated Academy*, 84–8; Chen, *Seeds from the West*.

10 Gilmartin, *Engendering the Chinese Revolution*, 100–3.

11 Hichens, *That Which Is Hidden*, 251, 318, 513. Some of these references are to Hong Kong; I assume that Hichens has on occasion mixed up Hong Kong and Shanghai in the novel. On how I am using this novel, see chapter 13.

12 Hichens, *That Which Is Hidden*, 531.

13　This paragraph is based on the portrait of Li in Hichens, *That Which Is Hidden*, 320, 531, and elsewhere, as well as on Ou-fan Lee, *Shanghai Modern*.

14　Ou-fan Lee, *Shanghai Modern*, 5; Jackson, *Shaping Modern Shanghai*, 1, 11. On fashion see Ou-fan Lee, *Shanghai Modern*; Dong, "Who Is Afraid of the Chinese Modern Girl?" See also Lu, *Beyond the Neon Lights*. Quotation from Smith, "China Awakened," 35. On Smith see Paddle, "For the China of the Future."

15　Carroll, "Problem of Glands and Secretions."

16　Jackson, *Shaping Modern Shanghai*, 2–19; Denison and Yu Ren, *Building Shanghai*, 130–3. On interwar Shanghai see also Yeh, *Shanghai Splendor*; Gilmartin, *Engendering the Chinese Revolution*; Denison and Yu Ren, *Building Shanghai*.

17　Long, "To the Yen-an Station," 53. The China United Apartments as of 2021 was still standing and was the Pacific Hotel Shanghai.

18　Hirschfeld, *Weltreise*, 69. See also Hsu, "Ellis Effect."

19　Rupp, *Sapphistries*, 149–51.

20　Chiang, "Epistemic Modernity and the Emergence of Homosexuality in China." On Chinese sexology see also Rocha, "Translation and Two 'Chinese Sexologies'"; Chiang, "Double Alterity and the Global History of Sexuality"; Chiang, *After Eunuchs*.

21　Hirschfeld's last two books, *World Journey* and *Racism*, were in English, but he resisted having his other work translated into English. Harry Benjamin repeatedly tried to connect him to interested English publishers, and Hirschfeld passed. See their correspondence in HHAfS-Humboldt. On the other hand, he may simply have not wanted Benjamin involved in translations, as he seems to have agreed to have Norman Haire translate some of his work: See a letter from Haire about this, dated January 16, 1928, in the Charlotte Wolff Papers, Wellcome Library, PSY/WOL/6/8/4, file 1 of 2.

22　Hirschfeld, *Weltreise*, 90. I have taken the account of Hirschfeld and Li's meeting from Hirschfeld, *Weltreise*. Li has a slightly different version in his unpublished manuscript: he says they met at St. John's University. Since Hirschfeld wrote down his recollections much closer to the event, I have gone with his version. See Li, unpublished manuscript, unnumbered p. 15, Li Shiu Tong Nachlass.

23　"Mrs. Peter Wong to Head Chinese Women's Club," *China Press*, June 9, 1931.

24　Dong, "Who Is Afraid of the Chinese Modern Girl?" The Chinese Women's Club's doings were the subject of regular reporting in Shanghai's English press. See, among others, Mrs. Z.D. Zau, "Activities of Chinese Women's Club Told by Chairman of Committee," *China Weekly Review*, December 25, 1937; "'Joint Committee' Entertained," *North-China Herald and Supreme Court & Consular Gazette*, January 29, 1941.

25 Gilmartin, *Engendering the Chinese Revolution*, 16.

26 "Mrs. Peter Wong to Head Chinese Women's Club," *China Press*, June 9, 1931; Paddle, "For the China of the Future."

27 "Knowledge and Freedom of Sex Speaker's Creed: Dr. Magnus Hirschfeld Discusses Sexology Before Chinese Women," *China Press*, May 12, 1931.

28 "Knowledge and Freedom of Sex Speaker's Creed."

29 Victor Robinson, "In Honor of Magnus Hirschfeld," place of publication unclear, Charlotte Wolff Papers, PSY/WOL/6/8/4, file 1 of 2. This is the text of Robinson's introduction of Hirschfeld before the American Society of Medical History on December 4, 1930. "Stepchildren of nature" is Krafft-Ebing's term; see Oosterhuis, *Stepchildren of Nature*, 95.

30 In *Hirschfeld Archives*, 105, Bauer argues that Hirschfeld sometimes downplayed homosexuality as a theme in his lectures; I suspect that, rather, the press reports sometimes downplayed it.

31 Hirschfeld, *Weltreise*, 79–81. I assume Li translated because he served as Hirschfeld's translator; Hirschfeld does not say here who translated.

32 "An Eminent Psychologist."

33 Li, unpublished manuscript, unnumbered p. 15, Li Shiu Tong Nachlass, Box 1.

34 On this see chapters 12 and 13.

35 See the Benjamin-Hirschfeld correspondence, HHAfS-Humboldt.

36 "Researches of the Sexual Science: A Famous Erudite in Athens; Who Is Dr. Hirschfeld," *VRADINI*, March 20, 1932; translated and quoted in Vyras, "Magnus Hirschfeld in Greece," 20.

37 Dora Russell to Charlotte Wolff, undated [1981?], Charlotte Wolff Papers, PSY/WOL/6/8/1.

38 Heinz Liehr to Charlotte Wolff, April 29, 1981, Charlotte Wolff Papers, PSY/WOL/6/8/4, file 1 of 2.

39 Wolff, *Magnus Hirschfeld*, 432.

40 Rolf Italiaander to Charlotte Wolff, April 24, 1981, Charlotte Wolff Papers, PSY/WOL/1/4, folder 1 of 3.

41 Hirschfeld, *Weltreise*, 193.

42 Hirschfeld, *Weltreise*, 146.

43 For rumpled, see the many photographs and Benjamin, "Reminiscences," 4.

44 Hirschfeld, *Weltreise*, 245.

45 Hirschfeld, *Weltreise*, 69.

46 Hirschfeld, *Weltreise*, 259–60.

47 Hirschfeld, *Testament, Heft II*, 142. Metaphorically the nickname meant "Fine Disciple," but it also had a possible homoerotic reading, according to D.E. Mungello. See *Western Queers in China*, 127–8.

48 Hirschfeld, *Weltreise*, 93.

49 Hirschfeld, *Weltreise*, 93.

50 Hirschfeld, *Weltreise*, 74.

51 Hirschfeld, *Weltreise*, 70.

52 Hirschfeld, *Weltreise*, 70.

53 Li, unpublished manuscript, unnumbered p. 15, Li Shiu Tong Nachlass, Box 1.

54 See chapter 13.

55 "Hirschfeld Hits Foreigners Idea of Superiority: Has Faith in Future of Chinese People to Make Good," *China Press*, June 11, 1931.

56 Hirschfeld, *Weltreise*, 60–1.

57 Hirschfeld, *Testament, Heft II*, 74.

58 Such as Hodann and Karl Besser – Hiller less so. Hirschfeld took his betrayal less seriously; he chalked it up to Hiller's infatuation with Linsert: Hirschfeld, *Testament, Heft II*, 56–8, 44–6, 74.

59 Hirschfeld, *Testament, Heft II*, 16.

60 Wolff, *Magnus Hirschfeld*, 431.

61 Wolff, *Magnus Hirschfeld*, 431.

62 Hirschfeld, *Testament, Heft II*, 126.

63 Lowrie, *Masters and Servants*, 54–60.

64 Hirschfeld, *Weltreise*, 89–90. See also *Geschlechtskunde* III, 531, where he gives it as "at least" 2.3 percent.

65 Hirschfeld, *Weltreise*, 76, 94.

66 Hirschfeld, *Weltreise*, 90.

67 Hirschfeld, *Weltreise*, 94–5.

68 Hirschfeld, *Weltreise*, 95–6.

69 See Eng, *Racial Castration*.

70 Hirschfeld, *Weltreise*, 112.

71 Hirschfeld, *Weltreise*, 89. Much has been written about Hirschfeld's view that to be homosexual meant to have characteristics of the opposite sex. It was controversial in homosexual emancipation circles in Germany, where men who cherished masculinity resented the implication that they were feminine. In Hirschfeld's early work, he is clear that to be a homosexual man means to be feminine; by the 1920s, gender nonconformity was a much less prominent part of his model: Marhoefer, *Sex and the Weimar Republic*, 142. Yet even here, in his late work, when pressed to define male homosexuality he includes femininity.

72 Hirschfeld, *Weltreise*, 69.

73 Hirschfeld, *Weltreise*, 69.

74 "Hirschfeld Hits Foreigners Idea of Superiority."

75 Chiang, "Epistemic Modernity and the Emergence of Homosexuality in China."

76 Hirschfeld, *Testament, Heft II*, 194.

77 Hirschfeld, *Weltreise*, 93.

78 Hirschfeld, *Weltreise*, 112.
79 Hirschfeld, *Weltreise*, 112.
80 See chapter 9.
81 Jackson, "The Raj on Nanjing Road."
82 Hirschfeld, *Weltreise*, 61.
83 Hirschfeld, *Weltreise*, 61.

4 The Fight against Sexual Oppression Is a Fight against Empire

 1 Hirschfeld, *Weltreise*, 240, 245, 250.
 2 Hirschfeld, *Weltreise*, 250.
 3 Hirschfeld, *Geschlechtskunde* II, 629; Petersson, "Hub of the Anti-Imperialist Movement," 50–1.
 4 Nehru, *Autobiography*, 161; Petersson, "Hub of the Anti-Imperialist Movement," 55.
 5 Hirschfeld, *Weltreise*, 250. On the household see Borghi, "Forgotten Feminisms."
 6 Gupte, "India."
 7 Hirschfeld, *Weltreise*, 236.
 8 Borghi, "Forgotten Feminisms."
 9 Hirschfeld, *Weltreise*, 259.
10 Bauer, *Hirschfeld Archives*, 10–12; see also 23, 29–31.
11 Hirschfeld, *Geschlechtskunde* II, 629.
12 Hirschfeld, *Weltreise*, 128.
13 Hirschfeld, *Weltreise*, 347.
14 For example, Hirschfeld, *Weltreise*, 156, 159, 251–2.
15 Hirschfeld, *Weltreise*, 156.
16 Hirschfeld, *Weltreise*, 127.
17 Hirschfeld, *Weltreise*, 66.
18 Hirschfeld, *Weltreise*, plate 12. See also Alexanderson, *Subversive Seas*.
19 Hirschfeld, *Weltreise*, 59.
20 Hirschfeld, *Weltreise*, 58–9.
21 Hirschfeld, *Weltreise*, 105.
22 Hirschfeld, *Weltreise*, 105.
23 Hirschfeld, *Weltreise*, 106.
24 See, for example, Hirschfeld, *Weltreise*, 62–5, 127.
25 Hirschfeld, *Weltreise*, 63.
26 Hirschfeld, *Weltreise*, 127.
27 On this see also Bauer, *Hirschfeld Archives*, 31–5; chapter 12.
28 Hirschfeld, *Weltreise*, 127–8.
29 For example, Hirschfeld, *Weltreise*, 259.
30 Hirschfeld, *Weltreise*, 98; see also 208–9, 156.

31 Hirschfeld, *Weltreise*, 127.
32 Hirschfeld, *Weltreise*, 135–6.
33 Hirschfeld, *Weltreise*, 61, 350; Hirschfeld, *Racism*, 112–15. He had this idea earlier: Hirschfeld, *Was eint und trennt das Menschengeschlecht?*, 15. On his criticisms of imperialism, see also Fuechtner, "Indians, Jews, and Sex," 114–15.
34 Hirschfeld, *Weltreise*, 350.
35 Hirschfeld, *Weltreise*, 127; see also 128–9, 125–6.
36 Hirschfeld, *Weltreise*, 128–30.
37 Hirschfeld, *Weltreise*, 126.
38 Hirschfeld, *Weltreise*, 126.
39 Hirschfeld, *Weltreise*, 126.
40 Hirschfeld, *Weltreise*, 127.
41 Hirschfeld, *Weltreise*, 127.
42 Clare, *Earthly Encounters*, 12–13. Hirschfeld also cites a 1929 article in a Vienna medical journal on this: see *Weltreise*, 128. He mentions Kant at *Weltreise*, 59.
43 Clare, *Earthly Encounters*, 10–13.
44 Daly, "British Occupation," 251.
45 Botman, "Liberal Age," 291.
46 Hirschfeld, *Weltreise*, 348–9.
47 Hirschfeld, *Weltreise*, 142.
48 Hirschfeld, *Weltreise*, 128.
49 Gandhi, "Loving Well," 90–3. See also Gandhi, *Affective Communities*. Jawaharlal Nehru and Carpenter had an indirect link via Fabian socialism. On Nehru and Fabian socialism see Mohan, "Jawaharlal Nehru and His Socialism."
50 "Stella Kramrisch, Indian-Art Experts and Professor, 97," *New York Times*, September 2, 1993; Hirschfeld, *Weltreise*, 211.
51 Hirschfeld, *Weltreise*, 211.
52 Hirschfeld, *Weltreise*, 212.
53 Hirschfeld, *Weltreise*, 61.
54 "Hirschfeld Hits Foreigners Idea of Superiority."
55 "Hirschfeld Hits Foreigners Idea of Superiority."
56 Li Shiu Tong, "Aufzeichnungen von Li Shiu Tong im roten Ringbuch, handschriftlich, verschieden farbige Stifte, unkorrigierte abschrift," transcribed by Ralf Dose, 43, in Li Shiu Tong Nachlass, Box 1. On these notes that Li made see chapter 13.
57 Hirschfeld, *Weltreise*, 63.
58 Hirschfeld, *Weltreise*, 119.
59 Hirschfeld, *Weltreise*, 65.
60 Hirschfeld, *Weltreise*, 250.

61 Herzer, *Magnus Hirschfeld und seine Zeit*, 66.

62 Dose, *Magnus Hirschfeld: The Origins of the Gay Liberation Movement*, 28; for other examples of how quiet he kept this even among acquaintances, see also Wolff, *Magnus Hirschfeld*, 419, 440–4.

63 Gandhi, "Loving Well," 89. See also Eng, *Racial Castration*, 136.

64 Vanita, "New Homophobia," 251. On same-sex love in India see Vanita and Kidwai, *Same-Sex Love in India*, and Vanita, *Queering India*.

65 Gandhi, "Loving Well," 94–5.

66 Gandhi, "From *Young India*, July 26, 1929," 255–6; see also Ruth Vanita's introduction to this letter at 253–5.

67 Malihabadi, "'There Will Never Be Another Like You' (Urdu)," 279.

68 Nehru, Speech in the Lok Sabha, September 16, 1954, in Nehru, *Oxford India Nehru*, 403–4.

69 Nehru, *Autobiography*, 512.

70 Nehru, *Autobiography*, 512.

71 Nehru, *Autobiography*, 512.

72 Nehru, *Autobiography*, 512.

73 Nehru to M.K. Gandhi, July 24, 1941, in Nehru, *Oxford India Nehru*, 708.

5 Was the Homosexual White? Analogy and the Making of the Sexual Minority

1 Hirschfeld, *Sappho und Sokrates*, unnumbered page, foreword to the second edition.

2 For this concept in Ulrichs see Tobin, *Peripheral Desires*, 86.

3 Hirschfeld, *Sappho und Socrates*, 14–15. Ulrichs makes a similar point: Tobin, *Peripheral Desires*, 88.

4 Marhoefer, *Sex and the Weimar Republic*, 142–3; on homosexual emancipation and disability see also 112–45, 208. This lasted well into the twentieth century; see Kunzel, "Queer History, Mad History, and the Politics of Health."

5 Foucault, *History of Sexuality*.

6 The most famous example is Ulrichs's correspondence with Krafft-Ebing, but Ulrichs was just one of many men who wrote the psychiatrist: Oosterhuis, *Stepchildren of Nature*.

7 One could both agree with the psychiatrist and hold the view that one was a member of a class. One man, for example, wrote to Krafft-Ebing about "our despised class": Beachy, "German Invention of Homosexuality," 817. For a different revision of Foucault's broadly sketched historical point that is far more exhaustive, see Spector, *Violent Sensations*.

8 Ross, "Beyond the Closet as a Raceless Paradigm," 165.

9 Samuels, "My Body, My Closet," 235.

10 Tobin, *Peripheral Desires*, 47–51, 83–92, 110.

11 Though other sorts of analogies persisted. One author analogized to Huguenots, for example: Hans Georg, "Der Invertierte und die Politik," *Der Freund (Die Freundschaft)* 1, no. 3 (1919).

12 Kurt – Leipzig, "Von der Freiheit!," *Die Freundschaft*, February 10, 1923. On *Friendship* magazine, see Marhoefer, *Sex and the Weimar Republic*, 40, 42–9.

13 On this see Samper Vendrell, *Seduction of Youth*; Marhoefer, *Sex and the Weimar Republic*, 38–42; Ramsey, "Rites of Artgenossen," 88–90; Crouthamel, *Intimate History of the Front*, 134–41.

14 Giovanni Nemo, "Zusammenschluss," *Die Freundschaft* 27 (1920).

15 Whisnant, *Male Homosexuality in West Germany*, 102–3, 193; Rupp, "Persistence of Transnational Organizing," 1037. Churchill notes that Cory read Hirschfeld and was influenced by him: "Transnationalism and Homophile Political Culture in the Postwar Decades," 36.

16 On Hiller, see Marhoefer, *Sex and the Weimar Republic*. On Hiller's involvement with the Scientific Humanitarian Committee and his working relationship with Hirschfeld, which broke down toward the end of the 1920s, see Marhoefer, *Sex and the Weimar Republic*, 129–43.

17 Grimmer, "Politics of *Geist*," 126–77; Saalmann, "Kurt Hiller und Mussolini." On Hiller's sexual liberalism see, for example, his defense of sadism and masochism: Hiller, "Recht und Sexuelle Minderheiten."

18 Hiller, "Ethische Aufgaben der Homosexuellen," 404.

19 Fink, *Defending the Rights of Others*, 67–9.

20 On the settlement's shortcomings with respect to minority protection, see Fink, *Defending the Rights of Others*, 359–62. On the failed appeals of anticolonial leaders, feminists, and African Americans to the peacemakers in 1919, see Fink, *Defending the Rights of Others*, 133; MacMillan, *Paris 1919*, 59.

21 Articles 86 and 91, Treaty of Versailles, quoted in Fink, *Defending the Rights of Others*, xvi.

22 On the history of these treaties see Fink, *Defending the Rights of Others*, 67–9, 359–62, 133; MacMillan, *Paris 1919*, 59.

23 See Fink, *Defending the Rights of Others*, 295 and elsewhere; Fink, "Defender of Minorities."

24 Hiller, "Sexualfreiheit und Proporz," 85.

25 Kroh, *Nationalistische Macht und nationale Minderheit*, 204–5. Germany's national minorities were not protected by an international treaty.

26 Wynot, "Poles in Germany," 174–5, 180–1.

27 Hiller, "Sexualfreiheit und Proporz," 85–7; Hans Janus, "Wen wählen wir?," *Die Freundschaft* 21 (1920); René Stelter, "Politik," *Die Freundschaft*, May 19, 1923. See also Steakley, *Homosexual Emancipation Movement in Germany*, 81; Marhoefer, *Sex and the Weimar Republic*, 6–7.

28 On how the movement tried to embrace mass politics see Marhoefer, *Sex and the Weimar Republic*, 38–42.

29 On the 1921 congress as the first of the WLSR see Dose, "World League for Sexual Reform," 1.

30 Hiller, "Recht und Sexuelle Minderheiten."

31 Röhl, *The Kaiser and His Court*, 198–9.

32 Hiller, "Recht und Sexuelle Minderheiten." For other examples of Hiller using the language of sexual minority see Kurt Hiller, "Zur Kampflage," *Blätter für Menschenrecht* 6 (May 1, 1923); Hiller, "Sexualstrafrecht in Deutschland," 96.

33 For other examples of minority language see Friedrich Radszuweit, "Vor der Entscheidung," *Blätter für Menschenrecht*, April 1, 1923; Hirschfeld, *Die Homosexualität des Mannes und des Weibes*, 373.

34 Zelénski, "Die Minderheit der Sexualen." This could be a reference to Hiller's 1928 speech in Copenhagen.

35 Mazower, "Strange Triumph of Human Rights."

36 Kurt Hiller, "Appeal to the Second International Congress for Sexual Reform on Behalf of an Oppressed Human Variety," 114.

37 Rupp, "Persistence of Transnational Organizing"; Churchill, "Transnationalism and Homophile Political Culture in the Postwar Decades."

38 For example, one of the wealthiest US groups is named the Human Rights Campaign, www.hrc.org (accessed March 18, 2018).

39 See Theilhaber, *Der Untergang der deutschen Juden*, 2–6, 48, 157; Gillerman, *Germans into Jews*, 53–77; Efron, *Defenders of the Race*.

40 Hiller, "Recht und Sexuelle Minderheiten."

41 Hiller, "Ethische Aufgaben der Homosexuellen," 403. See also Bauer's analysis of a similar use of the word "race" by Hirschfeld: *Hirschfeld Archives*, 16.

42 See Marhoefer, *Sex and the Weimar Republic*, 134–8.

43 Hirschfeld, *Testament, Heft II*, 56; On Hiller's infatuation with Richard Linsert see Marhoefer, *Sex and the Weimar Republic*, 113.

44 Hiller, "The Problem of Constitution," 24. Hiller rejected Nazi racism: Grimmer, "Politics of *Geist*," 172.

45 See Somerville, "Queer Loving," 336; Puar, *Terrorist Assemblages*, 117–18.

46 Eaton, "Homosexual Unmodified," 48–50; on this see also Somerville, "Queer Loving," 364n49; Somerville, *Queering the Color Line*, 9–10.

47 On this see also Ross, "Beyond the Closet as a Raceless Paradigm," 165, 167–8; Clare, "Biological Sex and the 'Overrepresentation of Man.'"

48 Eng, *Racial Castration*, 138.

49 Frankenberg, *White Women, Race Matters*, 6.

50 Schueller, "Analogy and (White) Feminist Theory," 71–2.

51 Dyer, "Matter of Whiteness," 10.

52 Puar, *Terrorist Assemblages*, 118.

53 Tobin makes this point: *Peripheral Desires*, 239; see also 236. I would note that not all of the authors glossed by Tobin on this are asserting that race is a biological reality.

54 Bay, *White Image in the Black Mind*, ch. 6.

55 Schueller, "Analogy and (White) Feminist Theory," 71.

56 Schueller, "Analogy and (White) Feminist Theory," 71. See Aitken and Rosenhaft, *Black Germany*.

57 See also Halley, "'Like Race' Arguments"; Jakobsen, "Queers Are Like Jews, Aren't They?"; Eng, "Freedom and the Racialization of Intimacy"; Peacock, "Race, the Homosexual, and the Mattachine Society of Washington."

58 See, among others, hooks, *Ain't I a Woman*, 7–9; Carby, "White Woman Listen!," 45–6. Alcoff, *Visible Identities*, 208–10, reviews some of this trouble.

59 See for example the Mattachine Society's 1951 statement of purpose: Blasius and Phelan, *We Are Everywhere*, 283; Tobin, *Peripheral Desires*, 239, 242; Konnoth, "Created in Its Image."

60 Haritaworn, *Queer Lovers and Hateful Others*, 23, 43–4, 108–9, 146–7, 150.

61 Peacock, "Race, the Homosexual, and the Mattachine Society of Washington," 278.

62 Tobin, *Peripheral Desires*, 239.

63 On this see also Carter, "Historical Methods and Racial Identification in U.S. Lesbian and Gay History," 45–6.

64 The same can be said of the relationship between male-dominated homosexual emancipation of the nineteenth century and feminism. See Tobin, *Peripheral Desires*, 162.

6 Magnus Hirschfeld's Theory of the Races

1 Hirschfeld, *Geschlechtskunde* I, 538–9.

2 Bauer, *Hirschfeld Archives*, 14.

3 See, for example, "Blick in die Bücherwelt," *Vorwärts*, August 10, 1930.

4 Bauer, *Hirschfeld Archives*, 14; Tobin, *Peripheral Desires*, 136; Herzer, *Magnus Hirschfeld und seine Zeit*, 381; Fredrickson, *Racism*, 162.

5 Dose, *Magnus Hirschfeld: The Origins of the Gay Liberation Movement*, 10; Lentin, "Fault on Both Sides?" On Firmin see Firmin, *Equality of the Human Races*; Fluehr-Lobban, "Anténor Firmin."

6 Hirschfeld, *Geschlechtskunde* II, 656.

7 Hirschfeld, *Racism*, 320.

8 Hirschfeld, *Racism*, 320.

9 Seeck, "Einführung," 13; Herrn, "Phantom Rasse," 116; Mancini, *Magnus Hirschfeld and the Quest for Sexual Freedom*, xvii; Marhoefer, *Sex and the Weimar Republic*, 216.

10 Funke, "Navigating the Past," 133; Fuechtner, "Indians, Jews," 111; Bauer, *Hirschfeld Archives*; Egelmeers, "Universal Fetishism?" See also Becker, "Tragik eines deutschen Juden," 28–46.

11 Rainer Herrn's work does approach Hirschfeld's writing on race as something like a coherent theory. I would submit that the present account is more complete. Herrn's aim is to distinguish Hirschfeld's eugenics from his thoughts on race. Thus Herrn, understandably, does not give a complete account of what Hirschfeld actually thought about race. I am nevertheless indebted to Herrn's work. See Herrn, "Phantom Rasse." See also Herzer, *Magnus Hirschfeld und seine Zeit*, 7, 37, 200–2, 352. Herzer argues, essentially, that Hirschfeld did not believe in races as such; this is not entirely the case, as Herzer inadvertently demonstrates at one point: *Magnus Hirschfeld und seine Zeit*, 201.

12 Hirschfeld, *Testament, Heft II*, 84.

13 Lorde, "Scratching the Surface," 31.

14 "Racism," *Oxford English Dictionary*, 3rd ed., June 2008.

15 Johnson, "Race Prejudice and the Negro Artist," 753, 764.

16 See chapter 7.

17 On Virchow and liberal anthropology see Evans, *Anthropology at War*; Zimmerman, "Anti-Semitism as Skill"; Zimmerman, *Anthropology and Antihumanism in Imperial Germany*.

18 Bauer, *Hirschfeld Archives*, 18, 64.

19 Herzer, *Magnus Hirschfeld und seine Zeit*, 38. On this see also chapter 2.

20 On Hirschfeld's admiration for Virchow, see Hirschfeld, *Racism*, 84–5, 233–4; Mancini, *Magnus Hirschfeld and the Quest for Sexual Freedom*, 19, 36–7; Wolff, *Magnus Hirschfeld*, 28; Herzer, *Magnus Hirschfeld und seine Zeit*, 36–8.

21 Evans, *Anthropology at War*, 49, 63; Zimmerman, "Anti-Semitism as Skill."

22 Zimmerman, *Anthropology and Antihumanism in Imperial Germany*, 158–62.

23 Matysik, *Reforming the Moral Subject*, 148; see also Evans, *Anthropology at War*, 75–7; and Zimmerman, *Anthropology and Antihumanism in Imperial Germany*. Unlike Evans, Zimmerman emphasizes continuities between liberal anthropology, the overtly racist anthropology of the 1920s, and National Socialism. For those interested in the debate, there is a review of it in Evans, *Anthropology at War*, 3–7.

24 Evans, *Anthropology at War*.

25 Evans, *Anthropology at War*, 57–80; Efron, *Defenders of the Race*, 24–6.

26 Hirschfeld, *Geschlechtskunde* II, 563–4. As Hirschfeld's thoughts here are expressed in such a convoluted way, readers may wish to see the last part of the passage in the original German: *Wogegen wir uns wenden, ist nur, daß Rassenmerkmale mit Wertvorzeichen versehen werden. Es gibt nicht gute oder schlechte Rasse oder Völker, sondern nur innerhalb jeder Rasse Menschen mit guten oder schlechten* (hübschen oder häßlichen, nützlichen oder schädlichen) *Eigenschaften. Nur auf die körperlichen, seelischen und geschlechtlichen Individualcharaktere (in Verbindung mit der familiären Abstammung) kommt es bei der Vererbung, bei der Liebeswahl und auch bei der Höherzüchtung des Menschengeschlechts an*" [emphasis in original].

27 Hirschfeld, *Racism*, 175. On "mimicry" see also Bauer, *Hirschfeld Archives*, 15–16.
28 Hirschfeld, *Racism*, 176.
29 Hirschfeld, *Racism*, 180.
30 Hirschfeld, *Racism*, 187.
31 Hirschfeld, *Racism*, 182–3.
32 Hirschfeld, *Racism*, 86. On Vohsen see Davis, *Colonialism, Antisemitism, and Germans of Jewish Descent*, 139–42.
33 Hirschfeld, *Geschlechtskunde* II, 564. For the original see the note above.
34 Hirschfeld, *Geschlechtskunde* II, 607.
35 Hirschfeld, *Geschlechtskunde* II, 607.
36 Hirschfeld, *Racism*, 56.
37 Hirschfeld, *Racism*, 101–3; Hirschfeld, *Geschlechtskunde* II, 623–4.
38 Hirschfeld, *Racism*, 86. On von Luschan see Zimmerman, *Anthropology and Antihumanism in Imperial Germany*.
39 That is, "nicht der Rassen-, sondern der Individual- und Sexualtypus eines Menschen entscheidet." Hirschfeld, *Geschlechtskunde* II, 562.
40 Hirschfeld, *Was eint und trennt das Menschengeschlecht?*, 4. See also Hirschfeld, *Geschlechtskunde: Auf Grund dreißigjähriger Forschung und Erfahrung bearbeitet*, vol. 3, *Einblicke und Ausblicke* (Stuttgart: Julius Püttmann, 1930), 72; Hirschfeld, *Racism*, 273. He is perhaps most convinced that races are mixtures in *Was eint und trennt das Menschengeschlecht?*, where he likens this notion of race-as-mixture to his theories of sex, gender, and sexuality as continuums, with each individual having a mixed expression of various factors. On this see also Herrn, "Magnus Hirschfelds Geschlechterkosmos," 189. Hirschfeld, however, by and large retains the idea of "races" as I described above; this is also noted by Becker, "Tragik eines deutschen Juden," 43–4.
41 Hirschfeld, *Racism*, 57. On this passage see also Bauer, *Hirschfeld Archives*, 15.
42 Hirschfeld, *Weltreise*, 194.
43 Hirschfeld, *Geschlechtskunde* II, 616–17.
44 Hirschfeld, *Geschlechtskunde* II, 607.
45 For example, Hirschfeld, *Geschlechtskunde* II, 617, 618–19.
46 Hirschfeld, *Racism*, 292.
47 Hirschfeld, *Racism*, 120.
48 Fabian, *Time and the Other*; Kang, "Herder's Idea of Historical Childhood," 26.
49 Hirschfeld, *Racism*, 116.
50 Hirschfeld, *Racism*, 84.
51 Hirschfeld, *Racism*, 84–5.
52 Von Luschan, "Anthropological View of Race," 21. On von Luschan see Matysik, *Reforming the Moral Subject*, 143–6; Smith, "W.E.B. DuBois, Felix von Luschan, and Racial Reform at the *Fin de Siècle*."
53 Von Luschan, "Anthropological View of Race," 22.

54 Hirschfeld, *Racism*, 86, 106, 234.

55 Hirschfeld, *Was eint und trennt das Menschengeschlecht?*, 14; Hirschfeld, *Racism*, 86, 110–11.

56 Adas, *Machines as the Measure of Men*.

57 See chapter 4.

58 For example, Hirschfeld, *Weltreise*, 60, 66.

59 See chapter 7.

60 Hirschfeld, *Was eint und trennt das Menschengeschlecht?*, 12.

61 Hirschfeld, *Weltreise*, 66–9.

62 Hirschfeld, *Weltreise*, 168.

63 See Boas, *Anthropology and Modern Life*, 18, 59, 110, 116–18, 133–4, 138, 157; Williams, *Rethinking Race*.

64 Hirschfeld, *Racism*, 162; see also Hirschfeld, *Weltreise*, 47: "The individual sexual type far outweighs the racial type in strength and significance." Refer also to Bauer's analysis of this quotation from *Racism* (*Hirschfeld Archives*, 16) and to Bauer's larger point that in *Racism*, Hirschfeld is more interested in the plight of homosexuals than in racism and, moreover, that he obscures the fact that racism and homophobia intersect.

65 Bauer, *Hirschfeld Archives*, 35. *Racism* seems to be a translation of a long essay Hirschfeld wrote after he completed *World Journey*. He titled it "Phantom Race" (*Phantom Rasse*) and published it in installments in 1934 and 1935 in a German-language leftist journal based in Prague, *Die Wahrheit*. On this see Herrn, "Phantom Rasse," 112–13, and the original essays. I did not compare the entire essay to the entire English-language book, but spot checks on the tenth and eleventh installments revealed that passages were word-for-word verbatim. Becker also notes the book and essay are basically identical: Becker, "Tragik eines deutschen Juden," 40. The Pauls seem to have made some additions and subtractions, and to have moved Hirschfeld's sections around. It is also possible that there was a German manuscript of the whole book that Hirschfeld edited after the essay came out and that that manuscript was lost. The Pauls perhaps suggest this in their introduction to the translation, where they write that before he died, he finished the book: *Racism*, 28. If there was a German-language manuscript aside from the essay in *Die Wahrheit*, it was never published.

66 Bauer, *Hirschfeld Archives*, 15–17.

7 Tea with Langston Hughes: Hirschfeld's Anti-Blackness and Queer Black New York

1 Van Vechten, *Splendid Drunken Twenties*, 313. On Carl Van Vechten see Bernard, *Carl Van Vechten and the Harlem Renaissance*; Bernard, *Remember Me to Harlem*.

2 The term "Harlem Renaissance" is lacking – the movement was a continu-
   ation of the long history of African American arts and letters rather than a
   "rebirth" and it did not only happen in Harlem: Bernard, "Introduction,"
   xv. On Harlem in this moment see also King, *Whose Harlem Is This, Anyway?*
3 On Hughes in the winter of 1930 see Rampersad, *Life of Langston Hughes*, 193–4.
4 For Johnson on the arts see Johnson, "Race Prejudice and the Negro Artist."
5 Hirschfeld, *Testament, Heft II*, 104; Langston Hughes to Carl Van Vechten,
   March 13, 1931, in Bernard, *Remember Me to Harlem*, 84; Carl Van Vechten
   Papers, Daybooks, Sunday, December 21, 1930, and Monday, December 29,
   1930; Pollack, *Aaron Copland*.
6 Bernard, *Carl Van Vechten and the Harlem Renaissance*, 17–19.
7 But see Clark, "Race, Homosocial Desire, and 'Mammon' in *Autobiography
   of an Ex-Colored Man*"; Rohy, *Lost Causes*, ch. 4.
8 On the debate about whether or not he was queer, see Rampersad, *Life of
   Langston Hughes*, 20, 34, 37, 66–71; Als, "Elusive Langston Hughes"; Bernard, "Introduction," xiii; Bernard, *Carl Van Vechten and the Harlem Renaissance*, 87–91; Tidwell, "Sounds of Silence"; Bennett, "Langston Hughes on
   the Open Road"; Wilson, "Queer Harlem, Queer Tashkent."
9 Stewart, *New Negro*; Holcomb, *Claude McKay, Code Name Sasha*.
10 On Larsen see Dean, "Gaze, the Glance, the Mirror." On Hurston see
   Smith, "Sexual Politics and the Fiction of Zora Neale Hurston."
11 For Nugent reading Krafft-Ebing see Wirth, *Gay Rebel of the Harlem Renaissance*, 8. On Locke's letter see Rampersad, *Life of Langston Hughes*, 68.
12 Fuechtner, "Indians, Jews, and Sex," 126. See also Bauer, *Hirschfeld Archives*, 21.
13 Aitken and Rosenhaft, *Black Germany*, 125–6.
14 This was the Deutsche Liga für Menschenrechte (DLfM). On its advocacy
   on behalf of Afro-Germans see Deutsche Liga für Menschenrechte, Berlin,
   an das Auswärtige Amt, February 27, 1930, Bundesarchiv Lichterfelde R
   1001/4457/7. The Communist Reichstag deputy Willi Münzenberg was involved with the DLfM: Rosenhaft, "Afrikaner und 'Afrikaner' im Deutschland
   der Weimarer Republik," 287–9. Münzenberg reportedly rented a room
   in Hirschfeld's Institute: Magnus Hirschfeld Gesellschaft, https://www.
   hirschfeld.in-berlin.de/institut/en/personen/pers_40.html (accessed June
   25, 2020). Linsert worked closely with Münzenberg: Marhoefer, *Sex and the
   Weimar Republic*, 115. Münzenberg organized the 1927 Brussels conference:
   Petersson, "Hub of the Anti-Imperialist Movement," 50.
15 El-Tayeb, *Schwarze Deutsche*; Oguntoye, *Eine afro-deutsche Geschichte*; Aitken
   and Rosenhaft, *Black Germany*; Möhle, "Betreuung, Erfassung, Kontrolle";
   Joeden-Forgey, "Nobody's People"; Lewerenz, "'Loyal Askari' and 'Black
   Rapist'"; Campt, "Converging Spectres of an Other Within"; Campt, *Other
   Germans*; Campt, "Family Matters"; Lennox, *Remapping Black Germany*; Mi-
   chael, *Black German*.

16 Gaines, *Uplifting the Race*.
17 Hughes in *The Nation* in June 1926, quoted in Wirth, *Gay Rebel of the Harlem Renaissance*, 14.
18 Wirth, *Gay Rebel of the Harlem Renaissance*, 14.
19 Wirth, *Gay Rebel of the Harlem Renaissance*, 22.
20 On respectability politics, queer sexuality, and the Black freedom struggle in the US see, among many others, Hammonds, "Toward a Genealogy of Black Female Sexuality"; Cohen, *Boundaries of Blackness*; Mumford, *Not Straight, Not White*, 11–38; Woolner, "Woman Slain in Queer Love Brawl."
21 Wirth, *Gay Rebel of the Harlem Renaissance*, 22. See also Bragg, "Augustus Granville Dill."
22 English, *Unnatural Selections*, 55–7.
23 See Als, "Elusive Langston Hughes."
24 "Whites More Sexy in Dancing than Negroes, Scientist Thinks," *Baltimore Afro-American*, February 14, 1931.
25 Hirschfeld, *Testament, Heft II*, 104; Hirschfeld, "An die Mitglieder des Kuratoriums der Dr. Magnus Hirschfeld-Stiftung, Berlin, zwischen San Francisco und Honolulu auf dem pazifischen Ozean, *Asama Maru*," March 6, 1931, in Hirschfeld, *Testament, Heft II*, 207–12, here 209. Hirschfeld also met Hughes's agent Maxim Lieber: Hirschfeld, *Testament, Heft II*, 104. See also Bauer, *Hirschfeld Archives*, 20–1.
26 Quoted in Bernard, "Introduction," xiv.
27 On Australians see Hirschfeld, *Weltreise*, 168.
28 Hirschfeld, *Geschlechtskunde* II, 619.
29 Hirschfeld, *Geschlechtskunde* I, 539.
30 Hirschfeld, *Geschlechtskunde* II, 656.
31 Hirschfeld, *Geschlechtskunde* II, 618.
32 Magnus Hirschfeld, "III. Brief, The New Yorker, Dec. 7, 1930" (published in *Sexus*), in Hirschfeld, *Testament, Heft II*, 206–7, here 206. He added the following observation: "Also the many Chinese launderers look like Japanese gentlemen in the subway." This is also a dismissive and distancing comment about both Japanese and Chinese men, one that seems at odds with what he wrote later in *World Journey*, after traveling in Japan and in China with Li.
33 Tompkins, *Racial Indigestion*, 90. Though Tompkins looks at the nineteenth century, this imagery persisted well into the twentieth: Tompkins, *Racial Indigestion*, 2; Pieterse, *White on Black*, 199–201 and elsewhere. On this see also hooks, "Eating the Other"; Hackenesch, *Chocolate and Blackness*; Florvil, *Mobilizing Black Germany*, 8.
34 Tompkins, *Racial Indigestion*, 8.
35 Tompkins, *Racial Indigestion*, 90.
36 Pieterse, *White on Black*; McClintock, *Imperial Leather*, 207–31.
37 Quoted in Florvil, *Mobilizing Black Germany*, 111; see also 8, 114–15, 222n31.

38 Hirschfeld, *Weltreise*, 165.

39 Tompkins, *Racial Indigestion*, 5.

40 Hirschfeld, "III. Brief, The New Yorker, Dec. 7, 1930," 206.

41 Hirschfeld, *Racism*, 121.

42 Tompkins, *Racial Indigestion*.

43 Baldwin, "On Being 'White' … And Other Lies."

44 Hirschfeld, *Die Homosexualität des Mannes und des Weibes*, 559–60, 610.

45 Hirschfeld, "An die Mitglieder des Kuratoriums," 211.

46 Hirschfeld, *Testament, Heft II*, 110–14.

47 Hirschfeld, *Testament, Heft II*, 114.

48 See, for example, Hirschfeld, *Testament, Heft II*, 122.

49 Hirschfeld, *Testament, Heft II*, 118–22.

50 On this see Wake, *Private Practices*.

51 Hirschfeld, *Testament, Heft II*, 114–16; emphasis in original.

52 Hirschfeld, *Testament, Heft II*, 116.

53 Hirschfeld, *Die Homosexualität des Mannes und des Weibes*, 559–60.

54 Hirschfeld, *Die Homosexualität des Mannes und des Weibes*, 550.

55 Hirschfeld, "An die Mitglieder des Kuratoriums," 209.

56 On the dates of that trip: Hirschfeld, *Racism*, 243.

57 Hirschfeld, *Die Homosexualität des Mannes und des Weibes*, 551.

58 Hirschfeld, *Die Homosexualität des Mannes und des Weibes*, 551.

59 Hirschfeld, *Racism*, 119. See also Hirschfeld, *Weltreise*, 66.

60 Hirschfeld, *Racism*, 112; see also 124.

61 Bauer argues Hirschfeld is blind or oblivious to white racism. My point is
    a little different – he saw it and spoke out against it, but it does not bother
    him all that much, though when subjected to the extremes of Nazi racism
    himself, it did, albeit in a self-interested way. For Bauer's argument see
    Hirschfeld Archives.

62 Herzer, *Magnus Hirschfeld und seine Zeit*, 353.

63 Hirschfeld, "An die Mitglieder des Kuratoriums," 208.

64 Hirschfeld, *Racism*, 119.

65 "Whites More Sexy in Dancing than Negroes, Scientist Thinks."

66 McCabe, "Multifaceted Politics of Primitivism in Harlem Renaissance Writing."

67 Hirschfeld, *Racism*, 113.

68 Hirschfeld, *Racism*, 182.

69 Hirschfeld, *Testament, Heft II*, 211.

70 Hirschfeld, *Testament, Heft II*, 168.

71 Hirschfeld, *Racism*, 234.

72 Avery, *Up from Washington*, 9–10.

73 Hirschfeld, *Geschlechtskunde* II, 618–9; Avery, *Up from Washington*, 226.

74 Appiah, *Lines of Descent*, 27–8; Stewart, *New Negro*, 192 and following.

75 Lewis, *W.E.B. Du Bois*, 98.

76 Avery, *Up from Washington*, 226.
77 Pickens, *Kind of Democracy the Negro Race Expects*, 5.
78 Pickens, *Kind of Democracy the Negro Race Expects*, 6.
79 For Pickens on this see *Kind of Democracy the Negro Race Expects*, 6.
80 Du Bois, "African Roots of War"; Bay, *White Image in the Black Mind*, 207.
81 Hirschfeld, *Geschlechtskunde* II, 618–9.
82 Hirschfeld, *Geschlechtskunde* II, 619.
83 See Smith, "Friedrich Ratzel and the Origins of Lebensraum."
84 Hirschfeld, *Racism*, 110–12.
85 Hirschfeld, *Weltreise*, 288.
86 Herzer, *Magnus Hirschfeld und seine Zeit*, 42.
87 Hirschfeld, *Weltreise*, 8, 332.
88 Hirschfeld, *Weltreise*, 332.
89 Hirschfeld, *Weltreise*, 331.
90 Hirschfeld, *Weltreise*, 296.

8 Making Jews White

 1 The first wave of immigration or *aliyah* began in 1882, a response to po-
     groms in the Russian Empire following the assassination of Alexander II:
     Gelvin, *Israel-Palestine Conflict*, 56–7. On the Templers see Gelvin, *Israel-
     Palestine Conflict*, 28, 66.
 2 Hirschfeld, *Weltreise*, 356–7.
 3 Hirschfeld, *Weltreise*, 350. He never considered immigrating to Palestine,
     however, in part because of the difficulty of learning Hebrew: Hirschfeld,
     Weltreise, 361.
 4 On the translation of his lectures see Hirschfeld, *Weltreise*, 362. I am con-
     jecturing here – Hirschfeld does not write that he enjoyed walking on
     the beach, but given that he loved the sea and did walk along Tel Aviv's
     beaches, I feel safe in assuming that he enjoyed it.
 5 On European seaside spa towns as the model: Weiss, "Beach of Their
     Own," 15–16.
 6 Hirschfeld, *Weltreise*, 363.
 7 Hirschfeld, *Weltreise*, 363.
 8 Hirschfeld, *Weltreise*, 363–4.
 9 Weiss, "Beach of Their Own," 18–20.
10 Weiss, "Beach of Their Own," 20–2.
11 Bauer argues that in his descriptions of Palestine, Hirschfeld rejected the
     idea that Jews were a race: Bauer, *Hirschfeld Archives*, 120. Fuechtner con-
     tends that Hirschfeld critiqued the idea that Jews had racial characteristics
     and argued that, rather, what seemed like group characteristics were fash-
     ioned by environment and would change: Fuechtner, "Indians, Jews, and

Sex," 125. I respectfully disagree. I find it helpful in making sense of what he wrote about Jews and whiteness by considering his larger theory of race, which I have laid out in this and proceeding chapters.

12 Goldstein, *Price of Whiteness*, 11–31 and elsewhere. On German Jews and race thinking and race science around this time, see Efron, *Defenders of the Race*; Gillerman, *Germans into Jews*. See also Noam Pianko on relationships between race ideas and the notion of Jewish peoplehood: Pianko, *Jewish Peoplehood*, 94–105; and Susan Glenn on the persistence, into the twenty-first century, of what she calls a secular "blood logic": Glenn, "In the Blood?" On whiteness and Jewish identity see also Naar, "Our White Supremacy Problem."

13 Goldstein, *Price of Whiteness*, 18.

14 See Painter, *History of White People*.

15 Rogoff, "Is the Jew White?," 224.

16 Benton-Cohen, *Inventing the Immigration Problem*, 1–2.

17 Benton-Cohen, *Inventing the Immigration Problem*, 14.

18 Quoted in Rogoff, "Is the Jew White?," 224.

19 Rogoff, "Is the Jew White?," 224.

20 Evans, *Anthropology at War*, 84–5; Goldstein, *Price of Whiteness*, 119–20; Zimmerman, *Anthropology and Antihumanism in Imperial Germany*, 135–46. Note, however, that even in the case of the Schulstatistik (a massive survey of the racial composition of Germany directed by none other than Virchow), Virchow, long a foe of antisemitism, did not assume that to construe Jews as a race meant to validate antisemitism: Zimmerman, *Anthropology and Antihumanism in Imperial Germany*, 137. On the Schulstatistik see also Evans, *Anthropology at War*, 74–5.

21 Goldstein, *Price of Whiteness*, 119–20.

22 Pianko, *Jewish Peoplehood*, 94; Stratton, "Colour of Jews," particularly 59–60. I do not entirely agree with Stratton's analysis of ideas about Jews and race in Australia, but here he gives a good example of Australian Jews asserting that they were not a race. For another example of this debate about race among Jewish thinkers in the US in 1911, see Rogoff, "Is the Jew White?," 220–1.

23 Rogoff, "Is the Jew White?," 201, 207–8.

24 Hirschfeld, *Weltreise*, 358. Bauer reads this quotation differently. I argue in contrast that this comment on the whiteness and yet mixed-ness of Tel Avivers does not mean, as Bauer contends, that Hirschfeld "disagreed ... with racial definitions of Jewishness." See Bauer, *Hirschfeld Archives*, 120.

25 See, for example, de Gobineau, *Inequality of Human Races*, 146. On this see also Painter, *History of White People*.

26 I cited this quotation earlier as well: Hirschfeld, *Geschlechtskunde* II, 607.

27 For example, Rogoff, "Is the Jew White?," 212–18.

28 Rogoff, "Is the Jew White?," 205 and elsewhere. Rogoff (205) however notes that some of this literature held Jews to be a mixed race, with mixing being a marker of racial degradation.

29 De Gobineau, *Inequality of Human Races*, 122–3, 146.

30 De Gobineau, *Inequality of Human Races*, 211–12, 146, 151, 204.

31 Rogoff, "Is the Jew White?," 203–4.

32 See, for example, how Australia's white supremacist immigration rules applied to Jews, particularly to Sephardic Jews: Stratton, "Colour of Jews," particularly 61, 63. I do not agree with all of Stratton's conclusions. On whiteness and Ashkenazi prejudice against Sephardic Jews see Naar, "Our White Supremacy Problem."

33 Hirschfeld, *Weltreise*, 278.

34 Hirschfeld, *Weltreise*, 278. This passage came to my attention thanks to the work of Fuechtner; see her analysis of it: "Indians, Jews, and Sex," 125. We have somewhat different takes on the passage; Hirschfeld's thoughts on race versus culture do not seem inconsistent when one foregrounds his belief in Jewish whiteness.

35 Hirschfeld, *Geschlechtskunde* II, 633.

36 Hirschfeld, *Weltreise*, 357.

37 Hirschfeld, *Weltreise*, 357–8.

38 Frübis, "Die 'Reinheit' der Jüdin," 114.

39 Ofek and Schütz, *Hermann Struck*.

40 Steinweis, *Studying the Jew*, 26, 30.

41 Steinweis, *Studying the Jew*, 26.

42 Hirschfeld, *Weltreise*, 286.

43 Hirschfeld, *Weltreise*, 366.

44 Hirschfeld, *Geschlechtskunde* II, 641.

45 On Eden and Cedar Paul and left-wing eugenics see Paul, "Eugenics and the Left," 567.

46 Hirschfeld, *Racism*, 201.

47 Hirschfeld, *Testament, Heft II*, 168.

48 For a self-referential mention of whiteness, see Hirschfeld, *Racism*, 85, where he refers to people of non-white races who have "skins ... darker than our own."

49 On his Jewish identity (or lack thereof) see Dose, *Magnus Hirschfeld: Deutscher – Jude – Weltbürger*, 34; Becker, "Tragik eines deutschen Juden"; Bauer, *Hirschfeld Archives*, 120.

50 Hirschfeld, *Testament, Heft II*, 136, 134, 162.

51 Hirschfeld, *Testament, Heft II*, 130.

52 On his plans for his funeral: Hirschfeld, *Testament, Heft II*, 168. On his secularism and critiques of Christianity, for example, Hirschfeld, *Weltreise*, 353–5. On Christmas see, for example, Hirschfeld, *Testament, Heft II*, 130.

53 See chapter 3.

54 Hirschfeld, *Testament, Heft II*, 134.

55 Hirschfeld, *Testament, Heft II*, 140.

56 Gelvin, *Israel-Palestine Conflict*, 86–9.

57 Gelvin, *Israel-Palestine Conflict*, 87–91.

58 Gelvin, *Israel-Palestine Conflict*, 87–8, 90–1.

59 Hirschfeld, *Weltreise*, 381–4.

60 Hirschfeld, *Weltreise*, 358, 391.

61 Magnus Hirschfeld to Ernst Maass, April 12, 1933, in Hirschfeld, *Testament, Heft II*, 220. Though Hirschfeld chose not to migrate to Palestine, other sex reformers did: Leng, "Limits of Transnationalism."

62 Hirschfeld, *Weltreise*, 384, 386.

63 Hirschfeld, *Weltreise*, 363. On this phrase see chapter 2.

64 On Hirschfeld, Zionism, and the struggle over Palestine in 1932, see also Bauer's cogent remarks: Bauer, *Hirschfeld Archives*, 120–3.

65 See chapter 5. To my knowledge, Tobin was the first to publish on the foundational nature of the analogy to Jews, and his work on it is extremely useful reading on this. He however writes that though Hirschfeld did so much to articulate the minoritizing model, he did not write explicitly about Jews as analogous to homosexuals: Tobin, *Peripheral Desires*, 93. Tobin also sees the significance of this analogy differently than I do: *Peripheral Desires*, 92–7.

66 Max Danielsen, "Unsere Presse," *Die Freundschaft*, April 24–30, 1920.

67 Hiller, "Ethische Aufgaben der Homosexuellen," 403–4. I cited portions of this passage in chapter 5 as well.

68 Hiller, "Ethische Aufgaben der Homosexuellen," 403–4.

69 On Friedländer see Steakley, *Homosexual Emancipation Movement in Germany*, 43–9.

70 Steakley, "Cinema and Censorship in the Weimar Republic"; Steakley, *"Anders als die Andern."* See also Malakaj, "Richard Oswald, Magnus Hirschfeld, and the Possible Impossibility of Hygienic Melodrama."

71 *Different from the Others (Anders als die Andern)*, Kino International/Filmmuseum Muenchen, 2004. Translation from the film.

72 Magnus, *Jewish Emancipation in a German City*, 103–4; Katz, "Term 'Jewish Emancipation.'"

73 Niewyk, *Jews in Weimar Germany*, 100. On Hirschfeld's father: Herzer, *Magnus Hirschfeld und Seine Zeit*, 17–20.

74 Magnus, *Jewish Emancipation in a German City*, 2.

75 Niewyk, *Jews in Weimar Germany*, 2.

76 Herzer, *Magnus Hirschfeld und seine Zeit*, 21.

77 Hirschfeld, "Jahresbericht 1906–1908," 660–1. See also Hirschfeld, *Die Homosexualität des Mannes und des Weibes*, 959, 985.

78 Magnus Hirschfeld and Richard Linsert, "Die Homosexualität," in *Sitteng-eschichte des Lasters: Die Kulturepochen und Ihre Leidenschaften*, ed. Leo Schidrowitz (Vienna: Verlag für Kulturforschung, 1927), 255.

79 Hirschfeld and Linsert, "Die Homosexualität," 255.

80 Magnus Hirschfeld, "Schuldig geboren," in *Sexual-Katastrophen: Bilder aus dem modernen Geschlechts- und Eheleben*, ed. Ludwig Levy-Lenz (Leipzig: A.H. Payne, 1926), 5.

81 Hirschfeld, *Die Homosexualität des Mannes und des Weibes*, 1026.

82 Hirschfeld, *Die Homosexualität des Mannes und des Weibes*, 969.

83 Quoted in Hirschfeld, *Die Homosexualität des Mannes und des Weibes*, 976.

84 As reported in the *Leipziger Volkszeitung*, October 1, 1920, quoted in "Aus der Bewegung," *Jahrbuch für sexuelle Zwischenstufen mit besonderer Berücksichtigung der Homosexualität* 20, nos. 3 and 4 (1920): 122–3.

85 "Aus der Bewegung," 123–7.

86 Marhoefer, *Sex and the Weimar Republic*, 178–9; see also Herzog, *Sex After Fascism*, 20–2.

87 Gilman, "Struggle of Psychiatry with Psychoanalysis"; Haeberle, "Jewish Contribution to the Development of Sexology"; Brandhorst, "From Neo-Malthusianism to Sexual Reform"; Crozier, "All the World's a Stage." (One wishes that Crozier had taken a more critical view of the antisemitism facing Norman Haire.) On Jews and sexology see also von Braun, *Gibt es eine "jüdische" und eine "christliche" Sexualwissenschaft?*

88 Hirschfeld, *Racism*, 290.

89 Hirschfeld, *Racism*, 134–5, 139–41.

90 Herrn, "'Phantom Rasse,'" 116.

91 Marhoefer, *Sex and the Weimar Republic*, 6–7, 134–6.

92 Hirschfeld, *Weltreise*, 375.

93 Hirschfeld, *Weltreise*, 375.

9 Magnus Hirschfeld's Queer Eugenics

1 Hirschfeld, *Geschlechtskunde* III, 47.

2 For details see Grossmann, *Reforming Sex*.

3 Ladd-Taylor, *Fixing the Poor*, 85.

4 Marhoefer, *Sex and the Weimar Republic*, 95–7.

5 Hirschfeld, *Geschlechtskunde* III, 47.

6 Hirschfeld, *Geschlechtskunde* II, 435–7; *Geschlechtskunde* III, 39–40.

7 Hirschfeld, *Geschlechtskunde* III, 39–40.

8 Burleigh, *Death and Deliverance*, 23.

9 See Ladd-Taylor, *Fixing the Poor*, 84–6.

10 Schoen, *Choice and Coercion*, 93–5; quotation at 94.

11 Magnus Hirschfeld, Andreas Gaspar, and Institut für Sexualwissenschaft, *The Sexual History of the World War* (New York: Panurge Press, 1934), 350.

12 On his study see below and Hirschfeld, *Geschlechtskunde* III, 15, 30.

13 Hirschfeld, *Geschlechtskunde* III, 31.

14 Beginning in 1983, the debate was about whether Hirschfeld's eugenics were partly to blame for Nazi eugenic programs, including the mass murders of disabled people. See Seeck, *Durch Wissenschaft zur Gerechtigkeit?*; Seeck, "' ... Dunstkreis der Täter'?"; Leng, "Magnus Hirschfeld's Meanings."

15 Leng, "Magnus Hirschfeld's Meanings," 112–14. Herzer probably goes the farthest of recent apologists for Hirschfeld on this score when he argues that what Hirschfeld meant by "eugenics" was what we in the early twenty-first century called prenatal counseling, prenatal testing, and medically indicated abortion: *Magnus Hirschfeld und seine Zeit*, 8, 313.

16 Seeck, "' ... Dunstkreis der Täter'?," 321. Herrn makes this point as well: Herrn, "'Phantom Rasse.'"

17 Herzer, *Magnus Hirschfeld*, 36; see also 9–11; Herzer, *Magnus Hirschfeld und seine Zeit*, 312.

18 Tobin writes that "Hirschfeld always insisted on voluntary eugenics, not coercive state-run policies": *Peripheral Desires*, 96. Herzer says the same: *Magnus Hirschfeld und seine Zeit*, 201, 245. Later, to the contrary, Herzer shows that Hirschfeld approved of compulsory sterilization in cases involving mentally disabled people: Herzer, *Magnus Hirschfeld und seine Zeit*, 312.

19 As Evans suggests: "Introduction: Why Queer German History?," 378.

20 Hirschfeld, *Geschlechtskunde* II, 659.

21 Hirschfeld, *Weltreise*, vii.

22 Galton, *Inquiry into Human Faculty and Its Development*, 1–2. See also Galton, "Eugenics."

23 English, *Unnatural Selections*, 1.

24 Rogoff, "Is the Jew White?," 206.

25 For Hirschfeld's thoughts on Galton in particular, see *Geschlechtskunde* II, 540–1.

26 See Schoen, *Choice and Coercion*; Stern, *Eugenic Nation*; McLaren, *Our Own Master Race*; Vicenti Carpio, "Lost Generation"; Dyck, *Facing Eugenics*.

27 Dikötter, "Race Culture," 467.

28 Etzemüller, "Sozialstaat, Eugenik und Normalisierung in skandinavischen Demokratien"; Sonn, "Your Body Is Yours"; Adams, *Wellborn Science*; Dikötter, "Race Culture"; Gerodetti, "From Science to Social Technology"; Broberg and Roll-Hansen, *Eugenics and the Welfare State*; Ordover, *American Eugenics*; Stern, *Eugenic Nation*; McLaren, *Our Own Master Race*.

29 Hirschfeld, *Geschlechtskunde* II, 595, 649.

30 Schwartz, *Sozialistische Eugenik*; Weiss, "Race Hygiene Movement in Germany," 9–10.

31 English, *Unnatural Selections*, 35–64.

32 Hirschfeld, *Weltreise*, 140.

33 Hirschfeld, *Weltreise*, 140.

34 Quoted in Hirschfeld, *Weltreise*, 140.

35 Quoted in Hirschfeld, *Weltreise*, 140.

36 Hirschfeld, *Geschlechtskunde* II, 560–1.

37 Hirschfeld, *Racism*, 174.

38 Hirschfeld, *Was eint und trennt das Menschengeschlecht?*, 5.

39 Hirschfeld, *Geschlechtskunde* II, 562. Another similar example is at Hirschfeld, *Was eint und trennt das Menschengeschlecht?*, 3.

40 Hirschfeld, *Geschlechtskunde* II, 539.

41 Hirschfeld, *Von einst bis jetzt*, 158.

42 Magnus Hirschfeld, "Über Sexualwissenschaft," *Zeitschrift für Sexualwissenschaft* 1, no. 1 (1908): 9. Note that he occasionally used the word "race" to mean the human race: Hirschfeld, *Geschlechtskunde* II, 600–3.

43 An endorsement of this core principle of Galton's is the implication of Hirschfeld's approving quotations of Luther Darwin, Francis Galton, and Charles Darwin in *Geschlechtskunde* II, 540–1.

44 Hirschfeld, *Die Homosexualität des Mannes und des Weibes*, 735–6; on Hirschfeld, eugenics, and male-male sex work, see Marhoefer, *Sex and the Weimar Republic*, 129–45.

45 Hirschfeld, *Was eint und trennt das Menschengeschlecht?*, quotations at 3, 13. See also Leng, "Magnus Hirschfeld's Meanings," 98, 105, 107–10, 115n106.

46 Hirschfeld, *Geschlechtskunde* III, 31, 58; Hirschfeld, "Das Erbgericht, Betrachtungen zum deutschen Sterilisationgesetz," 318–19; Hirschfeld, "Über amtliche Ehevermittlung."

47 Hirschfeld, *Geschlechtskunde* III, 55–8. Women were thought to reach sexual maturity faster than men: Marhoefer, *Sex and the Weimar Republic*, 122.

48 Hirschfeld, *Geschlechtskunde* III, 58. On ideas about syphilis damaging the "quality" of the German population, see Marhoefer, "Among Abnormals," 168.

49 Hirschfeld, *Geschlechtskunde* III, 58–9.

50 Hirschfeld, *Geschlechtskunde* III, 24–5, 42, 47. On alcoholism see Hirschfeld, *Geschlechtskunde* III, 9; Hirschfeld, *Geschlechtskunde* I, 149–63.

51 Hirschfeld, "Das Erbgericht," 318.

52 See Pross, "Attitude of German Émigré Doctors Towards Medicine Under National Socialism."

53 Hirschfeld, "Das Erbgericht," 314.

54 Ladd-Taylor, *Fixing the Poor*, 230.

55 Hirschfeld, *Geschlechtskunde* III, 52–4.

56 To see states that had laws and basic data on sterilization in those states, including the number of people reported sterilized through 1963, see Ladd-Taylor, *Fixing the Poor*, 230.

57 Hirschfeld, "An die Mitglieder des Kuratoriums," 208–9.

58 Gosney and Popenoe, *Sterilization for Human Betterment.*

59 Stern, *Eugenic Nation,* 72, 90.

60 Stern, *Eugenic Nation,* 72–3.

61 Ladd-Taylor, "Eugenics, Sterilisation, and Modern Marriage in the USA." On Popenoe and the Human Betterment Foundation see also Stern, *Eugenic Nation.*

62 Popenoe and Hill Johnson, *Applied Eugenics,* 720. On its influence: Ladd-Taylor, *Fixing the Poor,* 85.

63 Stern, *Eugenic Nation,* 94–5.

64 Popenoe and Johnson, *Applied Eugenics,* 714.

65 Popenoe and Johnson, *Applied Eugenics,* 345, 723–6, 759, 769–70, 777–9.

66 Popenoe and Johnson, *Applied Eugenics,* 695.

67 Popenoe and Johnson, *Applied Eugenics,* 694–5.

68 Popenoe and Johnson, *Applied Eugenics,* 914–16.

69 Hirschfeld, "Das Erbgericht," 311.

70 Hirschfeld, *Testament, Heft II,* 96.

71 Marhoefer, *Sex and the Weimar Republic,* 24, 116; Einstein, *Collected Papers of Albert Einstein,* 16:445.

72 Hirschfeld, *Testament, Heft II,* 209. On Mooney see Johnson, *1916 Preparedness Day Bombing;* on reformers and the sex starvation of prisoners see Rosenblum, *Beyond the Prison Gates,* 201–25.

73 Hirschfeld, "An die Mitglieder des Kuratoriums," 209.

74 Stern, *Eugenic Nation,* 92.

75 On Steinach and Hirschfeld see Sutton, *Sex Between Body and Mind.*

76 Blue, "Strange Career of Leo Stanley," 229.

77 Blue, "Strange Career of Leo Stanley," 224, 226, 231, 233.

78 Too zealous: Stern, *Eugenic Nation,* 92.

79 Leng, "Magnus Hirschfeld's Meanings," 114.

80 Huonker, *Diagnose: "Moralisch defekt";* van der Meer, "Eugenic and Sexual Folklores and the Castration of Sex Offenders in the Netherlands." Note that at times what was happening was a conflation of "castration" and "sterilization" as we would define them.

81 Boag, *Same-Sex Affairs,* 212–14.

82 On the case of "F.S.," see Otto Kaus, "Der Fall Böters," *Das Tage-Buch,* March 7, 1925: 338–43; Marhoefer, "Among Abnormals," 105–6.

83 On Boeters see Kaus, "Der Fall Böters"; Burleigh, *Death and Deliverance,* 36–42; Marhoefer, "Among Abnormals," chapter 2.

84 Hirschfeld, *Geschlechtskunde* III, 42–3.

85 Hirschfeld, *Geschlechtskunde* III, 47–8.

86 Hirschfeld, *Die Homosexualität des Mannes und des Weibes,* 734–6; Marhoefer, *Sex and the Weimar Republic,* 126–7, 138–45. I would not classify pedophiles

as "queer," but it is perhaps relevant here that Hirschfeld supported cas-
trating them: Hirschfeld, *Geschlechtskunde* III, 39–40, 48–9.

87 See Marhoefer, *Sex and the Weimar Republic;* see also Lybeck, *Desiring Emancipation,* 166–9 and elsewhere.
88 Hirschfeld, *Geschlechtskunde* III, 762.
89 Hirschfeld debunks the notion that homosexuality is a sign of degeneration and provides a long list of actual signs of degeneration: Hirschfeld,
Geschlechtskunde III, 15–18. Oregon, for example, expanded its bureaucracy
of eugenic sterilization to perform forced castrations, which advocates understood not as a way to prevent "inferior" men from having children but as
a way to end their queer behavior or as a punishment. The program targeted
incarcerated men who had sex with men. See Boag, *Same-Sex Affairs,* 207–16.
90 For these details on von Römer see Marhoefer, *Sex and the Weimar Republic,*
137.
91 Hirschfeld, *Geschlechtskunde* III, 15.
92 See Marhoefer, *Sex and the Weimar Republic,* 136–8.
93 Hirschfeld, *Geschlechtskunde* III, 30.
94 Hirschfeld, *Geschlechtskunde* III, 30.
95 Hirschfeld, *Geschlechtskunde* III, 511; see also 29–30. He writes at length
about "intersexual variations" and "hermaphroditism": see Hirschfeld,
Geschlechtskunde I, 545 and following; see also elsewhere (refer to the index
entry in *Geschlechtskunde* V, 166).
96 Hirschfeld, *Geschlechtskunde* III, 30.
97 Hirschfeld, quoted in Marhoefer, *Sex and the Weimar Republic,* 137. On this
see also Hirschfeld, "Über Sexualwissenschaft," 14.
98 Hirschfeld, *Geschlechtskunde* III, 15.
99 Hirschfeld, *Geschlechtskunde* III, 55.
100 Hirschfeld, *Weltreise,* 307.
101 See, for instance, Hirschfeld, *Sappho und Sokrates,* 17.
102 Ellis, *My Life.*
103 Hirschfeld, *Weltreise,* 307. Sutton shows that earlier in his career, Hirschfeld
did seriously entertain the possibility of curing homosexuality, only to reject it: Sutton, *Sex Between Body and Mind,* 60–4, 70–5, 86–90.
104 Hirschfeld, *Weltreise,* 160–1.
105 Hirschfeld, *Weltreise,* 161; Hirschfeld, "Über Sexualwissenschaft," 3. On the
uniqueness of German-speaking Europe in this respect see also Beachy,
"German Invention of Homosexuality."
106 Hirschfeld, *Weltreise,* 161.
107 Alexanderson, *Subversive Seas,* 101.
108 See Lowrie, *Masters and Servants.*
109 Alexanderson, *Subversive Seas,* 15–16.
110 See Alexanderson, *Subversive Seas,* 12–22.

111 Alexanderson, *Subversive Seas*, 19.
112 Hirschfeld, *Weltreise*, 159–60.
113 Hirschfeld, *Weltreise*, 160.
114 Hirschfeld, *Weltreise*, 160–1.
115 Hirschfeld, *Weltreise*, 161.
116 Hirschfeld, *Weltreise*, 161.
117 Edelman, *No Future*. Thanks to a peer reviewer for pointing this out.

10 "And What about Women?"

1 Hirschfeld, *Weltreise*, 134.
2 A number of critics have pointed out Hirschfeld's sexism and the gender-exclusionary nature of the model. See Bruns, "Kontroversen zwischen Freud, Blüher und Hirschfeld"; Wolff, *Magnus Hirschfeld*, 87–8, and see also 90; Bauer, *Hirschfeld Archives*, 48–50.
3 Hirschfeld, *Racism*, 156–7.
4 See, for example, Hirschfeld, *Die Homosexualität des Mannes und des Weibes*, 495–6.
5 Hirschfeld, *Die Homosexualität des Mannes und des Weibes*, 495–6.
6 Tobin, *Peripheral Desires*, 238–9; Bauer, *Hirschfeld Archives*, 48–51, 116; Sutton and Leng, "Forum Introduction," 64.
7 For an example of Hirschfeld's cursory treatment of female homosexuality in comparison to his lavish attention to male homosexuality, see Hirschfeld, *Die Homosexualität des Mannes und des Weibes*, 559–60.
8 Quoted in Sutton, *Sex Between Body and Mind*, 145.
9 See Sutton on interwar female sexologists: *Sex Between Body and Mind*, 145–72; see also Leng on female sexologists: *Sexual Politics and Femininst Science*.
10 Leng, *Sexual Politics and Feminist Science*; Sutton, *Sex Between Body and Mind*, 166–7. An exception to the common story of male scientists ignoring female collaborators may possibly be the collaboration between Dora Russell and Norman Haire in the final years of the World League for Sexual Reform. See Crozier, "All the World's a Stage"; Weisskopf, "Der Brünner Sexualkongreß."
11 Sutton, *Sex Between Body and Mind*, 170–1. On the relationship between sexology and psychoanalysis in this moment see Sutton, *Sex Between Body and Mind*, 209: the two fields still had important areas of intersection and yet also distinctions.
12 A rare exception: he cites Anna Rüling on female homosexuality: Hirschfeld, *Die Homosexualität des Mannes und des Weibes*, 497. On Rüling see Leidinger, "Anna Rüling"; Leng, *Sexual Politics and Feminist Science*. On Hirschfeld and citation see Bauer, *Hirschfeld Archives*, 117 and elsewhere. If I may, a brief note on my sense of the politics of citation insofar as this book

goes: Writing in a subfield – queer history – where some (not all) men no-toriously cite neither work by women nor work about women, I have been guided by a contrary inclination, that is, to endeavor to read and to cite as widely as I can. On citations see also Ahmed, *Living a Feminist Life*, 15–16.

13   Wolff, *Magnus Hirschfeld*, 87–8.

14   Chauncey, *Gay New York*, 78.

15   Hirschfeld, *Weltreise*, 91–2. On Li as a sporting type see Hichens, *That Which Is Hidden*, 145.

16   In the Weimar period, there were no women in the leadership at all. It seems there was greater gender diversity before the First World War; a few women are listed as members, or even chairs, and before the war female authors occasionally contributed to the WhK's *Jahrbuch*. On the female chairs see Leng, *Sexual Politics and Feminist Science*, 53.

17   Hirschfeld, *Testament, Heft II*, 108. On Fürst Chiavacci see also Max Planck Institute for the History of Science, "Sidonie Fürst."

18   See, for example, the letterhead Hirschfeld used to write Benjamin in February 1930: Hirschfeld to Benjamin, February 4, 1930, HHAfS-Humboldt, which lists Sanger, Stöcker, and Kollontai as members of the WLSR's International Committee. Of the three, his professional world intersected most with Stöcker's. Jonathan Høegh von Leunbach wrote Kollontai in 1928 and told her she had been named to the WLSR's International Committee: Healey, "Homosexual Existence and Existing Socialism," 370n16. It is not clear that Kollontai had anything else to do with the WLSR, and she was certainly not a major participant. On Leunbach see Brandhorst, "From Neo-Malthusianism to Sexual Reform." On Kollontai's popularity in sex re-form circles in Weimar Germany see Usborne, *Politics of the Body in Weimar Germany*. On Stöcker see Leng, *Sexual Politics and Feminist Science*; Dickin-son, *Sex, Freedom, and Power in Imperial Germany*; Usborne, *Politics of the Body*; Sutton, *Sex Between Body and Mind*, 145–72.

19   Sanger, *Selected Papers of Margaret Sanger*, 13–14, 287; Hirschfeld, "An die Mitglieder des Kuratoriums," 208.

20   See chapter 1.

21   Sanger, *Selected Papers of Margaret Sanger*, 140–1. Sanger and Hirschfeld also ran competing international groups: see Dose, "World League for Sexual Reform." Sanger did not want to work with what she considered the overly radical sex reform movement – she also avoided Helene Stöcker: Sanger to How-Martyn, April 4, 1929, in *Selected Papers of Margaret Sanger*, 158, 161n16. In 1928, Harry Benjamin thought Hirschfeld was not even in touch with Sanger; he offered to connect them: Benjamin to Hirschfeld, June 15, 1928, HHAfS-Humboldt.

22   Riese and Leunbach, *Sexual Reform Congress*, 9. The letterhead Hirschfeld used to write Benjamin in February 1930 lists her: Hirschfeld to Benjamin, February 4, 1930, HHAfS-Humboldt.

23 See Riese and Leunbach, *Sexual Reform Congress*, 216; Braker, "Helene Stöcker's Pacifism," 456; Leng, *Sexual Politics and Feminist Science*, 197–8.

24 Hirschfeld, *Von einst bis jetzt*, 191.

25 Wolff, *Magnus Hirschfeld*, 88.

26 See, for example, Hirschfeld, *Geschlechtskunde* I, 481–8.

27 Riese and Leunbach, *Sexual Reform Congress*, 10.

28 Quoted in Grossmann, "Magnus Hirschfeld, Sexualreform und die Neue Frau," 207.

29 Hirschfeld, *Geschlechtskunde* I, 481.

30 See Bauer, *Hirschfeld Archives*, 113–23.

31 Bauer, *Hirschfeld Archives*, 116–17.

32 Hirschfeld, *Weltreise*, 262.

33 Herzer, *Magnus Hirschfeld und seine Zeit*, 93–4. See also Hirschfeld, "Über Sexualwissenschaft," 15.

34 Sutton, *Sex Between Body and Mind*, 165–6.

35 Herzer, *Magnus Hirschfeld und seine Zeit*, 94–5.

36 Herzer, *Magnus Hirschfeld und seine Zeit*, 95–6.

37 See chapter 6.

38 Herzer, *Magnus Hirschfeld und seine Zeit*, 96.

39 Hirschfeld, *Was eint und trennt das Menschengeschlecht?*, 3.

40 Hirschfeld, *Was eint und trennt das Menschengeschlecht?*, 6, 10.

41 Rupp, *Sapphistries*, 7–8, 143; Canaday, *Straight State*, 12–13; Lorway, *Namibia's Rainbow Project*, 64–85. On this and on the dearth of work in the field of queer history on queer women (queer white women and especially queer women of color and queer women living outside the US), see Kunzel, "Power of Queer History," 1577–9.

42 Halperin, "Introduction," 5.

43 Rich, "Compulsory Heterosexuality and Lesbian Existence."

44 Lybeck, *Desiring Emancipation*; Chaplin, "Utopian Gaiety"; Cahn, *Coming on Strong*, 164–84; Cahn, "From the 'Muscle Moll' to the 'Butch' Ballplayer"; Sinnott, "Dormitories and Other Queer Spaces"; Frydman, "Freedom's Sex Problem"; Marhoefer, "'The Book Was a Revelation, I Recognied Myself in It.'" Queer women's lives in the twentieth century were profoundly shaped by both sexism and racism, as was the anti-queer animus they navigated: Woolner, "Woman Slain in Queer Love Brawl."

45 Bauer, *Hirschfeld Archives*, 49–50.

46 Herzer, *Magnus Hirschfeld und seine Zeit*, 8.

47 Hirschfeld, "I. Brief," 204.

48 Oguntoye, "Mein Coming-out als schwarze Lesbe in Deutschland"; Lorde, "Showing Our True Colors"; Opitz [Ayim], Oguntoye, and Schultz, *Showing Our Colors*; Florvil, "Emotional Connections"; Florvil, *Mobilizing Black Germany*, 25–52; Michaels, "Impact of Audre Lorde's Politics and Poetics

on Afro-German Women Writers"; De Veaux, *Warrior Poet*, 327 and elsewhere; Lennox, "Introduction," 4–5. See also Schultz's film *Audre Lorde*. On queer women in Afro-German organizing and in Lorde's Berlin circle, see Oguntoye, "Mein Coming-out als schwarze Lesbe in Deutschland"; Florvil, "Distant Ties," 82; Michaels, "Impact of Audre Lorde's Politics and Poetics on Afro-German Women Writers," 30; Lennox, "Introduction," 6.

49 Oguntoye, "Mein Coming-out als schwarze Lesbe in Deutschland," 162–3.
50 Oguntoye, *Eine afro-deutsche Geschichte*. On Oguntoye's activism see also a recent interview with her: Maurer, "Der ewige Kampf gegen Rassismus," as well as Florvil, "Emotional Connections" and *Mobilizing Black Germany*.
51 Florvil, "Emotional Connections," 137.
52 Lorde, "Scratching the Surface," 31.
53 De Veaux, *Warrior Poet*, 83–5.
54 Lorde, "I Am Your Sister," 61.
55 For her influence in Germany see Oguntoye and Gammon, "Lesben und ihr Kampf um Anerkennung."

11 The Exile

1 Hirschfeld, *Testament, Heft II*, 136; see also the stamp in his passport, which is in the MHG archive.
2 Magnus Hirschfeld to Harry Benjamin, March 16, 1932, HHAfS-Humboldt. Hirschfeld and Giese probably met sometime around 1914–18. In 1934 Hirschfeld wrote to Benjamin that Giese had worked at the Institute for almost twenty years. (The Institute opened in 1919.) Magnus Hirschfeld to Harry Benjamin, June 3, 1934, HHAfS-Humboldt.
3 Wolff, *Magnus Hirschfeld*, 187–8, 432.
4 Giese to Haire, May 17, 1933, in Hirschfeld, *Testament, Heft II*, 221.
5 Hirschfeld, *Weltreise*, 69.
6 See Herzer, *Magnus Hirschfeld und seine Zeit*, 65–6, including n79, 370–1.
7 See Hirschfeld, *Testament, Heft II*, 28–30, 50; Franz Wimmer to Magnus Hirschfeld, October 26, 1932, in Hirschfeld, *Testament, Heft II*, 216. Wimmer was one of only three non-relatives (aside from Giese and Li) to whom Hirschfeld left money in his will: Soetaert, "Succession Hirschfeld," 40 and elsewhere.
8 Hirschfeld, *Testament, Heft II*, 62.
9 Wolff, *Magnus Hirschfeld*, 432.
10 Giese to Max Hodann, quoted in Soetaert, "Succession Hirschfeld," 26.
11 I base this conclusion on the Hichens novel; see chapter 12.
12 Traute Hodann to Fritz and Paulette Brupbacher, April 2, 1934, quoted in Dose, "Magnus Hirschfeld in Frankreich," 12.
13 Vyras, "Magnus Hirschfeld in Greece," 20.

14 Vyras, "Magnus Hirschfeld in Greece," 21; Hirschfeld, *Testament, Heft II*, 136.

15 Vyras, "Magnus Hirschfeld in Greece," 21–2 (translations from Greek are by Vyras).

16 Vyras, "Magnus Hirschfeld in Greece," 22.

17 Vyras, "Magnus Hirschfeld in Greece," 23.

18 Vyras, "Magnus Hirschfeld in Greece," 24.

19 Hirschfeld, *Testament, Heft II*, 136.

20 Hirschfeld, *Testament, Heft II*, 136. It is not clear whether Giese also went on to Vienna. See Dose's note in Hirschfeld, *Testament, Heft II*, 138n373.

21 Hirschfeld, *Testament, Heft II*, 136.

22 Hirschfeld, *Testament, Heft II*, 128–30.

23 Kaplan, *Between Dignity and Despair*.

24 Li, unpublished manuscript, unnumbered p. 15, Li Shiu Tong Nachlass, Box 1.

25 Li, unpublished manuscript, unnumbered p. 5, Li Shiu Tong Nachlass, Box 1.

26 Hirschfeld to Benjamin, April 11, 1932, HHAfS-Humboldt.

27 On Röhm see Marhoefer, *Sex and the Weimar Republic*, 146–73. On the Eulenburg scandal see Domeier, *Eulenburg Affair*.

28 See Kuiper, "Tolstoyans on a Mountain."

29 See chapter 7.

30 Bergemann, Dose, and Keilson-Lauritz, *Magnus Hirschfelds Exil-Gästebuch*, 181.

31 Hirschfeld began writing *Weltreise* when he arrived in Vienna in April 1932 from Greece (by train through Skopje): *Testament, Heft II*, 136–8. He sent *Weltreise* to the publisher early in 1933, about a year after he began it, while he was in Zurich: Hirschfeld, *Testament, Heft II*, 164; Hirschfeld, *Weltreise*, vii. Li appears to have been with him for much of that period.

32 Hirschfeld, *Testament, Heft II*, 140; see also 158. For where he lived in Zurich see Hirschfeld, *Testament, Heft II*, 140n375.

33 Vordtriede, *Das verlassene Haus*, 245. Vordtriede remembered hearing this in 1934, but by then Hirschfeld was in France and not often, if ever, in Zurich, so I assume he meant the period 1932–3. I assume Li and he were friends because Li introduced him to Hichens: Hichens, *Yesterday*, 392. Vordtriede was the model for the character Max in Hichens's novel: Werner Vordtriede, *Das verlassene Haus*, 24–5. Vordtriede was queer and may have had an affair with Hichens; in any event they got very close, see Hichens, *Yesterday*, 407 and following; Vordtriede, *Das verlassene Haus*, 36, 38, 41, 44, and elsewhere.

34 Hirschfeld, *Testament, Heft II*, 138.

35 Bergemann, Dose, and Keilson-Lauritz, *Magnus Hirschfelds Exil-Gästebuch*, 113.

36 Li, unpublished manuscript, unnumbered p. 12, Li Shiu Tong Nachlass, Box 1.

37 Li, unpublished manuscript, unnumbered p. 15, Li Shiu Tong Nachlass, Box 1.

38 Weisskopf, "Der Brünner Sexualkongreß," 31.

39 Weisskopf, "Der Brünner Sexualkongreß," 31.

40 Hirschfeld, *Geschlechtskunde* I, 546.

41 Hirschfeld, *Geschlechtskunde* III, 511; see also chapter 9.

42 Elkan's note on the back of the photograph: E. Elkan papers, SA/FPA/A23/1/1-14, Wellcome Library.

43 E. Elkan papers, SA/FPA/A23/1/1-14; on Giese see Elkan to Margaret Howard, October 12, 1971, E. Elkan papers; Weisskopf, "Der Brünner Sexualkongreß"; Bauer, *Hirschfeld Archives*, 123.

44 Hirschfeld, *Testament, Heft II*, 142.

45 Hirschfeld, *Testament, Heft II*, 142.

46 Hirschfeld, *Testament, Heft II*, 158.

47 Hirschfeld, *Testament, Heft II*, 164; Hirschfeld, *Weltreise*, vii.

48 Hirschfeld, *Testament, Heft II*, 158; Hirschfeld to Leunbach and Haire, March 1933, in Hirschfeld, *Testament, Heft II*, 219.

49 Hirschfeld to Haire and Leunbach, May 13, 1933, Norman Haire Papers (3.20), University of Sydney Library.

50 On his sisters losing their housing see Hirschfeld, *Testament, Heft II*, 174.

51 Dose, *Magnus Hirschfeld: The Origins of the Gay Liberation Movement*, 20.

52 See Li's recollection that Hirschfeld did not feel safe in Zurich after the fascists took power in Berlin: Li, unpublished manuscript, unnumbered p. 1, Li Shiu Tong Nachlass, Box 1.

53 Hirschfeld, *Testament, Heft II*, 170.

54 Hirschfeld, *Testament, Heft II*, 170.

55 Li, unpublished manuscript, unnumbered p. 15, Li Shiu Tong Nachlass, Box 1.

56 On the flight see Hirschfeld to Haire and Leunbach, May 13, 1933; on his passport see Dose's note: Hirschfeld, *Testament, Heft II*, 170n434.

57 Hirschfeld, *Testament, Heft II*, 170.

58 Soetaert, "Succession Hirschfeld," 19; Hirschfeld to Benjamin, August 8, 1933, HHAfS-Humboldt.

59 Hirschfeld to Benjamin, August 8, 1933, HHAfS-Humboldt.

60 Hirschfeld, *Testament, Heft II*, 170.

61 Magnus Hirschfeld and Edmond Zammert, April 7, 1934, Charlotte Wolff Papers, PSY/WOL/6/8/4, file 1 of 2.

62 Hirschfeld to Norman Haire, September 15, 1933, and October 10, 1933, Charlotte Wolff Papers, PSY/WOL/6/8/4, file 1 of 2.

63 Li, unpublished manuscript, unnumbered p. 1, Li Shiu Tong Nachlass, Box 1.

64 Karl Giese and Tao Li (Li Shiu Tong) to Max Reiss, May 1935, Sammlung Max Reiss.

65 Hirschfeld, *Testament, Heft II*, 174.

66 Hirschfeld, *Testament, Heft II*, 174, 184.

67 Hirschfeld, *Testament, Heft II*, 184.

68 Hirschfeld, *Testament, Heft II*, 194.

69 Soetaert, "Succession Hirschfeld," 26; Hirschfeld, *Testament, Heft II*, 178–80; Hiller, "Persönliches über Magnus Hirschfeld," 5.

70 Hirschfeld, *Testament, Heft II*, 178–80.

71 This was Albert Moll. Dose, "Magnus Hirschfeld in Frankreich," 22–3.

72 Li, unpublished manuscript, unnumbered p. 2, Li Shiu Tong Nachlass, Box 1. Hirschfeld's Paris troubles may have been compounded by an attack on him by Moll. See Sutton, *Sex Between Body and Mind*, 11.

73 Hirschfeld, *Testament, Heft II*, 176: "meines erlebnis- u. arbeitsreichen Lebens."

74 Baldwin, *Giovanni's Room*, 162.

75 Hirschfeld does not note this in the December 1934 entry in the *Testament, Heft II*, but it was the case; his lack of angst about his finances in that entry – despite the Nazi seizure of many of his assets – and the subsequent renting of the Gloria Mansions apartment attest to this. On his improved finances see Soetaert, "Succession Hirschfeld," 19.

76 Hirschfeld, *Testament, Heft II*, 194.

77 Hirschfeld, *Testament, Heft II*, 182, 192.

78 Hirschfeld, *Testament, Heft II*, 194.

79 On the aborted plans for the second lecture tour see the Hirschfeld-Benjamin correspondence in HHAfS-Humboldt. On how managers did not want to take Hirschfeld on thanks to his topic and reputation, see Benjamin to Hirschfeld, March 24, 1932, and Benjamin to Hirschfeld, August 22, 1932, both in HHAfS-Humboldt.

80 Hirschfeld to Benjamin, April 29, 1934, HHAfS-Humboldt.

81 The first letters in the Haeberle collection date to 1926 and seem to reflect a new professional relationship. See, for example, Hirschfeld to Benjamin, February 16, 1926, HHAfS-Humboldt.

82 Benjamin to Hirschfeld, May 23, 1934, HHAfS-Humboldt.

83 Hirschfeld to Benjamin, June 3, 1934, HHAfS-Humboldt; emphasis in original.

84 Hirschfeld to Benjamin, June 3, 1934, HHAfS-Humboldt.

85 When Benjamin nixed the idea of a joint medical practice, Hirschfeld said he could live modestly off his royalties anyway: Hirschfeld to Benjamin, June 3, 1934, HHAfS-Humboldt.

86 Hirschfeld to Ernst Maass, April 12, 1933, in Hirschfeld, *Testament, Heft II*, 220.

87 Sutton, *Sex Between Body and Mind*, 206–7; Herzer, *Magnus Hirschfeld und Seine Zeit*, 386.

88 Hirschfeld, *Testament, Heft II*, 196.

89 Claudia Schoppmann wrote the Zurich police in the 1990s and got a list of Li's registrations in the city: Stadt Zürich an Schoppmann, Li Shiu Tong Nachlass, Box 1.

90 Magnus Hirschfeld to Max Reiss, March 30, 1935, Sammlung Max Reiss.

91 Li, unpublished manuscript, unnumbered p. 1, Li Shiu Tong Nachlass, Box 1.

 92 Hichens, *That Which Is Hidden*, 401.
 93 Hirschfeld to Haire, March 15, 1935, Norman Haire Papers (3.20), University of Sydney Library.
 94 Hirschfeld to Reiss, March 30, 1935, Sammlung Max Reiss.
 95 Magnus Hirschfeld to Li Shiu Tong, April 21, 1932, in "Magnus Hirschfeld's letzter Brief an Li Shiu Tong," 14. On his new secretary Robert Kirchberger see Bergemann, Dose, and Keilson-Lauritz, *Magnus Hirschfelds Exil-Gästebuch*, 214–15.
 96 Bergemann, Dose, and Keilson-Lauritz, *Magnus Hirschfelds Exil-Gästebuch*, 195.
 97 Giese and Li to Reiss, May 1935, Sammlung Max Reiss; Soetaert, "Succession Hirschfeld," 24; Herzer, *Magnus Hirschfeld und seine Zeit*, 384.
 98 Giese and Li to Reiss, May 1935; Soetaert, "Succession Hirschfeld," 24, 29.
 99 Magnus Hirschfeld, "Testament," in Hirschfeld, *Testament, Heft II*, 224. Emphasis underlined in the original.
100 Soetaert, "Succession Hirschfeld," 18, 29.
101 Hirschfeld, *Testament, Heft II*, 18, 80, 82, 152.
102 Giese and Li to Reiss, May 1935. Li signed this letter but Giese wrote it. See also Soetaert, "Succession Hirschfeld," 30.
103 Hiller, "Persönliches über Magnus Hirschfeld," 5.

12 Li Shiu Tong's Queer Masculinities

 1 For this attire see Hichens, *That Which Is Hidden*, 666.
 2 Hichens, *That Which Is Hidden*, 138.
 3 Hichens, *That Which Is Hidden*, 105.
 4 Hichens, *That Which Is Hidden*, 136–9.
 5 I am assuming this because it figures so often in Hichens's novel.
 6 Hichens, *Yesterday*, 392.
 7 See Hichens, *That Which Is Hidden*, 31; Freeman, "What Kind of Love Came to Professor Guildea?"
 8 See Lynn M. Thomas's point on this, albeit in a different context, that of African women's history: Thomas, "Historicising Agency."
 9 Muñoz, "Ephemera as Evidence"; Arondekar et al., "Queering Archives."
10 Freeman, "What Kind of Love Came to Professor Guildea?," 340.
11 Freeman, "What Kind of Love Came to Professor Guildea?," 341–2.
12 Canaday, *Straight State*, 71.
13 Rolf Italiaander knew Hirschfeld and was a friend of Hichens's: Italiaander to Wolff, April 24, 1981, Charlotte Wolff Papers, PSY/WOL/1/4, folder 1 of 3; Italiaander to Wolff, April 8, 1981, Charlotte Wolff Papers, PSY/WOL/1/4, folder 1 of 3.
14 Hichens, *Yesterday*, 393.
15 Li, unpublished manuscript, unnumbered p. 2, Li Shiu Tong Nachlass, Box 1.

16 Hichens, *That Which Is Hidden*, 373.

17 Hichens, *That Which Is Hidden*, 531.

18 Hichens, *That Which Is Hidden*, 540, 259–60, 339–40.

19 See the scene at the Widder: Hichens, *That Which Is Hidden*, 262–88.

20 Hichens, *That Which Is Hidden*, 7.

21 Shimizu, *Straitjacket Sexualities.*

22 Fung, "Films About Interracial Relationships."

23 There was one among the books in his apartment when he died; it and the
    rest of his library was eventually acquired by the Magnus Hirschfeld Ge-
    sellschaft and is now at the MHG archive in Berlin.

24 Hichens, *That Which Is Hidden*, 269; Hirschfeld, *Weltreise*, 336.

25 Refer to the photos in Hirschfeld, *Weltreise*, and Bergemann, Dose, and
    Keilson-Lauritz, *Magnus Hirschfelds Exil-Gästebuch.*

26 Shimizu, *Hypersexuality of Race*, 22.

27 See Nguyen's review of these arguments and expansion on them: *View from
    the Bottom*, 18–21. See also Nash, *Black Body in Ecstasy.*

28 Nguyen, *View from the Bottom*, 19.

29 A word on Li as a student: In his own manuscript as well as in this novel,
    Li claims the mantle of "student." His experience as Hirschfeld's student
    came decades before the propagation in the 1960s of the "model minority"
    stereotype of Asian Americans, a stereotype about diligence and academic
    success, and though his identity as a star student probably makes readers
    think of that racialized trope, he did not see it in those terms. By the time
    that racialization of Asian Americans emerged, Li was living in Hong Kong
    and was no longer in school. Li probably saw his scholastic career chiefly in
    terms of class and racialization – having a Western education, in English,
    at prominent universities in Europe and the US distinguished him from
    working-class Chinese people who were also living outside of China. On
    the "model minority" see Chou and Feagin, *Myth of the Model Minority.* US
    immigration policy, racist as it was, screened in favor of well-off Chinese
    intellectuals such as Li, who lived in the US for several years: Hsu, *Good
    Immigrants.*

30 See, for example, Hichens, *That Which Is Hidden*, 609.

31 Eng, *Racial Castration*, 2–3 and elsewhere.

32 Hichens, *That Which Is Hidden*, 645.

33 Hichens, *That Which Is Hidden*, 646–7.

34 Hichens, *That Which Is Hidden*, 645, 647–9, 668; Eng, *Racial Castration.*

35 Hichens, *That Which Is Hidden*, 609.

36 For the car and flower, see Hichens, *That Which Is Hidden*, 284, 545, 596.
    For the hat and shoes, see the photos in Bergemann, Dose, and Keil-
    son-Lauritz, *Magnus Hirschfelds Exil-Gästebuch*, 123, 167.

37 Hirschfeld, *Testament, Heft II*, 194.

38 "L'Amour et la Science par le Docteur Magnus Hirschfeld."

39 This photograph is in the Max Reiss collection (Sammlung Max Reiss), and given when Hirschfeld knew Riess it seems likely taken in France, though there is at least one photo in the collection that was taken on the world journey.

40 Bergemann, Dose, and Keilson-Lauritz, *Magnus Hirschfelds Exil-Gästebuch*, 106.

41 For the minor queer characters see Hichens, *That Which Is Hidden*, 349 and following, 554 and following.

42 Hichens, *Yesterday*, 247–8, 317–19.

43 Hichens, *That Which Is Hidden*, 214–15.

44 Hichens, *That Which Is Hidden*, 220.

45 On this see Freeman, "What Kind of Love Came to Professor Guildea?"

46 Muñoz, *Disidentifications*, 1–34; Sedgwick, *Touching Feeling*, 149–50.

47 *Oxford English Dictionary Online*, s.v. "gay, adj., adv., and n.," https://www.oed.com/view/Entry/77207?rskey=0sX5z2&result=1&isAdvanced=false (accessed November 11, 2021); s.v. "queer, adj.1," https://www.oed.com/view/Entry/156236?rskey=sODGiE&result=2 (accessed November 11, 2021); Hichens, *That Which Is Hidden*, 430–1, 339–40, 513, 646–7.

48 Hichens, *That Which Is Hidden*, 189, 193–4, 430–1.

49 Hichens, *That Which Is Hidden*, 596; see also 598–9, 604.

50 Hichens, *That Which Is Hidden*, 500.

51 Hichens, *That Which Is Hidden*, 294; see also 148–9 and elsewhere.

52 Hichens, *That Which Is Hidden*, 10.

53 Hichens, *That Which Is Hidden*, 95, 104, 138, 268.

54 Stadt Zürich an Schoppmann, Li Shiu Tong Nachlass, Box 1.

55 Stadt Zürich an Schoppmann, Li Shiu Tong Nachlass, Box 1; reference staff, Harvard University Archives, to author, email, October 3, 2018. The information on Harvard is from Li's entry in Harvard's Alumni Directory. His student records at Harvard will be open for research in July 2024.

56 Stadt Zürich an Schoppmann, Li Shiu Tong Nachlass, Box 1; Dose, "In memoriam," 11–12.

57 Stadt Zürich an Schoppmann, Li Shiu Tong Nachlass, Box 1.

58 Participation Certificate, *SS. President Cleveland*, May 19, 1969, Li Shiu Tong Nachlass, Box 1.

59 Dose, "In memoriam," 20; Mitchell, "Global Diasporas and Traditional Towns"; Skeldon, "Emigration and the Future of Hong Kong"; Carroll, *Concise History of Hong Kong*, 149–66.

13 Li Shiu Tong's Defiant Sexology

1 Dose, "In memoriam," 20. (My account is indebted to Dose's research on Li's life after Hirschfeld.) Registration of Death, Province of British Columbia Ministry of Health and Ministry Responsible for Seniors, Division of Vital Statistics, Document Control Number 100229921, Registration

Number 93-022617. See also Li's letters with his brother S.S. Li, Li Shiu Tong Nachlass, Box 1. Li's apartment was at 1060 Barcley Street: Dose, "In memoriam."

2 Dose, "In memoriam," 9.

3 Dose, "In memoriam," 9, 13.

4 Dose, "In memoriam," 9–10, 12–13. I have truncated parts of the story. For a longer version see Dose, "In memoriam."

5 The only other scholarship on it is Dose's "In memoriam."

6 Li, unpublished manuscript, unnumbered p. 3, Li Shiu Tong Nachlass, Box 1.

7 Li, "Aufzeichnungen von Li Shiu Tong im roten Ringbuch, handschrift-lich, verschieden farbige Stifte, unkorrigierte abschrift," 43, Li Shiu Tong Nachlass, Box 1. This document is Ralf Dose's transcription of Li's notes. Hereafter it is cited as "Aufzeichnungen von Li Shiu Tong im roten Ringbuch." For a more comprehensive account of Li's unpub-lished work than I am giving here, see Ralf Dose, "Notizen zu Li Shiu Tongs Aufzeichnungen," Li Shiu Tong Nachlass, Box 1. See also Dose, "In memoriam."

8 Li, unpublished manuscript, unnumbered p. 4, Li Shiu Tong Nachlass, Box 1.

9 On "just reading" see Marcus, *Between Women*, 3 and elsewhere; on "reading along the grain" see Stoler, *Along the Archival Grain*; and on its implications for queer history see Kunzel's comments in Arondekar et al., "Queering Archives," 215.

10 Li, "Aufzeichnungen von Li Shiu Tong im roten Ringbuch," 1, Li Shiu Tong Nachlass, Box 1.

11 My own decision to smush together two genres, intellectual history and bi-ography, in this book probably frames my perception that Li did the same, but nevertheless.

12 Li, "Aufzeichnungen von Li Shiu Tong im roten Ringbuch," 26, Li Shiu Tong Nachlass, Box 1.

13 Li, "Aufzeichnungen von Li Shiu Tong im roten Ringbuch," 74, 76, Li Shiu Tong Nachlass, Box 1.

14 Li, unpublished manuscript, unnumbered p. 1, Li Shiu Tong Nachlass, Box 1.

15 In my quotations of him I have mostly corrected his inconsequential spell-ing and grammar errors. In some cases these were left in to preserve mean-ing or authenticity.

16 Li, unpublished manuscript, unnumbered pp. 2, 5, 8, Li Shiu Tong Nachlass, Box 1.

17 Li, unpublished manuscript, unnumbered p. 11, Li Shiu Tong Nachlass, Box 1.

18 Li, "Aufzeichnungen von Li Shiu Tong im roten Ringbuch," 25, Li Shiu Tong Nachlass, Box 1.

19 Li, unpublished manuscript, unnumbered p. 7, Li Shiu Tong Nachlass, Box 1.

20 S.S. Li to Li Shiu Tong, undated, postmarked March 15, 1975, Li Shiu Tong Nachlass, Box 1.

21 Li, "Aufzeichnungen von Li Shiu Tong im roten Ringbuch," 34, Li Shiu Tong Nachlass, Box 1.

22 Li, "Aufzeichnungen von Li Shiu Tong im roten Ringbuch," 75, Li Shiu Tong Nachlass, Box 1.

23 Li, unpublished manuscript, unnumbered p. 15, Li Shiu Tong Nachlass, Box 1.

24 Muñoz, "Ephemera as Evidence," 6. See also Freedman, "Burning of Letters Continues."

25 On reading photographs see Marhoefer, "Lesbianism, Transvestitism, and the Nazi State," 1173n26; Evans, "Seeing Subjectivity."

26 See also three photos in which they appear to be touching: Bergemann, Dose, and Keilson-Lauritz, *Magnus Hirschfelds Exil-Gästebuch*, 106–7, 119.

27 Bergemann, Dose, and Keilson-Lauritz, *Magnus Hirschfelds Exil-Gästebuch*, 122–3.

28 Bergemann, Dose, and Keilson-Lauritz, *Magnus Hirschfelds Exil-Gästebuch*, 99.

29 Bergemann, Dose, and Keilson-Lauritz, *Magnus Hirschfelds Exil-Gästebuch*, 122–3, 166–7.

30 Li, unpublished manuscript, unnumbered p. 3, Li Shiu Tong Nachlass, Box 1.

31 Li, "Aufzeichnungen von Li Shiu Tong im roten Ringbuch," 26, Li Shiu Tong Nachlass, Box 1.

32 Li, unpublished manuscript, unnumbered p. 7, Li Shiu Tong Nachlass, Box 1.

33 Li, "Aufzeichnungen von Li Shiu Tong im roten Ringbuch," 27, Li Shiu Tong Nachlass, Box 1.

34 Li, unpublished manuscript, unnumbered p. 7, Li Shiu Tong Nachlass, Box 1.

35 Li, "Aufzeichnungen von Li Shiu Tong im roten Ringbuch," 31, Li Shiu Tong Nachlass, Box 1.

36 Li, "Aufzeichnungen von Li Shiu Tong im roten Ringbuch," 34, Li Shiu Tong Nachlass, Box 1.

37 Li, "Aufzeichnungen von Li Shiu Tong im roten Ringbuch," 69, Li Shiu Tong Nachlass, Box 1.

38 Li, unpublished manuscript, unnumbered p. 7, Li Shiu Tong Nachlass, Box 1.

39 Li, "Aufzeichnungen von Li Shiu Tong im roten Ringbuch," 36, Li Shiu Tong Nachlass, Box 1.

40 Li, "Aufzeichnungen von Li Shiu Tong im roten Ringbuch," 68, Li Shiu Tong Nachlass, Box 1.

41 Li, "Aufzeichnungen von Li Shiu Tong im roten Ringbuch," 39, Li Shiu Tong Nachlass, Box 1.

42 Li, unpublished manuscript, unnumbered p. 3, Li Shiu Tong Nachlass, Box 1.

43 Li, unpublished manuscript, unnumbered p. 1, Li Shiu Tong Nachlass, Box 1.

44 Li, "Aufzeichnungen von Li Shiu Tong im roten Ringbuch," 34, Li Shiu Tong Nachlass, Box 1.

45 Li, "Aufzeichnungen von Li Shiu Tong im roten Ringbuch," 21–2, Li Shiu Tong Nachlass, Box 1.

46 Li, "Aufzeichnungen von Li Shiu Tong im roten Ringbuch," 39, Li Shiu Tong Nachlass, Box 1.

47 Li, "Aufzeichnungen von Li Shiu Tong im roten Ringbuch," 13, Li Shiu Tong Nachlass, Box 1.

48 See "L'Amour et la Science par le Docteur Magnus Hirschfeld." Note the *Voilà* article came out in installments in three issues of the magazine.

49 Li, unpublished manuscript, unnumbered p. 11, Li Shiu Tong Nachlass, Box 1.

50 Gutterman, *Her Neighbor's Wife*, 240–3.

51 Li, "Aufzeichnungen von Li Shiu Tong im roten Ringbuch," 56, Li Shiu Tong Nachlass, Box 1.

52 Kinsey, Pomeroy, and Martin, *Sexual Behavior in the Human Male*, 660. Li's notes just say "Kinsey 659, 660" but the corresponding pages in *Sexual Behavior in the Human Female* do not match the themes in Li's book.

53 Li, "Aufzeichnungen von Li Shiu Tong im roten Ringbuch," 72, Li Shiu Tong Nachlass, Box 1.

54 For the rare exception, see his comments on Tunis in chapter 2.

55 Heinrich Pudor, quoted in Hirschfeld, *Homosexualität*, 198.

56 Hirschfeld, *Homosexualität*, 200, 208. In *Geschlechtskunde* III, he writes that homosexuals make up at least 2.3 percent of the population and bisexuals make up an additional 4 percent: 531.

57 Li, unpublished manuscript, unnumbered p. 3, Li Shiu Tong Nachlass, Box 1.

58 Li, unpublished manuscript, unnumbered p. 12; Li, "Aufzeichnungen von Li Shiu Tong im roten Ringbuch," 12, Li Shiu Tong Nachlass, Box 1.

59 Li, unpublished manuscript, unnumbered p. 13, Li Shiu Tong Nachlass, Box 1.

60 Dose, "In memoriam," 21.

61 Fung, "Asians: Gay and Proud."

62 Warner, *Never Going Back*, 327.

63 "HIV Is Not Just a White Thing: Asian Support – AIDS Project," *Angles*, January 1994. See also Warner, *Never Going Back*, 255–6. On queer Asian Canadian experience see also Kojima, Catungal, and Diaz, "Introduction."

64 Fung, "Looking for My Penis," 237.

65 Fung, "Looking for My Penis," 252n10.

66 Li, unpublished manuscript, unnumbered p. 13, Li Shiu Tong Nachlass, Box 1.

67 Li, unpublished manuscript, unnumbered p. 15, Li Shiu Tong Nachlass, Box 1. Note that I gave a portion of this quotation earlier in this chapter.

68 Thanks to Stephanie Clare to pointing this out and for the Foucault reference: Gallagher and Wilson, "Sex, Power, and the Politics of Identity," 26.

69 Nguyen, *View from the Bottom*, 4.

70 Fung, "Asians: Gay and Proud."

71 See among many others who make this and related points, some in different contexts of racialization, Kumashiro, "Supplementing Normalcy and Otherness," 501–2; Carby, "White Woman Listen!"; Decena, "Tacit Subjects."

Conclusion: Li Shiu Tong's Berlin and Magnus Hirschfeld's America

1 See, for example, Griffiths, *Ambivalence of Gay Liberation*, 21, 145; Ewing, "Color Him Black"; Boovy, "Belonging in Black and White"; Ferguson, *One-Dimensional Queer*; Peacock, "Race, the Homosexual, and the Mattachine Society of Washington."

2 See, for example, Mumford's masterful examination of Lorraine Hansberry, James Baldwin, and Bayard Rustin: Mumford, *Not Straight, Not White*, 11–38.

3 Marhoefer, *Sex and the Weimar Republic*.

4 Zhou, "On the Arrest of Homosexuals," 142.

5 See Sutton, *Sex Between Body and Mind*, 202–9; Grossmann, *Reforming Sex*, 166–88.

6 Hirschfeld scholars have not noted this. See, for example, Dose, *Magnus Hirschfeld: The Origins of the Gay Liberation Movement*, 8–9.

7 Kunzel, *Criminal Intimacy*, 48–9.

8 Kunzel, *Criminal Intimacy*, 59.

9 Lvovsky, "Queer Expertise," ch. 1.

10 Herzog, *Cold War Freud*; Kunzel, "'Durable Homophobia' of Psychoanalysis."

11 Kunzel, "Queer History, Mad History, and the Politics of Health," 315.

12 A search for his name in the Hathi Trust database turns up hundreds of books in English in the 1950s. On the development of sexology in the United States see Stein, *Measuring Manhood*; Irvine, *Disorders of Desire*.

13 London, *Libido and Delusion*, 20; Caprio and Brenner, *Sexual Behavior*, 59, 365; London and Caprio, *Sexual Deviations*, xiii, 19–20, 40.

14 Caprio, *Female Homosexuality*, 108; see also 265, where a lesbian reports reading Hirschfeld.

15 They were *Sexual Pathology*, which first appeared in 1932 and was unauthorized (Harry Benjamin to Magnus Hirschfeld, September 20, 1933, HHAfS; Dose, *Magnus Hirschfeld: The Origins of the Gay Liberation Movement*, 9), and *Sexual Anomalies and Perversions* (London: Francis Aldor, 1944). Norman Haire edited an English edition of some of his work: *Sexual Anomalies and Perversions: Physical and Psychological Development, Diagnosis and Treatment: A Summary of the Works of Magnus Hirschfeld* (London: Encyclopaedic Press, 1952).

16 For example, Jeannette Howard Foster cites his work in English and German: Foster, *Sex Variant Women in Literature*, 387. So do London and Caprio: *Sexual Deviations*, 684–5.

17 Foster, *Sex Variant Women in Literature*, 84.

18 Foster, *Sex Variant Women in Literature*, 84, 150–2; see also 281.

19 Rado, "A Critical Examination of the Concept of Bisexuality," 177. On Rado see "Dr. Sandor Rado Dies at 82."

20 Moore, *Nature and Treatment of Mental Disorders*, 317. Moore deals with Hirschfeld's work throughout this book.

21 Moore, *Nature and Treatment of Mental Disorders*, 317.

22 Bauer, "Sexology Backward," 137.

23 For Kinsey's mention of von Römer see Kinsey, Pomeroy, and Martin, *Sexual Behavior in the Human Male*, 619. Kinsey, Pomeroy, and Martin mention Hirschfeld in four places in *Sexual Behavior in the Human Male* and Hirschfeld is mentioned in thirty-eight places in Kinsey, Pomeroy, Martin, and Gebhard, *Sexual Behavior in the Human Female*. Most of these are citations of prior art in the notes.

24 Kinsey, Pomeroy, and Martin, *Sexual Behavior in the Human Male*, 620, 618.

25 Kinsey, Pomeroy, and Martin, *Sexual Behavior in the Human Male*, 639. The line about sheep and goats is a reference to the description of the last judgment in Matthew 25:31–46.

26 Bauer, "Sexology Backward."

27 Bauer, "Sexology Backward," 140.

28 Benjamin, "Reminiscences," 4.

29 Rupp, "Persistence of Transnational Organizing"; Churchill, "Transnationalism and Homophile Political Culture in the Postwar Decades"; Wolfert,

"Gegen Einsamkeit und 'Einsiedelei,'" 42. Kurt Hiller was personally involved in German and Swiss homophile groups: see Wolfert, *"Gegen Einsamkeit und 'Einsiedelei,'"* 76; Whisnant, *Male Homosexuality in West Germany*, 77–8; Kennedy, *Ideal Gay Man*, 62, 74, 186.

30 Mattachine Society statement of purpose of 1951 in Blasius and Phelan, *We Are Everywhere*, 283.

31 On Cory (Edward Sagarin) see Murray, "Donald Webster Cory (1913–1986)."

32 Cory, *Homosexual in America*, 237.

33 Cory, *Homosexual in America*, 3.

34 Cory, *Homosexual in America*, 4.

35 Rupp suggests as much: Rupp, "Persistence of Transnational Organizing," 1027, 1037. Whisnant also traces the idea to Cory and dates it after 1945: *Male Homosexuality in West Germany*, 102–3, 193. For Cory's influence in West Germany see Whisnant, *Male Homosexuality in West Germany*, 103. On Cory see also Churchill, "Transnationalism and Homophile Political Culture in the Postwar Decades."

36 Cory had read Hirschfeld in German: Churchill, "Transnationalism and Homophile Political Culture in the Postwar Decades," 36.

37 Kunzel, "Queer History, Mad History, and the Politics of Health." Frank Kameny was a key activist in this movement. On his "sexual minority" rhetoric and analogies to Blackness, see Peacock, "Race, the Homosexual, and the Mattachine Society of Washington."

38 See, for example, Tobin, *Peripheral Desires*, 94. Here, moreover, I am grateful to have the opportunity to revise my thoughts on Hirschfeld's hero status at the end of my first book, where I wrote something similar. See Marhoefer, *Sex and the Weimar Republic*, 216.

39 On sex workers and on respectability in the work of Hirschfeld and his colleagues, see also Marhoefer, *Sex and the Weimar Republic*.

40 This paragraph is indebted to Alexis McGill Johnson's essay on Margaret Sanger: McGill Johnson, "I'm the Head of Planned Parenthood." Thanks to Taylor Soja for pointing it out.

41 Here I draw on many German studies scholars who are working beyond the national frame, on which see Byrd, "Orientations in German Studies."

42 Sedgwick, *Epistemology of the Closet*, 86, 88–9.

43 See Leff, *Well Worth Saving*.

44 On this see also Wake, *Private Practices*.

45 Clare, Grzanka, and Wuest, "Gay Genes in the Post-genomic Era." The Ganna et al. study results were misreported in favor of a genetic cause of homosexuality; see, for example, Belluck, "Many Genes Influence Same-Sex Sexuality, Not a Single 'Gay Gene.'" On how Ganna et al. remained

beholden to biological homosexuality see Wuest, "Dream of Bioessential-ism Is Alive in a Post-genomic Era."

46 Ganna et al., "Large-Scale GWAS Reveals Insights into the Genetic Archi-tecture of Same-Sex Sexual Behavior." On the study's exclusions see Clare, "Biological Sex and the 'Overrepresentation of Man.'" On the study's demonstration of non-genetic causes of queer behavior see Grzanka, "Programs of Life/Knowing Ourselves."

47 Oguntoye, "Mein Coming-out als schwarze Lesbe in Deutschland," 160.

48 On this see also Fatima El-Tayeb on the aim of queer-of-color critique: El-Tayeb, "Blackness and Its (Queer) Discontents," 253.

49 Such as Warner, "Introduction," xvi–xxi.

50 Butler, "Critically Queer."

51 Muñoz, *Disidentifications*, 5.

52 Muñoz, *Disidentifications*, 5.

53 Gallagher and Wilson, "Sex, Power, and the Politics of Identity," 26; Rich, "Compulsory Heterosexuality and Lesbian Existence."

Bibliography

Periodicals

Angles (Vancouver)
Atlanta Constitution
Baltimore Afro-American
Blätter für Menschenrecht
Chicago Defender
China Press
China Weekly Review
Davenport Democrat and Leader
Denton Journal
Die Freundin
Die Freundschaft / Der Freund
Medical Record
Modesto News-Herald
New England Journal of Medicine
New York Times
North-China Herald and Supreme Court and Consular Gazette
Ogden Standard-Examiner
San Antonio Light
Sexus: Internationale Vierteljahreszeitschrift für die gesamte Sexualwissenschaft und Sexualreform
Sheboygan Press
Das Tage-Buch
Der Transvestit

Films

Anders als die Andern. Directed by Richard Oswald. 1919; Kino International/ Filmmuseum Muenchen, 2004.

Audre Lorde: The Berlin Years. Directed by Dagmar Schultz. New York: Third
    World Newsreel, 2012.

Published Primary Sources

"L'Amour et la Science par le Docteur Magnus Hirschfeld Directeur de
    l'Institut de Sexualité de Berlin." *Voilà* no. 119 (July 1, 1933).
"Länder, die den gleichgeschlechtlichen Verkehr mehr oder weniger
    anerkennen." In *Jahrbuch für sexuelle Zwischenstufen mit besonderer
    Berücksichtigung der Homosexualität.* Leipzig: Max Spohr, 1899.
Benjamin, Harry. "Reminiscences." *Journal of Sex Research* 6, no. 1 (1970): 2–9.
Bergemann, Hans, Ralf Dose, and Marita Keilson-Lauritz, eds. *Magnus
    Hirschfelds Exil-Gästebuch 1933–1935.* Berlin: Hentrich and Hentrich, 2019.
Boas, Franz. *Anthropology and Modern Life.* New York: W.W. Norton, 1928.
Caprio, Frank S. *Female Homosexuality: A Psychodynamic Study of Lesbianism.*
    New York: Citadel Press, 1954.
Caprio, Frank S., and D.R. Brenner. *Sexual Behavior: Psycho-Legal Aspects.*
    New York: Citadel Press, 1961.
Cory, Donald Webster. *The Homosexual in America: A Subjective Approach.*
    New York: Greenberg, 1951.
de Gobineau, Arthur. *The Inequality of Human Races.* Translated by Adrian
    Collins. New York: Putnam, 1915.
Du Bois, W.E.B. "The African Roots of War." *The Atlantic*, May 1915.
– *The Souls of Black Folk.* 1903; Project Gutenberg, 1996 (updated 2021).
    https://www.gutenberg.org/files/408/408-h/408-h.htm.
Einstein, Albert. *The Collected Papers of Albert Einstein.* Vol. 16, *The Berlin Years:
    Writings and Correspondence June 1927–May 1929*, edited by Diana Kormos
    Buchwald, Ze'ev Rosenkranz, József Illy, Daniel J. Kennefick, A.J. Dennis
    Lehmkuhl, Tilman Sauer, and Jennifer Nollar James. Princeton, NJ:
    Princeton University Press, 2021.
Ellis, Havelock. *My Life: Autobiography of Havelock Ellis.* Whitefish, MT: Kessinger,
    2010.
Firmin, Anténor. *The Equality of the Human Races (Positivist Anthropology).*
    Translated by Asselin Charles. New York: Garland, 2000.
Foster, Jeannette Howard. *Sex Variant Women in Literature: A Historical and
    Quantitative Survey.* New York: Vantage Press, 1956.
Galton, Francis. "Eugenics: Its Definition, Scope and Aims." In *The Idea of
    Race*, edited by Robert Bernasconi and Tommy L. Lott, 79–83. Indianapolis:
    Hackett Publishing, 2000.
– *Inquiries into Human Faculty and Its Development.* New York: MacMillan: 1883.
Gandhi, M.K. "Reply to a Query." In *Same-Sex Love in India*, edited by Ruth
    Vanita and Saleem Kidwai, 255–6. New York: St. Martin's Press, 2000.

Gosney, E.S., and Paul Popenoe. *Sterilization for Human Betterment: A Summary of Results of 6,000 Operations in California, 1909–1929.* New York: Macmillan, 1929.

Hichens, Robert. *That Which Is Hidden.* New York: Doubleday, Doran, 1940.

– *Yesterday: The Autobiography of Robert Hichens.* London: Cassell, 1947.

Hiller, Kurt. "Appeal to the Second International Congress for Sexual Reform on Behalf of an Oppressed Human Variety." Translated by John Lauritsen. In *The Early Homosexual Rights Movement (1864–1935),* edited by John Lauritsen and David Thorstad, 106–14. Rev. ed. Ojai, CA: Times Change Press, 1995.

– "Ethische Aufgaben der Homosexuellen." *Jahrbuch für sexuelle Zwischenstufen mit besonderer Berücksichtigung der Homosexualität* 13, no. 4 (1913): 399–410.

– "Persönliches über Magnus Hirschfeld." *Der Kreis* 16, no. 5 (1948): 3–6.

– "The Problem of Constitution." Translated by O.S. Griffiths. In *After Nazism – Democracy?,* edited by Kurt Hiller, 9–77. London: Lindsay Drummond, 1945.

– "Recht und Sexuelle Minderheiten: Rede, gehalten im Rahmen der 'Internationalen Tagung für Sexualreform auf sexualwissenschaftlicher Grundlage,' Berlin, Virchow-Langebeck-Haus, 19. September 1921." In *§175: Die Schmach des Jahrhunderts!,* edited by Kurt Hiller, 105–18. Hanover: Paul Steegemann, 1922.

– "Sexualfreiheit und Proporz." *Vierteljahresberichte des Wissenschaftlich-humanitären Komitees während der Kriegszeit* 18, nos. 2–3 (April–July 1918): 83–7.

– "Sexualstrafrecht in Deutschland." *Die neue Generation* 25, no. 3 (March 1929): 92–8.

Hirschfeld, Magnus. "Das Erbgericht, Betrachtungen zum deutschen Sterilisationsgesetz." *Die Sammlung* I (1934): 309–19 (Nendeln, Liechtenstein: Kraus Reprint, 1970).

– *Geschlechtskunde: Auf Grund dreißigjähriger Forschung und Erfahrung bearbeitet.* Vol. 1, *Die körperseelischen Grundlagen.* Stuttgart: Julius Püttmann, 1926.

– *Geschlechtskunde: Auf Grund dreißigjähriger Forschung und Erfahrung bearbeitet.* Vol. 2, *Folgen und Folgerungen.* Stuttgart: Julius Püttmann, 1928.

– *Geschlechtskunde: Auf Grund dreißigjähriger Forschung und Erfahrung bearbeitet.* Vol. 3, *Einblicke und Ausblicke.* Stuttgart: Julius Püttmann, 1930.

– *Geschlechtskunde: Auf Grund dreißigjähriger Forschung und Erfahrung bearbeitet..* Vol. 4, *Bilderteil.* Stuttgart: Julius Püttmann, 1930.

– *Geschlechtskunde: Auf Grund dreißigjähriger Forschung und Erfahrung bearbeitet.* Vol. 5, *Registerteil.* Stuttgart: Julius Püttmann, 1930.

– *Die Homosexualität des Mannes und des Weibes.* 2nd ed. Berlin: Louis Marcus, 1920.

– "Jahresbericht 1906–1908." In *Jahrbuch für sexuelle Zwischenstufen unter besonderer Berücksichtigung der Homosexualität,* vol. 9, edited by Magnus Hirschfeld, 621–63. Leipzig: Max Spohr, 1908.

– "Magnus Hirschfeld's letzter Brief an Li Shiu Tong: Transkription und Anmerkungen." Edited by Ralf Dose. *Mitteilungen der Magnus-Hirschfeld-Gesellschaft* 37/38 (2007): 13–14.
– "Phantom Rasse: Ein Hirngespinst als Weltgefahr," 10. Fortsetzung, *Die Wahrheit*, February 1, 1935.
– "Phantom Rasse: Ein Hirngespinst als Weltgefahr," 11. Fortsetzung, *Die Wahrheit*, February 20, 1935.
– *Racism.* Translated and edited by Eden and Cedar Paul. London: Victor Gollancz, 1938.
– *Sappho und Sokrates: Wie erklärt sich die Liebe der Männer und Frauen zu Personen des eigenen Geschlechts?* 3rd ed. Leipzig: Max Spohr, 1922.
– "Schuldig geboren." In *Sexual-Katastrophen: Bilder aus dem modernen Geschlechts- und Eheleben*, edited by Ludwig Levy-Lenz, 1–105. Leipzig: A.H. Payne, 1926.
– *Testament, Heft II.* Edited by Ralf Dose. Berlin: Hentrich and Hentrich, 2013.
– *Transvestites: The Erotic Drive to Cross-Dress.* Translated by Michael A. Lombardi-Nash. Amherst, NY: Prometheus Books, 1991.
– "Über Sexualwissenschaft." *Zeitschrift für Sexualwissenschaft* 1, no. 1 (1908): 1–19.
– "Über amtliche Ehevermittlung." In *Sexual Reform Congress: World League for Sexual Reform Proceedings of the Third Congress*, edited by Norman Haire, 661. London: Kegan Paul, Trench, Trubner and Co., 1930.
– *Von einst bis jetzt: Geschichte einer homosexuellen Bewegung 1897–1922.* Edited by Manfred Herzer and James Steakley. Berlin: Rosa Winkel, 1986.
– *Was eint und trennt das Menschengeschlecht?* Berlin: Arbeitsgemeinschaft für Staatsbürgerliche und Wirtschaftliche Bildung, 1919.
– *Die Weltreise eines Sexualforschers.* Brugg, Switzerland: Bözberg, 1933.
– *Women East and West: Impressions of a Sex Expert.* Translated by O.P. Green. London: William Heinemann, 1935.
Hirschfeld, Magnus, Andreas Gaspar, and Institut für Sexualwissenschaft. *The Sexual History of the World War.* New York: Panurge Press, 1934.
Hirschfeld, Magnus, and Richard Linsert. "Die Homosexualität." In *Sittengeschichte des Lasters: Die Kulturepochen und Ihre Leidenschaften*, edited by Leo Schidrowitz, 253–318. Vienna: Verlag für Kulturforschung, 1927.
Hössli, Heinrich. *Eros: Die Männerliebe der Griechen, ihre Beziehungen zur Geschichte, Erziehung, Literatur und Gesetzgebung aller Zeiten.* Berlin: Rosa Winkel, 1996.
Hughes, Langston, and Carl Van Vechten. *Remember Me to Harlem: The Letters of Langston Hughes and Carl Van Vechten.* Edited by Emily Bernard. New York: Vintage, 2001.
Isherwood, Christopher. *Christopher and His Kind: 1929–1939.* New York: Farrar, Straus and Giroux, 1976.
Johnson, James Weldon. "Race Prejudice and the Negro Artist." In *James Weldon Johnson: Writings*, edited by William L. Andrews, 753–65. New York: Penguin, 2004.

Karsch-Haack, Ferdinand. *Das gleichgeschlechtliche Leben der Naturvölker.* 1911;
    repr., New York: Arno Press, 1975.
Kinsey, Alfred, Wardell Pomeroy, and Clyde Martin. *Sexual Behavior in the
    Human Male.* Philadelphia: W.B. Saunders, 1948.
Kinsey, Alfred, Wardell Pomeroy, Clyde Martin, and Paul Gebhard. *Sexual
    Behavior in the Human Female.* Philadelphia: W.B. Saunders, 1953.
Krafft-Ebing, Richard von. *Der Conträrsexuale vor dem Strafrichter.* Leipzig: Franz
    Deuticke, 1895.
London, Louis Samuel. *Libido and Delusion.* Washington, DC: Mental Therapy
    Publications, 1945.
London, Louis Samuel, and Frank S. Caprio. *Sexual Deviations.* Washington, DC:
    Linacre Press, 1960.
Lorde, Audre. *I Am Your Sister: Collected and Unpublished Writings of Audre Lorde.*
    Edited by Rudolph P. Byrd, Johnnetta Betsch Cole, and Beverly Guy-Sheftall.
    Oxford: Oxford University Press, 2009.
– "I Am Your Sister: Black Women Organizing Across Sexualities." In *I Am Your
    Sister: Collected and Unpublished Writings of Audre Lorde,* edited by Rudolph
    P. Byrd, Johnnetta Betsch Cole, and Beverly Guy-Sheftall, 57–63. Oxford:
    Oxford University Press, 2009.
– "Scratching the Surface: Some Notes on Barriers to Women and Loving."
    Black Scholar 9, no. 7 (April 1978): 31–5.
– "Showing Our True Colors." *Callaloo* 14, no. 1 (January 1991): 67–71.
– *Sister Outsider: Essays and Speeches by Audre Lorde.* 1984; repr., Freedom, CA:
    Crossing Press, 1996.
Moore, Thomas Verner. *The Nature and Treatment of Mental Disorders.* 2nd ed.
    New York: Grune and Stratton, 1951.
Nehru, Jawaharlal. *An Autobiography.* 1936; repr., Bombay: Allied Publishers, 1962.
– *The Oxford India Nehru.* Edited by Uma Iyengar. Oxford: Oxford University
    Press, 2007.
Pickens, William. *Bursting Bonds.* Boston: Jordan and More, 1923.
– *The Kind of Democracy the Negro Race Expects.* Baltimore: Herald Printing, 1918.
Popenoe, Paul, and Roswell Hill Johnson. *Applied Eugenics.* New York:
    Macmillan, 1918; Project Gutenberg, 2006.
Rado, Sandor. "A Critical Examination of the Concept of Bisexuality." In *Sexual
    Inversion: The Multiple Roots of Homosexuality,* edited by Judd Marmor, 175–89.
    New York: Basic Books, 1965.
Riese, Hertha, and J.H. Leunbach, eds. *Sexual Reform Congress* (Proceedings of
    the Second Congress of the World League for Sexual Reform, Copenhagen,
    1928). Copenhagen: Levin and Munksgaard, 1929.
Sanger, Margaret. *The Selected Papers of Margaret Sanger.* Vol. 4, edited by Esther
    Katz, Peter Engelman, and Cathy Moran Hajo. Urbana: University of Illinois
    Press, 2016.

Smith, A. Viola. "China Awakened." *National Women Lawyers Journal*, 1937, 33–9.

Stekel, Wilhelm. *Sex and Dreams: The Language of Dreams*. Boston: R.G. Badger, 1922.

Tessmann, Günter. "Die Homosexualität bei den Negern Kameruns." In *Jahrbuch für sexuelle Zwischenstufen mit besonderer Berücksichtigung der Homosexualität* 21 (July and October 1921): 121–38.

Theilhaber, Felix A. *Der Untergang der deutschen Juden: Eine volkswirtschaftliche Studie*. Munich: Ernst Reinhardt, 1911.

Thompson, Dorothy. "Governor Stratton Was Right." *Sheboygan Press*, August 8, 1957.

Tridon, André. *Psychoanalysis and Love*. New York: Brentano's, 1922.

Van Vechten, Carl. *The Splendid Drunken Twenties: Selections from the Daybooks, 1922–1930*. Edited by Bruce Kellner. Urbana: University of Illinois Press, 2003.

von Bülow, F.J. *Deutsch-Südwestafrika: Drei Jahre im Lande Hendrik Witboois; Schilderungen von Land und Leuten*. Berlin: Ernst Sigfried Mittler und Sohn, 1896.

von Luschan, Felix. "Anthropological View of Race." In *Papers on Inter-racial Problems Communicated to the First Universal Races Congress*, edited by G. Spiller, 13–24. London: P.S. King and Son, 1911.

Vordtriede, Werner. *Das verlassene Haus: Tagebuch aus dem amerikanischen Exil 1938–1947*. Vienna: Carl Hanser, 1975.

Weisskopf, Josef. "Der Brünner Sexualkongreß." In *Sexus: Internationale Vierteljahreszeitschrift für die gesamte Sexualwissenschaft und Sexualreform* 1 (1933): 26–33.

Zelénski, Boy. "Die Minderheit der Sexualen." *Blätter für Menschenrecht*, May 1931.

Zhou Zuoren. "On the Arrest of Homosexuals." In *Zhou Zuoren: Selected Essays*, translated by David Pollard, 140–5. Hong Kong: Chinese University Press, 2006.

Secondary Literature

Abinales, Patricio N., and Donna J. Amoroso. *State and Society in the Philippines*. New York: Rowman and Littlefield, 2005.

Adams, Mark B., ed. *The Wellborn Science: Eugenics in Germany, France, Brazil, and Russia*. Oxford: Oxford University Press, 1990.

Adas, Michael. *Machines as the Measure of Men: Science, Technology, and Ideologies of Western Dominance*. Ithaca, NY: Cornell University Press, 2015.

Ahmed, Sara. *Living a Feminist Life*. Durham, NC: Duke University Press, 2017.

Aitken, Robbie, and Eve Rosenhaft. *Black Germany: The Making and Unmaking of a Diaspora Community, 1884–1960*. Cambridge: Cambridge University Press, 2013.

Alcoff, Linda Martín. *Visible Identities: Race, Gender, and the Self.* New York: Oxford, 2005.

Aldrich, Robert. *Colonialism and Homosexuality.* New York: Routledge, 2003.

Alexanderson, Kris. *Subversive Seas: Anticolonial Networks Across the Twentieth-Century Dutch Empire.* Cambridge: Cambridge University Press, 2019.

Als, Hilton. "The Elusive Langston Hughes." *New Yorker,* February 16, 2015. https://www.newyorker.com/magazine/2015/02/23/sojourner

Amin, Kadji. *Disturbing Attachments: Genet, Modern Pederasty, and Queer History.* Durham, NC: Duke University Press, 2017.

Appiah, Anthony Kwame. *Lines of Descent: W.E.B. Du Bois and the Emergence of Identity.* Cambridge, MA: Harvard University Press, 2014.

Arondekar, Anjali, Ann Cvetkovich, Christina B. Hanhardt, Regina Kunzel, Tavia Nyong'o, Juana María Rodríguez, Susan Stryker, Daniel Marshall, Kevin Murphy, and Zeb Tortorici. "Queering Archives: A Roundtable Discussion." *Radical History Review* 122 (2015): 211–31.

Avery, Sheldon. *Up from Washington: William Pickens and the Negro Struggle for Equality, 1900–1954.* Newark: University of Delaware Press, 1989.

Baldwin, Davarian L., and Minkah Makalani, eds. *Escape from New York: The New Negro Renaissance Beyond Harlem.* Minneapolis: University of Minnesota Press, 2013.

Baldwin, James. *Giovanni's Room.* New York: Vintage Books, 2013.

– "On Being 'White' … And Other Lies." In *Black on White: Black Writers on What It Means to Be White,* edited by David Roediger, 177–80. New York: Schocken, 1998.

Bauer, Heike. *The Hirschfeld Archives: Violence, Death, and Modern Queer Culture.* Philadelphia: Temple University Press, 2017.

– "'Not a Translation but a Mutilation': The Limits of Translation and the Discipline of Sexology." *Yale Journal of Criticism* 16, no. 2 (October 2003): 381–405.

– ed. *Sexology and Translation: Cultural and Scientific Encounters Across the Modern World.* Philadelphia: Temple University Press, 2015.

– "Sexology Backward: Hirschfeld, Kinsey and the Reshaping of Sex Research in the 1950s." In *Queer 1950s: Rethinking Sexuality in the Postwar Years,* edited by Heike Bauer and Matt Cook, 133–49. Basingstoke, UK: Palgrave Macmillan, 2012.

Bay, Mia. *The White Image in the Black Mind: African-American Ideas about White People, 1830–1925.* New York: Oxford University Press, 2000.

Beachy, Robert. *Gay Berlin: Birthplace of a Modern Identity.* New York: Vintage, 2015.

– "The German Invention of Homosexuality." *Journal of Modern History* 82, no. 4 (December 2010): 801–38.

Becker, Sophinette. "Tragik eines deutschen Juden: Anmerkungen zu drei politischen Schriften von Magnus Hirschfeld." In *Sexualität und Gesellschaft:*

Festschrift für Volkmar Sigusch, edited by Martin Dannecker and Reimut Reiche, 28–46. Frankfurt: Campus Verlag, 2000.

Belluck, Pam. "Many Genes Influence Same-Sex Sexuality, Not a Single 'Gay Gene.'" *New York Times*, August 29, 2019.

Bennett, Juda. "Langston Hughes on the Open Road: Compulsory Heterosexuality and the Question of Presence." In *Montage of a Dream: The Art and Life of Langston Hughes*, edited by John Edgar Tidwell and Cheryl R. Ragar, 68–85. Columbia: University of Missouri Press, 2007.

Benton-Cohen, Katherine. *Inventing the Immigration Problem: The Dillingham Commission and Its Legacy*. Cambridge, MA: Harvard University Press, 2018.

Berlin Museum. *Eldorado: Homosexuelle Frauen und Männer in Berlin 1850–1950; Geschichte, Alltag und Kultur*. Berlin: Edition Heinrich, 1992.

Bernard, Emily. *Carl Van Vechten and the Harlem Renaissance: A Portrait in Black and White*. New Haven, CT: Yale University Press, 2012.

– "Introduction." In *Remember Me to Harlem: The Letters of Langston Hughes and Carl Van Vechten*, edited by Emily Bernard, xiii–xvii. New York: Vintage, 2001.

– ed. *Remember Me to Harlem: The Letters of Langston Hughes and Carl Van Vechten*. New York: Vintage, 2001.

Bland, Lucy, and Laura Doan, eds. *Sexology in Culture: Labelling Bodies and Desires*. Chicago: University of Chicago Press, 1998.

– eds. *Sexology Uncensored: The Documents of Sexual Science*. Chicago: University of Chicago Press, 1998.

Blasius, Mark, and Shane Phelan, eds. *We Are Everywhere: A Historical Sourcebook of Gay and Lesbian Politics*. New York: Routledge, 1997.

Blue, Ethan. "The Strange Career of Leo Stanley: Remaking Manhood and Medicine at San Quentin State Penitentiary, 1913–1951." *Pacific Historical Review* 78, no. 2 (2009): 210–41.

Boag, Peter. *Same-Sex Affairs: Constructing and Controlling Homosexuality in the Pacific Northwest*. Berkeley: University of California Press, 2003.

Boovy, Bradley. "Belonging in Black and White: Race, Photography, and the Allure of *Heimat* in West German Gay Magazines from the 1950s." *Seminar: A Journal of Germanic Studies* 54, no. 4 (November 2018): 428–41.

– "Troubling Sameness." *Women in German Yearbook* 32 (2016): 152–62.

Borghi, Elena. "Forgotten Feminisms: Gender and the Nehru Household in Early-Twentieth-Century India." *Gender & History* 29, no. 2 (2017): 254–72.

Botman, Selma. "The Liberal Age, 1923–1952." In *Modern Egypt, From 1517 to the End of the Twentieth Century*, edited by M.W. Daly, 285–308. Cambridge: Cambridge University Press, 1998.

Bragg, Susan. "Augustus Granville Dill (1881–1956)." BlackPast, June 11, 2008. https://www.blackpast.org/african-american-history/dill-augustus-granville -1881-1956/.

Braker, Regina. "Helene Stöcker's Pacifism: International Intersections." *Peace & Change* 23, no. 4 (October 1998): 455–65.

Brandhorst, Henny. "From Neo-Malthusianism to Sexual Reform: The Dutch Section of the World League for Sexual Reform." *Journal of the History of Sexuality* 12, no. 1 (January 2003): 38–67.

Bravmann, Scott. *Queer Fictions of the Past: History, Culture, and Difference.* New York: Cambridge University Press, 1997.

Bristow, Joseph. "Symonds's History, Ellis's Heredity: *Sexual Inversion.*" In *Sexology in Culture: Labelling Bodies and Desires,* edited by Lucy Bland and Laura Doan, 79–99. Chicago: University of Chicago Press, 1998.

Broberg, Gunnar, and Nils Roll-Hansen, eds. *Eugenics and the Welfare State: Sterilization Policy in Denmark, Sweden, Norway, and Finland.* East Lansing: Michigan University Press, 1996.

Bruns, Claudia. "Kontroversen zwischen Freud, Blüher und Hirschfeld." In *Dämonen, Vamps und Hysterikerinnen: Geschlechter- und Rassenfigurationen in Wissen, Medien und Alltag um 1900,* edited by Ulrike Auga, Claudia Bruns, Dorothea Dornhof, and Gabriele Jähnert, 161–84. Bielefeld: transcript Verlag, 2014.

– "The Politics of Masculinity in the (Homo-)Sexual Discourse (1880–1920)." *German History* 23, no. 3 (August 2005): 306–20.

– *Politik des Eros: Der Männerbund in Wissenschaft, Politik und Jugendkultur, 1880–1934.* Cologne: Böhlau, 2008.

– "Toward a Transnational History of Racism: Wilhelm Marr and the Interrelationships between Colonial Racism and German Anti-Semitism." In *Racism in the Modern World: Historical Perspectives on Cultural Transfer and Adaptation,* edited by Manfred Berg and Simon Wendt, 122–39. New York: Berghahn, 2011.

Bryant, Andrea Dawn, Nichole M. Neuman, David Gramling, and Ervin Malakaj. "Announced but Not Enacted: Anti-Racist German Studies as Process." *Applied Linguistics* 42, no. 2 (2021): 347–54.

Burleigh, Michael. *Death and Deliverance: "Euthanasia" in Germany c. 1900–1945.* New York: Cambridge University Press, 1994.

Butler, Judith. "Critically Queer." *GLQ: A Journal of Lesbian and Gay Studies* 1, no. 1 (1993): 17–32.

Byrd, Vance. "Orientations in German Studies." In "Does German Cultural Studies Need the Nation-State Model" by Yael Almog et al. *German Quarterly* 92, no. 4 (2019): 431–503.

Cahn, Susan K. *Coming on Strong: Gender and Sexuality in Women's Sport.* 2nd ed. Springfield: University of Illinois Press, 2015.

– "From the 'Muscle Moll' to the 'Butch' Ballplayer: Mannishness, Lesbianism, and Homophobia in U.S. Women's Sport." *Feminist Studies* 19, no. 2 (Summer 1993): 343–68.

Campt, Tina. "Converging Spectres of an Other Within: Race and Gender in Prewar Afro-German History." *Callaloo* 26, no. 2 (April 2003): 322–41.

— "Family Matters: Race, Gender and Belonging in Black German Photography." *Social Text* 27, no. 1 (March 2009): 83–114.

— *Other Germans: Black Germans and the Politics of Race, Gender and Memory in the Third Reich.* Ann Arbor: University of Michigan Press, 2004.

Campt, Tina, and Michelle M. Wright, eds. "Reading the Black German Experience." Special issue, *Callaloo* 26, no. 2 (April 2003).

Canaday, Margot. *The Straight State: Sexuality and Citizenship in Twentieth-Century America.* Princeton, NJ: Princeton University Press, 2009.

Capó, Julio. *Welcome to Fairyland: Queer Miami before 1940.* Chapel Hill: University of North Carolina Press, 2017.

Carby, Hazel V. "White Woman Listen! Black Feminism and the Boundaries of Sisterhood." In *Black British Feminism: A Reader,* edited by Heidi Safia Mirza, 45–53. London: Routledge, 1997.

Carroll, John. *A Concise History of Hong Kong.* Lanham, MD: Rowman and Littlefield, 2007.

— *Edge of Empires: Chinese Elites and British Colonials in Hong Kong.* Cambridge, MA: Harvard University Press, 2005.

Carroll, Peter J. "'A Problem of Glands and Secretions': Female Criminality, Murder, and Sexuality in Republican China." In *Sexuality in China: Histories of Power and Pleasure,* edited by Howard Chiang, 99–124. Seattle: University of Washington Press, 2018.

Carter, Julian. "Historical Methods and Racial Identification in U.S. Lesbian and Gay History." In *Connexions: Histories of Race and Sex in North America,* edited by Jennifer Brier, Jim Downs, and Jennifer L. Morgan, 38–58. Chicago: University of Illinois Press, 2016.

Chaplin, Tamara. "Utopian Gaiety: French Lesbian Activism and the Politics of Pleasure (1974–2016)." In *Making Waves: French Feminisms and Their Legacies 1975–2015,* edited by Margaret Atack, Alison S. Fell, Diana Holmes, and Imogen Long, 115–28. Liverpool, UK: Liverpool University Press, 2019.

Chauncey, George. *Gay New York: Gender, Urban Culture, and the Making of the Gay Male World, 1890–1940.* New York: Basic Books, 1995.

Cheang, Sarah. "Women, Pets, and Imperialism: The British Pekingese Dog and Nostalgia for Old China." *Journal of British Studies* 45, no. 2 (2006): 359–87.

Chen, Kaiyi. *Seeds from the West: St. John's Medical School, Shanghai, 1880–1952.* Chicago: Imprint Publications, 2001.

Cheung, King-Kok. "The Woman Warrior Versus the Chinaman Pacific: Must a Chinese American Critic Choose Between Feminism and Heroism?" In *Maxine Hong Kingston's The Woman Warrior: A Casebook,* edited by Sau-Ling C. Wong, 113–34. Oxford: Oxford University Press, 1999.

Chiang, Howard. *After Eunuchs: Science, Medicine, and the Transformation of Sex in Modern China.* New York: Columbia University Press, 2018.

– "Double Alterity and the Global History of Sexuality: China, Europe, and the Emergence of Sexuality as a Global Possibility." *e-pisteme* 2, no. 1 (2009): 33–52.

– "Epistemic Modernity and the Emergence of Homosexuality in China." *Gender & History* 22, no. 3 (October 2010): 629–57.

– "Liberating Sex, Knowing Desire: *Scientia Sexualis* and Epistemic Turning Points in the History of Sexuality." *History of the Human Sciences* 23, no. 5 (November 2010): 42–69.

Chou, Rosalind, and Joe Feagin. *The Myth of the Model Minority: Asian Americans Facing Racism.* New York: Routledge, 2016.

Chu, Andrea Long, and Emmett Harsin Drager. "After Trans Studies." *TSQ: Transgender Studies Quarterly* 6, no. 1 (2019): 103–16.

Chu, Richard T. *Chinese and Chinese Mestizos of Manila: Family, Identity, and Culture, 1860s–1930s.* Leiden: Brill, 2010.

Chung, Yuehtsen Juliette. *Struggle for National Survival: Chinese Eugenics in a Transnational Context.* New York: Routledge, 2002.

Churchill, David S. "Transnationalism and Homophile Political Culture in the Postwar Decades." *GLQ: A Journal of Lesbian and Gay Studies* 15, no. 1 (January 2009): 31–65.

Clare, Stephanie. "Biological Sex and the 'Overrepresentation of Man.'" In Stephanie Clare, Patrick R. Grzanka, and Joanna Wuest, "Gay Genes in the Post-genomic Era: A Roundtable." Special issue, *GLQ: A Journal of Gay and Lesbian Studies*, edited by Greta LaFleur and Benjamin Kahan (forthcoming).

– *Earthly Encounters: Sensation, Feminist Theory, and the Anthropocene.* Albany: SUNY Press, 2019.

– "'Finally, She's Accepted Herself!' Coming Out in Neoliberal Times." *Social Text* 35, no. 2 (2017): 17–38.

Clare, Stephanie, Patrick R. Grzanka, and Joanna Wuest. "Gay Genes in the Post-genomic Era: A Roundtable." Special issue, *GLQ: A Journal of Gay and Lesbian Studies*, edited by Greta LaFleur and Benjamin Kahan (forthcoming).

Clark, Anna. *Desire: A History of European Sexuality.* New York: Routledge, 2008.

Clark, Cheryl. "Race, Homosocial Desire, and 'Mammon' in *Autobiography of an Ex-Colored Man.*" In *Professions of Desire*, edited by George Haggerty and Bonnie Zimmerman, 84–97. New York: MLA, 1995.

Cleves, Rachel Hope. "From Pederasty to Pedophilia: Sex Between Children or Youth and Adults in U.S. History." *History Compass* 16, no. 1 (2017): 1–9.

– *Unspeakable: A Life Beyond Sexual Morality.* Chicago: University of Chicago Press, 2020.

Cohen, Cathy J. *The Boundaries of Blackness: AIDS and the Breakdown of Black Politics.* Chicago: University of Chicago Press, 1999.

Cohn, Don J. "A Pride of Pekingese: Bite Foreign Devils Instantly." *China Heritage*, February 18, 2018. http://chinaheritage.net/journal/a-pride -of-pekingese.

Cole, Douglas. *Franz Boas: The Early Years, 1858–1906*. Seattle: University of Washington Press, 1999.

Collins, Patricia Hill, and Sirma Bilge. *Intersectionality*. Cambridge: Polity Press, 2016.

Crenshaw, Kimberlé. "Demarginalizing the Intersection of Race and Sex: A Black Feminist Critique of Antidiscrimination Doctrine, Feminist Theory, and Antiracist Politics." *University of Chicago Legal Forum* 1, no. 8 (1989): 139–67.

– "Mapping the Margins: Intersectionality, Identity Politics, and Violence Against Women of Color." *Stanford Law Review* 43, no. 6 (July 1991): 1241–99.

Crompton, Louis. "The Myth of Lesbian Impunity: Capital Laws from 1280 to 1791." *Journal of Homosexuality* 1–2, no. 6 (1981): 11–25.

Crouthamel, Jason. *An Intimate History of the Front: Masculinity, Sexuality, and German Soldiers in the First World War*. New York: Palgrave Macmillan, 2014.

Crozier, Ivan. "'All the World's a Stage': Dora Russell, Norman Haire, and the 1929 London World League for Sexual Reform Congress." *Journal of the History of Sexuality* 12, no. 1 (January 2003): 16–37.

– ed. *Sexual Inversion: A Critical Edition; Havelock Ellis and John Addington Symonds*. London: Palgrave Macmillan, 2008.

Daly, M.W. "The British Occupation, 1882–1922." In *Modern Egypt: From 1517 to the End of the Twentieth Century*, edited by M.W. Daly, 239–51. Cambridge: Cambridge University Press, 1998.

Davis, Christian. *Colonialism, Antisemitism, and Germans of Jewish Descent in Imperial Germany*. Ann Arbor: University of Michigan, 2012.

De Veaux, Alexis. *Warrior Poet: A Biography of Audre Lorde*. London: W.W. Norton, 2004.

Dean, Elizabeth. "The Gaze, the Glance, the Mirror: Queer Desire and Panoptic Discipline in Nella Larsen's *Passing*." *Women's Studies* 48, no. 2 (2019): 97–103.

Decena, Carlos Ulises. "Tacit Subjects." *GLQ: A Journal of Lesbian and Gay Studies* 14, nos. 2–3 (June 2008): 339–59.

– *Tacit Subjects: Belonging and Same-Sex Desire Among Dominican Immigrant Men*. Durham, NC: Duke University Press, 2011.

Denison, Edward, and Guang Yu Ren. *Building Shanghai: The Story of China's Gateway*. Hoboken, NJ: Wiley-Academy, 2006.

Dennert, Gabriele, Christiane Leidinger, and Franziska Rauchut, eds. *In Bewegung bleiben: 100 Jahre Politik, Kultur und Geschichte von Lesben*. Berlin: Querverlag, 2007.

Dickinson, Edward Ross. *Sex, Freedom, and Power in Imperial Germany, 1880–1914*. New York: Cambridge University Press, 2014.

Dikötter, Frank. "Race Culture: Recent Perspectives on the History of Eugenics." *American Historical Review* 103, no. 2 (April 1998): 467–78.

Doan, Laura, and Chris Waters. "Introduction." In *Sexology Uncensored: The Documents of Sexual Science*, edited by Lucy Bland and Laura Doan, 41–4. Chicago: University of Chicago Press, 1998.

Dobler, Jens. *Von anderen Ufern: Geschichte der Berliner Lesben und Schwulen in Kreuzberg und Friedrichshain.* Berlin: Bruno Gmünder Verlag, 2003.

– *Zwischen Duldungspolitik und Verbrechensbekämpfung: Homosexuellenverfolgung durch die Berliner Polizei von 1848 bis 1933.* Frankfurt: Verlag für Polizeiwissenschaft/Lorei, 2008.

Domeier, Norman. *The Eulenburg Affair: A Cultural History of Politics in the German Empire.* Translated by Deborah Lucas Schneider. Rochester, NY: Camden House, 2015.

Dong, Madeleine Y. "Who Is Afraid of the Chinese Modern Girl?" In *The Modern Girl Around the World: Consumption, Modernity, and Globalization*, edited by Alys Eve Weinbaum, Lynn M. Thomas, Priti Ramamurthy, Uta G. Poiger, Madeleine Yue Dong, and Tani E. Barlow, 194–219. Durham, NC: Duke University Press, 2008.

Dose, Ralf. "In memoriam Li Shiu Tong (1907–1993) zu seinem 10. Todestag am 5.10.2003." *Mitteilungen der Magnus-Hirschfeld-Gesellschaft* 35/36 (2003): 7–21.

– *Magnus Hirschfeld: Deutscher – Jude – Weltbürger.* Teetz, Germany: Hentrich and Hentrich, 2005.

– *Magnus Hirschfeld: The Origins of the Gay Liberation Movement.* Translated by Edward H. Willis. New York: Monthly Review Press, 2014.

– "Magnus Hirschfeld in Frankreich." In *Magnus Hirschfelds Exil-Gästebuch*, edited by Hans Bergemann, Ralf Dose, and Marita Keilson-Lauritz, 11–25. Berlin: Hentrich and Hentrich, 2019.

– "Vorbemerkungen." In Magnus Hirschfeld, *Testament, Heft II*, edited by Ralf Dose, 4–10. Berlin: Hentrich and Hentrich, 2013.

– "The World League for Sexual Reform: Some Possible Approaches." Translated by Pamela Selwyn. *Journal of the History of Sexuality* 12, no. 1 (January 2003): 1–15.

Duman, Tülin. "Eine Minderheit unter vielen." *taz.de*, July 3, 2010.

Dutton, Ron. "The Mystery of Li Shiu Tong." *Xtra*, October 15, 2003. https://xtramagazine.com/power/the-mystery-of-li-shiu-tong-43055.

Dyck, Erika. *Facing Eugenics: Reproduction, Sterilization, and the Politics of Choice.* Toronto: University of Toronto Press, 2013.

Dyer, Richard. "The Matter of Whiteness." In *White Privilege: Essential Readings on the Other Side of Racism*, 2nd ed., edited by Paula Rothenberg, 9–14. New York: Worth Publishers, 2005.

Eaton, Mary. "Homosexual Unmodified: Speculations on Law's Discourse, Race, and the Construction of Sexual Identity." In *Legal Inversions: Lesbians,*

Gay Men, and the Politics of Law, edited by Didi Herman and Carl Stychin, 46–76. Philadelphia: Temple University Press, 1995.

Edelman, Lee. *No Future: Queer Theory and the Death Drive*. Durham, NC: Duke University Press, 2004.

Efron, John. *Defenders of the Race: Jewish Doctors and Race Science in Fin-de-Siècle Europe*. New Haven, CT: Yale University Press, 1994.

Egelmeers, Wouter. "Universal Fetishism? Emancipation and Race in Magnus Hirschfeld's 1930 Sexological Visual Atlas." *Journal of the History of Sexuality* 30, no. 1 (2021): 23–47.

El-Tayeb, Fatima. "Blackness and Its (Queer) Discontents." In *Remapping Black Germany*, edited by Sara Lennox, 243–58. Amherst: University of Massachusetts Press, 2017.

– *European Others: Queering Ethnicity in Postnational Europe*. Minneapolis: University of Minnesota Press, 2011.

– "'Gays Who Cannot Properly Be Gay': Queer Muslims in the Neoliberal European City." *European Journal of Women's Studies* 19, no. 1 (2012): 79–95.

– *Schwarze Deutsche: Der Diskurs um "Rasse" und nationale Identität 1890–1933*. Frankfurt: Campus, 2001.

Eng, David L. "Freedom and the Racialization of Intimacy: *Lawrence v. Texas* and the Emergence of Queer Liberalism." In *A Companion to Lesbian, Gay, Bisexual, Transgender, and Queer Studies*, edited by George Haggerty and Molly McGarry, 38–59. Hoboken, NJ: Wiley-Blackwell, 2007.

– *Racial Castration: Managing Masculinity in Asian America*. Durham, NC: Duke University Press, 2001.

Eng, David L., Jack Halberstam, and José Estaban Muñoz. "What's Queer About Queer Studies Now?" *Social Text* 23, nos. 3–4 (December 2005): 1–17.

Eng, David L., and Alice Y. Hom, eds. *Q&A: Queer in Asian America*. Philadelphia, PA: Temple University Press, 1998.

English, Daylanne K. *Unnatural Selections: Eugenics in American Modernism and the Harlem Renaissance*. Chapel Hill: University of North Carolina Press, 2004.

Etzemüller, Thomas. "Sozialstaat, Eugenik und Normalisierung in skandinavischen Demokratien." *Archiv für Sozialgeschichte* 43 (2003): 492–510.

Evans, Andrew. *Anthropology at War: World War I and the Science of Race in Germany*. Chicago: University of Chicago Press, 2010.

Evans, Jennifer V. "Introduction: Why Queer German History?" *German History* 34, no. 3 (September 2016): 371–84.

– *Life Among the Ruins: Cityscape and Sexuality in Cold War Berlin*. London: Palgrave Macmillan, 2011.

– "Seeing Subjectivity: Erotic Photography and the Optics of Desire." *American Historical Review* 118, no. 2 (2013): 430–62.

Evans, Jennifer, and Jane Freeland. "Rethinking Sexual Modernity in Twentieth-Century Germany." *Social History* 37, no. 3 (August 2012): 314–27.

Evans, Richard. *The Coming of the Third Reich.* New York: Penguin, 2003.

Ewing, Christopher. "'Color Him Black': Erotic Representations and the Politics of Race in West German Homosexual Magazines, 1949–1974." *Sexuality & Culture* 21, no. 2 (June 2017): 382–403.

– "'Toward a Better World for Gays': Race, Tourism, and the Internationalization of the West German Gay Rights Movement, 1969–1983." *Bulletin of the German Historical Institute* 61 (2017): 109–34.

Fabian, Johannes. *Time and the Other: How Anthropology Makes Its Object.* New York: Columbia University Press, 2014.

Faderman, Lillian. *The Gay Revolution: The Story of the Struggle.* New York: Simon and Schuster, 2015.

Faderman, Lillian, and Brigitte Ericksson. *Lesbians in Germany: 1890's–1920's.* Tallahassee: Naiad Press, 1990.

Farrow, Kenyon. "Is Gay Marriage Anti-Black???" In *Against Equality: Queer Critiques of Gay Marriage*, edited by Against Equality Collective and Ryan Conrad, 21–32. Oakland, CA: AK Press, 2010.

Fass, Paula S. "Making and Remaking an Event: The Leopold and Loeb Case in American Culture." *Journal of American History* 80, no. 3 (December 1993): 919–51.

Ferguson, Roderick A. *Aberrations in Black: Toward a Queer of Color Critique.* Minneapolis: University of Minnesota Press, 2003.

– *One-Dimensional Queer.* Cambridge: Policy Press, 2019.

Fields, Karen E., and Barbara Jeanne Fields. *Racecraft: The Soul of Inequality in American Life.* New York: Verso, 2012.

Fink, Carole. "Defender of Minorities: Germany in the League of Nations, 1926–1933." *Central European History* 5, no. 4 (1972): 330–57.

– *Defending the Rights of Others: The Great Powers, the Jews, and International Minority Protection, 1878–1938.* New York: Cambridge University Press, 2004.

Fischel, Joseph. "Of Polymaths and Pederasts: Reflections on Rachel Hope Cleves's *Unspeakable.*" *Notches*, April 13, 2021. https://notchesblog .com/2021/04/13/of-polymaths-and-pederasts-reflections-on-rachel-hope -clevess-unspeakable.

Fisher, Kate, and Jana Funke. "The Age of Attraction: Age, Gender, and the History of Modern Male Homosexuality." *Gender & History* 31, no. 2 (2019): 266–83.

– "'Let Us Leave the Hospital; Let Us Go on a Journey Around the World': British and German Sexual Science and the Global Search for Sexual Variation." In *A Global History of Sexual Science, 1880–1960*, edited by Veronika Fuechtner, Douglas Haynes, and Ryan Jones, 51–69. Berkeley: University of California Press, 2017.

Florvil, Tiffany. "Beyond Shorelines: Audre Lorde's Queered Belonging." Black Perspectives, February 15, 2021. https://www.aaihs.org/beyond -shorelines-audre-lordes-queered-belonging.

– "'Distant Ties': May Ayim's Transnational Solidarity and Activism." In *To Turn the Whole World Over: Black Women and Internationalism*, edited by Keisha N. Blain and Tiffany M. Gill, 74–100. Urbana: University of Illinois Press, 2019.

– "Emotional Connections: Audre Lorde and Black German Women." In *Audre Lorde's Transnational Legacies*, edited by Sabine Broeck and Stella Bolaki, 135–47. Boston: University of Massachusetts Press, 2015.

– *Mobilizing Black Germany: Afro-German Women and the Making of a Transnational Movement*. Urbana: University of Illinois Press, 2020.

Fluehr-Lobban, Carolyn. "Anténor Firmin: Haitian Pioneer of Anthropology." *American Anthropologist* 102, no. 3 (September 2000): 449–66.

Foucault, Michel. *The History of Sexuality*. Vol. 1, *An Introduction*. Translated by Robert Hurley. New York: Vintage, 1990.

Frank, Gelya. "Jews, Multiculturalism, and Boasian Anthropology." *American Anthropologist* 99, no. 4 (September 1997): 731–45.

Frankenberg, Ruth. *White Women, Race Matters: The Social Construction of Whiteness*. Minneapolis: University of Minnesota Press, 1993.

Fredrickson, George M. *Racism: A Short History*. Princeton, NJ: Princeton University Press, 2015.

Freedman, Estelle. "'The Burning of Letters Continues': Elusive Identities and the Historical Construction of Sexuality." *Journal of Women's History* 9, no. 4 (1998): 181–200.

Freeman, Nick. "What Kind of Love Came to Professor Guildea? Robert Hichens, Oscar Wilde, and the Queer Ghosts of Hyde Park." *Modern Language Review* 111, no. 2 (April 2016): 333–51.

Frydman, Hannah. "Freedom's Sex Problem: Classified Advertising, Law, and the Politics of Reading in Third Republic France." *French Historical Studies* 44, no. 4 (October 2021): 675–709.

Frübis, Hilla. "Die 'Reinheit' der Jüdin." *Metis: Zeitschrift für historische Frauen- und Geschlechterforschung* 6, no. 11 (1997): 106–22.

Fuechtner, Veronika. "Indians, Jews, and Sex: Magnus Hirschfeld and Indian Sexology." In *Imagining Germany Imagining Asia: Essays in Asian-German Studies*, edited by Veronika Fuechtner and Mary Rhiel, 111–30. Rochester, NY: Camden House, 2013.

Fuechtner, Veronika, Douglas E. Haynes, and Ryan M. Jones, eds. *A Global History of Sexual Science 1880–1960*. Oakland: University of California Press, 2017.

Fuechtner, Veronika, and Mary Rhiel, eds. *Imagining Germany Imagining Asia: Essays in Asian-German Studies*. Rochester, NY: Camden House, 2013.

Fung, Richard. "Asians: Gay and Proud." *The Asianadian* 2, no. 3 (1979–80): 30. http://www.richardfung.ca/index.php?/articles/asians-gay-and-proud

– "Films About Interracial Relationships." *Fuse* (Winter 1992). http://www.richardfung.ca/index.php?/articles/films-about-interracial-relationships-1991.

– "Looking for My Penis: The Eroticized Asian in Gay Video Porn." In
    A Companion to Asian American Studies, edited by Kent A. Ono, 235–53.
    Hoboken, NJ: Blackwell, 2005.

Funke, Jana. "Navigating the Past: Sexuality, Race, and the Uses of the Primitive
    in Magnus Hirschfeld's *The World Journey of a Sexologist.*" In *Sex, Knowledge, and
    Receptions of the Past*, edited by Kate Fisher and Rebecca Langlands, 111–34.
    Oxford: Oxford University Press, 2015.

– "'We Cannot Be Greek Now': Age Difference, Corruption of Youth and the
    Making of *Sexual Inversion.*" *English Studies* 94, no. 2 (2013): 139–53.

Gaines, Kevin K. *Uplifting the Race: Black Leadership, Politics and Culture in the
    Twentieth Century.* Chapel Hill: University of North Carolina Press, 1996.

Gallagher, B., and A. Wilson. "Sex, Power, and the Politics of Identity (Interview
    with Michel Foucault, Toronto, June 1982)." *The Advocate*, August 7, 1984:
    26–30, 58.

Gandhi, Leela. *Affective Communities: Anticolonial Thought, Fin-de-Siècle Radicalism,
    and the Politics of Friendship.* Durham, NC: Duke University Press, 2006.

– "Loving Well: Homosexuality and Utopian Thought in Post/Colonial India."
    In *Queering India: Same-Sex Love and Eroticism in Indian Culture and Society*,
    edited by Ruth Vanita, 87–99. London: Routledge, 2002.

Ganna, Andrea, Karin J.H. Verweif, Michel G. Nivard, Robert Maier, Robbee
    Wedow, Alexander S. Busch, Abdel Abdellaoui, et al. "Large-Scale GWAS
    Reveals Insights into the Genetic Architecture of Same-Sex Sexual Behavior."
    Science 365, no. 6456 (2019).

Gearhardt, Nan. "Rethinking Trans History and Gay History in Early Twentieth-
    Century New York." *QED: A Journal in GLBTQ Worldmaking* 6, no. 1 (2019):
    26–47.

Gelvin, James L. *The Israel-Palestine Conflict: One Hundred Years of War.*
    Cambridge: Cambridge University Press, 2014.

Gerodetti, Natalia. "From Science to Social Technology: Eugenics and Politics
    in Twentieth-Century Switzerland." *Social Politics* 13, no. 1 (February 2006):
    59–88.

Giles, Geoffrey. "'The Most Unkindest Cut of All': Castration, Homosexuality
    and Nazi Justice." *Journal of Contemporary History* 27, no. 1 (January 1992):
    41–61.

Gillerman, Sharon. *Germans into Jews: Remaking the Jewish Social Body in the
    Weimar Republic.* Stanford, CA: Stanford University Press, 2009.

Gilman, Sander. *The Jew's Body.* New York: Routledge, 1991.

– "The Struggle of Psychiatry with Psychoanalysis: Who Won?" *Critical Inquiry*
    13, no. 2 (1987): 293–313.

Gilmartin, Christina. *Engendering the Chinese Revolution: Radical Women,
    Communist Politics, and Mass Movements in the 1920s.* Berkeley: University of
    California Press, 1995.

Glenn, Susan A. "In the Blood? Consent, Descent, and the Ironies of Jewish Identity." *Jewish Social Studies* 8, nos. 2–3 (2002): 139–52.

Goldstein, Eric L. *The Price of Whiteness: Jews, Race, and American Identity.* Princeton, NJ: Princeton University Press, 2006.

Griffiths, Craig. *The Ambivalence of Gay Liberation: Male Homosexual Politics in 1970s West Germany.* Oxford: Oxford University Press, 2021.

– "Between Triumph and Myth: Gay Heroes and Navigating the schwule Erfolgsgeschichte." *helden. heroes. héros. E-Journal zu Kulturen des Heroischen,* special issue 1 (2014): 54–60.

Grimmer, Ian. "The Politics of *Geist*: German Intellectuals and Cultural Socialism, 1890–1920." PhD diss., University of Chicago, 2010.

Grossmann, Atina. "Magnus Hirschfeld, Sexualreform und die Neue Frau: Das Institut für Sexualwissenschaft und das Weimarer Berlin." In Kotowski and Schoeps, *Der Sexualreformer Magnus Hirschfeld,* 201–16.

– *Reforming Sex: The German Movement for Birth Control and Abortion Reform, 1920–1950.* New York: Oxford University Press, 1995.

Guettel, Jens-Uwe. "The Myth of the Pro-Colonialist SPD: German Social Democracy and Imperialism Before World War I." *Central European History* 45, no. 3 (September 2012): 452–84.

Gupte, Prajakta. "India: 'The Emergency' and the Politics of Mass Sterilization." *Education About Asia* 22, no. 3 (2017): 40–4.

Gutterman, Lauren Jae. *Her Neighbor's Wife: A History of Lesbian Desire within Marriage.* Philadelphia: University of Pennsylvania Press, 2019.

Grzanka, Patrick R. "Programs of Life/Knowing Ourselves." In Stephanie Clare, Patrick R. Grzanka, and Joanna Wuest, "Gay Genes in the Post-genomic Era: A Roundtable." Special issue, *GLQ: A Journal of Gay and Lesbian Studies,* edited by Greta LaFleur and Benjamin Kahan (forthcoming).

Hackenesch, Silke. *Chocolate and Blackness: A Cultural History.* Frankfurt: Campus, 2017.

Haeberle, Erwin J. "Der transatlantische Pendler: Ein Interview mit Harry Benjamin." *Sexualmedizin* 14, no. 1 (1985): 44–7.

– "The Jewish Contribution to the Development of Sexology." *Journal of Sex Research* 18, no. 4 (November 1982): 305–23.

– "A Movement of Inverts: An Early Plan for a Homosexual Organization in the United States." *Journal of Homosexuality* 10, nos. 1–2 (December 1984): 127–33.

Hájková, Anna. "Den Holocaust queer erzählen." *Sexualitäten Jahrbuch,* 2018: 86–110.

– "Queere Geschichte und der Holocaust." *Aus Politik und Zeitgeschichte* 38–9 (2018): 42–7.

Halili, Servando. *Iconography of the New Empire: Race and Gender Images and the American Colonization of the Philippines.* Diliman, Quezon City: University of Philippines Press, 2006.

Halley, Janet. "'Like Race' Arguments." In *What's Left of Theory? New Work on the Politics of Literary Theory*, edited by Judith Butler, John Guillory, and Kendall Thomas, 40–74. New York: Routledge, 2000.

Halperin, David M. "Introduction: The War on Sex." In *The War on Sex*, edited by David M. Halperin and Trevor Hoppe, 1–61. Durham, NC: Duke University Press, 2017.

Hammonds, Evelynn M. "Toward a Genealogy of Black Female Sexuality: The Problematic of Silence." In *Feminist Genealogies, Colonial Legacies, Democratic Futures*, edited by M. Jacqui Alexander and Chandra Talpade Mohanty, 93–104. New York: Routledge, 1997.

Haritaworn, Jin. *Queer Lovers and Hateful Others: Regenerating Violent Times and Places*. London: Pluto Press, 2015.

– "Women's Rights, Gay Rights and Anti-Muslim Racism in Europe: Introduction." *European Journal of Women's Studies* 19, no. 1 (February 2012): 73–8.

Haritaworn, Jin, Adi Kuntsman, and Silvia Posocco, eds. *Queer Necropolitics*. New York: Routledge, 2014.

Hartman, Saidiya. "Venus in Two Acts." *Small Axe* 12, no. 2 (2008): 1–14.

– *Wayward Lives, Beautiful Experiments: Intimate Histories of Social Upheaval*. New York: Norton, 2019.

Healey, Dan. "Homosexual Existence and Existing Socialism: New Light on the Repression of Male Homosexuality in Stalin's Russia." *GLQ: A Journal of Lesbian and Gay Studies* 8, no. 3 (2002): 349–78.

Heineman, Elizabeth. "Consuming Sex: A Photo-Essay on the Legacy of Magnus Hirschfeld in the West German Erotica Industry, 1945–1975." In *Not Straight from Germany: Sexual Publics and Sexual Citizenship Since Magnus Hirschfeld*, edited by Michael Taylor, Annette Timm, and Rainer Herrn, 332–74. Ann Arbor: University of Michigan Press, 2017.

Herrn, Rainer. "'Phantom Rasse. Ein Hirngespinst als Weltgefahr': Anmerkungen zu einem Aufsatz Magnus Hirschfeld." In *Durch Wissenschaft zur Gerechtigkeit? Textsammlung zur kritischen Rezeption des Schaffens von Magnus Hirschfeld*, edited by Andreas Seeck, 111–24. Münster: Lit Verlag, 2003.

– *Schnittmuster des Geschlechts: Transvestitismus und Transsexualität in der frühen Sexualwissenschaft*. Gießen: Psychosozial-Verlag, 2005.

– "Magnus Hirschfelds Geschlechterkosmos: Die Zwischenstufentheorie im Kontext hegemonialer Männlichkeit." In *Männlichkeiten und Moderne: Geschlecht in den Wissenskulturen um 1900*, edited by Ulrike Brunotte and Rainer Herrn, 173–96. Bielefeld: transcript Verlag, 2007.

Herrn, Rainer, and Michael Taylor. "Magnus Hirschfeld's Interpretation of the Japanese *Onnagata* as Transvestites." *Journal of the History of Sexuality* 27, no. 1 (2018): 63–100.

Herzer, Manfred. "Karl Heinrich Ulrichs und die Idee des WhK: Zu einem unbekannten Ulrichs-Text." *Mitteilungen der Magnus-Hirschfeld-Gesellschaft* 10 (June 1987): 34–8.

– *Magnus Hirschfeld: Leben und Werk eines jüdischen, schwulen und sozialistischen Sexologen.* Frankfurt am Main: Campus, 1992.

– *Magnus Hirschfeld und seine Zeit.* Berlin: de Gruyter, 2017.

Herzog, Dagmar. *Cold War Freud: Psychoanalysis in an Age of Catastrophes.* Cambridge: Cambridge University Press, 2017.

– *Sex After Fascism: Memory and Morality in Twentieth-Century Germany.* Princeton, NJ: Princeton University Press, 2005.

– *Sexuality in Europe: A Twentieth-Century History.* Cambridge: Cambridge University Press, 2011.

Hill, Darryl. "Sexuality and Gender in Hirschfeld's *Die Transvestiten*: A Case of the 'Elusive Evidence of the Ordinary.'" *Journal of the History of Sexuality* 14, no. 3 (July 2005): 316–32.

Hobson, Emily. *Lavender and Red: Liberation and Solidarity in the Gay and Lesbian Left.* Oakland: University of California Press, 2016.

Hochberg, Gil, ed. "Queer Politics and the Question of Palestine/Israel." Special issue, *GLQ: A Journal of Lesbian and Gay Studies* 16, no. 4 (October 2010).

Holcomb, Gary Edward. *Claude McKay, Code Name Sasha: Queer Black Marxism and the Harlem Renaissance.* Gainesville: University Press of Florida, 2007.

hooks, bell. *Ain't I a Woman: Black Women and Feminism.* 1981; repr., New York: Routledge, 2014.

– "Eating the Other: Desire and Resistance." In *Black Looks: Race and Representation*, 21–40. Cambridge, MA: South End, 1999.

Hsu, Madeline. *The Good Immigrants: How the Yellow Peril Became the Model Minority.* Princeton, NJ: Princeton University Press, 2017.

Hsu, Rachel Hui-Chi. "The 'Ellis Effect': Translating Sexual Science in Republican China, 1911–1949." In *A Global History of Sexual Science 1880–1960*, edited by Veronika Fuechtner, Douglas E. Haynes, and Ryan M. Jones, 186–209. Berkeley: University of California Press, 2017.

Hull, Isabel V. *Absolute Destruction: Military Culture and the Practices of War in Imperial Germany.* Ithaca, NY: Cornell University Press, 2005.

Hunt, Lynn. "Pornography and the French Revolution." In *The Invention of Pornography: Obscenity and the Origins of Modernity, 1500–1800*, edited by Lynn Hunt, 301–40. New York: Zone Books, 1993.

Huonker, Thomas. *Diagnose: "Moralisch defekt"; Kastration, Sterilisation und Rassenhygiene im Dienst der Schweizer Sozialpolitik und Psychiatrie 1890–1970.* Zurich: Orell Füssli, 2003.

Irvine, Janice. *Disorders of Desire: Sexuality and Gender in Modern American Sexology.* Philadelphia, PA: Temple University Press, 2005.

Jackson, Isabella. "The Raj on Nanjing Road: Sikh Policemen in Treaty-Port Shanghai." *Modern Asian Studies* 46, no. 6 (November 2012): 1672–1704.

– *Shaping Modern Shanghai: Colonialism in China's Global City.* Cambridge: Cambridge University Press, 2018.

Jakobsen, Janet. "Queers Are Like Jews, Aren't They? Analogy and Alliance Politics." In *Queer Theory and the Jewish Question*, edited by Daniel Boyarin, Daniel Itzkovitz, and Ann Pellegrini, 64–89. New York: Columbia University Press.

Joeden-Forgey, Elisa. "Nobody's People: Colonial Subjects, Race Power and the German State, 1884–1945." PhD diss., University of Pennsylvania, 2004.

Johnson, Jeffrey A. *The 1916 Preparedness Day Bombing: Anarchy and Terrorism in Progressive Era America.* Critical Moments in American History. New York: Routledge, 2017.

Kang, Taran. "Herder's Idea of Historical Childhood." *German Studies Review* 40, no. 1 (February 2017): 23–40.

Kaplan, Marion. *Between Dignity and Despair: Jewish Life in Nazi Germany.* Oxford: Oxford University Press, 1999.

Kates, Gary. "Jews into Frenchmen: Nationality and Representation in Revolutionary France." *Social Research* 56, no. 1 (1989): 213–32.

Katz, Jacob. "The Term 'Jewish Emancipation': Its Origin and Historical Impact." In *Studies in Nineteenth-Century Jewish Intellectual History*, edited by Alexander Altmann, 1–25. Cambridge, MA: Harvard University Press, 1964.

Keilson-Lauritz, Marita. *Die Geschichte der eigenen Geschichte: Literatur und Literaturkritik in den Anfängen der Schwulenbewegung.* Berlin: Rosa Winkel, 1997.

Kennedy, Hubert. *The Ideal Gay Man: The Story of Der Kreis.* Binghamton, NY: Haworth Press, 1999.

– *The Life and Works of Karl Heinrich Ulrichs, Pioneer of the Modern Gay Movement.* Boston: Alyson, 1988.

King, Shannon. *Whose Harlem Is This, Anyway? Community Politics and Grassroots Activism During the New Negro Era.* New York: New York University Press, 2015.

Kissack, Terence. *Free Comrades: Anarchism and Homosexuality in the United States, 1895–1917.* Oakland, CA: AK Press, 2008.

Kojima, Dai, John Paul Catungal, and Robert Diaz. "Introduction: Feeling Queer, Feeling Asian, Feeling Canadian." *Topia* 38 (2017): 69–80.

Kokula, Ilse. *Jahre des Glücks, Jahre des Leids: Gespräche mit älteren lesbischen Frauen; Dokumente.* Kiel: Frühlings Erwachen, 1986.

– *Weibliche Homosexualität um 1900 in zeitgenössischen Dokumenten.* Munich: Verlag Frauenoffensive, 1981.

Kollenbroich, James. *Our Hour Has Come: The Homosexual Rights Movement in the Weimar Republic.* Saarbrücken: VDM, 2007.

Konnoth, Craig. "Created in Its Image: The Race Analogy, Gay Identity, and Gay Litigation in the 1950s–1970s." *Yale Law Journal* 119, no. 2 (November 2009): 316–72.

Kotowski, Elke-Vera, and Julius H. Schoeps, eds. *Der Sexualreformer Magnus Hirschfeld: Ein Leben im Spannungsfeld von Wissenschaft, Politik und Gesellschaft.* Berlin: Bebra Wissenschaft, 2004.

Koven, Seth. *Slumming: Sexual and Social Politics in Victorian London.* Princeton, NJ: Princeton University Press, 2006.

Kroh, Peter Jan Joachim. *Nationalistische Macht und nationale Minderheit: Jan Skala (1889–1945); Ein Sorbe in Deutschland.* Berlin: Homilius, 2009.

Kuiper, Yme. "Tolstoyans on a Mountain: From New Practices of Asceticism to the Deconstruction of the Myths of Monte Verità." *Journal of Religion in Europe* 6, no. 4 (2013): 464–81.

Kumashiro, Kevin. "Supplementing Normalcy and Otherness: Queer Asian American Men Reflect on Stereotypes, Identity, and Oppression." *International Journal of Qualitative Studies in Education* 15, no. 5 (1999): 491–508.

Kunzel, Regina. *Criminal Intimacy: Prison and the Uneven History of Modern American Sexuality.* Chicago: University of Chicago Press, 2010.

– "The 'Durable Homophobia' of Psychoanalysis: Forum on Dagmar Herzog's *Cold War Freud.*" *Modern Intellectual History* 17, no. 1 (2020): 215–19.

– "The Power of Queer History." *American Historical Review* 123, no. 5 (December 2018): 1560–82.

– "Queer History, Mad History, and the Politics of Health." *American Quarterly* 69, no. 2 (June 2017): 315–19.

Kurimay, Anita. *Queer Budapest: 1873–1961.* Chicago: University of Chicago Press, 2020.

Ladd-Taylor, Molly. "Eugenics, Sterilisation and Modern Marriage in the USA: The Strange Career of Paul Popenoe." *Gender & History* 13, no. 2 (2001): 298–327.

– *Fixing the Poor: Eugenic Sterilization and Child Welfare in the Twentieth Century.* Baltimore: Johns Hopkins University Press, 2020.

Lang, Birgit, and Katie Sutton. "The Queer Cases of Psychoanalysis: Rethinking the Scientific Study of Homosexuality, 1890s–1920s." *German History* 34, no. 3 (September 2016): 419–44.

Leck, Ralph M. *Vita Sexualis: Karl Ulrichs and the Origins of Sexual Science.* Springfield: University of Illinois Press, 2016.

Leff, Laurel. *Well Worth Saving: American Universities' Life-and-Death Decisions on Refugees from Nazi Europe.* New Haven, CT: Yale University Press, 2019.

Leidinger, Christiane. "'Anna Rüling': A Problematic Foremother of Lesbian Herstory." *Journal of the History of Sexuality* 13, no. 4 (October 2004): 477–99.

Leng, Kirsten. "Culture, Difference, and Sexual Progress in Turn-of-the-Century Europe: Cultural Othering and the German League for the Protection of Mothers and Sexual Reform, 1905–1914." *Journal of the History of Sexuality* 25, no. 1 (January 2016): 62–82.

– "The Limits of Transnationalism: The Case of Max Marcuse." In *A Global History of Sexual Science 1880–1960*, edited by Veronika Fuechtner, Douglas E. Haynes, and Ryan M. Jones, 422–43. Berkeley: University of California Press, 2017.

– "Magnus Hirschfeld's Meanings: Analysing Biography and the Politics of Representation." *German History* 35, no. 1 (March 2017): 96–116.

– *Sexual Politics and Feminist Science: Women Sexologists in Germany, 1900–1933.* Ithaca, NY: Cornell University Press, 2018.

Lennox, Sara. "Introduction." In *Remapping Black Germany: New Perspectives on Afro-German History, Politics, and Culture*, edited by Sara Lennox, 1–32. Boston: University of Massachusetts Press, 2016.

– ed. *Remapping Black Germany: New Perspectives on Afro-German History, Politics, and Culture.* Boston: University of Massachusetts Press, 2016.

Lentin, Alana. "Fault on Both Sides? Racism, Anti-Racism and the Persistence of White Supremacy." *ABC Religion and Ethics*, February 27, 2018. http://www .abc.net.au/religion/articles/2018/02/27/4809171.htm.

Levine, Philippa. *Prostitution, Race and Politics: Policing Venereal Disease in the British Empire.* New York: Routledge, 2003.

Lewerenz, Susann. "'Loyal Askari' and 'Black Rapist': Two Images in the German Discourse on National Identity and Their Impact on the Lives of Black People in Germany, 1918–45." In *German Colonialism and National Identity*, edited by Michael Perraudin, Jürgen Zimmerer, and Katy Heady, 173–83. New York: Routledge, 2011.

Lewis, David L. *W.E.B. Du Bois: A Biography.* New York: Henry Holt, 2009.

Lim, Eng-Beng. *Brown Boys and Rice Queens: Spellbinding Performance in the Asias.* New York: New York University Press, 2014.

Long, Kelly Ann. "To the Yen-an Station: The Life and Writing of Helen Foster Snow (A.K.A. Nym Wales)." PhD diss., University of Colorado, 1998.

Lorway, Robert. *Namibia's Rainbow Project: Gay Rights in an African Nation.* Bloomington: Indiana University Press, 2015.

Love, Heather. *Feeling Backward: Loss and the Politics of Queer History.* Cambridge, MA: Harvard University Press, 2009.

Lowrie, Claire. *Masters and Servants: Cultures of Empire in the Tropics.* Manchester, UK: Manchester University Press, 2016.

Lu, Hanchao. *Beyond the Neon Lights: Everyday Shanghai in the Early Twentieth Century.* Berkeley: University of California Press, 1999.

Lücke, Martin. *Männlichkeit in Unordnung: Homosexualität und männliche Prostitution in Kaiserreich und Weimarer Republik.* Frankfurt: Campus, 2008.

Lvovsky, Anna. "Queer Expertise: Urban Policing and the Construction of Public Knowledge About Homosexuality, 1920–1970." PhD diss., Harvard University, 2015.

Lybeck, Marti M. *Desiring Emancipation: New Women and Homosexuality in Germany, 1890–1933.* Albany: State University of New York Press, 2014.

– "Writing Love, Feeling Shame: Rethinking Respectability in the Weimar Homosexual Women's Movement." In *After the History of Sexuality: German Genealogies with and Beyond Foucault,* edited by Scott Spector, Helmut Puff, and Dagmar Herzog, 156–68. New York: Berghahn, 2012.

MacMillan, Margaret. *Paris 1919: Six Months That Changed the World.* New York: Random House, 2003.

Mader, D.H. "The Greek Mirror: The Uranians and Their Use of Greece." In *Same-Sex Desire and Love in Greco-Roman Antiquity and in the Classical Tradition of the West,* edited by Beert C. Verstraete and Vernon Provencal, 377–420. New York: Harrington Park Press, 2005.

Magnus, Shulamit. *Jewish Emancipation in a German City: Cologne, 1789–1871.* Stanford, CA: Stanford University Press, 1997.

Malakaj, Ervin. "Richard Oswald, Magnus Hirschfeld, and the Possible Impossibility of Hygienic Melodrama." *Studies in European Cinema* 14, no. 3 (2017): 216–30.

Malakaj, Ervin, and Regine Criser. *Diversity & Decolonization in German Studies.* New York: Palgrave Macmillan, 2020.

Malihabadi, Josh. "'There Will Never Be Another Like You.'" Translated by Saleem Kidwai. In *Same-Sex Love in India,* edited by Ruth Vanita and Saleem Kidwai, 274–82. New York: St. Martin's Press, 2000.

Mancini, Elena. *Magnus Hirschfeld and the Quest for Sexual Freedom.* New York: Palgrave Macmillan, 2010.

Marcus, Sharon. *Between Women: Friendship, Desire, and Marriage in Victorian England.* Princeton, NJ: Princeton University Press, 2009.

– *The Drama of Celebrity.* Princeton, NJ: Princeton University Press, 2019.

Marhoefer, Laurie. "Among Abnormals: The Queer Sexual Politics of Germany's Weimar Republic, 1918–1933." PhD diss., Rutgers University, 2008.

– "'The Book Was a Revelation, I Recognized Myself in It': Lesbian Sexuality, Censorship, and the Queer Press in Weimar-era Germany." *Journal of Women's History* 27, no. 2 (2015): 62–86.

– "Homosexuality and Theories of Culture." In *Was ist Homosexualität? Forschungsgeschichte, gesellschaftliche Entwicklungen und Perspektiven,* edited by Florian Mildenberger, Jennifer Evans, Rüdiger Lautmann, and Jakob Pastötter, 255–69. Hamburg: Männerschwarm, 2014.

– "Lesbianism, Transvestitism, and the Nazi State: A Microhistory of a Gestapo Investigation, 1939–1943." *American Historical Review* 121, no. 4 (2016): 1167–95.

– "Queer Fascism and the End of Gay History." *Notches,* June 19, 2018. https://notchesblog.com/2018/06/19/queer-fascism-and-the-end-of-gay-history/.

– *Sex and the Weimar Republic: German Homosexual Emancipation and the Rise of the Nazis.* Toronto: University of Toronto Press, 2015.

Markowitz, Sally. "Pelvic Politics: Sexual Dimorphism and Racial Difference." *Signs* 26, no. 2 (2001): 389–414.

Martin, Brian. "Panthers, Palms, and Desert Passions: Balzac and Napoleon in Egypt." In *Queer Exoticism: Examining the Queer Exotic Within*, edited by David Powell and Tamara Powell, 47–62. Newcastle upon Tyne: Cambridge Scholars, 2010.

Matsuda, Matt. *Empire of Love: Histories of France and the Pacific*. New York: Oxford University Press, 2005.

Matysik, Tracie. *Reforming the Moral Subject: Ethics and Sexuality in Central Europe, 1890–1930*. Ithaca, NY: Cornell University Press, 2008.

Maurer, Jakob. "Der ewige Kampf gegen Rassismus – Gespräch mit einer Afrodeutschen." *Frankfurter Rundschau*, June 14, 2020. https://www.fr.de /politik/deutschland-rassismus-schwarze-muss-kontinuierlich-verlernt -werden-13796550.html.

Max Planck Institute for the History of Science. "Sidonie Fürst." University Women's International Networks Database. http://uwind.mpiwg-berlin.mpg .de/de/fm13-dab-detail/65 (accessed April 24, 2021).

Mazower, Mark. "The Strange Triumph of Human Rights, 1933–1950." *Historical Journal* 47, no. 2 (June 2004): 379–98.

McCabe, Tracy. "The Multifaceted Politics of Primitivism in Harlem Renaissance Writing." *Soundings: An Interdisciplinary Journal* 80, no. 4 (December 1997): 475–97.

McClintock, Anne. *Imperial Leather: Race, Gender, and Sexuality in the Colonial Context*. New York: Routledge, 1995.

McGill Johnson, Alexis. "I'm the Head of Planned Parenthood: We're Done Making Excuses for Our Founder." *New York Times*, April 17, 2021.

McKenna, Kevin. "Safer Sex: Gay Politics and the Remaking of Liberalism in Seattle, 1966–1995." PhD diss., University of Washington, 2017.

McLaren, Angus. *Our Own Master Race: Eugenics in Canada, 1885–1945*. Toronto: McClelland and Stewart, 1990.

Mendoza, Victor Román. *Metroimperial Intimacies: Fantasy, Racial-Sexual Governance, and the Philippines in U.S. Imperialism, 1899–1913*. Durham, NC: Duke University Press, 2015.

Meyerowitz, Joanne. *How Sex Changed: A History of Transsexuality in the United States*. Cambridge, MA: Harvard University Press, 2004.

Michael, Theodor. *Black German: An Afro-German Life in the Twentieth Century*. Translated by Eve Rosenhaft. Liverpool: Liverpool University Press, 2017.

Michaels, Jennifer. "The Impact of Audre Lorde's Politics and Poetics on Afro-German Women Writers." *German Studies Review* 29, no. 1 (February 2006): 21–40.

Micheler, Stefan. *Selbstbilder und Fremdbilder der "Anderen": Männer begehrende Männer in der Weimarer Republik und der NS-Zeit*. Konstanz: UVK, 2005.

Mildenberger, Florian G. *… in der Richtung der Homosexualität verdorben: Psychiater, Kriminalpsychologen und Gerichtsmediziner über männliche Homosexualität 1850–1970.* Hamburg: MännerschwarmSkript, 2002.
– "Per scientiam ad iustitiam? Werk und Wirkung von Magnus Hirschfeld (1869–1935)." *Aschkenas* 28, no. 1 (2018): 85–117.
Miller, James, and Andrés Gómez Bravo. "Why We Shouldn't Cancel Foucault: Even If He Did Have Sex with Underage Boys in a Tunisian Cemetery in the Sixties." *Public Seminar*, April 8, 2021. https://publicseminar.org/essays/why-we-shouldnt-cancel-foucault/.
Miller, James A., Susan D. Pennybacker, and Eve Rosenhaft. "Mother Ada Wright and the International Campaign to Free the Scottsboro Boys, 1931–1934." *American Historical Review* 106, no. 2 (April 2001): 387–430.
Mills, Robert. *Seeing Sodomy in the Middle Ages.* Chicago: University of Chicago Press, 2015.
Mitchell, Katharyne. "Global Diasporas and Traditional Towns: Chinese Transnational Migration and the Redevelopment of Vancouver's Chinatown." *Traditional Dwellings and Settlements Review* 11, no. 2 (2000): 7–18.
Mohan, Jag. "Jawaharlal Nehru and His Socialism." *India International Centre Quarterly* 2, no. 3 (July 1975): 183–92.
Möhle, Heiko. "Betreuung, Erfassung, Kontrolle: Afrikaner aus den deutschen Kolonien und die 'Deutsche Gesellschaft für Eingeborenenkunde' in der Weimarer Republik." In *Die (koloniale) Begegnung: AfrikanerInnen in Deutschland 1880–1945; Deutsche in Afrika 1880–1918*, edited by Marianne Bechhaus-Gerst and Reinhard Klein-Arendt, 225–36. Frankfurt am Main: Peter Lang, 2003.
Molnar, Nicholas Trajano. *American Mestizos, the Philippines, and the Malleability of Race: 1898–1961.* Columbia: University of Missouri Press, 2017.
Moore, R.I. *The Formation of a Persecuting Society: Authority and Deviance in Western Europe, 950–1250.* 2nd ed. Malden, MA: Blackwell, 2007.
Morgensen, Scott Lauria. *Spaces Between Us: Queer Settler Colonialism and Indigenous Decolonization.* Minneapolis: University of Minnesota Press, 2011.
Morris-Reich, Amos. *The Quest for Jewish Assimilation in Modern Social Sciences.* New York: Routledge, 2008.
Mühlhahn, Klaus. "A New Imperial Vision? The Limits of German Colonialism in China." In *German Colonialism in a Global Age*, edited by Geoff Eley and Bradley Naranch. Durham, NC: Duke University Press, 2014.
Mumford, Kevin J. *Interzones: Black/White Sex Districts in Chicago and New York in the Early Twentieth Century.* New York: Columbia University Press, 1997.
– *Not Straight, Not White: Black Gay Men from the March on Washington to the AIDS Crisis.* Chapel Hill: University of North Carolina Press, 2016.
Mungello, D.E. *Western Queers in China: Flight to the Land of Oz.* New York: Rowman and Littlefield, 2012.
Muñoz, José Esteban. *Disidentifications: Queers of Color and the Performance of Politics.* Minneapolis: University of Minnesota Press, 1999.

– "Ephemera as Evidence: Introductory Notes to Queer Acts." *Women & Performance: A Journal of Feminist Theory* 8, no. 2 (1996): 5–16.

Murray, Stephen O. "Donald Webster Cory (1913–1986)." In *Before Stonewall: Activists for Gay and Lesbian Rights in Historical Context*, edited by John Dececco and Vern L. Bullough, 333–43. New York: Routledge, 2002.

Musser, Amber Jamilla. *Sensational Flesh: Race, Power, and Masochism*. New York: New York University Press, 2014.

– *Sensual Excess: Queer Femininity and Brown Jouissance*. New York: New York University Press, 2018.

Naar, Devin. "Our White Supremacy Problem: Exposing the Roots of Intra-Jewish Prejudice." *Jewish Currents*, Spring 2019: 10–21.

Najmabadi, Afsaneh. *Women with Mustaches and Men without Beards: Gender and Sexual Anxieties of Iranian Modernity*. Berkeley: University of California Press, 2005.

Nash, Jennifer. *The Black Body in Ecstasy: Reading Race, Reading Pornography*. Durham, NC: Duke University Press, 2014.

Nguyen, Tan Hoang. *A View from the Bottom: Asian American Masculinity and Sexual Representation*. Durham, NC: Duke University Press, 2014.

Niewyk, Donald L. *The Jews in Weimar Germany*. Baton Rouge: Louisiana State University Press, 1980.

Ofek, Ruthi, and Chana Schütz, eds. *Hermann Struck, 1876–1944*. Tefen, Israel: Open Museum, 2007.

Oguntoye, Katharina. *Eine afro-deutsche Geschichte: Zur Lebenssituation von Afrikanern und Afro-Deutschen in Deutschland von 1884 bis 1950*. Berlin: Hoho, 1997.

– "Mein Coming-out als schwarze Lesbe in Deutschland." In *In Bewegung bleiben: 100 Jahre Politik, Kultur und Geschichte von Lesben*, edited by Gabriele Dennert, Christiane Leidinger, and Franziska Rauchut, 160–3. Berlin: Querverlag, 2007.

Oguntoye, Katharina, and Carolyn Gammon. "Lesben und ihr Kampf um Anerkennung." *Regenbogen-Portal.de*, https://www.regenbogenportal.de /informationen/lesben-und-ihr-kampf-um-anerkennung (accessed May 19, 2021).

Oosterhuis, Harry. *Stepchildren of Nature: Krafft-Ebing, Psychiatry, and the Making of Sexual Identity*. Chicago: University of Chicago Press, 2000.

Opitz, May [May Ayim], Katharina Oguntoye, and Dagmar Schultz, eds. *Showing Our Colors: Afro-German Women Speak Out*. Translated by Anne V. Adams. Boston: University of Massachusetts Press, 1991.

Ordover, Nancy. *American Eugenics: Race, Queer Anatomy, and the Science of Nationalism*. Minneapolis: University of Minnesota Press, 2003.

Osorio, Ruth. "Embodying Truth: Sylvia Rivera's Delivery of Parrhesia at the 1973 Christopher Street Liberation Day Rally." *Rhetoric Review* 36, no. 2 (April 2017): 151–63.

Ou-fan Lee, Leo. *Shanghai Modern: The Flowering of a New Urban Culture in China 1930–1945*. Cambridge, MA: Harvard University Press, 1999.

Paddle, Sarah. "'For the China of the Future': Western Feminists, Colonisation and International Citizenship in China in the Inter-War Years." *Australian Feminist Studies* 16, no. 36 (November 2001): 325–41.

Painter, Nell Irvin. *The History of White People*. New York: W.W. Norton, 2011.

Paul, Diane. "Eugenics and the Left." *Journal of the History of Ideas* 45, no. 4 (October 1984): 567–90.

Peacock, Kent W. "Race, the Homosexual, and the Mattachine Society of Washington, 1961–1970." *Journal of the History of Sexuality* 25, no. 2 (May 2016): 267–96.

Pellegrini, Ann. *Performance Anxieties: Staging Psychoanalysis, Staging Race*. New York: Routledge, 1997.

Perez, Hiram. "You Can Have My Brown Body and Eat It, Too!" *Social Text* 23, nos. 3–4 (December 2005): 171–91.

Petersson, Fredrik. "Hub of the Anti-Imperialist Movement: The League Against Imperialism and Berlin, 1927–1933." *Interventions: International Journal of Postcolonial Studies* 16, no. 1 (January 2014): 49–71.

Pianko, Noam. *Jewish Peoplehood: An American Innovation*. New Brunswick, NJ: Rutgers University Press, 2015.

Pieterse, Jan Nederveen. *White on Black: Images of Africa and Blacks in Western Popular Culture*. New Haven, CT: Yale University Press, 1992.

Plötz, Kirsten. *Einsame Freundinnen? Lesbisches Leben während der zwanziger Jahre in der Provinz*. Hamburg: MännerschwarmSkript, 1999.

Pollack, Howard. *Aaron Copland: The Life and Work of an Uncommon Man*. New York: Henry Holt, 1999.

Poon, Shuk-Wah. "Dogs and British Colonialism: The Contested Ban on Eating Dogs in Colonial Hong Kong." *Journal of Imperial and Commonwealth History* 42, no. 2 (2014): 308–28.

Pross, Christian. "The Attitude of German Émigré Doctors Towards Medicine Under National Socialism." *Social History of Medicine: Journal of the Society for the Social History of Medicine* 22, no. 3 (2009): 531–52.

Puar, Jasbir K. *Terrorist Assemblages: Homonationalism in Queer Times*. Durham, NC: Duke University Press, 2007.

Puff, Helmut. *Sodomy in Reformation Germany and Switzerland 1400–1600*. Chicago: University of Chicago Press, 2003.

Ragan, Bryant T. "The Enlightenment Confronts Homosexuality." In *Homosexuality in Modern France*, edited by Jeffrey Merrick and Bryant T. Ragan, 8–29. New York: Oxford University Press, 1996.

Rampersad, Arnold. *The Life of Langston Hughes*, Vol. 1, *1902–1941: I, Too Sing America*. New York: Oxford University Press, 1986.

Ramsey, Glenn. "The Rites of Artgenossen: Contesting Homosexual Political Culture in Weimar Germany." *Journal of the History of Sexuality* 17, no. 1 (January 2008): 85–109.

Reddy, Chandan. *Freedom with Violence: Race, Sexuality, and the US State.* Durham, NC: Duke University Press, 2011.

Rich, Adrienne. "Compulsory Heterosexuality and Lesbian Existence." *Signs* 5, no. 4 (1980): 631–60.

Rocha, Leon Antonio. "Translation and Two 'Chinese Sexologies': *Double Plum* and *Sex Histories*." In *Sexology and Translation: Cultural and Scientific Encounters Across the Modern World,* edited by Heike Bauer, 154–73. Philadelphia: Temple University Press, 2015.

Rogoff, Leonard. "Is the Jew White? The Racial Place of the Southern Jew." *American Jewish History* 85, no. 3 (September 1997): 195–230.

Röhl, John C.G. *The Kaiser and His Court: Wilhelm II and the Government of Germany.* Cambridge: Cambridge University Press, 1994.

Rohy, Valerie. *Anachronism and Its Others: Sexuality, Race, Temporality.* Albany: SUNY Press, 2010.

– *Lost Causes: Narrative, Etiology, and Queer Theory.* Oxford: Oxford University Press, 2014.

Rosenblum, Warren. *Beyond the Prison Gates: Punishment and Welfare in Germany, 1850–1933.* Studies in Legal History. Chapel Hill: University of North Carolina Press, 2008.

Rosenhaft, Eve. "Afrikaner und 'Afrikaner' im Deutschland der Weimarer Republik: Antikolonialismus und Antirassismus zwischen Doppelbewusstsein und Selbsterfindung." In *Phantasiereiche: Zur Kulturgeschichte des deutschen Kolonialismus,* edited by Birthe Kundrus, 282–304. Frankfurt: Campus, 2003.

Rosenkranz, Bernhard, and Gottfried Lorenz. *Hamburg auf anderen Wegen: Die Geschichte des schwulen Lebens in der Hansestadt.* Hamburg: Lambda, 2005.

Ross, Marlon B. "Beyond the Closet as a Raceless Paradigm." In *Black Queer Studies: A Critical Analogy,* edited by E. Patrick Johnson and Mae G. Henderson, 161–89. Durham, NC: Duke University Press, 2005.

Rottmann, Andrea. "Queer Home Berlin? Making Queer Spaces and Selves in the Divided City, 1945–1970." PhD diss., University of Michigan, 2019.

Ruggiero, Guido. *The Boundaries of Eros: Sex Crime and Sexuality in Renaissance Venice.* New York: Oxford University Press, 1985.

Rupp, Leila J. "The Persistence of Transnational Organizing: The Case of the Homophile Movement." *American Historical Review* 116, no. 4 (October 2011): 1014–39.

– *Sapphistries: A Global History of Love Between Women.* New York: New York University Press, 2009.

Rydström, Jens. *Sinners and Citizens: Bestiality and Homosexuality in Sweden, 1880–1950.* Chicago: University of Chicago Press, 2003.

Saalmann, Dieter. "Kurt Hiller und Mussolini." *Orbis litterarum* 38, no. 2 (June 1983): 150–67.

Said, Edward. *Orientalism.* New York: Vintage, 1979.

Samper Vendrell, Javier. "Adolescence, Psychology, and Homosexuality in the Weimar Republic." *Journal of the History of Sexuality* 27, no. 3 (September 2018): 395–419.

– "The Case of a German-Jewish Lesbian Woman: Martha Mosse and the Danger of Standing Out." *German Studies Review* 41, no. 2 (2018): 335–53.

– *The Seduction of Youth: Print Culture and Homosexual Rights in the Weimar Republic.* Toronto: University of Toronto Press, 2020.

Samuels, Ellen. "My Body, My Closet: Invisible Disability and the Limits of Coming-Out Discourse." *GLQ: A Journal of Lesbian and Gay Studies* 9, nos. 1–2 (April 2003): 233–55.

Schader, Heike. *Virile, Vamps und wilde Veilchen: Sexualität, Begehren und Erotik in den Zeitschriften homosexueller Frauen im Berlin der 1920er Jahre.* Königstein/Taunus: Ulrike Helmer, 2004.

Schmidt, Heike I. "Colonial Intimacy: The Rechenberg Scandal and Homosexuality in German East Africa." *Journal of the History of Sexuality* 17, no. 1 (2008): 25–59.

Schoen, Johanna. *Choice and Coercion: Birth Control, Sterilization, and Abortion in Public Health and Welfare.* Chapel Hill: University of North Carolina Press, 2005.

Schoppmann, Claudia. *Der Skorpion: Frauenliebe in der Weimarer Republik.* Hamburg: Frühlings Erwachen, 1985.

– *Nationalsozialistische Sexualpolitik und weibliche Homosexualität.* Pfaffenweiler: Centaurus, 1997.

Schueller, Malini Johar. "Analogy and (White) Feminist Theory: Thinking Race and the Color of the Cyborg Body." *Signs* 31, no. 1 (September 2005): 63–92.

Schwartz, Michael. *Sozialistische Eugenik: Eugenische Sozialtechnologien in Debatten und Politik der deutschen Sozialdemokratie 1890–1933.* Bonn: J.H.W. Dietz, 1995.

Sears, Clare. *Arresting Dress: Cross-Dressing, Law, and Fascination in Nineteenth-Century San Francisco.* Durham, NC: Duke University Press, 2015.

Sedgwick, Eve Kosofsky. *Epistemology of the Closet.* Berkeley: University of California Press, 2008.

– *Touching Feeling: Affect, Pedagogy, Performativity.* Durham, NC: Duke University Press, 2002.

Seeck, Andreas. "' … Dunstkreis der Täter'? Zur kritischen Hirschfeldrezeption." In Kotowski and Schoeps, *Der Sexualreformer Magnus Hirschfeld,* 317–28.

– ed. *Durch Wissenschaft zur Gerechtigkeit? Textsammlung zur kritischen Rezeption des Schaffens von Magnus Hirschfeld.* Münster: Lit Verlag, 2003.

– "Einführung." In *Durch Wissenschaft zur Gerechtigkeit? Textsammlung zur kritischen Rezeption des Schaffens von Magnus Hirschfeld,* edited by Andreas Seeck, 7–23. Münster: Lit Verlag, 2003.

Shimizu, Celine Parreñas. *The Hypersexuality of Race: Performing Asian/American Women on Screen and Scene.* Durham, NC: Duke University Press, 2007.

– *Straitjacket Sexualities: Unbinding Asian American Manhoods in the Movies*. Palo Alto, CA: Stanford University Press, 2012.

Sibalis, Michael David. "The Regulation of Male Homosexuality in Revolutionary and Napoleonic France, 1789–1815." In *Homosexuality in Modern France*, edited by Jeffrey Merrick and Bryant Ragan, 80–101. New York: Oxford University Press.

Sigusch, Volkmar. *Geschichte der Sexualwissenschaft*. Frankfurt: Campus, 2008.

– *Karl Heinrich Ulrichs: Der erste Schwule der Weltgeschichte*. Berlin: Rosa Winkel, 2000.

Sinnott, Megan. "Dormitories and Other Queer Spaces: An Anthropology of Space, Gender, and the Visibility of Female Homoeroticism in Thailand." *Feminist Studies* 39, no. 2 (January 2013): 333–56.

Skeldon, Ronald. "Emigration and the Future of Hong Kong." *Pacific Affairs* 63, no. 4 (1990–1): 500–23.

Smith, Barbara. "Sexual Politics and the Fiction of Zora Neale Hurston." *Radical Teacher* 8 (1978): 26–30.

Smith, John David. "W.E.B. DuBois, Felix von Luschan, and Racial Reform at the *Fin de Siècle*." *Amerikastudien* 47, no. 1 (2002): 23–38.

Smith, Woodruff D. "Friedrich Ratzel and the Origins of Lebensraum." *German Studies Review* 3, no. 1 (February 1980): 51–68.

Snorton, C. Riley. *Black on Both Sides: A Racial History of Trans Identity*. Minneapolis: University of Minnesota Press, 2017.

Soetaert, Hans P. "*Succession Hirschfeld*: The Handling and Settlement of Magnus Hirschfeld's Estate in Nice (France), 1935–1936." In *Mitteilungen der Magnus-Hirschfeld-Gesellschaft* 50/51 (September 2014): 13–77.

Somerville, Siobhan B. "Queer Loving." *GLQ: A Journal of Lesbian and Gay Studies* 11, no. 3 (June 2005): 335–70.

– *Queering the Color Line: Race and the Invention of Homosexuality in American Culture*. Durham, NC: Duke University Press, 2000.

– "Scientific Racism and the Emergence of the Homosexual Body." *Journal of the History of Sexuality* 5, no. 2 (1994): 243–66.

Sonn, Richard. "Your Body Is Yours: Anarchism, Birth Control, and Eugenics in Interwar France." *Journal of the History of Sexuality* 14, no. 4 (October 2005): 415–32.

Spector, Scott. *Modernism Without Jews? German-Jewish Subjects and Histories*. Bloomington: Indiana University Press, 2017.

– *Violent Sensations: Sex, Crime and Utopia in Vienna and Berlin, 1860–1914*. Chicago: University of Chicago Press, 2016.

Steakley, James D. *"Anders als die Andern": Ein Film und seine Geschichte*. Hamburg: Männerschwarm, 2007.

– "Cinema and Censorship in the Weimar Republic: The Case of *Anders als die Andern*." *Film History* 11, no. 2 (January 1999): 181–203.

- *The Homosexual Emancipation Movement in Germany*. 1975; repr., Salem, NH: Ayer, 1993.
- *The Writings of Dr. Magnus Hirschfeld: A Bibliography*. Toronto: Canadian Gay Archives, 1985.
Steidele, Angela. *In Männerkleidern: Das verwegene Leben der Catharina Margaretha Linck alias Anastasius Lagrantinus Rosenstengel, hingerichtet 1721*. Berlin: Insel Verlag, 2021.
Stein, Melissa. *Measuring Manhood: Race and the Science of Masculinity, 1830–1934*. Minneapolis: University of Minnesota Press, 2015.
Steinmetz, George. *The Devil's Handwriting: Precoloniality and the German Colonial State in Qingdao, Samoa, and Southwest Africa*. Chicago: University of Chicago Press, 2007.
Steinweis, Alan E. *Studying the Jew: Scholarly Antisemitism in Nazi Germany*. Cambridge, MA: Harvard University Press, 2006.
Stern, Alexandra Mina. *Eugenic Nation: Faults and Frontiers of Better Breeding in Modern America*. Berkeley: University of California Press, 2005.
Stewart, Jeffrey C. *The New Negro: The Life of Alain Locke*. Oxford: Oxford University Press, 2018.
Stoler, Ann Laura. *Along the Archival Grain: Epistemic Anxieties and Colonial Common Sense*. Princeton, NJ: Princeton University Press, 2010.
- *Carnal Knowledge and Imperial Power: Race and the Intimate in Colonial Rule*. Berkeley: University of California Press, 2002.
- *Race and the Education of Desire: Foucault's History of Sexuality and the Colonial Order of Things*. Durham, NC: Duke University Press, 1995.
Stratton, Jon. "The Colour of Jews: Jews, Race and the White Australia Policy." *Journal of Australian Studies* 20, nos. 50–1 (January 1998): 51–65.
Stryker, Susan. "My Words to Victor Frankenstein Above the Village of Chamounix: Performing Transgender Rage." *GLQ: A Journal of Lesbian and Gay Studies* 1, no. 3 (June 1994): 237–54.
- *Transgender History: The Roots of Today's Revolution*. New York: Seal Press, 2017.
Stümke, Hans-Georg. *Homosexuelle in Deutschland: Eine politische Geschichte*. Munich: Beck, 1989.
Sutton, Katie. "Female Masculinities and Conflicting Lesbian Identities in Anna Elisabet Weirauch's *Der Skorpion*." In *Quer durch die Geisteswissenschaften: Perspektiven der Queer Theory*, edited by E. Haschemi Yekani and B. Michaelis, 267–81. Berlin: Querverlag, 2005.
- "From Sexual Inversion to Trans: Transgender History and Historiography." In *Was ist Homosexualität? Forschungsgeschichte, gesellschaftliche Entwicklungen und Perspektiven*, edited by Florian Mildenberger, Jennifer Evans, Rüdiger Lautmann, and Jakob Pastötter. Hamburg: Männerschwarm, 2014.
- *The Masculine Woman in Weimar Germany*. New York: Berghahn, 2011.
- *Sex Between Body and Mind*. Ann Arbor: University of Michigan, 2019.

– "Sexological Cases and the Prehistory of Transgender Identity Politics in Interwar Germany." In *Case Studies and the Dissemination of Knowledge*, edited by Joy Damousi, Birgit Lang, and Katie Sutton, 85–103. New York: Routledge, 2015.

– "Sexology's Photographic Turn: Visualizing Trans Identity in Interwar Germany." *Journal of the History of Sexuality* 27, no. 3 (September 2018): 442–79.

– "Trading Transvestite Cases in Sexology, Psychoanalysis, and Weimar Sexual Subcultures." In *Intercultural Encounters in German Studies*, edited by Alan Corkhill and Alison Lewis, 323–40. St. Ingbert, Germany: Röhrig Universitätsverlag, 2014.

– "'We Too Deserve a Place in the Sun': The Politics of Transvestite Identity in Weimar Germany." *German Studies Review* 35, no. 2 (May 2012): 335–54.

Sutton, Katie, and Kirsten Leng. "Forum Introduction: Rethinking the Gendered History of Sexology." *Gender & History* 31, no. 2 (July 2019): 256–65.

Taylor, Michael, Annette Timm, and Rainer Herrn. *Not Straight from Germany: Sexual Publics and Sexual Citizenship Since Magnus Hirschfeld*. Ann Arbor: University of Michigan Press, 2017.

Terry, Jennifer. *An American Obsession: Science, Medicine and Homosexuality in Modern Society*. Chicago: University of Chicago Press, 2010.

Thamann, Rolf. *"Keine Liebe ist an sich Tugend oder Laster": Heinrich Hössli (1784–1864) und sein Kampf für die Männerliebe*. Zurich: Chronos, 2014.

Thomas, Lynn M. "Historicising Agency." *Gender & History* 28, no. 2 (2016): 324–39.

Tidwell, John Edgar. "The Sounds of Silence: Langston Hughes as a 'Down Low' Brother?" in *Montage of a Dream: The Art and Life of Langston Hughes*, edited by John Edgar Tidwell, Cheryl R. Ragar, and Arnold Rampersad, 55–67. Columbia: University of Missouri Press, 2007.

Tobin, Robert Deam. *Peripheral Desires: The German Discovery of Sex*. Philadelphia: University of Pennsylvania Press, 2015.

– "Sexology in the Southwest: Law, Medicine, and Sexuality in Germany and Its Colonies." In *A Global History of Sexual Science 1880–1960*, edited by Veronika Fuechtner, Douglas E. Haynes, and Ryan M. Jones, 141–62. Berkeley: University of California Press, 2017.

– "Widernatürliche Unzucht! Paragraph 175 in Deutsch-Südwestafrika." In *Crimes of Passion: Repräsentationen der Sexualpathologie im frühen 20. Jahrhundert*, edited by Oliver Böni and Jasper Johnstone, 277–300. Berlin: de Gruyter, 2015.

Tompkins, Kyla Wazana. *Racial Indigestion: Eating Bodies in the 19th Century*. New York: New York University Press, 2012.

Usborne, Cornelie. *The Politics of the Body in Weimar Germany*. London: Macmillan, 1992.

Vaid, Urvashi. *Irresistible Revolution: Confronting Race, Class and the Assumptions of LGBT Politics.* New York: Magnus Books, 2012.

– *Virtual Equality: The Mainstreaming of Gay and Lesbian Liberation.* New York: Anchor, 1996.

van der Meer, Theo. "Eugenic and Sexual Folklores and the Castration of Sex Offenders in the Netherlands (1938–1968)." *Studies in History and Philosophy of Biological and Biomedical Sciences* 39 (2008): 195–204.

Vanita, Ruth. "The New Homophobia: Ugra's *Chocolate.*" In *Same-Sex Love in India: Readings from Literature and History,* edited by Ruth Vanita and Saleem Kidwai, 246–52. New York: St. Martin's Press, 2000.

– ed. *Queering India: Same-Sex Love and Eroticism in Indian Culture and Society.* New York: Routledge, 2002.

Vanita, Ruth, and Saleem Kidwai, eds. *Same-Sex Love in India: Readings from Literature and History.* New York: St. Martin's Press, 2000.

Vicenti Carpio, Myla. "The Lost Generation: American Indian Women and Sterilization Abuse." *Social Justice* 31, no. 4 (2004): 40–53.

von Braun, Christina. *Gibt es eine "jüdische" und eine "christliche" Sexualwissenschaft? Sexualität und Säkularisierung.* Vienna: Picus, 2004.

Vyras, Panayiotis. "Magnus Hirschfeld in Greece." *Journal of Homosexuality* 34, no. 1 (September 1997): 17–29.

Wake, Naoko. *Private Practices: Harry Stack Sullivan, the Science of Homosexuality, and American Liberalism.* New Brunswick, NJ: Rutgers University Press, 2011.

Warner, Michael. "Introduction." In *Fear of a Queer Planet: Queer Politics and Social Theory,* edited by Michael Warner (for the Social Text Collective), vii–xxxi. Minneapolis: University of Minnesota Press, 1993.

Warner, Thomas. *Never Going Back: A History of Queer Activism in Canada.* Toronto: University of Toronto Press, 2002.

Weiss, Shayna. "A Beach of Their Own: The Origins of Gender Segregation in the Israeli Public Sphere." PhD diss., New York University, 2015.

Weiss, Sheila Faith. "The Race Hygiene Movement in Germany 1904–1945." In *The Wellborn Science: Eugenics in Germany, France, Brazil, and Russia,* edited by Mark B. Adams, 8–68. Oxford: Oxford University Press, 1990.

Wheeler, Leigh Ann. *How Sex Became a Civil Liberty.* New York: Oxford University Press, 2014.

Whisnant, Clayton J. *Male Homosexuality in West Germany: Between Persecution and Freedom, 1945–69.* New York: Palgrave Macmillan, 2012.

– *Queer Identities and Politics in Germany: A History 1880–1945.* New York: Harrington Park Press, 2016.

Whitbread, Helena, ed. *I Know My Own Heart: The Diaries of Anne Lister (1791–1840).* London: Virago, 1998.

– *No Priest but Love: The Journals of Anne Lister from 1824–1826.* New York: New York University Press, 1992.

Williams, Vernon J. *Rethinking Race: Franz Boas and His Contemporaries.* Lexington: University of Kentucky Press, 1996.

Wilson, Jennifer. "Queer Harlem, Queer Tashkent: Langston Hughes's 'Boy Dancers of Uzbekistan.'" *Slavic Review* 76, no. 3 (October 2017): 637–46.

Winkelmann, Marie. "Dangerous Intercourse: Race, Gender and Interracial Relations in the American Colonial Philippines, 1898–1946." PhD diss., University of Illinois at Urbana-Champaign, 2015.

Wirth, Thomas H. *Gay Rebel of the Harlem Renaissance: Selections from the Work of Richard Bruce Nugent.* Durham, NC: Duke University Press, 2002.

Wolfert, Raimund. "Annäherungen an Franziska Mann – Schriftstellerin und Briefpartnerin Ellen Keys." *Mitteilungen der Magnus-Hirschfeld-Gesellschaft* 58/59 (2017): 45–64.

– *"Gegen Einsamkeit und 'Einsiedelei'": Die Geschichte der Internationalen Homophilen Welt-Organisation.* Hamburg: Männerschwarm, 2009.

– "In Memoriam Karl Giese (1898–1938)." *Nachrichtenbrief der Kurt Hiller Gesellsachaft e.V.* 31 (2016): 5–8.

Wolff, Charlotte. *Bisexuality: A Study.* 2nd ed. London: Quartet Books, 1979.

– *Magnus Hirschfeld: A Portrait of a Pioneer in Sexology.* London: Quartet Books, 1986.

Woolner, Cookie. "'Woman Slain in Queer Love Brawl': African American Women, Same-Sex Desire, and Violence in the Urban North, 1920–1929." *Journal of African American History*, special issue 100, no. 3 (Summer 2015): 406–27.

Wuest, Joanna. "The Dream of Bioessentialism Is Alive in a Post-genomic Era." In Stephanie Clare, Patrick R. Grzanka, and Joanna Wuest, "Gay Genes in the Post-genomic Era: A Roundtable." Special issue, *GLQ: A Journal of Gay and Lesbian Studies*, edited by Greta LaFleur and Benjamin Kahan (forthcoming).

Wyndham, Diana. *Norman Haire and the Study of Sex.* Sydney: Sydney University Press, 2021.

Wynot, Edward. "The Poles in Germany, 1919–1939." *East European Quarterly* 30, no. 2 (June 1996): 171–86.

Yeh, Wen-Hsin. *The Alienated Academy: Culture and Politics in Republican China, 1919–1937.* Cambridge, MA: Harvard University Press, 2000.

– *Shanghai Splendor: Economic Sentiments and the Making of Modern China, 1843–1949.* Berkeley: University of California Press, 2007.

Zimmerman, Angela. *Alabama in Africa: Booker T. Washington, the German Empire, and the Globalization of the New South.* Princeton, NJ: Princeton University Press, 2010.

– *Anthropology and Antihumanism in Imperial Germany.* Chicago: University of Chicago Press, 2001.

– "Anti-Semitism as Skill: Rudolf Virchow's 'Schulstatistik' and the Racial Composition of Germany." *Central European History* 32, no. 4 (1999): 409–29.

Index

Lightning Source UK Ltd.
Milton Keynes UK
UKHW031850240123
415884UK00021B/247